The Power of
PRAYER™
for COUPLES

3 in 1 Collection

The Power of Prayer™ *to*
Change Your Marriage

The Power of a
Praying® Wife

The Power of a
Praying® Husband

STORMIE
OMARTIAN

HARVEST HOUSE PUBLISHERS

EUGENE, OREGON

THE POWER OF PRAYER™ FOR COUPLES
Copyright © 2009 by Stormie Omartian
Published by Harvest House Publishers
Eugene, Oregon 97402
www.harvesthousepublishers.com

ISBN 978-0-7369-3043-7

Cover design by Katie Brady Design, Eugene, Oregon

Compilation of:

The Power of Prayer™ to Change Your Marriage
Copyright © 2009 by Stormie Omartian
ISBN 978-0-7369-2515-0

The Power of a Praying® Wife
Copyright © 1997 by Stormie Omartian
ISBN 978-0-7369-1924-1

The Power of a Praying® Husband
Copyright © 2001 by Stormie Omartian
ISBN 978-0-7369-1976-0

Printed in the United States of America

9 10 11 12 13 14 15 16 17 18 / DP-SK / 10 9 8 7 6 5 4 3 2 1

The Power
of PRAYER™
to Change Your
MARRIAGE

STORMIE OMARTIAN

HARVEST HOUSE PUBLISHERS

EUGENE, OREGON

THE POWER OF PRAYER™ TO CHANGE YOUR MARRIAGE
Copyright © 2007 by Stormie Omartian
Published by Harvest House Publishers
Eugene, Oregon 97402
www.harvesthousepublishers.com

Omartian, Stormie.
    [Praying through the deeper issues of marriage]
    The power of prayer to change your marriage / Stormie Omartian.
       p. cm.
    Originally published: Praying through the deeper issues of marriage. c2007
    ISBN 978-0-7369-2515-0 (pbk.)
    1. Spouses—Religious life. 2. Prayer—Christianity. 3. Marriage—Religious aspects—Christianity.
I. Title.
    BV4596.M3O43 2009
    248.8'44—dc22

                                       2008017307

Printed in the United States of America

CONTENTS

With God's power working in us,
God can do much, much more than
anything we can ask or imagine.

EPHESIANS 3:20 NCV

THE POWER of PRAYER and the DEEPER ISSUES of MARRIAGE

Everyone desires to see some kind of positive change in their marriage. No two people are so perfect that they can't benefit from knowing more about what God has for them as a couple. No one is above needing a certain degree of transformation. Most people have had to deal with some kind of issue—whether large or small—between them and their spouse. And those who haven't may still face problems in their future unless something is done to prevent that from happening. But the good news is that when change is needed in marriage, the power of God through faithful prayer can change everything—even the issues we face that seem to be unchangeable.

You may be thinking, *Who, me? I don't have any issues. I don't see any of the 14 areas of prayer focus listed on the Contents page as being a problem in my marriage. Except...well...maybe one...or two...or more...but they are my husband's (wife's) problem, not mine.*

But please hear me out on this, because I believe that every married person will have to make a decision at some point in their lives on *each one* of these 14 areas as to whether they will *allow* them to *become* issues in their marriage or not. Just because they aren't a problem now doesn't mean they won't be in the future. In fact, these major concerns are traps that are easier to fall into than we might think, as recent statistics prove, suggesting that soon nearly half of all marriages will end in divorce. The common reasons given for these divorces are often found in this list of 14 potential problem areas.

This means that every marriage has a fifty-fifty chance of making it. Of course, there are exceptions. I'm sure there must be some couples who have never had a problem and their marriages have always been perfect. I have never met any of them, but they must be out there. And there are newly married couples for whom the glow has not worn off and reality has not set in, and they have not yet experienced the stresses, losses, and trials of life that can put a strain on any marriage. But this book is for them as well as those who have struggled. In fact, this book is for all of us who are married. Because it is not only about praying *through* struggles to find healing, restoration, and change. It is also about praying to *prevent* these struggles from ever developing into anything serious in the first place.

Thanks to countless letters, emails, phone calls, and contacts on my website, thousands of couples have told me about the problems they are facing in their marriages. Add to that the experiences I've had in my own marriage, and I have what I believe to be the 14 most common problems that lead to divorce. If we can conquer these, we will have divorce-proof marriages. But God has more for us in our marriages than just avoiding divorce. He wants us to be happy and fulfilled in them too. He is not glorified when we are married and miserable. He has a great purpose for each marriage, but His purpose can't be fully realized if the people in them are living in strife.

You would be surprised if you knew how many people there are who *appear* to have perfect marriages and yet are struggling with serious problems. Even the friends and family around them would never suspect they are having difficulties because of their ability to cover them up and present an amazingly strong front. Many people believe they can gut it out and live with the situation, but too often that proves unbearable. This is especially true as people get older and realize that nothing is changing in their marriage and they can't live as they have been for the rest of their lives.

I am thoroughly convinced that all of these problems could be avoided if we would truly understand what God wants for our marriages and how the enemy of our soul will always try to thwart that. And we help him by playing into his hand. But there is a way to hasten the demise of the enemy's plans and see God's plans for our marriages prevail.

If your marriage has already been challenged in any number of ways, the good news is that God has a plan to restore it to the way He intended it to be. And He wants you to partner with Him in order to see that happen. The way you do it is to live God's way and be in prayer every day for your mate and your marriage.

I know this works because my husband and I have at one time or another struggled with most of these issues ourselves. We have had times of communication breakdown between us that were so bad we didn't speak to each other for days, and then we only spoke what was absolutely necessary and nothing that bordered on real communication for months. My husband's anger and my supersensitive reaction to it nearly caused our marriage to be one of the 50 percent that didn't make it. We've had our seasons of unforgiveness, and we've both struggled with negative emotions such as depression, anxiety, and fear that permeated the atmosphere of our home. There have been seasons when we were so occupied with raising children that we completely forgot about us. We've had times of financial difficulty and disagreements over it. We've experienced a hardening of our hearts toward one another, and occasions when we each felt as though we were very low on the other's priority list. We have actually used the "D" word, threatening to get a divorce, even though neither of us really wanted that. I have personally felt at times that all hope was lost and we needed a miracle. And it was true, because outside of the Lord there was no hope. It took a miracle of God to turn things around. I saw God do a miracle by changing our hearts and teaching us to move into the wholeness He has for us.

How Our Past Affects the Present

The reason I was so sensitive to my husband's anger was because I was raised by a mentally ill mother who was angry about everything. She was angry because she thought her father—my grandfather—loved her older and younger sisters more than he loved her. She thought this because when she was 11, *her* mother died suddenly and tragically in childbirth and her father wasn't able to care for his three daughters. My mother had to live with other families, and she felt rejected because of it. This happened during the Depression when times were hard and money was scarce. People were just trying to cope with their own problems and didn't have the time, resources, or knowledge necessary to help a young child cope with hers.

When my mother was 19, she had rheumatic fever, and her mental illness manifested with anger and delusions after that. She became angry at people she thought were following her and trying to kill her. She could seem normal one minute and crazy the next. She was adept at hiding her dark side when she needed to, but she couldn't keep up the facade for long. Her illness always came out, usually when someone powerless and vulnerable was with her.

When my dad married her, he thought she was normal. That is, until they were driving to their honeymoon destination and she made him bypass the hotel where they were supposed to stay because she thought people were following her there to kill her. After driving to and fleeing from two more hotels in the same manner, my dad finally put his foot down. Upon arriving at the fourth hotel, he said, "This is enough. We're staying here." He was in love with her, and it seemed as though he was willing to put up with anything to be married to her.

My mother was beautiful. Everyone said she looked like Vivian Leigh in *Gone with the Wind*. I looked like my dad. In fact, when people would say, "Your mother looks like Vivian Leigh and you look like your dad," I felt hurt. I took it to mean that I resembled a guy instead of a girl. Once I became an adult and my friends had children who looked like their fathers, I realized it didn't mean that at all. So I suffered all those years for nothing. Anyway, I got her good eyes and teeth, and for that I am grateful.

My mother was always angry at my dad because he could never *do* enough, *be* enough, or *give* enough to suit her. And she took all this anger out on me when he was gone. We lived on an isolated ranch in Wyoming, miles from town and the nearest neighbor. My dad was gone a lot out in the fields rounding up and feeding cattle; mending fences; planting, irrigating, and harvesting crops; and working at a logging mill for extra money. Life on a ranch with no one to help is beyond a full-time job. It is many hard and burdensome jobs. When he was gone, my mother kept me locked in a small closet underneath the stairs where the basket of laundry was kept. I was safe in the closet from her physical abuse for a while, but other terrors lurked there. It was pitch-black inside except for a tiny ray of light coming from underneath the door. I always kept my legs pulled up into the basket so that any rats or mice claiming this closet as their home would not be able to touch me. I had once discovered a big snake coiled up in the house and that memory never left me. My dad killed the snake, but meeting that snake's mother in the closet was always an imminent possibility in my mind. I was terrified.

Once we moved from that ranch I was not locked in the closet anymore, but my mother became more and more physically and verbally abusive. I never knew when she would slap me hard across the face. That was her favorite thing to do, and it seemed to give her joy and satisfaction. I feel now that every time she did it, she was getting even with the mother and father who abandoned her, the family she lived with whom she thought didn't want her, and the God who never rescued her from the people she believed were trying to kill her.

By the time I was in my teens I knew she was mentally ill, but I often wondered to myself, *What if she is really telling the truth? What if Frank Sinatra and the pope had actually hired the mob to kill her like she said?* For a while I watched carefully to see if I could identify any of the shadowy figures she said were behind her everywhere she went, but as hard as I tried I never did see even one suspicious thing. When she started using foul language at the people she thought were watching her through the mirrors and TV, I could no longer even give her the benefit of the doubt. Many times when she was out in public—at the grocery store, for example—she would suddenly turn on some innocent person and verbally attack them, saying loudly that she knew what they were up to, she knew they were following her and trying to kill her, and she was going to report this to the police. If I was with her at those times, I quickly walked the other way and pretended I didn't know her. I didn't dare look at the faces of the people she was attacking to see how they were taking it. I can only imagine their fright as she could become quite scary.

As a result of living with her, I grew up with fear, anxiety, depression, hopelessness, loneliness, and a deep sadness in my heart that never went away. I never felt as though I were a part of anything or anyone. I needed acceptance and love, and I looked for both wherever and however I could find them. I tried everything to get rid of the pain I felt inside. I tried Eastern religions and occult practices, always attempting to find some kind of purpose and meaning for my life. I looked for love in all the wrong faces and became more and more depressed with the failure of each relationship.

In my twenties I found great work in television as a singer/dancer/actress, and drugs and alcohol were everywhere. I only took them when I wasn't working because I was too professional to do anything stupid enough to jeopardize my jobs. But a few times I way overdid the drugs and came dangerously close to accidentally killing myself.

When I was 28, my friend Terry, with whom I had been working a lot on recording sessions and television shows, took me to meet her pastor—Pastor Jack Hayford at The Church on the Way in California. He talked to me about Jesus in a way I had never heard before. He told me God had a purpose for my life, but I would never realize that purpose outside of the power of the Holy Spirit, who would live in me if I received Jesus as my Lord. He gave me three books to take home and read, one of which was the Gospel of John in a small book form, and I read them in the days following our meeting. Terry took me back to see Pastor Jack the following week, and I received the Lord in his office. That's when I began to see the plan God had for my life, and my years of purposelessness finally came to an end.

I had met a young man named Michael Omartian before I became a believer during a week of recording sessions that Terry and I were both singing on. But I was about to get married to another man who I knew was wrong for me, and I also knew that the marriage wouldn't last two years. But I was in desperate shape and wanted to feel what it was like to belong somewhere to someone, so I went ahead and married him. As it turned out, it felt like hell because it was the wrong place with the wrong person.

Amazingly, I saw Michael Omartian again in church a couple years later after that first marriage had ended. We started attending church together and dated about a year before we were married. During that time I prayed and prayed for God to show me if Michael was the one I should marry, and every time I did that I felt the peace of God assuring me that this was His will. I kept releasing Michael to the Lord, saying, "God, take him out of my life and close the door if we are not to be together." And I would have let him go if God had showed me to do so because I was well aware of how I had ruined my life doing things my own way. I wasn't going to trust my judgment now; I wanted only what God wanted. By the time we did get married, I was convinced it was the right thing to do. Because of that certainty, when Michael and I had problems in the years to come, I always remembered the assurance from God that we were supposed to be together.

The Problems Started Right Away

The greatest problem I saw in our marriage was my husband's anger. It was explosive, unpredictable, and always directed at me. Because of my past I was way too sensitive and fragile to take it or deal with it. At first I thought it was all my fault. I thought, *I must be a terrible person to make him so angry at me all the time.* I was trying the best I could, but it wasn't enough. I was already too broken and hurting to be able to stand up to it, or better yet to understand where he was coming from.

After we were married less than a year, I went through major deliverance from fear, depression, and anxiety with the help of a gifted pastor's wife named Mary Anne, who prayed for me. And that helped tremendously. Also, my husband and I went to Christian marriage counselors, and I began to see that Michael's anger was *his* problem, not mine. In fact, one of the marriage counselors we went to at the time said to me, "Michael would have this anger no matter whom he was married to. If he had married someone else, he would have directed his anger at her."

That knowledge helped me to not feel like a failure, but I still couldn't get on top of how beat up I felt when he would attack me with angry words. It was as though my mother were slapping me in the face all over again. It made me feel the same way—small and without value. His anger was like a snake hidden from sight, always coiled and ready to strike when I least expected it. It would become a deep issue that nearly destroyed our marriage.

For a long time I was mad at God for letting me marry someone who was like my mother in any way. I saw no signs whatsoever of Michael's anger before we were married, and I questioned why it was never revealed to me. I did see him battle with depression and feelings of failure, but I had those issues too, and I thought I could help him through them. I thought we would be there for each other. I mistakenly believed that because God had called us to be together that there wouldn't be any problems when we got married.

In Michael's defense, I believe now that his anger came from having dyslexia back in the days when people didn't know what that was. His mother told me she was very hard on him because he struggled so much in school and she thought he was being rebellious. Having been blessed with a dyslexic child myself, I now understand the frustration of the person who has it and the deep feelings of failure they have because they can't learn the same way everyone else does. I also understand it from a parent's perspective. Before the problem is diagnosed, you can't figure out why your child isn't doing as well as they should be doing in school. You know how bright the child is, how creative and gifted, and how amazing their memory is, but when it comes to reading they seem to shut off. They appear rebellious because it seems that they are refusing to do the work, but the truth is they can't. So while I definitely sympathize with what Michael's mother went through, I also felt sorry for Michael. He suffered with tremendously overwhelming feelings of failure and depression because of it.

I believe now that's where his anger came from. He was angry over the frustration of being a creative dyslexic in a rigid and uncreative educational system. He was angry at his mother for often being angry at him for something he couldn't do anything about. And he took his anger out on me.

I'm going to tell you more of our story later in the book, but I want to reveal to you now that it has a good ending. Our marriage has gone through many tough times, but we have been married for more than 34 years. My husband and I have changed a lot for the better, and I will be sharing with you how that happened. I'm not saying we are perfect. Far from it. But we are living proof that if you *want* to, you can change. And if you hang in there and keep praying, you can see things turn around. So if you want to protect your marriage from the things that can destroy it, or you long to restore the damage that has already been done, read on and see how to do it. You can find the success you desire in your marriage if you do things God's way and refuse to give up.

You Can Change and So Can He (She)

We are told over and over, "Don't even try to change your husband (wife) because he (she) will never change." Hearing those dire predictions repeatedly can make you feel hopeless. If your marriage is miserable because of something intolerable your spouse does, and you're told he (she) will never change, then what hope do you have for your future together? Here are five important truths about that from God's perspective.

1. The truth is, everyone needs to change. God says so. In fact, it's His will for our lives that we change because He wants each one of us to become more like Him. And that is a never-ending project, for we all fall far short of the glory of God (Romans 3:21-23). We will always need to submit to Him and not think so highly of ourselves that we feel we don't need to change. God is in the business of changing people. That's why, through our prayers and the power of the Holy Spirit, there is always hope for change.

2. The truth is, every person can change. *You* can change. And *your spouse* can change. Don't let anyone tell you otherwise. It's not that a person *can't* change. It's that they don't *want* to. Or they don't want to make the effort to do anything differently than they always have. Or they don't care to seek God about what changes He would like to see worked in them. Or they are so totally happy with themselves that they don't think they need to change. Never mind that everyone around them does.

People usually don't change because:

1. They aren't aware they need to.
2. They don't believe they have to.
3. They don't want to.
4. They don't know how to.
5. They don't feel they are able to.

3. The truth is, being married creates the perfect opportunity for change. When you are married, you find out how much you need to improve yourself. It is prideful and selfish for anyone to get married and think they are so perfect they don't need to change in any way. Each one of us always needs to change in many ways, some more than others, but God will start with the one who is willing. And the good news is, this is where His blessings will be directed first as well. Remember that both you and your husband (wife) *can* be changed. God is waiting for you to invite Him to do that. Marriage always inspires change.

4. The truth is, people cannot make someone else change. Never is that more true than in a marriage. A wife can't change her husband. A husband can't change his wife. But *God* can change both. We have to learn that it's not *our* job to change our spouse, anyway. It's the work of the Holy Spirit. No amount of criticizing and nagging will accomplish it, no matter how hard we try. God made each of us in *His* image, and He doesn't want us to try and make our spouse over into *our own* image. Our job is to accept our spouse as he (she) is and pray for the Lord to make the necessary changes in him (her). Meanwhile, as He is working on your spouse's heart, God will also be working in yours. In the process of praying for *him* (*her*), God will change *you*.

5. *The truth is, only God can work changes in us that last.* Only God can transform us. We just have to be willing to say, "Lord, I recognize that I am far from perfect, and I realize I need to be changed in order to become more like You. I know I can't change myself in any lasting way, but You can. Lord, change me into the person You want me to be and show me what I need to do. I praise You and thank You for the transformation You are working in me."

Only God can:

1.   Make someone aware they *need* to change.
2.   Help someone see they *have* to change.
3.   Encourage someone to *want* to change.
4.   Show someone *how* to change.
5.   Enable someone to *make* a change.

What Are "Issues," Exactly?

Every marriage has issues. Every marriage has difficult times of negotiating and compromising that, if not handled carefully, can allow a wedge to get in between the husband and wife. If not repaired, this division can grow with each new unresolved problem and eventually become a *great* divide. Issues that are allowed to grow deep can completely break a marriage apart. And it can happen so stealthily that you don't even see it coming until one day you wake up and wonder how you let it get this far. And then you don't know what to do to stop the divide from widening. You don't see how you can ever bring it all back together again because the damage seems irreparable. But in the Lord nothing is irreparable. And every division can be eliminated. It just takes knowing what you're dealing with.

First of all, it helps to understand exactly what the issues are. Knowing the definition of "issues" makes resolving them seem more reasonable and attainable. It keeps us from being overwhelmed by the emotions and reactions they bring up. An *issue* is *a point that is disputed*. It is *a matter that has to be decided*. It is *a question that has to be answered* in a way that is acceptable to both parties. Having an *issue* means you have *entered into a disagreement or a conflict* over something. It is *a particular point that you do not agree upon*.

To take issue with your spouse means to have a difference of opinion with him (her). It means the two of you are at variance over something, and it's causing you to enter into arguments, disagreements, or conflicts over it. For example, if a husband drinks alcohol from time to time and his wife doesn't think it's the right thing to do, then this is something they don't fully agree on. They have a difference of opinion. They have a point that needs to be decided. If the wife confronts her husband about this and asks him to stop and he continues to drink anyway, knowing that his wife does not approve of it, then this problem has not been decided in a way that is acceptable to both of them, and so it becomes an issue. It makes the wife feel that her husband doesn't care enough about her to stop doing something that deeply bothers her. It becomes a point of contention that can turn into a deal breaker with regard to their marriage.

The wife can do one of four things:

1. She can negotiate. She can resolve the issue with some kind of compromise, such as agreeing that he can have a glass of wine with dinner. But this compromise may not be enough to satisfy her if any kind of drinking is against her religious beliefs.

2. She can choose to be silent and not press the issue. However, she may become resentful over time, especially if his drinking begins to affect his performance, such as his ability to walk, talk, drive, work, or be a kind, decent, and productive human being.

3. She can enter into conflict with him. This means having unpleasant disagreements, arguments, or strife, especially if he did things while drinking that made her feel threatened, such as jeopardizing her physical safety, mental stability, or sense of emotional well-being. Or, if he caused her to see her entire life going down the drain and their future being threatened because of it.

4. She can pray for him. She can pray that his eyes will be opened to God's will and perspective, and that God will do whatever it takes to bring about necessary changes in his life.

I'm not picking on the husband here. It's the same when the wife is doing something—or *not* doing something—and the husband objects. It doesn't matter what the issues are; they have to be resolved in a way that is acceptable to *both* husband and wife. If they are not, these disagreements will become deeper and deeper. Every issue in a marriage must be confronted because they usually don't go away on their own without one or both people making a great effort. But there is a powerful way to deal with the issues of marriage that will not only keep them from becoming deeper, but will heal and eliminate them completely.

It Takes Three to Agree

In order for a marriage to not only survive, but also to be fulfilling and successful, there needs to be three parties involved: the husband, the wife, and God. The reason marriages have issues in the first place is because every married couple is made up of two *imperfect people*. One imperfect human plus another imperfect human equals one *imperfect marriage*. However, if you add the presence of a *perfect God* into this imperfect mix of two imperfect people, you then have unlimited possibilities for growing closer to the perfection God intended for the marriage relationship. Whether that happens or not is determined by how frequently and fervently God is invited to reign in the hearts of both the husband and wife. It has to do with being willing to have three agree.

You and your spouse can agree about something, but it can still be an issue if *God* doesn't agree with it. For example, if your spouse wants you to view a film that has sexually explicit scenes in it and you agree to it, this is a compromise you have *both* chosen, but it doesn't agree with *God's Word*. Therefore, G*od doesn't agree* with it. The two of you may be fine with it, but it offends God and violates His laws. If it is a point of contention with God, it will always be an issue in your lives together. It will inhibit all that God wants to do in each of you and in your marriage. You may agree on something together, but if it doesn't agree with God, it will open the door for problems that will undermine your marriage.

There are consequences for violating any law of God—whether ignorantly or knowingly. Some people think that God's laws don't apply to them, but that doesn't make the consequences for violating them any less destructive. They may believe they are innocent of any violation, but God doesn't see it that way. It's like the law of gravity. You can jump out a tenth-story window and deny the law of gravity all the way down, but the consequences are still going to be the same when you hit the ground. God's laws are for our benefit. Life works better for us when we live by them.

Sixteen Ways to Destroy Your Marriage

1. Stop communicating openly and honestly.

2. Be consistently angry, selfish, rude, and abusive.

3. Refuse to forgive your spouse for any offense, no matter how small.

4. Stay depressed and negative as much as possible.

5. Convince your spouse that your children are far more important to you than he (she) is.

6. Be consistently lazy and refuse to do much around the house or on your job.

7. Spend money foolishly and continually run up great debt.

8. Give place to addictions or annoying habits and defend your right to have them.

9. Don't care about what your spouse needs sexually as long as you get what you want.

10. Habitually look at explicit films, magazines, or advertising and compare your husband (wife) to the glorified images you see there, and especially mention others whom you find more attractive.

11. Allow your heart to grow hard toward your husband (wife) and refuse to ever say "I'm sorry," "Forgive me," or "I forgive you."

12. Make something other than God and your spouse your top priority.

13. Threaten to get a divorce every time something comes up between you and your spouse that needs to be worked out.

14. Have an affair or entertain an obsession of the heart over someone other than your husband (wife).

15. Move out of the home and don't try to reconcile your differences.

16. Give up and refuse to believe that God is a God of miracles who can restore love and hope.

It Can Happen to Anyone

Each of the above 16 ways to destroy a marriage can start as something small and turn into something big overnight, even in the best of relationships. You may have an idyllic marriage with the most perfect of mates and you may be close to perfection yourself, but so were Adam and Eve, and look what happened to them. I know a number of women—and men as well—who thought they had it all together in their marriage and didn't need to ask God to change their heart so they could be a better marriage partner. They didn't learn to intercede for their spouse. Sadly, they are all divorced now. In each case, their spouse left them. They neglected to take the necessary steps to prevent it, and they refused to do what was required to repair the damage.

Don't buy into the dangerous belief that you are immune to such problems in your marriage. Too many people have thought that and ended in divorce court. Or equally as bad, they have allowed their marriage to be filled with so much strife and unforgiveness that it became miserable, lifeless, and dead. They lost sight of the purpose God had for them in being married in the first place. And make no mistake, He does have a great purpose for your marriage.

Today there is an epidemic of despair, hopelessness, and pain because of marriages in crisis. There is no greater torment, outside of the death of a loved one, than that which is suffered when a marriage relationship has broken down. The sense of failure, guilt, sadness, and heartbreak over a divorce is unbearable. And staying in a miserable marriage is intolerable. Either choice is heartbreaking.

However, just like the *problem* can happen to *anyone,* so can the *solution* to it. I'm not going to tell you that the solution I have written about in this book is easy, but it's *doable.* And not just for the deeply spiritual and highly disciplined. It's doable for *everyone.* If *I* can do it, *you* can do it. *The reason it's doable* is because it is God's way and He will help you accomplish it if your heart is willing. *The reason it's not easy,* however, is because of this one thing—*the condition of our own heart has to be right,* and changing that can often seem impossible. It's hard to take our blinders off when we've grown so used to them that we don't even know they are there. Deeper issues develop in the heart first, so that is where we have to go to find the root of the problem, and that is where the healing begins.

God Has Given You Authority

God is sovereign. And He has sovereignly declared that He will not work independently of us in our lives. He's not going to just fix things for us without any input on our part. He wants to work through anyone who will move in the authority He has given us in prayer. Without us praying, He *won't* do it. Without His help and power, we *can't* do it.

Let's get some basic facts straight. If you believe Jesus Christ is the Son of God and you have invited Him into your life to rule there, then you are a child of God. That makes you the son or daughter of a King. You were born again into royalty. And you are destined to reign over the forces of evil. God has "delivered us from the power of darkness and conveyed us into the kingdom of the Son of His love" (Colossians 1:13).

Knowing Jesus and being God's child is where our authority in prayer begins. Praying is putting our authority into action. Satan has the power to destroy us, but we have been given authority over him. "Behold, I give you the authority to trample on *serpents* and *scorpions,* and over *all the power of the enemy,* and nothing shall by any means hurt you" (Luke 10:19, emphasis added).

As I mentioned earlier, I was raised in the wild lands of Wyoming, and I have had way more experience with snakes than I ever wanted. When I think of how many times I came close to rattlesnakes coiled and ready to strike—I have been just inches away a few times—it's a miracle I have never been bitten by one. Snakes slither silently in, and you don't realize they are there until suddenly you are upon them and they startle you. Scorpions are known for their sudden, painful, and venomous sting. If you would think of all the threats to your marriage as being like snakes and scorpions, it will help you to see their potential for pain and destruction. Whether it is something dangerous that sneaks silently into your marriage unnoticed at first, or something small but deadly that rises up and stabs you when you least expect it, leaving you wounded and poisoned, God will help you to face the enemy with courage. He will work His power through you so you can exercise your authority over the enemy through prayer in Jesus' name.

God has given us *free choice* concerning who we will allow to have authority in our lives. Will we respect God's authority, or will we give it to Satan? When we choose Jesus, He gives us authority over all situations in our lives. But if we don't submit to Him in obedience to His ways, in reverence for who He is and what He accomplished on the cross, we will not be able to move in the authority He paid for with His life. The only way to move into all God has for us is to be totally submitted to the authority of Jesus in our lives. We have *authority* over the enemy because of what Jesus did on the cross. When we learn to use our authority over the enemy in Jesus' name, incredible things happen in our lives and in our marriages.

In a powerful book about the authority we have in prayer, Dutch Sheets writes, "...strictly speaking, authority and power are not the same. Power is the 'strength or force' needed to rule; authority is the 'right' to do so. They are governmental twins and must operate in tandem; authority without power to enforce it is meaningless; power exercised without authority—the right to use that power—is usurpation and is morally wrong."* God not only gives us His *power* in prayer, He gives us *authority* as well.

Taking Authority over Your World

The best place to start taking authority over your world and your life is by praying regularly for your husband (wife) and for your marriage. Your prayers for your husband (wife) have great power in the spirit realm. The same enemy of your soul who wants to see *you* destroyed also wants to see *your marriage* destroyed. If you don't realize that, you will end up thinking that your spouse is the enemy and your fight is with him (her). While it's true he (she) may be *acting* like the devil sometimes, he (she) is not the enemy. Jesus won the victory over death and hell, so if you are living in hell in your marriage relationship, you have not yet moved into the victory God has for you.

Whenever you find yourself in a tough situation in your life or in your marriage, take authority over it with prayer in Jesus' name. Then praise God for the victory He has already won on your behalf. Thank Him that He has a way out of any situation, even when it appears completely hopeless.

When you pray with God-given authority, it releases the power of God to work in both of your lives. You can't necessarily change the strong will of your spouse, but when you pray for him (her), you invite God to create an atmosphere in the spirit realm around him (her) that helps him (her) to better see the truth.

---

* Dutch Sheets, *Authority in Prayer: Praying with Power and Purpose* (Bloomington, MN: Bethany House Publishers, 2006), p. 20.

Becoming More Than a Conqueror

God never said we wouldn't have problems. He said we *will*. We can count on it. And when you are married you will not only have *your* problems; you will have your spouse's problems as well. But the good news is that Jesus overcame those problems for us. When we align ourselves with Him in prayer and obedience, He will help us to either rise above our problems or walk through them successfully. He will give you the power to be more than a conqueror (Romans 8:37).

You may be wondering, *How can you be more than a conqueror? Either you conquer or you don't.* But even when one country conquers another, it can still be dealing with constant strife and problems in that conquered country. (You can probably think of at least one example in your lifetime where that has happened in the world.) In reality, to be able to conquer a country *without* strife or problems would take a miracle. In our lives, Jesus has done that miracle. He has already conquered death and hell and has secured the victory over the enemy without strife for us. We have to learn to walk in that victory.

God has a destiny for you and your husband (wife), not only as individuals but also as a couple. Every chapter in this book deals with a trap the enemy has set for you to fall into so that your marriage can be destroyed and you won't reach that destiny. The enemy of your soul and your marriage is also the enemy of your purpose, both individually and together as a couple. Jesus enables you to be more than a conqueror in your life and your marriage. You can not only conquer the territory God has for you, but you can also experience the miracle of peace in the process.

Learning to Pray with Power

I don't want to just talk to you *about* praying for yourself, your husband (wife), and your marriage, I want to teach you *how* to pray in power. I want to inspire you with great hope that things can change. I'm not talking about being religious, saying "church" words, speaking "Christianese," or quoting "catchy phrases" without any power accompanying them. I am talking about praying in a way that will bring results.

I can tell you how to swim, I can describe the water, and I can teach you all the correct moves, but at some point you are going to have to get in the water. Once you get into the stream of God's Spirit flowing through you as you pray, you are going to find yourself not only staying afloat, but also rising to the top of each wave of life that would normally overwhelm you.

One of God's greatest promises says that "all things work together for good to those who love God, to those who are the called according to His purpose" (Romans 8:28). But if you read the verses *before* that promise, you will see that the Bible is talking about prayer. In other words, all things work together for good if we are *praying*. Things are not promised to work out for good automatically. If there have been things in your life you feel did not work out for good, it's possible that somewhere, sometime, the people who should have been praying for you or your situation weren't.

You have the power to control your own destiny. You can choose heaven or hell as your eternal home. You can choose to give God control of your life and let Him move you into the purpose for which He created you. You can choose either to give up on your marriage or stay and fight for it in prayer.

What Jesus accomplished at the cross seems baffling and foolish to someone who has never been born again and had their spiritual blinders removed, but to us who believe, it is the greatest manifestation of God's power. "The message of the cross is foolishness to those who are perishing, but to us who are being saved it is the power of God" (1 Corinthians 1:18). When you invite Jesus into your life, that same power that resurrected Him will manifest and resurrect all the dead areas of your life—including your marriage.

God knows we need that. He knows we can't come up with a foolproof plan that will keep our marriages together. We are way too selfish and blind. We lack wisdom and the spirit of self-sacrifice. "The LORD knows the thoughts of man, that they are futile" (Psalm 94:11). He wants *us* to realize that too. He wants *us* to understand that we can't do it without Him. He wants us to believe that He is greater than any hurricane, flood, or tsunami of circumstances and emotions that would threaten to wash over your relationship.

God is even greater than your husband's anger or your wife's lack of interest in sex. He is greater than your wife's depression or your husband's inability to communicate. He is greater than your unforgiveness or your husband's (wife's) hardness of heart. God is powerful enough to help you get out of debt and free of addictions. He is stronger than your bad habits and weak willpower. He made you to be victorious over all that and more, but you cannot proceed "having a form of godliness but denying its power" (2 Timothy 3:5). You have to run to the cross with gratefulness for His sacrifice on your behalf and acknowledge God's power in your life.

God had a plan for your life before you were even born. He says it is He "who has saved us and *called us with a holy calling,* not according to our works, but *according to His own purpose* and grace which was given to us in Christ Jesus before time began" (2 Timothy 1:9, emphasis added). He called you for a purpose, but He still gives you a choice. You can choose *His* destiny for your life, or you can make your own. Let me give you a tip about this that will save you a lot of time and effort: The life *you try* to make happen will never be as good as the one you *let God* make happen.

What if I Am the Only One Praying?

Your prayers for your marriage have power, even when you are the only one praying. That's because the two of you are one in the eyes of God, and what one does affects the other—either for good or for bad. Of course, the power is even greater when the two of you pray together, but I don't want to belabor that point. If you have a husband (wife) who will pray with you, consider yourself blessed. Most people don't have that.

What if you are the only person in the marriage who is a believer? Or only you are really living God's way? Or only you are willing to submit to God's perfecting process? Or are willing to work on the relationship? What if you understand the enemy's attack on your marriage and your spouse doesn't get it? Can *your* prayers alone save the marriage? I believe they can. In fact, I have heard of miracles in that regard. Don't allow anything other than God to rule in your marriage when you can take authority over it—even by yourself—and expect to see answers to your prayers.

Every marriage has two hearts that need to be changed, issues that need to be dealt with, and two completely different perspectives. In order for two different individuals to truly become one, they have to align themselves with God and each other. You have to be willing to let God transform you into the person He created you to be. Of course, if your husband or wife is sold out to their own selfish desires and determined to rebel against the ways of God, or be abusive enough to destroy the relationship, there is only so much you can do. But if your spouse has any desire at all to preserve the marriage, your prayers can pave the way for God to do miracles.

The good news is that God will still bless *your* life, even if your spouse has to go through some things until he (she) gets it. The problem is that what happens to your spouse happens to you. Everything he (she) does affects you in some way. But when you pray, God can rescue you from any situation—even your spouse's mistakes or sins. You can even be rescued from any negative aspect of your marriage while God works through your prayers to restore it.

Seek Godly Counsel When You Need It

There may be times in your marriage when it seems as though your prayers are not being heard. Or you feel so upset that you can't pray. Or you are at an impasse and unable to get beyond the great disconnect between you and your spouse. Or there is so much hurt and strife between you that you can't even talk. That's when you need the help of a good, godly marriage counselor. And you may need more than one in a lifetime of being married because "in a multitude of counselors there is safety" (Proverbs 24:6).

Keep in mind that any deeper issue can threaten a marriage seriously enough to cause a divorce. That's why I strongly suggest that if even one of the issues addressed in this book is already negatively affecting your marriage to the point where you or your spouse are miserable or are contemplating divorce because of it, find a godly and wise counselor who is willing to work with you both in order to save the marriage. And I say "godly" because not all "Christian counselors" necessarily give godly advice.

My husband and I once sent a Christian couple who are close friends of ours to a Christian counselor we had seen ourselves. This counselor had given us godly counsel at an impasse in our marriage and it helped us tremendously. However, when we sent this couple to him years later, he told them that their problem was so serious that they should get divorced. When the couple told us what happened, we were shocked and greatly disappointed. Fortunately, this couple was committed to staying married and didn't take this counselor's advice. They ended up going to our pastor instead and he helped them recover. This was more than 15 years ago, and their marriage is still going strong to this day. There are many great Christian counselors out there. Ask God to lead you to the right one and keep praying the prayers in this book.

I am aware that the expense of counseling can make you think about it carefully, but the cost of divorce is far greater in the long run. If you absolutely cannot afford even two or three sessions with a professional counselor, ask at your church if there is a person or a couple who are gifted in Christian marriage counseling and who are knowledgeable, mature, trustworthy believers who know that divorce is not the best answer to the deeper issues of marriage and who would be willing to help you save your relationship.

Can Prayer Keep These Things from Happening?

Of course, it would be best to pray about the deeper issues of marriage before any of them ever develop. Or better yet would be to pray about them *before* you walk down the aisle. However, even though it would be wonderful to have all these things resolved *before* you get married, I believe it is actually impossible. That's because you and your spouse have never before lived together as man and wife. And this is true even if you have lived together before marriage. No man or woman truly understands their own limits and capabilities before they have made that public declaration and have entered into this legally binding lifetime commitment. When you do that, you are forced to deal with issues in yourself and in your spouse because they deeply affect your lives together.

We all put our best foot forward when we are dating, but it's impossible to do that every day for the rest of our lives. Everyone has good days and bad days, weaknesses and strengths, times of patience and times of not so much. Everyone has moments when they let words slip out of their mouth that shouldn't have been spoken, and times they should have said or done something and didn't. But marriage provides a base in which you can give one another the security to come face-to-face with who you really are and have the freedom to be set free to heal and grow. That's why praying in advance of these things happening doesn't mean that difficult things won't ever happen, but if something does, you will be able to survive these times successfully, knowing God is using them to perfect both of you.

Remember the Good Times

Where I live in Tennessee, the fall season is exquisite. When the colors change, they are breathtaking shades of red, purple, orange, fuchsia, yellow, and one color that is a combination of coral and magenta that is so beautiful it defies description. It's similar to the most astounding sunset you've ever seen. Sometimes when I am driving in this colorful season, I want to pull over to the side of the road and just breathe in the hues. Standing in the midst of them gives me life.

It is the memory of those beautiful colors of fall that get me through the winter. When everything is dark and gray and stark, I think back to those fall colors and know I will see them again.

That's the way it is in a marriage too. It is the memory of the good times—the colorful and happy times—that can get you through the tough times—the dark and gray seasons. You remember what it *can* be, and that spurs you to not give up. Good memories encourage you to hang on and keep praying.

That being said, there is a surprising beauty about the winter too. It's stark nakedness. It's crisp monotones of black and gray and white. The leaves are off the trees, and the season exposes what is really there. You can see everything that the leaves were covering up before. You notice the bare bones of the supporting structure. That's the way it is in a marriage as well. The tough times expose what you are really made of—what's strong and what is weak. What is good and what isn't. They help you see what's really there. If you go through a season of difficulty and look at it from a perspective of growing deeper, of changing in the ways God wants you to change, of working things out and coming to new conclusions, of new and better compromises between you and your spouse, and of refusing to compromise with the laws of God, then you can always find beauty in the season you're in.

God Has More for You Than You Can Imagine

The thing you have to remember is that God has more for you than you can imagine. I know this is hard to comprehend because we can imagine some amazing things. We can dream big. But even considering your greatest dream for yourself, what God has for you is far greater. The Bible says: "Eye has not seen, nor ear heard, nor have entered into the heart of man the things which God has prepared for those who love Him" (1 Corinthians 2:9). It's true as a married couple too. You may have trouble imagining your marriage being better than your greatest dream for it, but it can be. The reason I know this is true is because it is God's will for your life. It's what He wants for you. I have seen God do miracles in my own marriage and in the lives of countless married couples I have prayed with and heard from over the years. I'm not saying our marriage is perfect, but it's a lot better than I thought it could ever be at this point. And I know it's because of the power of God working through our prayers.

The Cold Hard Facts

Now, you need to be sitting down for this. This may be the part where you throw the book across the room and say, "I'm not doing that," just as some of you did when you read the first chapter of my book *The Power of a Praying Wife*, where I told wives that you have to stop praying the "Change him, Lord" prayer for your husband and start praying "Change me, Lord" instead. Don't blame me for that. It was definitely not my idea. I liked the "Change him, Lord" prayer. Never mind that it wasn't getting answered. Most of us liked that prayer because we didn't think *we* were the ones who needed changing. But God says we *all* need to be changed, and He will start with whoever is *willing* to be changed. So, if you don't like this next part, take it up with God. This is *His* idea, not mine. But at least hear me out on this because it works. Prayer gets answered this way. And what I have learned is that you will have to accept this truth at some point in your life anyway, so you might as well do it now.

Okay. Here it is. Brace yourself.

The bottom line in saving, improving, and enriching your marriage is that you have to *be willing to have a repentant heart.*

Wait! Don't throw the book. I know what you're thinking. You're thinking, *My husband (wife) is the one who really needs to repent, so why should I have to do it? Besides, I'm a good person. I haven't murdered anyone or robbed a bank. Why do I need to repent?* But God says we *all* need to. That's because we all fall far short of what God wants for us in the way we think, act, and live our lives. And for the most part we don't understand the true meaning of having a repentant heart. It doesn't mean you have necessarily done something blatantly bad, although it *can* mean that. Rather, it means you are willing to let God show you where you have not done things perfectly and then respond by prostrating yourself before Him and asking for His forgiveness.

We have to get to the point in our marriage where we live with a repentant heart all the time. A heart that says *I am willing to see my errors, and no matter how I have been offended by the things my spouse has done, I will clean house on my own soul. I will pray to have eyes to see the truth about myself before I pray the same for my husband (wife).*

How often does God want to do amazing things in our lives and our marriages, but because we don't pray with a repentant heart, those things don't happen? God said of Israel that *they* would determine whether He could *bless* them or whether they would receive *curses* instead (Deuteronomy 28, emphasis added). He was ready to bless them, but they didn't listen. Instead, they arrogantly went their own way and chased after idols. We, likewise, determine whether we will have blessings or misery in our marriage by whether we will listen to God or chase after what feels good. Whether we will self-righteously think we don't ever need to repent of anything because we see worse sins in our spouse, or we will bite the bullet and repent of every bad thought or action as we humbly come before God in prayer.

I just heard on the news that more and more married couples are choosing to continue living together after they divorce and lead separate lives. Their reason is that "it's cheaper that way." But I have an idea. Why not do what it takes to stay together and actually learn to love and enjoy one another? It can be done with hearts that are *repentant enough* to be *willing* to let God *change them.* Even if you are the only one with a willing heart, your humble prayers can pave the way for God to do miracles in you and in your marriage relationship. Are you ready to pray for a change? Are you ready to protect your marriage relationship so it will last a lifetime?

If COMMUNICATION BREAKS DOWN

The most difficult thing about a marriage is that there are *two* people in it. And we all know that the problem is usually with the other person. If we were just trying to work things out by ourselves, we could certainly do a good job of it, but we have to fit our dreams, desires, hopes, abilities, mind-sets, assumptions, needs, and habits in with those of our spouse. And that takes three things: Communication, communication, and communication.

Verbally, emotionally, and physically.

The foundation of a good marriage that will last a lifetime has to be built by communication. It is the way intimacy is established. Anytime communication is shut off, intimacy suffers greatly. And a marriage without intimacy is dying. You and your spouse must each be able to have a sense of closeness in your marriage—an assurance you are on the same team. Without good communication, you won't have that.

The closest relationship you will ever have is with your spouse because you share everything. Not being able to communicate with him (her)—or he (she) not being able to communicate with you—paves the way for an intolerable existence. Not knowing what your spouse is thinking or feeling makes building a life together impossible. If neither of you know what the other's internal plans and visions are for the future, how can you move into it together?

How can you show your commitment to the relationship if you never share that with your spouse? How do you get the sense that you are always going to be there for each other if you don't talk? If you don't express your fears and inner turmoil, how can you receive the encouragement you need? If there isn't good verbal communication, then there isn't an emotional connection, and that means there won't be good physical intimacy, either. That part of your life together will then become an act without feeling or passion. If *one* of you believes that the communication is not good in your relationship, then some changes have to be made.

Time for a Change

Have you ever felt as though your life is stuck in one place? That you cannot move beyond where you are? Things can become that way in a marriage too. You can get into a rut. You can feel stuck in a relationship that isn't growing, isn't getting better, and isn't going anywhere. And only one of you—or perhaps neither of you—is willing to change anything in order to make it better.

God is a God of change. Although *He* is unchanging—*He* is the same yesterday, today, and forever—He doesn't want *us* to be like that. That's because *He* doesn't *need* to change. *We do. He* is *perfect. We're not.* He wants us to always be changing because He desires that we become more and more like Him. If we are resistant to being changed, then we are resistant to God because God is all about changing *us.*

If one or both people in a marriage are resistant to the changing, transforming, and perfecting work of the Holy Spirit, then there are certain to be bad habits that develop. Our flesh is like that—it's always headed toward the destructive. The longer these bad habits go on, the more entrenched they become. But the good news is that any stronghold of bad habits can be broken in an instant by the power of God, no matter how long they have been there. Even bad habits with regard to communication in your marriage can be completely eliminated. Anyone can learn to communicate better if they are willing to make the effort.

Marriage is not something you enter into to see what you can get *out* of it. It's something you ask yourself every day what you can put *into* it. Marriage is a covenant relationship, which means it is supposed to be a commitment until death parts us. Unfortunately, too often the *marriage* dies before the *people* in them do. *Getting* married is just the very beginning of your relationship. *Being* married frees you to feel secure enough to let your true self show—for better or for worse—so you can see where you need God's healing and transformation. *Staying* married depends on you both being able to communicate with one another.

The only way you can keep growing together and not apart is by good communication. What other way can love and respect be shown? How else can you really be on the same team? What would happen in a football game if the quarterback never communicated with the rest of the team? It would be a disaster. They would never reach their goal. They would never experience victory. It's the same in a marriage. That's why it is entirely selfish and destructive to refuse to communicate with your spouse for whatever reason.

Right from the Start

From the beginning God had the marriage relationship in mind. Even though Adam was able to communicate with God every day, God saw that this wasn't enough. God said, "It is not good that man should be alone; I will make him a helper comparable to him" (Genesis 2:18). He could have created another man so Adam would have a golfing buddy, but He didn't. He created a woman who was "comparable to him." That means she wasn't merely an airhead with a great body. She *complemented* him. She *helped* him. And he needed her *companionship* and *support*. He needed someone to *communicate* with him on his level. If Adam could have done it all by himself, he wouldn't have needed Eve.

God made Eve from the rib He took out of Adam (Genesis 2:21-22). That means a man will always have something missing without his wife. She completes him. And, likewise, a woman has a natural sense of belonging at a man's side as his support. I've known a number of single men and women for years who are now in their sixties and have never married, and no matter how many friends they had in their life, they still suffered with bouts of severe loneliness. And this only increased with age. I know there are exceptions to that, such as the men and women who have devoted their lives to God's service and because of His grace didn't suffer with that kind of loneliness. But most single people *do* struggle with it. Right from the start God recognized a man's and a woman's deep need to commune with one another.

I took a survey of women before I wrote *The Power of a Praying Husband,* and one of the most important things women wanted was that their husbands would talk to them more. This is a very big issue in a marriage. You may have been married 30 years to a poor communicator—or you may be one yourself—but God can change both of you. We *all* can learn to communicate better.

I know a couple who spend more time in silence than they do talking. They argue so much when they talk that they have chosen to not communicate at all. This is an unnatural way to live. If you have that kind of situation, you are not fulfilling the plan God has for your marriage. Communication is more about *serving God's will* than it is your own. It's more about doing *what's right* than it is deciding *who's right.* If you want to glorify God in your marriage, pray that the two of you will have good communication. That takes two hearts caring enough about one another to refuse to be selfish.

If your husband (wife) doesn't want to change right now, then be glad that God can change *you first* while you pray for the Holy Spirit to work on *him* (*her*). God can help *you* to not be so easily hurt by your spouse's poor communication skills. The Lord can give *you* such joy and excitement about *your* life in Him that you don't feel rejected when your husband (wife) is silent. If *you* are the one who has trouble communicating, ask God to give you a heart for your spouse that desires to express your love and thoughts openly.

You and your spouse became one in God's eyes the day you were married (Ephesians 5:31), but there is still a process of becoming one in your everyday lives together from then on. The day-to-day living out of this concept of total unity doesn't just happen; it takes time and effort. *Both* husband and wife have to compromise in order to do it. When one person stops putting forth any effort to talk things out or make the marriage better, it becomes a nightmare for the other. If only one is communicating and the other is not, the marriage is headed for serious problems. One person trying to carry the entire weight of a marriage relationship will work for only so long.

The Reason I Know How Important Communication Is

If you're like me and have already experienced divorce, you know the horrible pain of it and don't want to ever go through it again. You also know that when you are contemplating a divorce, you make a list in your mind of all the things that will change, and you ask yourself, *Is it worth it? Do the gains balance out the losses?* If communication is bad—or if the only communication is negative—you end up thinking you don't have much to lose and everything to gain.

When I was married the first time, before I became a believer, there was no communication in our relationship at all. Not only were we not on the same page, we weren't even in the same book. I came to the point where I felt as though I were living in hell, and I was ready to give up anything in order to feel hope, relief, and some degree of peace again. I wanted out so badly that I walked away from everything, taking only the possessions I brought into the marriage in the first place, even though I worked for two years to support him while he stayed home and watched TV. I didn't want to live another day in that slow death, and I saw no way whatsoever that life could ever be any different.

In his culture, men did not lift a finger to help around the house—or anywhere else, for that matter. Nor did they work, apparently. I found that I could not physically work 10- to 12-hour days and then come home to do *all* the cooking and *all* the cleaning because that was what he demanded. He daily evaluated my performance and recited the ways I had not lived up to the standards of his mother. He wanted me to be her and I just couldn't. He spent hours every day at her house while I worked, and he would still be there when I came home at night. It was like living alone again, except not as much fun. And I wasn't strong enough to take the constant criticism without any encouragement or sense of being loved. In his defense, he was probably trying to make me into the wife he wanted, and I was not a whole enough person at that time to be able to be all that.

He wasn't a believer, and he became extremely angry when he found out I had become one. After we had been married less than a year, I started going to church by myself every Sunday, which he thought was a waste of time when I could be cleaning or working another job to support him. One Sunday afternoon I came home from church feeling especially uplifted in my spirit, and I tried to talk to him about the Lord. He became irate and told me in a loud and threatening voice that I was forbidden to ever speak the name of Jesus in *his* house again and never as long as I was with *him*. It was the final straw that broke the back of my thinly spined marriage. I had been hanging on to the edge of a cliff by a delicate branch and had finally found hope and a reason to live, and now he was going to chop off the branch. It was like cutting off the air I breathed.

Soon after that I decided to do what he demanded and never speak the name of Jesus in *his* house or in *his* presence again. That meant, of course, I had to leave his house and his presence. After I left him I felt free to not only breathe, but to speak the name of Jesus whenever I wanted. It was liberating.

When I got married again, it was different. The most important difference being that my second husband, Michael, was a believer. We went to church together. We prayed together. We went to Christian marriage counselors together. So there was always hope for change in both of us. And I believed that any problems we had could be easily fixed.

However, we each came into the marriage with deep insecurities. He felt like a failure because he couldn't live up to his mother's expectations. I felt like a failure because my mentally ill mother had no expectations of me whatsoever. When she told me repeatedly that I was worthless and would never amount to anything, I had no reason to doubt her, even though I desperately looked for one. So my husband was *angry* and depressed. I was *anxious* and depressed. We were two damaged people, and hurting each other was easy. Although we communicated well in the beginning, there would be lapses where he would lash out in anger and I thought he was being cruel, so I would withdraw out of hurt, causing him to believe I didn't care. Communication became more and more difficult as time went on, and it was miserable.

When our marriage came to the ultimate crisis point after years like this, I wanted to leave. But in prayer about it one day, the Lord showed me that if I would pray for my husband every day the way God wanted me to, He would use me as an instrument of healing and deliverance for our marriage. I said yes to that and learned to pray the way the Lord was showing me. As I did, I began to see changes—especially in our communication. It wasn't an overnight transformation. It was more like a day by day moving into the territory God had for us to conquer and not giving up when there were times of setback.

The suffering that happens in an unhappy marriage is horrendous because there is no escape. Unless you get a divorce and dissolve the relationship completely, you are stuck there and have to work it out. If your spouse isn't willing to do anything to make it better, it is a nightmare. That's why praying about having good communication is so important. Yes, it's very good to be reading the Word of God and attending church where there is good Bible teaching, but I've seen too many marriages in the church end in divorce. I've even seen too many people who were great Bible teachers leave their husbands or wives. I've also seen marriages between people who never go to church or read the Bible last a lifetime. So there has to be more to saving a marriage than any kind of pat answer like "read the Word and stay in church." Even though I believe these two things are a must, you still have to do more. You have to pray and pray. And you have to pray specifically about your communication, because without that your marriage doesn't have a chance. I want to share specifically some ways I learned to pray about our communication that made a difference in our relationship.

Pray That You Can Just Be Nice

How many marriages could be saved if both the husband and wife would just be nice to one another? It's called common decency. The Bible says, "Love edifies" (1 Corinthians 8:1). That means love builds up and makes stronger. Love doesn't speak mean-spirited and sarcastic words that tear down. *What* we say and the *manner* in which we say it can either communicate love or total disregard. Loveless words of criticism destroy a marriage relationship, so we have to ask ourselves if the satisfaction derived from saying them is really worth the hurt and destruction they cause. God doesn't think so. He says that real love "does not behave rudely, does not seek its own, is not provoked, thinks no evil" (1 Corinthians 13:5). There is no reason to treat your spouse badly. If you want to improve your marriage, just being nice is a good place to start.

When a person is not treated well by their spouse, it keeps them from feeling safe enough to share their deepest thoughts and emotions, and this shuts off an important part of their relationship. If you have already fallen into bad habits of critical and insensitive speech toward your spouse, repent of that now and ask God to change your heart. If your husband (wife) frequently directs negative and critical speech toward *you,* pray for an awakening in him (her). Pray that the grave consequences of such careless words will be revealed to his (her) understanding. I know it may seem pointless to do anything if *you* are the only one making the effort and your spouse seems to be doing nothing, but I have found that when *you* do the right thing, even when your spouse doesn't, God blesses *you*. And that makes a big difference.

Have you seen couples who are married but seem like strangers? I used to know a couple who must have memorized the old saying, "If you can't say something nice, then don't say anything" because they never said anything. At least not to each other. Theirs was a lifeless marriage. When one spouse is emotionally distant or noncommunicative, it forces the other to have to endure all struggles alone. When there is no compatibility, there is no one with whom to share life. And when some people realize that they cannot rely on their spouse to come through with friendship and emotional support, it becomes too easy to turn to another person who will. If you can't be nice, you can't be friends, and your marriage will be an endurance test.

Friends enjoy being with one another. They don't act like strangers. They don't say words to bring the other down and destroy any hope or joy. If you and your husband (wife) have not been good in the friendship department, ask God to help you change your ways. If you have been friends all along, ask God to show you how to be better friends than you have ever been in the past.

God says our words have power. If "death and life are in the power of the tongue," then we must choose our words carefully (Proverbs 18:21). Pray that God will help you and your spouse speak words to each other that are kind, loving, positive, good, uplifting, encouraging, and life-giving. Ask God to be in charge of your marriage, and tell Him you will do whatever it takes to see that it becomes all it was intended to be. Even if it means being nice when you don't feel like it.

Pray That You Will Always Be Truthful and Honest

A marriage absolutely must be based on trust. If you can't trust each other, then whom can you trust? That's why lying to your spouse is one of the worst things you can do to damage your relationship. The Bible says clearly, "Do not lie to one another, since you have put off the old man with his deeds" (Colossians 3:9). Every lie has dangerous and far-reaching consequences. "A false witness will not go unpunished, and he who speaks lies will not escape" (Proverbs 19:5). The worst consequence is that lying distances you from God. "He who tells lies shall not continue in my presence" (Psalm 101:7). Lying also distances you from one another and stops the flow of good things God has for you personally.

In a marriage, it's important to be both *truthful* and *honest*. And there is a difference between the two. When you tell a lie, you are not truthful, but it is possible to tell the truth and still not be honest. That happens when you are not forthcoming with the *whole* truth. You may not have actually told a lie, but you didn't reveal everything you needed to reveal. Now, you don't need to reveal every single thing to every person you see, because then no one would want to be around you. But you do need to be forthcoming with your spouse, because he (she) will be with you for the rest of your life.

You know if you have told a lie or not, but sometimes you can inadvertently be less than honest about your true feelings because you don't know how to express them fully. You are not entirely honest if you haven't shared your feelings and thoughts. *A person who never communicates with their spouse cannot be completely honest because total honesty requires good communication.* Of course, it's not good to be expressing every thought you have every moment you have one even with your spouse, because then he (she) won't want to be around you either. But God will give you discernment about that too, if you ask Him for it.

Here are some things to remember about being honest:

1. Be honest about how you feel regarding the things your spouse does. You have to express your feelings when something seriously bothers you about your spouse's actions. If you are not honest with him (her) about this, nothing will ever change. Then bitterness and anger will build up in your heart and lead to resentment and unforgiveness. You not only have to know *what* to say, but *when* to say it. And God will always be the best judge of that. So anytime you need to say something important to your husband (wife) that may be hard to hear, ask God to show you the right time to say it. Ask Him to prepare your spouse's heart to receive it and give you the perfect words to say so you can speak "the truth in love" (Ephesians 4:15). The Bible says that there is "a time to keep silence, and a time to speak" (Ecclesiastes 3:7). Ask God to help you know the difference between the two.

2. Be honest about the way you see things. It's important for each of you to share your thoughts, plans, fears, concerns, hopes, and dreams for the future. You have to get these things out of your heart and into the open. Job said, "I will speak, that I may find relief" (Job 32:20). And that's exactly what you will find too. If your husband (wife) is the kind of person with whom it's difficult to communicate, ask God to break down that barrier in his (her) heart. Outside of going to a counselor who will be able to help you both open up and talk, you need a move of the Holy Spirit to do that, so pray for one. A husband and wife are constantly adjusting to each other in their marriage because no two people *are* the same or *stay* the same. (Even though at times it may seem as though nothing ever changes.) But they can never adjust properly to each other if they don't know what adjustments to make. If you are not honest with your spouse about these things, you can easily make wrong assumptions and incorrect adjustments.

3. Be honest about your past. When I first realized that Michael and I were getting serious, I knew I couldn't go any further in my relationship with him without being completely forthcoming about my past. But before I told him everything, I prayed that God would prepare his heart to receive it and give me the right words and time to say it.

He already knew about my mother, even though he didn't fully comprehend the seriousness of her mental illness until after we were married and we went to visit my parents for a weekend. But there were other things I had to tell him, and I didn't know whether he would totally reject me because of them. But he was completely accepting of what I told him and said it didn't change his mind about me at all. It was a great relief to get it out in the open and off my shoulders.

I've known other people who had secrets from their past that they never revealed to their spouse until well after they were married, and this late revelation shook the level of trust that had been established early on. Being totally honest about your past helps you to live more successfully in the present. It helps you to better move into the future God has for you. You don't want to always be looking over your shoulder to see if something is coming back to haunt you. The sooner you are forthcoming, the better.

4. Be honest about everything you are doing. I know a man who is constantly lying to his wife about the things he does. They don't have a close relationship, and his dishonesty could very well lead to a divorce in the future. Every lie breaks down trust. And when a husband or wife loses trust, the foundation of their marriage crumbles. Of course, trust can be restored again when the one who is lying confesses and truly repents. If you have to lie about what you are doing, then your priorities are completely out of order. You are not putting God first and your husband (wife) second above all else.

TEN THINGS THAT ARE TRUE ABOUT TELLING THE TRUTH

1. *Truth is what you must choose to think about.* "Finally, brethren, whatever things are true...meditate on these things" (Philippians 4:8).

2. *Truth is a decision you make about the words you speak.* "My mouth will speak truth; wickedness is an abomination to my lips" (Proverbs 8:7).

3. *Truth is the way you choose to walk.* "I have chosen the way of truth; Your judgments I have laid before me" (Psalm 119:30).

4. *Truth liberates you.* "You shall know the truth, and the truth shall make you free" (John 8:32).

5. *Truth protects you.* "Stand therefore, having girded your waist with truth, having put on the breastplate of righteousness" (Ephesians 6:14).

6. *Truth purifies your soul.* "Since you have purified your souls in obeying the truth through the Spirit in sincere love of the brethren, love one another fervently with a pure heart" (1 Peter 1:22).

7. *Truth pleases God.* "I have no greater joy than to hear that my children walk in truth" (3 John 1:4).

8. *Truth can be branded in your heart.* "Let not mercy and truth forsake you; bind them around your neck, write them on the tablet of your heart" (Proverbs 3:3).

9. *Truth brings you into God's light.* "He who does the truth comes to the light, that his deeds may be clearly seen, that they have been done in God" (John 3:21).

10. *Truth in your heart invites a greater sense of God's presence when you pray.* "The LORD is near to all who call upon Him, to all who call upon Him in truth" (Psalm 145:18).

Pray That God's Love Will Be Poured into Your Heart

The best way to have good communication with your spouse is to first be in good communication with God. If it's true that "out of the abundance of the heart the mouth speaks" (Matthew 12:34), then you have to ask God to fill your heart abundantly with His love every day so that the words you speak are loving. The Bible says that "no man can tame the tongue. It is an unruly evil, full of deadly poison" (James 3:8). Left to ourselves, we will naturally say hurtful and destructive words. The Bible also says, "The preparations of the heart belong to man, but the answer of the tongue is from the LORD" (Proverbs 16:1). We can prepare our heart by being in the presence of God in prayer, in worship, and by reading His Word.

When truth is hard to hear in a marriage, ask God for a greater portion of His love with which to communicate it. Whenever you speak from a bad attitude or a loveless heart, it cuts off your spouse's ability to hear what you're saying. Ask God to give you wisdom to say the right things the right way. "The heart of the wise teaches his mouth, and adds learning to his lips" (Proverbs 16:23). When you make an effort to speak words that communicate love, it pays off. It pleases God, and there is always great reward in that.

Don't let animosity swell up and become a flood pouring over your relationship. Dam up arguments with honest communication and loving words. "The beginning of strife is like releasing water; therefore stop contention before a quarrel starts" (Proverbs 17:14). Ask God to make your heart so filled with His love that your words will be like healing waters of encouragement and restoration instead of an open floodgate that produces serious water damage.

Pray That You Can Understand the Signs

We have a little white long-haired Chihuahua. He is actually my daughter's dog, but she wasn't able to take him with her when she moved out because of her work and travel schedule. I guess that makes him our grand-dog. His name is Wrigley, but Michael and I call him "The Great I Want." That's because unless he is sleeping, Wrigley always wants something. Wrigley communicates his wants by sitting up on his hind legs and putting his paws together as though he is praying, and he waves them up and down while relentlessly squeaking. He can balance that way for longer than you ever dreamed possible. You can ignore the sitting up and the praying hands, but there is no way you are going to ignore the squeaking. It will drive you crazy. The only way to get him to stop is to ask him simple questions about all the things he usually wants and see how many times his paws go up and down. Because he always wants *everything,* his paws will go up and down at least one or two times for anything you say. There are key words we have to speak, such as "Outside?" "Dinner?" "Hold you?" "Bed?" "Blanket?" "Bone?" "Biscuit?" "Toy?" "Walk?" "Ride?" He understands all of these perfectly.

Do you want to go *outside?* Do you want *dinner?* Do you want me to *hold you?* Do you want a *biscuit?* Do you want your *bone?* Do you want to go for a *ride?* Actually, we've learned not to say "ride" unless we are committed to taking him on one. Because no matter how much he needs to go "outside" or how hungry he is for "dinner," a "ride" takes precedence over everything. And once you said the "R" word, if you didn't follow through you would be squeaked to death.

When you ask Wrigley these questions, you have to be very discerning as to how many times his praying paws go up and down. One time for "bone," two times for "dinner," two times for "hold you." And so on through the entire cycle because all his wants are relative. The word that gets the greatest up and down movement of the praying paws indicates what he wants most. The only word he doesn't respond to is "bath." I tried throwing that word in a couple times, and Wrigley was frozen in silence with a look on his face that said *Don't see me. Don't see me.* One time when he desperately had to go outside, he waved his paws at least six times in the space of two seconds and we knew it was an emergency.

The thing is, the expression on Wrigley's face never changes when he is doing his praying paws, so you cannot tell by looking at his face what he wants. And his squeaks all have the same intensity. It's the subtle signals in his body language that you have to take into consideration in order to discern what it is he is after.

The point in all this is that sometimes we have to look very carefully at the body language of our spouse in order to figure out what he (she) wants and what is going on inside him (her). We have to ask the right questions and be able to discern his (her) reaction to them. We have to read between the lines. Ask God to enable you to recognize the vital signs in your husband (wife). Ask God to help *you* communicate so clearly that your husband (wife) doesn't have to search for helpful signs in your body language.

Pray That You Will Enjoy Doing Things Together

What do you and your husband (wife) like to do together? If you can think of something, that's good. But if you are struggling to think of even one thing, then this is a problem for your relationship. In order to have good communication you must have things you enjoy doing together, even if it's something as simple as sitting together watching the sunset or reading books or taking walks or going out to eat. If you work together, you still need something to do together outside of work.

My husband and I tried golfing together for a short period of time. We tried tennis too. But my husband's goal was to win at all costs and mine was to just have fun. I didn't like risking my life trying to have fun. So we gave that up.

At this stage in our lives, due to a miraculous answer to my husband's prayers, we both like football. (Watching, not playing.) He bought me a book called *Football for Dummies,* took me to games, and was willing to explain the same thing over and over and over until I got it. Not an easy task for an impatient type A, but this was important to him and so he persevered. And it paid off because I love the game. Now we watch football games together on TV and attend them in person when our team is in town. If you knew how much I used to think that this was the biggest waste of time, you would realize how miraculous this is. Michael and I had *both* been praying that we would have something we like to do together. And *he* won. I still have to shop alone.

Pray That You Will Grow Closer with Each New Stage of Life

There are many stages of life and marriage, and you need to pray that you and your spouse will grow together through them instead of apart. You don't want to wake up one morning and find that you're in bed with a stranger and realize that he (she) is the person you married. Sometimes situations change. Perhaps your spouse was originally the main wage earner in the family, but then for one reason or another, *you* became the main wage earner. Or when children arrived on the scene, the perfect husband didn't turn out to be the perfect father. Or what used to be the perfect wife suddenly becomes the perfect mother *instead*. Or the children leave home. Or they come *back home* after they have finally left home. Or there are job changes, health changes, or financial changes. All these things can affect communication or cause serious miscommunication.

The proof of love for your spouse is the willingness to make changes as your lives progress together. Ask God to enable you both to always be sensitive to what is going on in the other in each stage of life, and to make any adjustments necessary in how you communicate. That way you'll continue to grow together.

Pray That You Will Honor One Another

Don't you hate it when you are with another couple and one of them says something critical, demeaning, or dishonoring about the other? Nothing causes people to feel more uncomfortable than a husband or wife making unkind jabs at one another in front of them. And it can force *you* into the awkward position of having to take sides in the matter, which you really can't because no one knows the inner workings of someone else's marriage. Sometimes the one who appears to be the charming and wonderful person is actually the offending person who is nice to everyone but their spouse. And the spouse who appears bitter or nasty has actually been pushed to the edge of what she (he) can take.

Husbands are especially exhorted to give honor to their wives, and the consequence of failing to do so is not having their prayers answered. "Husbands, likewise, dwell with them with understanding, giving *honor* to the wife, as to the weaker vessel, and as being heirs together of the grace of life, *that your prayers may not be hindered*" (1 Peter 3:7, emphasis added). This consequence is about as serious as it can get and should not be taken lightly.

Husbands are also admonished to *love* their wives, and wives are to *respect* their husbands and *submit* to them (Ephesians 5:22-33). For wives, godly submission is something you willingly do. It's not something your husband forces you to do. That's slavery. Submission is communicated in a godly way by showing respect to your husband. But a wife finds submitting to her husband far *easier* if he is submitted to God, which is the way God wants it. She finds it *harder* to do if he is not submitted to God or if he has disrespected her in any way. Ask God to help you and your husband (wife) to unfailingly show honor, respect, appreciation, and love to one another—*especially* in front of other people.

TEN THINGS TO REMEMBER ABOUT THE WORDS YOU SPEAK

1. ***Choose your words carefully.*** "Let no corrupt word proceed out of your mouth, but what is good for necessary edification, that it may impart grace to the hearers" (Ephesians 4:29).

2. ***Gentle words have more power than harsh words.*** "A gentle tongue breaks a bone" (Proverbs 25:15).

3. ***You have to think before you speak.*** "The heart of the righteous studies how to answer, but the mouth of the wicked pours forth evil" (Proverbs 15:28).

4. ***Don't talk too much.*** "In the multitude of words sin is not lacking, but he who restrains his lips is wise" (Proverbs 10:19).

5. ***Your words can cause you to stumble.*** "We all stumble in many things. If anyone does not stumble in word, he is a perfect man, able also to bridle the whole body" (James 3:2).

6. ***Kind words are life-giving.*** "Pleasant words are like a honeycomb, sweetness to the soul and health to the bones" (Proverbs 16:24).

7. ***Your words can bring about great destruction.*** "The tongue is a little member and boasts great things. See how great a forest a little fire kindles!" (James 3:5).

8. ***If you want a good life, watch what you say.*** "He who would love life and see good days, let him refrain his tongue from evil, and his lips from speaking deceit" (1 Peter 3:10).

9. ***Your words can be inspired by the enemy.*** "The tongue is a fire, a world of iniquity. The tongue is so set among our members that it defiles the whole body, and sets on fire the course of nature; and it is set on fire by hell" (James 3:6).

10. ***Your unkind words hurt you more than they hurt your spouse.*** "By your words you will be justified, and by your words you will be condemned" (Matthew 12:37).

Pray That You Both Will Have Ears to Hear

A big part of communicating is learning to listen. That means not doing all the talking. It means asking God to give you ears to hear and a heart that is willing to receive what your spouse is saying. Often you can "bear one another's burdens, and so fulfill the law of Christ" by simply *listening* to your spouse talk about what his (her) burdens are (Galatians 6:2). If you are married to someone who is too self-absorbed to listen, or refuses to listen because it might give the appearance of not being in control, or doesn't value what you have to say, pray that God will give him (her) ears to hear. Believe me, there is a greater impact when God convicts someone of not listening than there is when *you* try to do it.

Sometimes we *think* we know what the other person is saying, but God says not to answer too soon before you fully listen. "He who answers a matter before he hears it, it is folly and shame to him" (Proverbs 18:13). Listening means not talking while the other talks. How can you "rejoice with those who rejoice, and weep with those who weep" if you don't listen well enough to know if they're weeping or rejoicing? (Romans 12:15). If it seems your spouse never listens to you—or if your husband (wife) is always saying that *you* don't listen to him (her)—ask God to give you both a heart to hear. He loves answering that prayer.

Pray That the Enemy's Plan to Disrupt Communication Will Not Succeed

Always keep in mind that the enemy of your soul is also the enemy of your marriage, and therefore the enemy of your communication. Have you ever had something come between you and your spouse just when everything seems to be going well and break down the lines of communication so that you suddenly find yourselves completely missing each other? Suddenly there will be confusion or an argument or a distortion of what is being said, and you can't understand the reason for it. Disrupting the lines of communication between a husband and wife is one of the enemy's most common tactics. This can happen in even the best of marriages and in subtle ways so you think it's you. Ask God to keep you both aware of the enemy's hand trying to stir up strife and misunderstandings between you. Don't allow it to happen. If you see that it already has, declare that because *God* is *for* you, no one can be against you—not even the two of you.

Prayers for My Marriage

Prayer for Protection

Lord, I invite Your presence to dwell in our marriage. I pray that You would protect my husband (wife) and me from any kind of breakdown of communication. Enable us to always share our thoughts and feelings and refuse to be people who don't talk. Teach us to trust each other enough to share our deepest hopes, dreams, fears, and struggles with one another. Help us to spend time communicating with *You* every day so that our communication with each other will always be good. Teach us how to openly express love for one another, and keep us from any laziness or selfishness that would cause us to neglect to do that. Help us to refuse to speak words that tear down, but only words that build up (Ephesians 4:29).

Deliver us from any temptation to lie to each other about anything or deal falsely with one another (Leviticus 19:11). Help us to be totally honest and open about everything. Teach us to speak with truth, wisdom, instruction, and understanding. We don't want to be "always learning and never able to come to the knowledge of the truth" (2 Timothy 3:7).

Teach us to listen to one another and recognize the signs in each other that give us greater understanding. Help us find things we enjoy doing together so that we will grow closer and not apart. Enable us to be able to communicate love, appreciation, and honor to each other at all times. Teach us to recognize the enemy's plan to steal, rob, and destroy our marriage. Enable us to understand his methods and see his attempts to stir up strife and miscommunication between us. Help us to take instant authority over any attack he brings against us—especially in the area of communication. Help us to settle all matters of disagreement between us in a loving, compromising, and considerate manner. Enable us to always be in unity with You and with each other. In Jesus' name I pray.

Prayer for Breakthrough in Me

Lord, I invite Your presence to dwell in me and change me where

I need to be changed. Reveal any times where I have not said the right words or communicated the right things to my husband (wife) and I will confess it as sin, for I know I fall far short of Your glory (Romans 3:23). Teach me how to communicate openly and honestly so I will speak excellent, right, and truthful words (Proverbs 8:6-9). I know I cannot live in Your presence if I don't speak the truth in my heart (Psalm 15:1-3). Take away any deceit in my heart and any perversity in my mind so that evil will be far from me (Proverbs 17:20).

I pray that Your love will be so much in my heart that it comes out in everything I say. Give me the right words for every situation. Help me to remember to show appreciation to my husband (wife) for the good things he (she) does. Open my eyes if I am not seeing all of them. Give me ears to really hear what my husband (wife) is saying so that I can bear some of his (her) burdens by simply listening. Make me quick to hear and slow to speak (James 1:19). Give me the wisdom to have a good sense of timing.

Lord, You are greater than anything I face and stronger than all that opposes me and our marriage. Thank You that You have given me authority over the enemy. I pray I will always recognize his hand in our lives so that I will not allow any of his evil intentions to disrupt us. I pray that "my mouth shall speak wisdom, and the meditation of my heart shall give understanding" (Psalm 49:3). I thank You in advance for the answers to my prayers. In Jesus' name I pray.

Prayer for Breakthrough in My Husband (Wife)

LORD, I THANK YOU FOR MY HUSBAND (WIFE) and pray that You would open his (her) heart to all that You have for him (her) and for our marriage together. Help him (her) to know You better, to understand Your ways, and to see things from Your perspective. Help him (her) to view the two of us the way You do. Make changes in him (her) that need to be made so that nothing will hinder him (her) from fulfilling the purpose and destiny You have for his (her) life and our lives together.

Lord, fill my husband's (wife's) heart with Your love so that it overflows in the words he (she) speaks. Help him (her) to understand the consequences for any careless or hurtful words. Help us both to be more discerning about what wounds the heart of the other. Speak through us so that our words to each other will be *Your* words. Help us to be instruments of Your peace and grace every time we speak to each other. Convict my husband's (wife's) heart of times he (she) has said words that have hurt me and did not glorify You. Enable him (her) to speak words of life and not death, words that build up and not tear down. Increase his (her) knowledge of Your ways so that he (she) will refuse to speak negatively. Help him (her) to communicate openly, and not allow a cold silence to exist between us.

Lord, help my husband (wife) to be honest about everything. Convict his (her) heart about any lies he (she) has told me or anyone else, and break down any thought in him (her) that lying is acceptable, or that there are different versions of the truth. Strengthen him (her) to resist the father of all lies and refuse to fall into any temptation to lie (John 8:44). Help him (her) to stop all deceit (1 Peter 2:1). May he (she) refuse to be snared by his (her) own words (Proverbs 6:2). May there be no division between us, because we are of the same mind and have the same good judgment (1 Corinthians 1:10). Where he (she) has not communicated well in the past, help him (her) to do so now. Thank You that You are our rock and our Redeemer, and You can redeem all things (Psalm 78:35). In Jesus' name I pray.

Truth to Stand On

Let the words of my mouth and the meditation of my heart
be acceptable in Your sight, O Lord, my strength and my Redeemer.

Psalm 19:14

Though I speak with the tongues of men and of angels, but have not love,
I have become sounding brass or a clanging cymbal.

1 Corinthians 13:1-3

We all stumble in many things. If anyone does not stumble in word,
he is a perfect man, able also to bridle the whole body.

James 3:2

Husbands ought to love their own wives as their own bodies;
he who loves his wife loves himself...
and let the wife see that she respects her husband.

Ephesians 5:28,33

Wives, submit to your own husbands, as to the Lord...Husbands love
your wives, just as Christ also loved the church and gave Himself for her.

Ephesians 5:22,25

If ANGER, RUDENESS, *or* ABUSE POISONS YOUR RELATIONSHIP

Arguments happen in every marriage. Every one of us can get angry sometimes. But it's possible to argue without venting anger at one another. It's possible to express anger in a civilized and godly manner and not attack your spouse or children. If you frequently see anger rising up in either you or your spouse, it's a sign of trouble ahead. Anger always turns off communication, so if one or both of you can't get control of your anger, then the distance between you is bound to grow. The quickest way to put a halt to all meaningful and constructive communication in your marriage is to direct your anger toward your spouse. Do it enough times and it will not only damage your spouse's soul, but also *yours* as well.

The anger I am talking about in this chapter is not expressed in an infrequent heated argument or a rare spirited disagreement. It is something that resides deep within a person that seems to have a life of its own. It festers and churns and always maintains a readiness to surge and strike at any moment, for any reason. And the degree of manifestation of the anger is way out of proportion to the offense. Some little thing can trigger it, and suddenly rage will come forth when least expected over what seems to be a nonissue. Anger looks for a reason and a way to attack and hurt, and there seems to be great satisfaction in it because this is what anger lives to do. There appears to be little if any recognition in the angry person of what their anger does to those toward whom it is directed. In the angry person's mind anger is always justified because he (she) deserves to be angry for whatever reason.

A person's frequent anger can be explained, but it is never justified. I am not talking about an incident happening that would make anyone angry. I am talking about someone who has an angry spirit inside of them that they give place to because it gives them the opportunity to be in control and get their way. It forces their spouse and children to walk on eggshells because they are always afraid that it is going to erupt again. This is no way to live—especially not in a marriage, where there is no escape.

One of the most common complaints I hear from women struggling in their marriages is a problem with anger in their husbands. I occasionally hear it from men as a complaint about their wives, but it seems that more women suffer because of their husband's anger. I have never seen any good come from one spouse venting their anger on the other, but I have seen a whole lot of devastation. That's why God has plenty to say about anger in His Word.

How to Inherit the Wind

The Bible says that "he who troubles his own house will inherit the wind" (Proverbs 11:29). That means a person who constantly stirs up strife in his own family will never find all the success and blessing the Lord has for him. It means even when that person does get anything, it will blow through his fingers like the wind and he won't be able to hold on to it.

Anything you do that upsets your spouse and children troubles your house. Using anger to control your spouse troubles your house. Raising your voice in explosive, loud, demeaning words troubles your house. Being rude and abusive troubles your house. While anger hurts the person it is directed toward, there are serious consequences for the angry person as well.

The anger I am talking about can drive a person to go beyond what is acceptable behavior. That kind of anger directed at your spouse is always selfish, and it will cause deep resentment. No one wants to be ruled by someone's anger—especially not from a spouse. Every angry outburst directed at a family member kills something in that person. It will eventually kill love, erode hope, and destroy the relationship.

We can be angry about something that happened. Anger's good when it's in response to a violation of human rights, social injustice, or irreverence for the things of God. It is not good when communicating with your husband (wife). We can have temporary anger toward someone we think is an offender, but we cannot sin in the process. The Bible says, " 'Be angry, and do not sin': do not let the sun go down on your wrath, nor give place to the devil" (Ephesians 4:26-27). That means no attacking or hurting.

When angry words and actions beat up the soul of a family member, even if their body is untouched, it destroys their sense of who God made them to be. It hurts them in a grievous way and sucks love out of their heart. The Bible says, "Put off all these: anger, wrath, malice, blasphemy, filthy language out of your mouth" (Colossians 3:8). Pray that neither you nor your spouse will ever trouble your family with anger.

When Your Love Fails, God's Won't

The first commandment says that the *most important thing* you can do is *love God.* The second commandment says that the *next most important thing* you can do is *love others* as you love yourself (Matthew 22:37-39). And the *most important person* to love above all others is your *spouse.*

A husband is supposed to love his wife (Ephesians 5:25), and a wife her husband (Titus 2:4). Loving your spouse is one of the ways you love and serve the Lord. God wants you as a married couple to love each other the way He loves you. But who can love the way Jesus loves *us?* He laid down His life for us. Who can love like that every day? When you get up every morning. When you see each other after a hard day. When one or both of you are definitely not at your best. *The only way you can truly love each other as God intended and Jesus demonstrated is to be filled afresh with the Holy Spirit every day.* Selfless love, which is a fruit of the Spirit, comes by having the Spirit of love poured in you.

Christ demonstrated His love for the church by sacrificing Himself for her. (The "church" in the Bible refers to all of us who are believers in Jesus, not to a building.) He didn't get angry and yell at the church or be mean to the church or criticize and put down the church. He loved the church and gave Himself for her. This is the kind of love God wants you to have for your spouse. But this kind of love cannot be conjured up in the flesh. It takes the enablement of the Holy Spirit and the infilling of your heart with His love.

No matter what happens in your life or your marriage, the Holy Spirit will always fill your heart afresh with God's love if you ask Him to. Or, if you spend time in God's presence in prayer, praise and worship, and in His Word, you will be infused with His love. When you love because Jesus commanded you to and the Holy Spirit has filled your heart with God's love, it's far different than trying to conjure up a feeling of love in the flesh when you don't feel like it. By being filled with God's love—which is far greater than human love—you will have the ability to love your husband (wife) the way God wants you to, no matter what is happening.

Feelings of love in a marriage can rise and fall and come and go. Human love ebbs and flows. It changes because of emotions, circumstances, and seasons. The love God wants us to have for our spouse is something that stays steady. It is a constant stream that pours from heaven into the human soul and overflows to those around them. But we can't love that way without *His* help. That's why we have to stay connected to the Lord and tap into that love every day by spending time with *Him*. The only way you can always be patient, kind, loving, and *not easily angered* is if you are plugged into God. The only way for God's love to consistently flow out of you toward your spouse is to be filled to overflowing with it.

God's love is the fountainhead from which a good marriage flows. *Loving your husband or wife is the most important thing you can do next to loving God, because you have to become like God to do it.* The love of God will keep you from being selfish, demanding, critical, angry, rude, or abusive. When God's love is in your heart, you will want to be patient and kind, and you won't want to insist on having your own way. You will be happy to say you're sorry, and you won't care about keeping a record of wrongs. In the flesh this is not possible, but with God it is.

If you want to stay in love with your spouse, stay in love with the Lord first. That flow of love found in Christ can touch you wherever you are and create an atmosphere of love, peace, and harmony within you that will overflow into your relationship with your husband (wife).

God Cares About the Way You Treat Your Spouse

It matters to God how you treat your spouse, and you will be called to account for it. Knowing that should make us all watch what we do and say. Knowing that should also help us to be more forgiving.

The way I reacted to my husband's anger was to withdraw from him. But that meant that while Michael would get all of his anger out of *his* system, it would still be stuck in *mine*. Eventually, when I was finally able to see the ultimate consequences for not treating your spouse with love and kindness, I began to feel sorrier for him than I did for myself. I saw that as long as I repented of any unforgiveness I had, I would be free. There would be consequences only in *his* life, not *mine*. I prayed for him to see the truth about his anger—how it displeased the Lord—and how he would bear the consequences for it. Even though it hurt me every time he was angry, I still loved him enough to not want to see him suffer because of it.

If you are married to someone who is often angry and takes his (her) anger out on you, know that this kind of behavior is hurting him (her) more than it is you. It may hurt you now, but it will hurt him (her) for a lifetime if it does not stop. It will shut off the blessings God wants to bring into his (her) life. He (she) will have delayed his (her) destiny because of anger. "Do not let your mouth cause your flesh to sin, nor say before the messenger of God that it was an error. Why should God be angry at your excuse and destroy the work of your hands?" (Ecclesiastes 5:6). Pray for your husband (wife) to be free of anger.

Anger Is a Work of the Flesh

It's not that you can never get angry at one another. But if it happens in a hurtful way, there must be genuine repentance on the angry person's part—that means having the intention of never doing that again—and there must be complete forgiveness from the spouse to whom the anger was directed. If those two things do not happen, the damage from that anger will be as if a hole was shot through the fabric of your relationship. Enough holes like that, and they will weaken the relationship so badly that only a miracle of God can keep it from ripping apart. We can only escape the consequences of our anger—which is sin—by the forgiveness of God and the power of the Holy Spirit.

An angry person *can* get free of his own anger because God sent His Son, Jesus, to save us from the consequences of our sins (Romans 8:2). When we receive Jesus, the Holy Spirit enables us to "not walk according to the flesh, but according to the Spirit" (Romans 8:4). In other words, because of the Holy Spirit in us, we have the power to reject all works of the flesh. But we have to *want* that, because if we don't, we will set our desires on constant fleshly gratification.

There is never a time when anger directed at your spouse will please God. It will always be fleshly minded and God hates it. "To be carnally minded is death, but to be spiritually minded is life and peace. Because the carnal mind is enmity against God; for it is not subject to the law of God, nor indeed can be. So then, those who are in the flesh cannot please God" (Romans 8:6-8). No one who has any sense of who God is wants to be in the position of not pleasing Him.

When you are giving place to a *sin,* you invite the spirit associated with it to have a *place* in your *life.* For example, if you tell enough lies, you invite a lying spirit to operate in your life. Then you start lying even when you have no reason to, and lying becomes a habit you can't break. In the same way, if you allow yourself to frequently give place to feelings of anger at your spouse or your children, you will end up with an angry spirit that can surface and attack at any time. When you don't control your anger, anger will control *you.* Only the power of the Holy Spirit can set you free from a spirit of anger. But you cannot be set free from something you don't even recognize that you have invited into your life.

Everyone gets angry sometimes. Some people get angry *all* the time. Those people have an angry spirit. They can't hold their anger in. A person who has an angry spirit always has it bubbling just under the surface waiting for some perceived imperfection in someone or some situation to summon it forth. It can explode in a moment of weakness on those around them. To be able to communicate without anger takes someone who can control his own spirit and is not controlled by their flesh. It takes a person of mercy instead of a person of wrath. "The merciful man does good for his own soul, but he who is cruel troubles his own flesh" (Proverbs 11:17).

If we live according to our flesh—that is giving the flesh what it wants when it wants it—we reap death. The death of our relationships and the death of the future God wants us to move into. If we want to see our marriages live, we have to put to death the constant gratifying of our flesh. And that's what giving place to anger is. If we want to see our purpose and future be fulfilled, we have to live according to the Spirit and not the flesh. "If you live according to the flesh you will die; but if by the Spirit you put to death the deeds of the body, you will live. For as many as are led by the

Spirit of God, these are sons of God" (Romans 8:13-14). We don't have to be a slave to our flesh by giving place to anger. When we are led by God's Spirit, we are truly children of God, and we will inherit the blessings God has for us.

Seven Things That Are True About Anger

1. **You are able to stop being angry.** "Cease from anger, and forsake wrath; do not fret—it only causes harm" (Psalm 37:8).

2. **Anger stirs up strife and causes you to sin.** "An angry man stirs up strife, and a furious man abounds in transgression" (Proverbs 29:22).

3. **Taking control of anger makes you stronger.** "He who is slow to anger is better than the mighty, and he who rules his spirit than he who takes a city" (Proverbs 16:32).

4. **It is to your benefit to let some things go instead of getting angry.** "The discretion of a man makes him slow to anger, and his glory is to overlook a transgression" (Proverbs 19:11).

5. **Only fools are quick to get angry.** "Do not hasten in your spirit to be angry, for anger rests in the bosom of fools" (Ecclesiastes 7:9).

6. **Angry people are never good to be around.** "Make no friendship with an angry man, and with a furious man do not go" (Proverbs 22:24).

7. **Angry words inspire more anger.** "A soft answer turns away wrath, but a harsh word stirs up anger" (Proverbs 15:1).

If You Are the One Who Has an Anger Problem

There is an epidemic of anger in marriages today. If anger is expressed frequently without repentance and forgiveness, it erodes all that has been established in the relationship and builds a wall between the husband and wife that will eventually become insurmountable. Anger has consequences, and they are never more apparent than in a marriage.

If you are the one with anger, you can make an intelligent decision to not be ruled by it. The hurt you inflict on the soul of someone God has given you to love will bring consequences you won't want to experience. Stop directing anger at your spouse and start directing it at the enemy of your soul and your marriage. No matter what happens in your life, don't respond to it in anger. Take it to God first. See where it's coming from. Ask God if displaying your anger will be glorifying to Him.

As with all negative emotions, anger begins in the mind. What you do and say comes out of what takes root in your mind. So fill your mind with the right things.

> Summing it all up, friends, I'd say you'll do best by filling your minds and meditating on things true, noble, reputable, authentic, compelling, gracious—the best, not the worst; the beautiful, not the ugly; things to praise, not things to curse. Put into practice what you learned from me, what you heard and saw and realized. Do that, and God, who makes everything work together, will work you into His most excellent harmonies (Philippians 4:8-9 MSG).

Don't let anger control you. Control *it* instead. When you let anger control you, you constantly blame your spouse for the things that upset you. Anger makes you blind to the feelings of other people. It causes you to hurt people you love. When you are angry you can't see anything except your own feelings. That's why most angry people have no clue as to how hurtful their anger is and what it's doing to their spouse and children.

If your husband (wife) makes you angry, ask God to reveal to you if this is something He wants you to be angry about. If not, ask Him to take it away. If so, ask Him to give you a calm spirit, the right words, and perfect timing so you can confront your spouse in a godly way about what has angered you. Then, with the leading of the Holy Spirit, calmly express your feelings without attacking your husband (wife). Write out your feelings *first* so you can delete any words you might regret.

Try to remember that both of you are on the same side and have a common enemy, so be angry at the enemy. Don't ever take revenge. It will only make you sick. Let *God* punish the offender if it's necessary. God says, "Vengeance is Mine" and He means it (Deuteronomy 32:35). Lashing out at your spouse with the desire to hurt will only punish you.

If Your Spouse Is the One with the Anger Problem

Common courtesy is required in a marriage. Why should a person be polite, considerate, and kind to everyone else, and rude, inconsiderate, and mean to the family they are supposed to love? If your spouse treats a stranger with more courtesy than he (she) does you, then he (she) is committing a sin that will grieve the Holy Spirit. This is not a good position to be in. If you are the one being treated that way, know that God does not want you to deal with your spouse's angry spirit. If you have been hurt and deeply wounded as a result of your spouse's anger, turn to God to save, heal, and deliver you and give you peace.

Most people with an anger problem don't see themselves as angry; they see themselves as right. They feel completely justified in what they say and do because they think they have a right to be angry. And the more self-centered they are, the more they feed off their own anger.

If there is an anger problem in your spouse, take it to God immediately. Ask Him to give you His perspective on it. If it is minor and a rare occurrence and you should just overlook it, ask God to help you do so. If it is a problem, ask God to show you how to confront it. Letting any issue go unresolved is dangerous—this is especially true of anger. Pray for your husband (wife) to be completely free of it. One of the greatest things you can give your spouse is your commitment to pray for him (her). Your prayers are a gift that will help him (her) get his (her) anger under control. "A gift in secret pacifies anger" (Proverbs 21:14).

When Anger Becomes Abuse

If a person gives *place* to anger and goes with it wherever it takes them, and if they say and do whatever feels good at the moment as they release that anger toward their spouse, it is abuse. There is a difference between simply getting angry about something, and letting anger become a weapon that crushes a person's heart, beats down their spirit, or hurts their physical body. Someone who will allow their anger to go that far has a mental and emotional disorder and needs professional help. In order to be free of that kind of anger disorder and the abuse that comes as a result of it, they also need the power of the Holy Spirit to cleanse their heart and deliver them from this selfish work of the flesh.

Abusive people love their anger to the point of actually looking for ways to be angry. Anger empowers them and fuels the fire they love to fan into flame. It gives them what they perceive as control. But actually, anger illustrates their utter lack of control. Lashing out and yelling at someone God has given you to love is sin. Abuse is sin.

Any words spoken in explosive anger can be abusive. A loudly raised voice and poor choice of words can cut like a knife into a person's soul. Angry outbursts are loveless and full of the desire to hurt. The verbal abuser doesn't try to see it from the perspective of the person they are abusing. They don't care to know how badly their anger makes the recipient of their anger feel because all they care about is how *they* feel themselves. If there have been times when your spouse's angry outbursts have killed something in you, that's abuse. Or if there are times when your own angry words have destroyed something in your spouse or your children, that is abuse. Abuse destroys lives.

You are in a battle for your marriage, but the battle is not with your spouse. If he (she) is the one firing the shots at you and you are being forced to defend or protect yourself, give the situation *your* best shot in prayer. Ask God to deliver your husband (wife) from the evil spirit troubling him (her) (1 Samuel 16:14-23). Ask God to give you the ability to stay calm in the midst of the battle. Ask Him to help you to resist striking back.

All that being said, I am definitely not saying to stop defending or protecting yourself if you are in harm's way. *I'm not telling any wife to stay in her marriage if her mental or physical health is in danger, and especially not if her life is being threatened in any way whatsoever.* Abuse of any kind goes against all that God is and all that He has for you. No one is required to take it. If you are afraid of what your spouse might do to harm you or your children, make plans to get free. Find a place to go and people to help you move out. I have known of too many people who waited too long and suffered devastating consequences. Don't be one of those statistics.

If your husband is physically abusing you, call a domestic violence hotline. You will usually find it listed under "Community Services" or "Emergency Services" at the beginning of your phone book. They understand the situation and can help you make the right decisions as to what to do about it. If you need to leave home for your own safety or the safety of your children, they will help you do that. Even if you don't end up leaving, it is good to have a plan. You need a safe place to go, a way to get there, someone to help, money you can have access to, and the legal papers and possessions you need to take with you.

Physical abuse doesn't go away on its own. It only gets worse. If you don't want to help yourself, then think about helping your husband by leaving and not returning until he gets help and is cured. Being destroyed by someone who has an emotional disorder such as uncontrolled anger is not the kind of self-sacrifice or martyrdom God is looking for. Don't enable your husband to suffer the consequences of his own sin of abuse. Help him get the healing needed to become a whole person.

There is no excuse for abuse. It is never justified. A man who physically or emotionally abuses his wife is emotionally sick and has a serious problem. Of all emotional disorders, anger can be by far the most destructive. It is more destructive than depression, anxiety, or fear because it is usually directed at the spouse in some abusive and destructive way. Don't fool around with this; it's too dangerous. He needs professional help and fast. A man who beats his wife and children in any way should be removed from them completely. Even if the abuse is only verbal, it is still extremely damaging. Scars happen internally as well as externally. Anger and abuse is the problem of the person who has it and not the fault of the one abused. No possible action or words of yours deserve violent, angry outbursts. Do not blame yourself.

You are not saved by your husband (wife) or your marriage. You are saved by Jesus Christ. While I am not advocating divorce, you should still know that you will not lose your salvation if you end up getting divorced. In an abusive situation, you may lose your life if you don't.

Seek Good Christian Counseling

If you or your spouse has an anger problem, even if it has not progressed to abuse, seek counseling together as soon as possible. If nothing else, you may need a referee. If your spouse refuses to go, seek it for yourself. Don't ignore signs that suggest something is broken and needs to be fixed. Find a good Christian counselor who does not believe "the abused person asked for it," or that "you have to stay in an abusive relationship because God said to submit to your husband." Both of these views are not only unbelievably out of touch with reality, but are cruel, wrong, and ungodly. Find a counselor who truly knows God's ways and values your individual lives as God does.

Seven Things That Are True About Being a Fool

1. *A fool thinks he is always right.* "The way of a fool is right in his own eyes, but he who heeds counsel is wise" (Proverbs 12:15).

2. *A fool cares only about himself.* "A fool has no delight in understanding, but in expressing his own heart" (Proverbs 18:2).

3. *A fool finds it easy to quarrel.* "It is honorable for a man to stop striving, since any fool can start a quarrel" (Proverbs 20:3).

4. *A fool trusts himself completely.* "He who trusts in his own heart is a fool, but whoever walks wisely will be delivered" (Proverbs 28:26).

5. *A fool vents all his feelings.* "A fool vents all his feelings, but a wise man holds them back" (Proverbs 29:11).

6. *A fool's words will do him harm.* "The words of a wise man's mouth are gracious, but the lips of a fool shall swallow him up" (Ecclesiastes 10:12).

7. *A fool destroys himself.* "Fools are undone by their big mouths; their souls are crushed by their words" (Proverbs 18:7 MSG).

If You Love Your Calling, Then Love Your Spouse

You and your husband (wife) are called together, and neither of you will completely accomplish the great purpose God has for you without the other. God made man and woman in His image. God's image is expressed in *both* male and female, and when you become one with your spouse spiritually, you begin to experience a measure of God's image in you that you wouldn't experience as fully without your mate.

The fact that you are designed to serve God together doesn't mean you have to be attached at the hip. You don't have to go every place together and do everything together. In fact, you can be separated as far as being on opposite sides of the world and still complement each other. You are still individuals with gifts and talents unique only to you, but God will combine those talents to bring out the best in each of you, and you will be an important part of each other's calling. God designed the two of you to complete each other. But your personality differences—especially if you are opposites—will either be the greatest blessing of your life or the greatest battle of your life, depending on whether you live in the Spirit or in the flesh. If you recognize that you are called together, it will help you appreciate each other's gifts, talents, abilities, and strengths, and you will know that directing anger toward your spouse is inappropriate.

PRAYERS FOR MY MARRIAGE

Prayer for Protection

DEAR LORD, HELP MY HUSBAND (WIFE) and me to be "slaves of righteousness" so we will always do the right thing and not allow anger to control our lives in any way (Romans 6:19). Keep us from ever using anger as a weapon to hurt one another so that it doesn't drive a wedge between us. Fill our hearts full of Your love and peace so there is no room for anger. Teach us to pray about everything and make all of our needs known to You, knowing that when we do You have promised in Your Word to give us Your peace (Philippians 4:6-7).

Lord, enable us to always see the best in one another and not the worst. Teach us to find things to praise about each other and not complain about, so that we can be brought into harmony with You and each other in our marriage (Philippians 4:8-9). Help us to always "pursue the things which make for peace" and the things by which we may edify one another (Romans 14:19). Enable us to exhibit the fruit of the Spirit—"love, joy, peace, longsuffering, kindness, goodness, faithfulness, gentleness, self-control"—and not a harvest of the flesh (Galatians 5:22-23). Take all anger from us and teach us to love each other from pure hearts and a good conscience (1 Timothy 1:5-6). In Jesus' name I pray.

Prayer for Breakthrough in Me

LORD, HELP ME TO DWELL ON the good and the positive in my life and in my husband (wife). I know that it is You who "looks deep inside people and searches through their thoughts" (Proverbs 20:27 NCV). Search the inner depths of my heart and expose anything that is not of You so I can be set free of it.

Lord, where I have directed anger toward my husband (wife) or held anger inside of me, I confess that as sin and ask You to forgive me and take all anger away. Heal any wounds that I have inflicted in him (her) with my words. Help me to speak good words and healing to my husband (wife), for I know that pleases You (Proverbs 15:23). Where I have shown anger toward any other family member,

I confess it to You as sin. Bring Your restoration to every situation where it is needed.

Thank You, Lord, that You will redeem my soul in peace from the battle that is against me (Psalm 55:18). I believe that You, the God of peace, "will crush Satan" under my feet shortly (Romans 16:20). Help me to live righteously because I know there is a connection between obedience to Your ways and peace (Psalm 85:10). Help me to "depart from evil and do good; seek peace and pursue it" (Psalm 34:14). Thank You that You will take away all anger in me and keep me in perfect peace, because my mind is fixed on You (Isaiah 26:3). In Jesus' name I pray.

Prayer for Breakthrough in My Husband (Wife)

LORD, I DON'T WANT TO ever feel that "my soul has dwelt too long with one who hates peace" (Psalm 120:6). Deliver me from anger in my husband (wife). Your Word says, "A wholesome tongue is a tree of life, but perverseness in it breaks the spirit" (Proverbs 15:4). Where I have ever felt that an angry spirit in my husband (wife) has hurt me or broken my spirit, I pray You would heal those wounds and take away any unforgiveness I have because of it.

I pray You would set my husband (wife) free from anger. Help him (her) to recognize a spirit of anger rising up in him (her) and reject it completely. Strengthen him (her) to be able to control his (her) mind and emotions and help him (her) to remember that "we do not wrestle against flesh and blood, but against principalities, against powers," and the rulers of darkness and wickedness (Ephesians 6:12). Teach him (her) to be slow to anger the way You are (James 1:19). Help him (her) to understand that anger never produces spiritual fruit (James 1:20). I pray that all anger in my husband (wife) will be evaporated by the power of the Holy Spirit, and that he (she) will have a strong desire to reject his (her) carnal side and become spiritually minded. Let there be no reason to fear his (her) anger and what he (she) might do. Help me trust that "I will both lie down in peace and sleep; for You alone, O LORD, make me dwell in safety" (Psalm 4:8).

I pray now that You, the God of all hope, will fill my husband (wife) with faith and hope by the power of the Holy Spirit (Romans

15:13). I pray You would lift up Your countenance upon him (her) and give him (her) Your peace (Numbers 6:26). I pray You would direct his (her) heart "into the love of God and into the patience of Christ" (2 Thessalonians 3:5). Help him (her) to flee anger and pursue righteousness, godliness, faith, love, patience, and gentleness (1 Timothy 6:11). In Jesus' name I pray.

TRUTH TO STAND ON

Be angry, and do not sin.
Meditate within your heart on your bed, and be still.

PSALM 4:4

So then, my beloved brethren,
let every man be swift to hear, slow to speak, slow to wrath;
for the wrath of man does not produce the righteousness of God.

JAMES 1:19-20

Beloved, let us love one another, for love is of God;
and everyone who loves is born of God and knows God…
In this is love, not that we loved God,
but that He loved us and sent His Son
to be the propitiation for our sins.
Beloved, if God so loved us,
we also ought to love one another.

1 JOHN 4:7,10-11

Above all things have fervent love for one another,
for love will cover a multitude of sins.

1 PETER 4:8

If you abide in Me, and My words abide in you,
you will ask what you desire, and it shall be done for you.

JOHN 15:7

3

If FORGIVENESS DOESN'T COME EASY

You know the feeling. You've already said "I forgive you" to your spouse. You've confessed your unforgiveness to the Lord and asked Him to cleanse your heart and set you free of it. But you still have that feeling. That feeling of not being able to let it go completely. You're trying to be forgiving, but you just cannot seem to do a thorough job of it. Unforgiveness is still there!

This happens when you have to forgive your spouse for the same things over and over again, and it gets harder instead of easier as time goes on. Layers of offenses have accumulated, and therefore layers of forgiveness are needed. We have to realize that in our lives—and especially in our marriages—forgiveness is ongoing; sometimes daily. We always need the *willingness* to forgive ready in our heart. And only a heart humbled by the forgiveness of God has the ability to completely forgive time and again.

You have to forgive your spouse the way Jesus has forgiven you (Ephesians 4:32). Jesus forgave you completely. No looking back. No remembering. It means not keeping a list of the ways you have been wronged. It means refusing to carry bitterness and resentment about anything. It means not allowing yourself to be an injustice collector who keeps one foot in the past, always brooding over what happened there. It means living each day free of bad memories and looking to the future with hope. True forgiveness means completely letting go of an offense and refusing to hold it against the offender. That kind of forgiveness is impossible without the Lord. We need God helping us to forgive every day.

In the beginning of your relationship, forgiving your spouse comes easy. But when you have to be forgiving time and again, you wonder if perhaps you are encouraging him (her) by *appearing* to condone his (her) actions. Sometimes you may be hesitant to forgive because you're afraid that in doing so you are setting yourself up for the same thing to happen again. But there is a clear line between enabling and forgiving. In other words, you can still confront your spouse about changing his (her) ways, and you pray for that to happen, but if he (she) doesn't do it, you refuse to let it eat at you and make you bitter. Forgiving does not mean you are giving the offender a free pass to commit the offense again and again. It does not mean you are inviting abuse or giving that person a license to walk all over you or continue to hurt you. It doesn't make you a doormat. *Forgiveness doesn't make the other person right; it makes you free.*

Ask God to Show You

Forgiveness is a decision we make, and we *know* if we made it or not. We don't accidentally forgive someone without realizing it. But it is possible to *not forgive* without realizing it. We think we've let it go when we haven't.

Mary Anne—the Christian counselor I had seen—had me confess my unforgiveness toward my mother. Months later she called me into her office and told me she felt I had unforgiveness toward my dad as well. I didn't think that was right, but she said to ask God about it anyway.

On my way home from her office I said, "Lord, do I have any unforgiveness in me toward my dad?"

I fully expected God to say, "Definitely not, My good and faithful servant." But instantly I was struck through the heart by the truth. God impressed upon me that I had truly not forgiven my father.

My father? I thought. *Why would I need to forgive him?*

In that moment I saw all the unforgiveness I had toward my dad for all those years of not protecting me from my mother. And he was the only one who could. He was never abusive to me, so I didn't think there was any reason to forgive him. But when my eyes were opened to the truth, I saw how my father had never rescued me from my mother's insanity, and I had held this against him without even realizing it.

I broke down and sobbed so hard I had to pull my car over to the side of the freeway. I confessed my unforgiveness toward my dad and asked God to forgive me. When I did that, I felt a release in my spirit that I had never felt before. Looking back now, I believe that if I had not *asked* God to reveal any unforgiveness in my heart, I doubt if I could have ever seen this on my own. We can't always see our unforgiving attitudes when we have them, but God will show us the truth if we will just ask Him to.

The Choice Is Yours

Forgiveness is a choice you have to make every day. You choose to *live* in forgiveness. And never is that more true than when you are married. Besides *loving* your husband (wife), the next most important thing you can do in your marriage is *forgive* him (her).

Even in the best of marriages, forgiveness is always necessary. For two completely different humans to live together in harmony, there are bound to be disappointments, misunderstandings, and hurts. We have to continually be "bearing with one another, and forgiving one another" (Colossians 3:13). We can't wait until our spouse deserves it or asks for it. Not forgiving is a killer. It kills your relationships. It kills your health. And it kills your joy. It also upsets your close walk with God.

When Jesus was asked by His disciples if we need to forgive others as many as *seven times,* He said that *seventy times seven* was more like it (Matthew 18:21-22). I did the math and that's 490 times. The point is, we need to forgive as often as necessary. You might be living with someone you have to forgive 490 times a day, but you will still have to forgive as often as it takes for your heart to be free.

In the prayer that Jesus taught us to pray, He said to *ask* God to forgive us, just as we *give* forgiveness to *others.* "Forgive us our debts, as we forgive our debtors" (Matthew 6:12). That means if we ask God for forgiveness for things we've done, while at the same time refusing to forgive our spouse, then we are not going to enjoy the full benefits of God's forgiveness to us. In other words, if we don't release others by forgiving them, we ourselves will not find the release we need to move on in our lives. Not forgiving will always hold us back. We will be attached to invisible unforgiveness ties, and though we may try hard, we won't be able to move beyond where we are to where we're supposed to be.

When you have been emotionally devastated by something your husband (wife) has said or done—or something he (she) did *not* say or do—sometimes the hurt is so great that you feel you can't get over it enough to forgive. The unforgiveness and bitterness can become so deeply rooted that it takes a major work of God to make you even *want* to forgive. When that happens, ask God to help you. Say, "God, help me to want to forgive my husband (wife). Help me to forgive him (her) completely." You have to do this "lest any root of bitterness springing up cause trouble, and by this many become defiled" (Hebrews 12:15). Bitterness is hard to get rid of, and it does the most damage to *you*.

Not only is it important to forgive your spouse, but it is also important to your marriage for you to forgive everyone else in your life. If you have any unforgiveness toward a family member, neighbor, friend, acquaintance, or coworker, it will take its toll on you personally. It will cause you to become bitter, and it will show on your face and be revealed in your voice when you speak. It will come out in your body in the form of sickness, disease, or disability of some sort. Our bodies, minds, and souls were not designed to live in unforgiveness. It destroys us from the inside out. It is a poison for which there is no antidote except total forgiveness. And it will affect your marriage whether you realize it or not, because unforgiveness comes out in your personality and people sense it, even if they don't know what it is.

Decide in Advance

I have learned that the best way to live is to decide in *advance* to be a person who forgives. It takes the pressure off because you don't have to try to make that decision every time something bad happens and you're reeling from disappointment, hurt, or your own anger.

Once I was finally convinced that not forgiving destroys you and forgiveness sets you free, I decided to be a forgiving person all the time. Once I made that decision, of course I was put to the test. The next time my husband became angry, instead of reacting to him in my normal negative way, I caught myself and remembered that I had made the decision to forgive him even for the future times when he gets that way. I already knew that I had not done anything deserving of this anger to my knowledge, so instead of withdrawing in hurt the way I usually would have, I pressed him for why he was angry and upset. As it turned out, it was something that had happened at work. When he told me about it, I could totally understand why he felt the way he did. I would have been upset too. What I did not understand was why he felt it was right to take it out on me. He later recognized it was wrong and apologized.

After I completely forgave my mother for the abuse I suffered at her hands, I wanted so much to go back to that time when she was an 11-year-old girl who lost her mother and was deprived of her father. I wished I could have comforted her and done something to take away the pain. Even though I knew she was with the Lord now, I wept for the devastating tragedies she had suffered.

I asked the Lord, "What good are these tears now that she's gone and nothing can be done?" I felt impressed that God wanted me to use this grief to help people understand that every person has a story in their past that has made them who they are. And only God knows the whole story. Every angry and cruel person has had some kind of mistreatment, pain, and tragedy in their past—sometimes a hurt so deep they can't even express or understand it—and they sometimes do terrible things to the very people they are supposed to love because of it. Their need to express it outweighs their sense of decency and compassion. It's as if a spirit of revenge takes over for them, and they vent their pain and frustration through their anger without even considering what it does to the heart and soul of the person on the receiving end. No matter how cruel or mean a person has been to you, releasing them with your forgiveness frees *you*. It releases you from them so you can move on without that bad memory keeping you stuck in the past.

After I was truly freed from the powerful effects of my husband's anger by deciding *in advance* of it ever happening again that I was going to forgive him, I felt sad for Michael when he became angry. I knew he was cutting off what God wanted to bring into his life and that he would be the loser because of it. I felt sorry for the little boy who was made to feel like a failure for something he didn't understand and couldn't help. I regret that I wasn't healed, whole, and mature enough sooner so I would not have taken his anger so personally. Even though it was directed at me, it had a history back before I even knew him. Only after God had worked complete forgiveness in my heart was I able to see all that.

You Are Being Followed

Because God is a God of mercy and His mercy endures forever, you can trust that He will have mercy on you (1 Chronicles 17:13). Therefore you can show mercy to your spouse by forgiving whenever he (she) does or says something that hurts or disturbs you.

David said, "Surely goodness and mercy shall follow me all the days of my life; and I will dwell in the house of the LORD forever" (Psalm 23:6). That means if goodness and mercy are following you, they are covering your back. When you see goodness and mercy in your rearview mirror, it makes it easier for you to show goodness and mercy to your spouse. Jesus said, "Blessed are the merciful, for they shall obtain mercy" (Matthew 5:7). If you want to continue to have mercy from God, you have to give it to others. The way you show mercy toward your spouse is by forgiving him (her) at all times.

God's mercy is far-reaching. "As the heavens are high above the earth, so great is His mercy toward those who fear Him; as far as the east is from the west, so far has He removed our transgressions from us" (Psalm 103:11-12). That is about as far-reaching as it gets. We will always have trouble extending that much mercy without the enablement of God. In other words, if on our own we can't find the mercy in us to be able to forgive completely, God will help us if we ask Him to. There are times when something in us wants to punish, get even, or hurt back instead of being merciful and forgiving. But when we do that we get locked up inside, just as if we are in a physical prison. Forgiveness is the only key to unlock that prison door and get free. And it starts with having a heart of mercy.

SEVEN THINGS THAT ARE TRUE ABOUT GOD'S MERCY

1. ***God's mercy is great.*** "Great is Your mercy toward me, and You have delivered my soul from the depths of Sheol" (Psalm 86:13).

2. ***When you have mercy the way He does, you find life.*** "He who follows righteousness and mercy finds life, righteousness and honor" (Proverbs 21:21).

3. ***God's mercy is abundant toward you.*** "The LORD is merciful

and gracious, slow to anger, and abounding in mercy" (Psalm 103:8).

4. *Forgiveness is an act of mercy.* "I desire mercy and not sacrifice, and the knowledge of God more than burnt offerings" (Hosea 6:6).

5. *God's mercy covers all your concerns.* "The LORD will perfect that which concerns me; Your mercy, O LORD, endures forever; do not forsake the works of Your hands" (Psalm 138:8).

6. *When you don't have mercy, you are not shown mercy.* "Judgment is without mercy to the one who has shown no mercy. Mercy triumphs over judgment" (James 2:13).

7. *God's mercy never ends.* "The LORD is good; His mercy is everlasting, and His truth endures to all generations" (Psalm 100:5).

Because God is merciful, He doesn't remember your sins once He forgives them. "I, even I, am He who blots out your transgressions for My own sake; and I will not remember your sins" (Isaiah 43:25). If you are having trouble forgiving your husband (wife), be honest with God about it. Job cried out honestly to God in his pain saying, "I will not restrain my mouth; I will speak in the anguish of my spirit; I will complain in the bitterness of my soul" (Job 7:11). We have a God who understands our pain when we pour it out to Him.

If you feel you can't forgive, ask God to penetrate your unforgiveness with His love. When we have to do the impossible, God says that the way it happens is "not by might nor by power, but by My Spirit" (Zechariah 4:6). This means that certain things will not be accomplished by human strength, but only by the power of God. The Holy Spirit will enable us to forgive even the unforgivable.

First Things First

The first thing the disciples did after they received the Holy Spirit was to forgive others (John 20:21-23). It is also the first thing we need to do as we come before God each day. Say, "Lord, show me where I have unforgiveness, and I will confess it to You as sin so I can be free from it." If you already know that you have unforgiveness in your heart, say, "Lord, take the burden of unforgiveness off my shoulders and help me to let go of it completely so I can walk free."

What's even harder is that God asks us to *bless* those who hurt us (Matthew 5:43-44). Sometimes it feels as though not killing them should be enough. But God wants more than restraint. He wants us to actually want good things for them. He want us to show mercy to someone who we think doesn't deserve it, just as He showed mercy to us when *we* didn't deserve it. The thing is, forgiving your spouse does not depend on him (her) asking you for forgiveness or showing any repentance. If we wait for that, we could wait a lifetime for something that may never happen.

Of all the horrible things that were done to Joseph, he was amazingly forgiving. He was sold into slavery by his jealous brothers, but he still found favor wherever he went. He ended up in prison falsely accused, but was eventually appointed second in command to Pharaoh. Through it all, Joseph knew that what others intended for evil, God was using for good. He eventually said that very thing to his brothers who had betrayed him (Genesis 50:20). When we have that kind of amazing willingness to forgive, God will use our very act of forgiveness to turn things around in our marriage. He can even restore a marriage that is dying if the people in it extend total forgiveness.

SEVEN THINGS THAT ARE TRUE ABOUT FORGIVING

1. ***Forgiving brings blessings to you.*** "Finally, all of you be of one mind, having compassion for one another; love as brothers, be tenderhearted, be courteous; not returning evil for evil or reviling for reviling, but on the contrary blessing, knowing that you were called to this, that you may inherit a blessing" (1 Peter 3:8-9).

2. ***Forgiving others paves the way for you to be forgiven.*** "Judge not, and you shall not be judged. Condemn not, and you shall not be condemned. Forgive, and you will be forgiven" (Luke 6:37).

3. ***Forgiving allows you to forget and move forward.*** "One thing I do, forgetting those things which are behind and reaching

forward to those things which are ahead, I press toward the goal for the prize of the upward call of God in Christ Jesus" (Philippians 3:13-14).

4. *Forgiving frees you to worship God with your whole heart.* "Therefore if you bring your gift to the altar, and there remember that your brother has something against you, leave your gift there before the altar, and go your way. First be reconciled to your brother, and then come and offer your gift" (Matthew 5:23-24).

5. *Forgiving proves that you are kind and tenderhearted.* "And be kind to one another, tenderhearted, forgiving one another, just as God in Christ forgave you" (Ephesians 4:32).

6. *Forgiving makes you Christlike.* "Even as Christ forgave you, so you must also do" (Colossians 3:13).

7. *Forgiving is the way you pursue peace and keep from becoming bitter.* "Pursue peace with all people, and holiness, without which no one will see the Lord: looking carefully lest anyone fall short of the grace of God; lest any root of bitterness springing up cause trouble, and by this many become defiled" (Hebrews 12:14-15).

When You Need to Forgive God

Blaming God for something is not the best position to take. Remember, He is the one with the lightning. It's better to talk to Him and tell Him honestly how you feel. Say, "Lord, I confess I am angry at You for requiring me to be married to someone who hurts me so much." Or, "Lord, I don't understand why he (she) is never required to change and I *am*." Or, "Lord, why doesn't my husband (wife) have any financial wisdom and why do I have to suffer for it?" Or, "Lord, why did You let me marry someone with an alcohol problem just like my dad had? Haven't I suffered enough?" Or, "Lord, why do I have to be the responsible one and he (she) can just float through life like a child?" God understands those feelings and He can take the honesty. You're not telling Him anything He doesn't already know. He is just waiting for you to share it with Him so He can set you free.

The best way to break down that unforgiveness toward God is to confess it and thank Him for His forgiveness toward you. In fact, whenever you feel unforgiveness toward anyone trying to grip your heart like a vise, lift up praise to God until you feel that thing break in your soul. It will transform your heart.

What Happens When We Don't Forgive?

Not forgiving interferes with the effectiveness of your prayer life (Mark 11:25). That means your prayers don't get answered. That means you can't experience the full benefits of God's forgiveness if you are not forgiving others—especially your spouse. That means God puts your blessings on hold and waits until you take care of that unfinished business.

Not forgiving evaporates your joy. When you don't forgive, it brings up a barrier to the joy God has for you. *No one is ever truly happy if they have unforgiveness in their heart.*

Not forgiving weakens your body. It eats away at you and eventually takes over and destroys your life from the inside. It makes you physically sick as well as spiritually crippled. When you forgive you release it into God's hand and healing comes for your body as well as your soul.

Not forgiving opens the door for the enemy to work in your life. We have to forgive "lest Satan should take advantage of us" (2 Corinthians 2:11). We invite the enemy in if we harbor unforgiveness. And when you treat your spouse as if he (she) is the enemy—or your spouse acts as if *you* are—you align yourselves with your true enemy and his plans for your future.

Not forgiving pollutes your soul. The Bible says, "Does a spring send forth fresh water and bitter from the same opening?" (James 3:11). If you have unforgiveness, the water in your soul will become bitter.

SEVEN MORE THINGS TO REMEMBER
ABOUT NOT FORGIVING

1. *Not forgiving will torture you.* " 'Should you not also have had compassion on your fellow servant, just as I had pity on you?' And his master was angry, and delivered him to the torturers until he should pay all that was due to him. So My heavenly Father also will do to you if each of you, from his heart, does not forgive his brother his trespasses" (Matthew 18:33-35).

2. ***Not forgiving causes you to entertain thoughts of revenge.*** "Do not say, 'I will do to him just as he has done to me; I will render to the man according to his work'" (Proverbs 24:29).

3. ***Not forgiving means you won't be forgiven by God.*** "But if you do not forgive men their trespasses, neither will your Father forgive your trespasses" (Matthew 6:15).

4. ***Not forgiving delays the answers to your prayers.*** "Whenever you stand praying, if you have anything against anyone, forgive him, that your Father in heaven may also forgive you your trespasses" (Mark 11:25).

5. ***Not forgiving means you see the failures of others, but not your own.*** "Why do you look at the speck in your brother's eye, but do not consider the plank in your own eye? Or how can you say to your brother, 'Let me remove the speck from your eye'; and look, a plank is in your own eye? Hypocrite! First remove the plank from your own eye, and then you will see clearly to remove the speck from your brother's eye" (Matthew 7:3-5).

6. ***Not forgiving means you are walking in darkness.*** "He who hates his brother is in darkness and walks in darkness, and does not know where he is going, because the darkness has blinded his eyes" (1 John 2:11).

7. ***Not forgiving means you are not pursuing what is best for your marriage.*** "See that no one renders evil for evil to anyone, but always pursue what is good both for yourselves and for all" (1 Thessalonians 5:15).

The Bottom Line

The bottom line is that forgiveness has to do with *repentance* and *love*. You have to *love* your spouse enough to *forgive* him (her) *and let it go.* And you have to *confess* your attitude of unforgiveness as a sin against God and *repent* of it. You have to be deeply sorry before the Lord that you were unforgiving because you know it displeases Him. You have to choose to forgive because you want to live God's way, because it's the right thing to do, and because it's the best thing for you. When you don't forgive, you feel separated from

God and you can't move ahead into the life God has for you. The truth is, *you* cannot be changed, *your husband (wife)* cannot be changed, and your *marriage* cannot be changed as long as you give place to unforgiveness in your heart.

I know that the last thing you may feel like doing is praying for your spouse if he (she) has hurt you, but that is what God wants you to do. In the process He will heal your pain because He is the God who "heals the brokenhearted and binds up their wounds" (Psalm 147:3). God will help you forgive so completely that you really don't think about those hurtful things anymore. As you pray, God will give you His heart of love. *You always grow to love the person you pray for.* Try it; you'll see. God wants you to live "not returning evil for evil or reviling for reviling, but on the contrary blessing, knowing that you were called to this, that you may inherit a blessing" (1 Peter 3:9). God isn't calling you to forgive so He can rub your nose in what offended or hurt you. He is asking you to forgive because when you do, you will inherit all that He has for you.

God does not violate a person's will who is determined to have a rebellious heart that refuses to take advice, seek counsel, or be open to the Lord's working in his (her) life. But your prayers for your spouse will still be rewarded with healing, release, strength, peace, and blessing for *you* when you pray for him (her), even if he (she) is not responding at the time. The Lord who loves *you* will "comfort *your* [heart] and establish *you* in every good word and work" (2 Thessalonians 2:17, emphasis added).

Forgiveness is not an option in our lives; it is a mandate. It is God's will for us every day. It doesn't depend on whether the person we must forgive is *repentant,* or *deserving* of it. It depends entirely on *us.* It is between *us* and *God.* We do it for the Lord, ultimately. Don't give up on forgiveness because you think you're just going to have to be doing it over and over again. Forgive because it is God's way and great good will come out of it. David said, "I would have lost heart, unless I had believed that I would see the goodness of the LORD in the land of the living" (Psalm 27:13). He wanted God's presence in his life enough to do whatever it took. I believe you want that too. Forgiving your husband (wife) is the best place to start.

PRAYERS FOR MY MARRIAGE

Prayer for Protection

LORD, I PRAY THAT YOU would help my husband (wife) and me to always be completely forgiving of one another. Help us to be humble enough to ask for forgiveness when we need to. And give us a heart to forgive freely—whether the other asks for it or not. Help us both to "grow in the grace and knowledge of our Lord and Savior Jesus Christ" (2 Peter 3:18), so that we will become forgiving like You are. Help us to forgive so that we will be forgiven (Luke 6:37).

Protect us from ourselves, Lord, so that we will not let our own flesh dictate whether we should hang on to offenses or let them go. Help us to love one another the way You love us, so that letting go of offenses will be easy. Help us to be merciful to one another, because we have Your goodness and mercy following us as You promised in Your Word (Psalm 23:6). Thank You that when we love each other Your way, You will bless us and show us Your favor by surrounding us like a protective shield (Psalm 5:12).

Lord, I know Your Word says that "if we say that we have no sin, we deceive ourselves, and the truth is not in us" (1 John 1:8). Help us to be undeceived about our own sins. Help us to live in truth and not be arrogant enough to think we have no sin in us. Help us to be quick to confess our sins to You and to one another. In Jesus' name I pray.

Prayer for Breakthrough in Me

THANK YOU, LORD, THAT I CAN DO *all* things through Christ who strengthens me, and therefore I have the strength to forgive my husband (wife) for anything that has hurt or disappointed me. Thank You that You are the God of forgiveness. Thank You for Your mercy and grace to me. Thank You that You have released me from any stronghold of unforgiveness. Take away any feelings in me that cause me to think I need to pay back hurt for hurt. I "strive to have a conscience without offense" toward You or my husband (wife) (Acts 24:16). Where I need to be forgiven, help me to apologize and receive forgiveness from my husband (wife).

Where there are places in me that harbor unforgiveness that I am not even aware of, please reveal those to me so I can confess them to You. I know that "You, Lord, are good, and ready to forgive, and abundant in mercy to all those who call upon You" (Psalm 86:5). I call upon You this day and ask You to forgive me for any unforgiveness I have toward anyone, especially my husband (wife). I know that You, Lord, are the only one who knows the whole story, so I refuse to be the judge of all that happens in my husband (wife). You are the one "who will both bring to light the hidden things of darkness and reveal the counsels of the [heart]" (1 Corinthians 4:5). Break any entrenched unforgiveness in me by the power of Your Spirit. Help me to love the way You do, so I can release all unforgiveness and be cleansed from all unrighteousness. In Jesus' name I pray.

Prayer for Breakthrough in My Husband (Wife)

LORD, I LIFT MY HUSBAND (WIFE) to You in prayer and ask You to help him (her) let go of any unforgiveness that he (she) harbors. I don't want him (her) to hang on to it and limit what You want to do in his (her) life. Help him (her) to forgive me for anything I have done—or *not* done—that was displeasing to him (her). I pray that You, "the God of patience and comfort," will grant to my husband (wife) the ability to be "like-minded" toward me so that we together may glorify You with a single-minded voice of unity (Romans 15:5-6). Give him (her) a heart of mercy toward me so that he (she) can truly let go of anything I have said or done that has hurt him (her).

You have said, Lord, that if we *don't* forgive people for their sins against us, You *won't* forgive us for *ours* (Matthew 6:14-15). Help my husband (wife) to become aware of anyone he (she) needs to forgive and enable him (her) to forgive that person completely, so that he (she) can move into the wholeness and restoration You have for him (her). Take away all thoughts of revenge or payback and make him (her) to be a forgiving person. In Jesus' name I pray.

Truth to Stand On

Whenever you stand praying, if you have anything
against anyone, forgive him that your Father in heaven may
also forgive you your trespasses.

MARK 11:25

Confess your trespasses to one another, and pray for one another,
that you may be healed. The effective, fervent prayer
of a righteous man avails much.

JAMES 5:16

Why do you judge your brother?
Or why do you show contempt for your brother?
For we shall all stand before the judgment seat of Christ.

ROMANS 14:10

If there is any consolation in Christ, if any comfort of love,
if any fellowship of the Spirit, if any affection and mercy,
fulfill my joy by being like-minded, having the same love,
being of one accord, of one mind.

PHILIPPIANS 2:1-2

Be submissive to one another, and be clothed with humility,
for God resists the proud, but gives grace to the humble.

1 PETER 5:5

4

If DEPRESSION *or* NEGATIVE EMOTIONS SPOIL *the* ATMOSPHERE

I think my depression started in the closet. That tiny dark space underneath the stairs in my parents' tiny old ranch house that had no running water, no bathroom, no electricity, and no heat in the bitter freezing Wyoming winters, except what came from an old coal-burning stove in the kitchen and a small stone fireplace in the living room. Upstairs, the two small bedrooms were always freezing, and it took forever till the sheets warmed up. Seeds of anxiety, sadness, fear, loneliness, and rejection were planted there like weeds that would grow deeper and more rampant every year of my early life until they would eventually suffocate all hope within me.

As far back as I can remember, I had that depressed feeling. I didn't know I was experiencing depression at the time; I thought it was just me. *This is the way I am,* I thought as I grew up. *I am a frightened, hopeless, lonely, hurting, anxious, and depressed person, and there is nothing I can do about it. No one can help me, nor does anyone want to, nor will anyone ever want to, or even be able to.*

I am not talking here about a chemical imbalance, although I probably had one. Terror, dread, sadness, and stress have a way of depleting your mind, body, and soul until you not only have a physical imbalance, but a spiritual and emotional one as well. And that's enough to depress anyone. I had gone to doctors and tried different medicines, but nothing ever worked for me. This was a deep wounding of the soul for which there is no cure outside of the power of God.

It wasn't until I received the Lord and began to learn of the wholeness He has for each of us that I became more aware that depressed, anxious, and afraid wasn't the way He made us to be. Depression, fear, and anxiety were not His will for my life. His promise for me was peace—if I would pray fervently and be thankful and worshipful of Him. "Be anxious for nothing, but in everything by prayer and supplication, with thanksgiving, let your requests be made known to God; and the peace of God, which surpasses all understanding, will guard your hearts and minds through Christ Jesus" (Philippians 4:6-7). That meant because of Jesus, I had a way out of anxiety, depression, and fear if I would learn to pray about everything. Every situation, condition, and relationship in my life would respond to prayer. Because of the power of God working through prayer, I eventually found deliverance and healing from all the negative emotions that crippled me. Sometimes just my own prayers alone were enough, but often the faith-filled prayers of others, praying *with* and *for* me, paved the way for miracles.

In my case, I went to our church for help at the suggestion of my husband. We had been married a few months, and I still couldn't shake the grip of depression, fear, and anxiety I was under. The first time I saw Mary Anne, the pastor's wife and counselor I mentioned earlier, I noticed she had the most beautiful eyes that sparkled like the ocean when the sun dances on the waves. I had heard she was especially gifted in the knowledge of God's Word and the understanding of the power of prayer, so when she asked me to fast and pray for three days—which was no easy feat for someone such as I, who had gone to bed hungry many nights as a child—I was willing to do it.

I went back to that same counseling office the following week after not having anything to eat or drink but water for three days, carrying a list Mary Anne had asked me to make of all the sins I could remember committing in my life. I was grateful when she didn't want to read it, but asked that I would present the list before God and confess it all at once. I also had to confess my unforgiveness toward my mother and renounce all my occult involvement. Even though I had completely stopped any practice or involvement with the occult when I received the Lord, I had never gone before the Lord and renounced those practices.

Once I confessed and renounced all that, Mary Anne and another pastor's wife prayed for me, and I literally felt the depression lift off of me. I am not exaggerating this. In fact, I am understating it so it won't be hard for you to believe. But I felt the depression lift off from me as though it were a heavy, wet, dark blanket. And the best part about the story is that it never came back. I am not saying I never felt depression again. There are many depressing things that happen in life. But I was never gripped or controlled by it again. I could always go to God in prayer and He would take it away.

This is not to say that if you are taking medication prescribed by a doctor for depression or anxiety that you are to suddenly stop taking it. To the contrary, this can be dangerous. That also doesn't necessarily sentence you to a lifetime of medication, either. I believe you can find wholeness without medicine. But there is no sin in taking prescribed medicine if you need it. Taking medicine doesn't make you any less holy than someone else who doesn't take anything. In a world spinning faster, with pressures increasing and the rigors of life becoming more monumental every day, it is no wonder we have gotten ourselves out of balance. Every *body* is different. Every *mind* and *soul* are different. Everyone's past is different, and each person's *reaction* to their past is different. Some of us are born depleted; some of us develop an imbalance later. It doesn't matter. What does matter is that you look to God as your healer and pray for healing. God will heal you in His way and time, and you can keep taking your medicine until that happens. You'll know when to stop, and a doctor can help you wean off of it if that's what you're supposed to do. If not, keep taking your medicine and praise God that it's working.

Whether you are taking medicine or not is entirely between you and God and your doctor. But I would tell you that medicine alone will never be enough. The only total cure for depression I have ever found is the love of God and His power working on your behalf to break all oppression on your life. And the love of God gives us hope. "Now hope does not disappoint, because the love of God has been poured out in our hearts by the Holy Spirit who was given to us" (Romans 5:5).

When the Problem Is Depression

It's normal to feel depressed about the things that happen in life from time to time. The loss of a job, a loved one, finances, or possessions. The experience of failure, disappointment, sickness, or accidents. But when you stay depressed, then it becomes a problem. You were not made to live in depression. Depression every day is not God's will for your life. When every day seems dark and gray and without joy or light, then it becomes a grip of hell in your life and must be broken.

When I received the Lord, I began to finally see a light at the end of the long dark tunnel of my life, but I still had depression. I was born again into the kingdom of God because I received Jesus and I know something happened to me that day, but I still had depression. I felt hope for the first time in my life, but I still lived under a heavy blanket of depression. Not everyone is instantly freed of every bondage the minute they receive the Lord. I have no doubt they can be, and I have no doubt that some are, but this is not most people's experience. There are way too many depressed Christians for this to be true. There are people who adamantly believe that if you are a true Christian you will never have depression. May I politely suggest that the people who are saying this are people who have never been depressed? They have been blinded by their own arrogance and legalism to the plight of others.

I have also heard it suggested that in light of the following verses, if we are really walking in the light then we wouldn't have to go through the darkness of depression. "God is light and in Him is no darkness at all. If we say that we have fellowship with Him, and walk in darkness, we lie and do not practice the truth" (1 John 1:5-6). They are saying that these verses bring into question our born-again status. Can we really be saved if we have depression? As one who has been depressed while being a born-again believer, this attitude makes me mad. Let me get something straight in case anyone has ever suggested that to you. *Yes, you can be born again and depressed at the same time!*

The verses above have to do with the *decision* to walk in fellowship with darkness. Being depressed does not mean you are *choosing* to walk in depression. Depression is something that you can have *on* you once you are a believer, but not *in* you. It can't possess you. It doesn't own you. The Holy Spirit is in you, not depression. Depression is not you. It may be on you like an oppression of the enemy designed to steal your joy and rob you of life, but you are not your depression. You can still have the light of the Lord *within* you and yet have the darkness of oppression settle *on* you and invade your life like an enemy encroaching on the territory of your being.

How Depression Feels

In case you have never been depressed yourself, let me describe it for you. It may help you to better understand your spouse if he (she) ever gets depressed. Job described what seemed like depression as "a land as dark as darkness itself, as the shadow of death, without any order, where even the light is like darkness" (Job 10:22). When you are depressed, even good things can't be enjoyed because they are tainted by that dark oppression. He said, "When I looked for good, evil came to me; and when I waited for light, then came darkness" (Job 30:26). In other words, it seems as though no matter what you do, it never gets better.

Perhaps no one ever struggled with depression more openly or wrote about it more clearly than King David. He knew depression well. Listen to what he said about the way he felt and see if this sounds like depression to you. "My life is spent with grief, and my years with sighing; my strength fails because of my iniquity, and my bones waste away" (Psalm 31:10). "Turn Yourself to me, and have mercy on me, for I am desolate and afflicted. The troubles of my heart have enlarged; bring me out of my distresses! Look on my affliction and my pain, and forgive all my sins" (Psalm 25:16-18). "Consider and hear me, O Lord my God; enlighten my eyes, lest I sleep the sleep of death" (Psalm 13:3). "Why are you cast down, O my soul? And why are you disquieted within me? Hope in God, for I shall yet praise Him for the help of His countenance" (Psalm 42:5). I especially appreciate the phrase "cast down" referring to a heavily burdened soul. That's exactly what it feels like—you have fallen in a pit far from hope.

David's solution to all this was to look up and put his hope in God. Sometimes we can feel as though God has abandoned us when we sink in depression and our prayers are not being answered. As a result, we feel separated from Him. But God has *not* abandoned us. He will comfort us when we turn to Him. Paul said, "God, who comforts the downcast, comforted us" (2 Corinthians 7:6).

David said, "I said in my haste, 'I am cut off from before Your eyes,'" but he also said, "*Nevertheless You heard the voice of my supplications when I cried out to You*" (Psalm 31:22, emphasis added). David knew deep despair and depression, but he also knew his hope was in God.

David said, "The pangs of death surrounded me, and the floods of ungodliness made me afraid. The sorrows of Sheol surrounded me; the snares of death confronted me" (Psalm 18:4-5). But he *also* said, "*You have delivered my soul from death, my eyes from tears, and my feet from falling*" (Psalm 116:8, emphasis added).

In the midst of David's sorrow he said, "*Yea, though I walk through the valley of the shadow of death, I will fear no evil; for You are with me; Your rod and Your staff, they comfort me*" (Psalm 23:4, emphasis added). "*Indeed, the darkness shall not hide from You, but the night shines as the day; the darkness and the light are both alike to You*" (Psalm 139:12, emphasis added). God can see plainly into the darkness that hangs over you. He sees the truth about you and your situation, and He wants you to see it too. That means "there is no darkness nor shadow of death where the workers of iniquity may hide themselves" (Job 34:22). That's because we have authority over all the power of the enemy.

When you feel as David did—"My spirit is overwhelmed within me; my heart within me is distressed" (Psalm 143:4), then say as David did, "*Hear me when I call, O God of my righteousness! You have relieved me in my distress; have mercy on me, and hear my prayer*" (Psalm 4:1, emphasis added).

This is the way depression feels to me. You feel distant from other people as if you are in another realm when you are around them. You are not on the same plane they are. You can be in the same room with them, but you feel as though there is a wall separating you from them, so you don't really make contact. It feels as if they are fading from you, as if the darkness around *you* is swallowing *them* up. When you speak, it's almost like an out of body experience. It's as if you are outside your body listening to yourself speak, but you are not really connecting to the other person. There is a barrier to their connecting with you. And it is your own depression. It is described in Psalms, saying, "Loved one and friend You have put far from me, and my acquaintances into darkness" (Psalm 88:18).

When you are depressed, it's hard to do anything, even the basic necessities for life. It takes all your energy just being depressed. You're tired all the time because fighting anxiety, fear, and depression is exhausting. You lose interest in activities and doing things that you would normally do. You are pessimistic about most things and you feel hopeless about everything else. You feel hopeless because there seems to be no way to rise above your predicament. When you don't believe your miserable situation will ever change, you can't see a reason to live. You wonder, *Why try?* At its worst, depression can make you feel suicidal, which means you see death as the only way out.

You feel as though you can't do anything that involves the future, even as close as the next day, so you live moment to moment. You are unable to think ahead and prepare in advance. You can't think clearly about things, and you find it hard to get anything done, so it's extremely difficult to keep your home straight or your closet clean. You have a difficult time planning anything because you will never feel good about what you are planning. You see no point to it. Depression can overshadow your ability to make solid and rational decisions. People may tell you to snap out of it, but you are powerless to do so on your own strength. That's why telling your spouse to "get over it" will only make them feel more hopeless.

We can also get depressed from being overextended, exhausted, malnourished, or sick. There is nothing more depressing than being sick or in pain. And any kind of loss can make us depressed too, such as the loss of a job, a person, a relationship, an ability, or a body part. The ultimate example of suffering loss was Job. He lost everything and said, "My heart is in turmoil and cannot rest; days of affliction confront me" (Job 30:27). Habits of the mind can keep us depressed because we are always focusing on a negative side of something or someone. Feeling helpless in the face of some threat or trauma makes us depressed.

When you are depressed, you have a strong need for physical touch and verbal affirmation, but this is the time when you find it hardest to communicate that need. It's difficult to communicate your need for love when you feel unlovable, unworthy, and unable to respond, but love is what you need most.

Don't ever feel that suffering from depression has separated you from God. It hasn't. The enemy wants you to believe that God is far from you and that's why you have to live in the darkness of depression. But God refers to the treasures of darkness saying, "I will give you the treasures of darkness and hidden riches of secret places, that you may know that I, the LORD, who call you by your name, am the God of Israel" (Isaiah 45:3). When you go through the dark times of depression, it forces you to walk closer to God. And that is a good thing. I have been there, and I have found that the treasure we find in darkness is *Him*. It's the promise of God's presence in the midst of our darkness. That means we don't have to be afraid of the dark, because His light will come into our darkness and He will reveal Himself to us.

TEN THINGS YOU NEED TO KNOW ABOUT DEPRESSION

1. ***God is with you in it.*** "Fear not, for I am with you; be not dismayed, for I am your God. I will strengthen you, yes, I will help you, I will uphold you with My righteous right hand" (Isaiah 41:10).

2. ***Even though you are in a struggle, you will not be destroyed.*** "We are hard-pressed on every side, yet not crushed; we are perplexed, but not in despair" (2 Corinthians 4:8).

3. ***God hears when you call to Him about it.*** "In my distress I called upon the LORD, and cried out to my God; He heard my voice from His temple, and my cry came before Him, even to His ears" (Psalm 18:6).

4. ***The Lord will be a light to you at all times.*** "The people who walked in darkness have seen a great light; those who dwelt in the land of the shadow of death, upon them a light has shined" (Isaiah 9:2).

5. ***God will bring you out of darkness.*** "For You are my lamp, O LORD; the LORD shall enlighten my darkness" (2 Samuel 22:29).

6. ***God wants you to trust in Him through it.*** "Who among you fears the LORD? Who obeys the voice of His Servant? Who walks in darkness and has no light? Let him trust in the name of the LORD and rely upon his God" (Isaiah 50:10).

7. ***Jesus understands your sorrow.*** Jesus was "despised and rejected by men, a Man of sorrows and acquainted with grief" (Isaiah 53:3).

8. ***God's presence will save you.*** "In all their affliction He was

afflicted, and the Angel of His Presence saved them; in His love and in His pity He redeemed them; and He bore them and carried them all the days of old" (Isaiah 63:9).

9. *You need to keep praying about it.* "Attend to my cry, for I am brought very low; deliver me from my persecutors, for they are stronger than I" (Psalm 142:6).

10. *Jesus has more for you than living with depression.* Jesus said, "The thief does not come except to steal, and to kill, and to destroy. I have come that they may have life, and that they may have it more abundantly" (John 10:10).

Rejection, Anxiety, Fear, Loneliness, and Other Negative Emotions

Feelings of rejection are often caused by something traumatic that has happened in the past—especially in childhood. Those of us who have been through difficult things in childhood often have a hard time sharing those things because they make you different. And you don't want to be different in any way when you're young. If you have had trouble accepting yourself or feeling accepted, you don't want to open the door of possibility for other people to reject you too. You have a constant internal life going on inside you that you don't share with others because you don't want to appear stupid, inferior, or rejectable.

I suffered with deep feelings of rejection because my mother told me from the time I was very young that I was worthless and no good and would never amount to anything. Because I believed her, the constant feeling of never being worth anything—always feeling unloved and uncared for—made me a magnet for every negative emotion there is.

Anxiety is a feeling of intense worry or fear that something bad is about to happen. You have a constant torturous uneasiness about the outcome of most events or situations. In the extreme, you feel anxious even when you are not sure why. At its worst, anxiety leads to panic attacks, which can grip you so strongly that you feel as though you are going to have a heart attack, stop breathing, and die.

When I was working as a singer, dancer, and actress on TV in my early twenties, I would have panic attacks so bad that I would go into the ladies' room and lock myself in a bathroom stall so I could double up against the door and hang on for dear life. If no one else was there I would cry. If someone was in the room, I would just hold my breath, try to gain control, and make myself breathe in and out. Although I didn't have a relationship with God then, I still said, "God, help me." In my mind I wasn't actually asking this distant being to take the anxiety away because I thought it was warranted since I was such a failure. And I continually feared that people were going to find out what a failure I was. All I was asking of God was that He would keep me from dying. I truly thought at the time that this was the most God could do. I thought that depressed, anxious, fearful, suicidal, and hopeless was just the way I was, and I didn't think He could make me into something I wasn't. What more could God possibly do than keep me alive?

Anxiety like this is usually unwarranted or greatly overblown in the face of the truth. When you are chronically uneasy because you think something bad is going to happen, you have no peace and it is uncomfortable to be around you. Jesus said not to have an anxious mind (Luke 12:29). Proverbs 12:25 says, "Anxiety in the heart of man causes depression, but a good word makes it glad." *The good word from God is that you don't have to be anxious about anything you can pray about.*

Fear is not something that comes from God. "God has not given us a spirit of fear, but of power and of love and of a sound mind" (2 Timothy 1:7). If we lay claim to the *love* God has for us, the *power* He has for us, and the *sound mind* He has for us, there will be no room for a spirit of fear. We don't invite a spirit of fear every time we are afraid, only when fear becomes a controlling factor in our lives. It's good to be afraid of danger when it is warranted. It's what will keep you from walking out into traffic or alone in a deserted place at night. But it's not good to have fear as a way of life.

The only kind of fear God wants us to have is to fear Him (1 Peter 2:17). That doesn't mean we are afraid of Him, but that we are afraid of what life would be like *without* Him. And the fear He is talking about is a deep reverence for Him and who He is. Don't live with fear when God says He has love, power, and a sound mind instead. Claim what God has for you.

Loneliness is painful. It causes an ache in your heart that can be unbearable. But you don't have to live with that when God is waiting to be close to you if you will draw close to Him. I used to live in the pain of loneliness even after I was married. One day, in an especially painful time of loneliness, God spoke to my heart that whenever I felt lonely I was to come to Him and He would take it away. I did that right then and the loneliness disappeared completely. Now I recognize any feelings of loneliness—which are rare for me now—as a signal that I need to be with God. Let it be that kind of sign to you as well. Jesus said, "Whatever you ask the Father in My name He will give you. Until now you have asked nothing in My name. Ask, and you will receive, that your joy may be full" (John 16:22-24). Ask God to set you free from loneliness and all other negative emotions.

TWELVE THINGS TO REMEMBER IN THE FACE OF NEGATIVE EMOTIONS

1. ***God knows what you are going through.*** "O Lord, You have searched me and known me. You know my sitting down and my rising up; You understand my thought afar off. You comprehend my path and my lying down, and are acquainted with all my ways. For there is not a word on my tongue, but behold, O Lord, You know it altogether" (Psalm 139:1-4).

2. ***God is there for you in your darkest hour.*** "Unto the upright there arises light in the darkness; He is gracious, and full of compassion, and righteous" (Psalm 112:4).

3. ***You don't have to live with the darkness of negative emotions.*** "I have come as a light into the world, that whoever believes in Me should not abide in darkness" (John 12:46).

4. ***God will rescue you when you cry out to Him.*** "They cried out to the Lord in their trouble, and He saved them out of their distresses" (Psalm 107:13).

5. ***You don't have to be afraid.*** "The Lord is my light and my salvation; whom shall I fear? The Lord is the strength of my life; of whom shall I be afraid?" (Psalm 27:1).

6. ***God will break through all bondage.*** "He brought them out of darkness and the shadow of death, and broke their chains in pieces" (Psalm 107:14).

7. *Even if you fall again, you will rise up yet another time.* "Do not rejoice over me, my enemy; when I fall, I will arise; when I sit in darkness, the LORD will be a light to me" (Micah 7:8).

8. *You have the power to cast off darkness and put on light.* "The night is far spent, the day is at hand. Therefore let us cast off the works of darkness, and let us put on the armor of light" (Romans 13:12).

9. *God keeps His eyes on you when you keep your eyes on Him.* "Behold, the eye of the LORD is on those who fear Him, on those who hope in His mercy, to deliver their soul from death, and to keep them alive in famine. Our soul waits for the LORD; He is our help and our shield. For our heart shall rejoice in Him, because we have trusted in His holy name. Let Your mercy, O LORD, be upon us, just as we hope in You" (Psalm 33:18-22).

10. *God will deliver you.* "He has delivered us from the power of darkness and conveyed us into the kingdom of the Son of His love" (Colossians 1:13).

11. *He will continue to deliver you until you are completely free.* "Yes, we had the sentence of death in ourselves, that we should not trust in ourselves but in God who raises the dead, who delivered us from so great a death, and does deliver us; in whom we trust that He will still deliver us" (2 Corinthians 1:9-10).

12. *God will comfort you.* "Sing, O heavens! Be joyful, O earth! And break out in singing, O mountains! For the LORD has comforted His people, and will have mercy on His afflicted" (Isaiah 49:13).

If the Problem Is with Your Spouse

While it is certainly no fun being depressed, it is definitely no fun being around someone who is depressed all the time, either. Life is hard enough on your own without having to deal with someone else's problems. But when you are married, your spouse's problems become yours as well. In my case, my husband and I both suffered from depression and anxiety in the beginning. However, I found healing for it in that first year we were married. Michael struggled with it longer.

A spouse who is controlled by depression, anxiety, or fear is very self-focused. He (she) is forced to think about himself (herself) most of the time, and therefore has little resource left to give to others—especially his (her) spouse. That's why your husband's (wife's) depression can make your life miserable too. And it will definitely affect your children, because they won't understand what it is and will think there is something wrong with them.

Often after a person gets married, all the weaknesses, negative emotions, and emotional disorders they have surface one by one. Those things can't be hidden for long in the closeness of a marriage. If you see that happening in you or your spouse, don't be afraid. God wants to set you both free from all that, and often these things don't come out until you are in a safe place. A marriage is a safe place—or at least it is supposed to be. It means that you are now with someone who loves you enough to commit to you. If there is anything wrong with you, God is not going to let you hang on to it. He won't allow you to continue with depression, anxiety, fear, bitterness, anger, or loneliness. It will be exposed because marriage shines a spotlight on those kinds of things and there is no place to hide. Who you are will be revealed. And God doesn't want you hiding anyway. He wants you free. When things surface in you or in your husband (wife), be willing to face what is exposed without fear. It is not the end of the good times; it is the beginning of the best times. Be willing to do what it takes to get free and become whole.

When your spouse is depressed, you end up not talking about things that need to be talked about. You avoid the depressed person because you don't know if what you say is going to make things worse. They appear weak to you because they don't have the ability to do things they need to do, which forces you to be the strong one and the decision maker. You can't go to them as a safe place where you can let down and share your thoughts, hopes, dreams, and fears because all they can focus on is getting through the day. Anxiety can be paralyzing, just as depression is, because if you believe that disaster is one step away from you, you won't want to take a step in any direction at all. Dreams for the future are put aside. The future is only tomorrow.

It will be much easier for you to deal with your spouse's depression if you don't see him (her) as a *depressed person* who can't seem to get over it.

See him (her), instead, as a *person God wants to heal*. If your spouse is on medication for depression, don't tell him (her) to get off of it. This could have serous ramifications and he (she) could end up feeling like a failure if it's necessary to resume taking it. As I said earlier, there is no failure in having to take medicine prescribed by a doctor. Some people take it all their lives, and if they are believers I am certain they are still going to heaven and are not walking in darkness. In fact, one of the best things you can do for your spouse is help him (her) find the right doctor who will prescribe the best medicine.

You may feel as though you don't know what to do to help your depressed husband (wife), but one thing you can always do is pray. And it will always make a big difference. You can also show your love and support. That means a lot to a depressed person. Assure your husband (wife) that depression is only temporary and there is an end to it. "Weeping may endure for a night, but joy comes in the morning" (Psalm 30:5).

How to Get Out of Depression and Other Negative Emotions

No matter what negative emotion it is, if it grips you and controls your life, you have to do whatever it takes to break the hold it has in you.

First of all, read God's Word every day. Read as much as you can. Speak it out loud. Find an appropriate verse and say it over and over until it is engraved upon your heart and you believe it. Say, "Thank you Lord, that Your word is a lamp to my feet and a light to my path" (Psalm 119:105). "Thank You for the sound mind You have given me."

Determine to take charge of your mind. Refuse to allow your emotions to rule you. Instead, you rule over them. Don't allow negative thoughts to dictate how you act, what you say or don't say, or what you do or don't do. Think about the good and positive things about your life.

Seek good Christian counseling. If negative emotions are a gripping problem for you and they don't respond to prayer as I have suggested here, there are good medical doctors, psychiatrists, and psychologists who can help you. Don't try to deal with your situation alone.

Pray without ceasing. Always have a dialogue going with God, but don't do all the talking. Listen too. God says you are to give the burden of your soul entirely to Him. If you pray instead of allowing negative emotions to control you, you can have the kind of peace in your heart that is beyond comprehension.

Praise and worship God. This is one of the most powerful things you can do. In fact, every time you begin to feel any negative emotion, worship God right where you are and you will feel that thing lift off of you. The wells of salvation are deep. There is so much that Jesus has saved you from. Draw spiritual water from those wells every day and you will find joy (Isaiah 12:3).

SEVEN THINGS DEPRESSION AND NEGATIVE EMOTIONS ARE NOT

1. They are not inevitable.
2. They are not a life sentence for you.
3. They are not a sign of failure.
4. They are not God's judgment on you.
5. They are not a license to withdraw from your spouse.
6. They are not an opportunity to be rude or mean to your spouse.
7. They are not a tool you use to control your spouse.

I believe God sometimes allows depression and other negative emotions in the lives of even strong believers because it forces us to draw closer to Him in order to walk through it. And He is glorified when we are set free of it. So cry out to God in your need for His love, peace, joy, and power, knowing that He longs to share Himself with you. Say, "Thank You, God, that You make us 'exceedingly glad with Your presence'" (Psalm 21:6).

Negative emotions are not something you have to live with. In fact, you must do whatever is necessary to get rid of them. They not only hurt you, they hurt your spouse and children as well. God has given you a way out of them through the power of prayer, praise, His Word, His presence, and His love. Bask in all that until you are free. And don't lose hope. Be confident of this, that "He who has begun a good work in you will complete it until the day of Jesus Christ" (Philippians 1:6). God won't give up on you, so don't give up on yourself or your spouse.

PRAYERS FOR MY MARRIAGE

Prayer for Protection

LORD, I THANK YOU THAT You show us the paths of life and "in Your presence is fullness of joy; at Your right hand are pleasures forevermore" (Psalm 16:11). Thank You that when we delight ourselves in You, You will cause us "to ride on the high hills of the earth" (Isaiah 58:14). I pray that You will keep my husband (wife) and me from all negative emotions. Help us to see that we never have to live with any of them. Where we have allowed anything such as depression, anxiety, fear, rejection, or loneliness to influence our lives, deliver us out of all that and keep it far from us.

I pray that even though we may go through times where we are hard-pressed on every side, we will not be crushed, nor will we be in despair (2 Corinthians 4:8). We will rejoice in Your Word and the comfort of Your presence. We will not forget that You have the power to set us free.

Your commandments are right and they make our hearts rejoice (Psalm 19:8). We were once in darkness, but now we are in Your light. Help us to always "walk as children of the light" (Ephesians 5:8). I pray we will always look to You and put our hope and expectations in You (Psalm 62:5). In Jesus' name I pray.

Prayer for Breakthrough in Me

LORD, I PRAY THAT YOU would "search me, O God, and know my heart; try me, and know my anxieties" (Psalm 139:23). Wherever I have allowed negative emotions to control me, deliver me forever from them. Show me things in my life that have been passed down in my family—attitudes, fears, prejudices, and even depression—and break these strongholds completely. Keep me from falling into habits of the heart that are learned responses to life. Lord, I pray for healing and deliverance from any depression, anxiety, fear, rejection, loneliness, or any other negative emotion that would seek to find permanent residence in my heart. You are the lamp of my soul, Lord, and I thank

You that You "will enlighten my darkness" (Psalm 18:28). Thank You that You will give me rest from my sorrow and fear (Isaiah 14:3).

Lord, take away all sadness or despair. Heal the hurt in my heart. Give me a garment of praise at all times and take away the spirit of heaviness. Make me to be a tree of strength. Plant me and feed me in Your Word so that Your glory will be revealed in me. Rebuild the places in me that have been damaged or ruined in the past. Lord, I pray that You would "send out Your light and Your truth! Let them lead me; let them bring me to Your holy hill and to Your tabernacle" (Psalm 43:3). May Your light in my life completely evaporate any black clouds around me so that they cannot keep me from sensing Your presence in my life. In Jesus' name I pray.

Prayer for Breakthrough in My Husband (Wife)

LORD, I LIFT MY HUSBAND (WIFE) up to You and ask that You would set him (her) free from depression, anxiety, fear, rejection, loneliness, or any other negative emotions that grips him (her). Thank You for Your promise to bring out Your "people with joy" and Your "chosen ones with gladness" (Psalm 105:43). Thank You that because of You, Jesus, "darkness is passing away, and the true light is already shining" in his (her) life (1 John 2:8). Help him (her) to keep his (her) eyes on You and take refuge in You knowing that You will not leave his (her) soul destitute (Psalm 141:8). Have mercy on him (her) and be his (her) helper! (Psalm 30:10). Anoint him (her) with Your "oil of gladness" (Psalm 45:7). Restore to him (her) the joy of Your salvation, and uphold him (her) "by Your generous Spirit" (Psalm 51:12). Set him (her) free from anything that holds him (her) other than You.

I say to my husband (wife) now, as You, Lord, said to Your people in Your Word, "Be strong and of good courage; do not be afraid, nor be dismayed, for the LORD your God is with you wherever you go" (Joshua 1:9). The Lord *loves* you and has given you *hope* and *grace,* and will *comfort* your heart and *establish* you in all things (2 Thessalonians 2:16-17). In Jesus' name I pray.

Truth to Stand On

We do not wrestle against flesh and blood,
but against principalities, against powers,
against the rulers of the darkness of this age,
against spiritual hosts of wickedness in the heavenly places.

EPHESIANS 6:12

He has delivered us from the power of darkness and conveyed
us into the kingdom of the Son of His love.

COLOSSIANS 1:13

He has sent Me to heal the brokenhearted…
to give them beauty for ashes, the oil of joy for mourning,
the garment of praise for the spirit of heaviness;
that they may be called trees of righteousness,
the planting of the LORD, that He may be glorified.

ISAIAH 61:1,3

There is no fear in love; but perfect love casts out fear,
because fear involves torment.
But he who fears has not been made perfect in love.

1 JOHN 4:18

You are my hiding place; You shall
preserve me from trouble; You shall
surround me with songs of deliverance.

PSALM 32:7

5

If CHILDREN START *to* DOMINATE YOUR LIVES

Nothing will change a marriage faster and more dramatically than the birth of a child. When children come along, the demands on you are far greater than anyone can really prepare you for. You no longer have time to focus entirely on each other because now you must focus on your child. That means there is a lot less time to be alone. One of you can't work as much, so there is less money. Or if you both try to keep working, you become exhausted. You realize you have to sacrifice all selfish pleasure in order to devote yourself to becoming a good parent. And all that can be overwhelming. But the good news is that all this forces you to grow up, establish firm priorities, and learn to take care of yourself because you can't afford to be sick.

It's important when the size of your family increases that you not lose sight of the fact that one day it will again just be the two of you. I know it's hard to think that far ahead when the children occupy all your time and attention now. In fact, it's easy to let children dominate your lives. And it can happen without you even realizing it. After all, in the beginning your child can't do one thing without you. Your husband (wife) can presumably take care of himself (herself). Your spouse can feed, bathe, and dress himself (herself). Your baby can't do anything without help. So right away, out of necessity, children come between the two of you because of the amount of time you need to devote to them. But that doesn't have to be bad. If the two of you share the load, it will bond you more closely together. Some parents become so focused on parenting that they think of nothing else, not even their spouse. While God wants us to love and care for our children to the best of our ability, He doesn't want us to make idols out of them. There is a fine line between the caring nurture that gives your children the best chance in life, and the other extreme of letting them become an obsession to the point that it jeopardizes your marriage. Allowing your spouse to feel neglected, overlooked, unimportant, unnecessary, or irrelevant doesn't help your marriage stay strong. And having your marriage fall apart doesn't help your children. We all need wisdom and revelation from God in order to find that balance.

Many conflicts can arise between a husband and wife over the raising of their children that are serious enough to lead to divorce. These conflicts may not happen in the busy infancy or toddler states, but rather later on in the complicated teenage years when more is at stake. I have found that the best way to raise your children and take the pressure off of you is to pray for them every step of the way. In my first book in the Power of a Praying series, *The Power of a Praying Parent,* I gave 30 ways to pray for your child. Such things as that they be protected, feel loved and accepted, maintain good family relationships, have godly friends and role models, have a desire to learn, have a sound mind, not be ruled by fear, not be addicted to anything, grow in faith, and become who God created them to be. Praying this way about your children means you don't have to be Supermom or Superdad, and that takes the pressure off your marriage. Praying *together* about your children is best, but praying alone has great benefits as well. Here are some things to pray about with regard to your marriage and raising children.

Pray to Agree on Discipline

How you discipline your children is a very important issue you have to decide together. It should not be one-sided, with one of you strict and the other lenient. If that is the case with you and your spouse, pray to find a happy meeting place somewhere between indulgent and permissive.

Seek God for wisdom and unity about how you are going to discipline your children for each offense. If *you* refuse to discipline your children, you force your *husband* (*wife*) to be the bad guy. Your husband (wife) will get very tired of being the bad guy while you look like your child's best friend. It will chip away at the foundation of your marriage until it is weakened or destroyed. Don't think for a moment that this is not a very deep issue. I have known too many marriages to break up over this serious situation.

In fact, I know a great couple who have been married nearly 25 years and their children are now teenagers. Recently the husband and wife have come into conflict over what to permit the children to do. The wife feels the husband is too permissive and the husband believes the wife is too strict. She felt that he was way too lenient when he found out that their children had experimented with drugs. She sees his permissiveness as a danger for their children, possibly jeopardizing their future. They have filed for divorce over this. Neither of them knows the Lord, but if they did, they could pray through this and come to a good solution. They could work this out so easily if humility, reliance on God, the power of prayer, and truly loving your spouse more than loving yourself were to come into play.

I can understand where she is coming from, but it would be so much better to go to Christian counseling than to break up the family. When she gets divorced, she will have completely lost control over what the children will be allowed to do when they are with the permissive spouse.

There are definitely times when you have a child endangered by the actions or inactions of a parent, but if you both are reasonable and sane people, you should be able to work this out. Especially if you pray. *Putting one another first before the children doesn't mean neglecting the children in any way.* It's just when raising them becomes an issue between you and your spouse, you have to work it out in a mutually acceptable manner. That takes prayer.

Pray to Agree on What Is Allowed

We have *two* long-haired Chihuahuas. Not by choice. Our daughter got our second grand-dog just before she went into her second year of college. Caring for her puppies was helpful to me at the time because having joint custody of these two fine examples of God's sense of humor made it easier for me when she left. It was like having a little part of her with us after she was gone, only furry. The one thing I have learned about Chihuahuas is that they are creatures of habit to the extreme. If they get to do something once, they think they have to do it all the time. Kids are a little like Chihuahuas when they are young. For example, they think that if they can come into your bed to sleep *one* night, they should be able to do it *every* night. Michael and I decided together when our first child was a baby that we did not want our children sleeping in our bed at night. We didn't want to make them feel bad about wanting to be near us, or to think that we were rejecting them, so our policy was that the one of us whose side of the bed the child came to in the middle of the night was the one who would carry or walk the child back to his or her bed and tuck them in and lay down beside them until they could get back to sleep or feel better about being in their room alone. It worked very well with each child because it only took a few times of doing that until the trip into our room didn't seem worth it to them. And then when they did come, we knew it was important.

It's not that we didn't love our children or couldn't stand to be with them. It's just that we couldn't sleep with them in bed with us. We would wake up tired and grumpy. We discovered a long time ago that not getting sleep wasn't good for our marriage. We also knew that "Chihuahua syndrome" in kids means that if you do it once, it immediately becomes a habit that is extremely hard to break.

Some people like their kids sleeping with them every night. I know some couples who have all their children and their big dogs sleeping in their bed with them and it doesn't bother them. Personally, that sounds like a nightmare, but if that works for them, great. The point is to be in agreement about it. You have to agree on the rules for your children. You have to come to some common conclusions so that there is balance in your boundaries.

Pray that you and your spouse can talk things out concerning your children. When you strongly disagree about something, pray that you both can get the mind of God on the issue. Often it's not a matter of wrong or right, but of personal preference. So if the two of you don't agree, there needs to be the working out of a compromise. And if you can't see how a compromise will ever work for you, know that God can change both of your hearts so you will do the right thing.

Communicate with your children what the rules are and why. Teach them about God's ways every day and pray with them about everything. Help them to see that prayer is a lifestyle, not something you only do in an emergency. If you are allowing your children to do things that your spouse objects to, and you continue doing it, that is putting your children before your husband (wife). What matters most is that your marriage stays strong and your intimacy doesn't get sacrificed on the altar of child obsession. You have to put each other first and come to some kind of agreement or compromise. Divorce is not good for a child, either.

Pray That You Will Have Time Alone Together

Everything you do affects your children. If you live God's way, they will benefit from that. "Oh, that they had such a heart in them that they would fear Me and always keep all My commandments, that it might be well with them and with their children forever!" (Deuteronomy 5:29). When we live God's way, our children will be kept free from the enemy's hand. "The posterity of the righteous will be delivered" (Proverbs 11:21). Likewise, if we live unrighteous lives, our children will suffer consequences for our sins.

One of the right things to do is to work on your marriage and find ways to make it better. Even though raising children takes up most of your time, you still *have* to find time to be alone together away from your children once a week, even if it's only for two hours to go to dinner. Pray that you can find someone you trust who will watch your children for a few hours once a week so that the two of you can go someplace where you are able to enjoy each other. Or take the children to someone else's house while you have a romantic time alone together at your own home.

Michael and I have two close friends, Bob and Sally, whom we met in church shortly after their first baby and ours were born. Sally and I traded babysitting favors, which was convenient for us because our children were exactly the same age and so we were set up for it. I took her daughter for three hours once a week, and she took my son for the same amount of time. Sometimes it was in the morning, sometimes in the afternoon, and sometimes it was an evening, which allowed for a date night. It was a lifesaver for all of us because none of us had any family members close by to help out the way many families do. And we all know how difficult it is to find trustworthy people who are willing and available to take care of our children.

Ask God to lead you to one or two trustworthy people who could take care of your child for a few hours once a week. Pay them so they will be more likely to say yes. Only God knows the truth about potential babysitters, so always ask Him for His peace—or lack thereof—with regard to whoever takes care of your child. Trust what the Holy Spirit whispers to your soul.

It's better to have a date night in your own home after your little darlings are in bed than it is to take a chance on a flaky babysitter.

Pray That You Can Agree on How Many Children—if Any—to Have

It's important that you come to some kind of agreement on how many children your hearts have room for—while always staying open to the plans of God and His surprises. Keep in mind that not having children can bring pressures too.

When one of you does not want to have any children, or you both want children but for one reason or another are not able to have them, this can also be a great source of stress in a marriage. I know a couple who decided not to have children because the husband had already raised a family with his first wife and didn't want to do it again. The wife in that marriage had to pray, "Lord, take away my desire for children if this is Your will. If it is not Your will, take away whatever fear my husband has that makes him not want children." In this case, the wife was able to come to terms with the fact that biological children were not in her future.

Another woman I know in the same situation devoted herself to mentoring spiritual children instead of having her own. In another case, the husband eventually changed his mind and they now have a child. Whatever your situation, and for whatever reason, pray that you and your spouse will be in unity and at peace with each other regarding this important matter.

Pray That the Two of You Will Stay Connected

Children change your marriage and your life. In the beginning you both have to accept that you are going to be too tired most days to sit down and discuss your feelings and dreams. You may be too exhausted at the end of the day to talk about much more than what the children need and how you can juggle the responsibilities of meeting those needs. Ask God to help you *both* in the midst of all that to stay connected to each other and still be good parents.

We all change through the seasons of life, and if you and your husband (wife) have not made any meaningful contact for years, then when the last child leaves home it will be especially difficult. You will feel like strangers and the house will be extremely empty. If you already have spent years totally focused on your careers, raising children, paying for a house, and keeping up with life, and you have lost contact with each other, just know that it is never too late to get that feeling of connection back. You have to talk together, spend time alone together, and reconnect.

If you're married to someone who is stubborn, stuck in his (her) ways, refusing to change, and incapable of stepping out of his (her) rut, then pray for him (her) to be set free. For his (her) own sake, as well as for yours, pray that he (she) will be delivered from stubbornness. Your future happiness together depends on it.

Pray That Both You and Your Children Will Honor Your Parents

God's commandment to honor your parents comes with a promise that says if you do, things will go well for you and you will have a long life (Ephesians 6:1-3). It is not only important to honor *your* parents, but your *husband's (wife's)* parents as well, no matter how difficult that may seem. Your graciousness to them will bring blessings upon you and your children that will be more far-reaching than you can imagine. Help your spouse to honor his (her) parents if he (she) has a hard time doing that. I have been extremely blessed in having a great mother- and father-in-law, although sadly they did not live nearly long enough. But I have heard horror stories from other people about the hurtful things that can happen in the delicate in-law relationship. Do whatever it takes to make peace with them. If they are deceased, do what you can to honor their memory to your children. If your children are married, do whatever it takes to love your daughter-in-law or son-in-law. Do whatever you need to do in order to make it easy for them to honor you. If there is any uneasiness in your relationship with them, pray that God will bring peace and love into your hearts for one another.

Even if your parents are deceased, honor them by saying positive things about them to your children. Honoring your parents has to do with having an attitude of appreciation toward them. Even if they were both the most horrible parents on earth, at least honor them for the fact that they gave you life.

While it's true you have to earn someone's respect, honor is not earned when it comes to your parents. It is commanded. Ask God to help you forgive them and to heal you from all past wounds. Honoring your parents does not mean allowing them to misbehave in a way that upsets you, your spouse, or your children. Honoring them may mean setting certain boundaries in your life that they cannot violate. If you pass down a heritage of honoring your parents to your children, it will be a legacy you will find beneficial when it comes time for them to honor you.

Honoring your parents will give you a long, good life, plus it will help you to be better parents to your children.

Pray That You Won't Blame Each Other if Something Bad Happens

Job regularly prayed for his children. "So it was, when the days of feasting had run their course, that Job would send and sanctify [*his children*], and he would rise early in the morning and offer burnt offerings according to the number of them all. For Job said, 'It may be that my sons have sinned and cursed God in their hearts.' Thus Job did regularly" (Job 1:5, emphasis added).

You may be saying to yourself, *A lot of good it did him to pray for his kids because he ended up losing all of them.* When they were all gathered together for dinner, a "great wind" hit the house and it collapsed on them, killing every one (Job 1:19). Here Job was, praying for his children and doing what he was supposed to be doing, and still something bad happened. But even so, Job's faith did not waver. He did not blame God.

If something happens to a child, too often we blame God. Or we beat ourselves up because we feel we are responsible for what happened. If a husband and wife blame each other, that will destroy the marriage, because no one can bear the blame for something happening to their children. Children are a guilt trip anyway, but especially if something goes wrong. A parent is always wondering if they have done too much or not enough. And if anything happens, such as poor grades, discipline problems at school, or they have an accident or get sick, you always blame yourself for either not being there or allowing them to be in a place or position where this could happen. And if on top of all that your spouse puts the blame on you for it, it's unbearable. When you are in the deepest pain of your life and not only is your spouse not there for you, but actually blames you, the relationship cannot bear the double-weight guilt.

God forbid that anything bad ever happen to one of your children, but if it does, don't blame your husband (wife). Don't blame God. Blame the enemy. Even if your spouse did something unwise, no one with any degree of sanity does anything to deliberately hurt their own children. Trust God in the situation and refuse to destry your spouse and your marriage by adding a heavy load of blame on him (her). Draw close to God and He will draw near to you. He is your source of healing and restoration, and His presence will bring healing to the situation.

Pray That You Will Be a Praying Parent

We can get prideful if we devote ourselves to becoming perfect parents. We can get even *more* prideful if we buy into the belief that we have raised perfect children. In fact, this is actually dangerous ground to walk on because God blesses those who are humble and He resists those who are prideful (James 4:6).

If you feel you don't know how to be a great parent on your own, then be glad. You will have to depend on God to help you raise your children. And He will always act in response to your prayers because you have more authority over your child in prayer than you know.

It is actually healthier for your marriage if you accept that you are not a perfect parent, but God is. He is the only one who knows what is best for your children. So consult Him every day and ask Him to help you to be the best parent you can be. This is far better than trying to figure it all out on your own. The best thing you can do for your children is pray *for* them and *with* them. *Teach them* to pray. Make prayer a natural part of their lives and it will serve them well all of their days. Being a *praying parent* is the best kind of parent of all, and it will take the pressure off of you trying to be the *perfect parent.*

Turn to God whenever you become discouraged while raising your children. God understands our weaknesses and temptation to give up. He says, "You're blessed when you're at the end of your rope. With less of you there is more of God and his rule" (Matthew 5:3 MSG). He wants you to come to Him and find His grace to help you with whatever you need. The more you experience God's love and grace, the more you are able to extend His love and grace to others—especially your husband (wife) and children.

Ten Great Things to Remember When Raising Your Children

1. *Start training them as soon as they are old enough and when they are older they will know better.* "Train up a child in the way he should go, and when he is old he will not depart from it" (Proverbs 22:6).

2. *Discipline them whenever they need it.* "Foolishness is bound up in the heart of a child; the rod of correction will drive it far from him" (Proverbs 22:15).

3. *Teach your children something from God's Word every day.* "These words which I command you today shall be in your heart. You shall teach them diligently to your children, and shall talk of them when you sit in your house, when you walk by the way, when you lie down, and when you rise up" (Deuteronomy 6:6-7).

4. *Trust that your children are not destined for trouble.* "They shall not labor in vain, nor bring forth children for trouble; for they shall be the descendants of the blessed of the Lord, and their offspring with them" (Isaiah 65:23).

5. *Pray fervently day and night for your children.* "Arise, cry out in the night, at the beginning of the watches; pour out your heart like water before the face of the Lord. Lift your hands toward Him for the life of your young children, who faint from hunger at the head of every street" (Lamentations 2:19).

6. *Give them godly training, not angry commands.* "You, fathers, do not provoke your children to wrath, but bring them up in the training and admonition of the Lord" (Ephesians 6:4).

7. *When you do what's right, your children will be blessed.* "The righteous man walks in his integrity; his children are blessed after him" (Proverbs 20:7).

8. *Keep praying when things get difficult and refuse to give up.* "I would have lost heart, unless I had believed that I would see the goodness of the Lord in the land of the living. Wait on the

LORD; be of good courage, and He shall strengthen your heart; wait, I say, on the LORD!" (Psalm 27:13-14).

9. ***Know that your children are God's reward to you, no matter what it feels like sometimes.*** "Behold, children are a heritage from the LORD, the fruit of the womb is a reward" (Psalm 127:3).

10. ***Trust that the Lord hears every prayer for your children.*** "For this child I prayed, and the LORD has granted me my petition which I asked of Him" (1 Samuel 1:27).

Pray That You Can Release Your Child into God's Hands

It's important to release your children to God so that you will have the peace of knowing they are in good hands. In an excerpt from *The Power of a Praying Parent,* I described what it means to release our children to God.

> We don't want to limit what God can do in our children by clutching them to ourselves and trying to parent alone. If we are not positive that God is in control of our children's lives, we'll be ruled by fear. And the only way to be sure that God *is* in control is to surrender our hold and allow Him full access to their lives. The way to do that is to live according to His Word and His ways and pray to Him about everything. We can trust God to take care of our children even better than we can. When we release our children into the Father's hands and acknowledge that He is in control of their lives and ours, both we and our children will have greater peace (pages 35-36).

Determine together with your spouse that you are going to partner with God to raise your children. When you trust your children to God and pray for them and ask for His help in raising them, you will have more peace. That will take that feeling of pressure and burden off your shoulders. Having greater peace about your children will bring greater peace in your marriage. And that is worth praying about.

PRAYER FOR MY MARRIAGE

Prayer for Protection

LORD, I PRAY FOR PROTECTION over my children and over our marriage. Help us to learn how to pray for our children so that we never leave any aspect of their lives to chance. Your Word says that "unless the LORD builds the house, they labor in vain who build it" (Psalm 127:1). So I invite You right now to build and establish our house, our family, and our marriage. I pray that we will never be divided or torn apart. Give me and my husband (wife) great wisdom and revelation about how to raise our children. Help us to talk things through and be in complete unity, especially in the area of discipline and privileges. Your Word says that You will reveal things we need to see when we reverence You (Psalm 25:14). Show us what we need to see about ourselves and each child.

Help us to always put You first in our lives and to make each other and our marriage a priority as we are busy tending to our children. Show us any time that we sacrifice each other to a point that is detrimental to our relationship. I know You are with us to save us, and Your love in us will bring peace and joy to our family (Zephaniah 3:17). Teach us how to pray for our children and to remember Your promise that whatever we ask in Your name, You will give to us (John 16:23). In Jesus' name I pray.

Prayer for Breakthrough in Me

LORD, HELP ME TO BE balanced in my parenting. Help me to not be obsessive about my children, but rather to relinquish control over their lives to You. Help me to find the balance between focusing too much on my children and neglecting my husband (wife), and the other extreme of neglecting my children in any way. Help me to put You first and my husband (wife) second in my life, so that my focus on our children doesn't come between those two relationships. Wherever there are disagreements between me and my husband (wife) as to how to raise and discipline our children, help us to be able to communicate well with each other and resolve whatever conflict we have.

Give me Your wisdom, revelation, and discernment. Give me Your strength, patience, and love. Teach me how to truly intercede for my children without trying to impose my own will when I pray. Teach me how to pray so I can lay the burden of raising them at Your feet and partner with You in training them in the way they should go. Increase my faith to believe for all the things You put on my heart to pray about for them. Lord, I know that I don't have the ability to be the perfect parent, but *You* do. I release my children into Your hands and pray that You would protect and guide them. Help me not to live in fear about my children because of all the possible dangers, but to live in peace trusting that You are in control. In Jesus' name I pray.

Prayer for Breakthrough in My Husband (Wife)

LORD, I PRAY FOR MY husband (wife) to find the perfect balance between being overly focused on the children and the other extreme of not spending enough time with them. Help him (her) to be willing to talk with me about the raising and disciplining of each child so we can be in complete unity about everything. Let no issues of child rearing change his (her) heart toward me or undermine our relationship. Help him (her) to see the need for us to spend time together alone so that we can stay strong and connected as a married couple.

Lord, You have said in Your Word that whatever we ask we receive from You, because we keep Your commandments and do things that are pleasing in Your sight (1 John 3:22). Help my husband (wife) to obey You and do what is right in Your sight so that his (her) prayers will be answered—especially for our children. Give him (her) wisdom and revelation about all aspects of child rearing and help him (her) to be a great father (mother) to our children. In Jesus' name I pray.

Truth to Stand On

The mercy of the LORD is from everlasting to everlasting
on those who fear Him, and His righteousness to children's
children, to such as keep His covenant, and to those who
remember His commandments to do them.

PSALM 103:17-18

If you then, being evil,
know how to give good gifts to your children,
how much more will your Father who is in heaven
give good things to those who ask Him!

MATTHEW 7:11

He has strengthened the bars of your gates;
He has blessed your children within you.

PSALM 147:13

My grace is sufficient for you,
for My strength is made perfect in weakness...
For when I am weak, then I am strong.

2 CORINTHIANS 12:9-10

All your children shall be taught by the LORD,
and great shall be the peace of your children.

ISAIAH 54:13

6

If FINANCES GET OUT *of* CONTROL

Can there be any greater pressure in a marriage than having financial problems? And what worse financial crisis can there be than sinking heavily into debt with no way to pay your bills? The sense of being caught in a vise that is always closing in on you is a horrible feeling. Not having enough money for rent, mortgage, the electric bill, or food is unbearably frightening. Those who have been there know how important it is to do whatever it takes to stay debt free and live within your means. In order to do that in a marriage, however, you need to pray that both you and your spouse will be of one mind with regard to handling money.

Some experts say that the number one cause of divorce today has to do with financial problems. I can see why. Money is a source of life. Without it we can't have a home, food, clothing, security, or a good future. So being married to someone who is irresponsible, foolish, selfish, stupid, or careless when it comes to money can cause you to feel as though your life is being sucked away. It makes you fear that no matter how hard you work, you will never have anything to show for it. It can cause any person to feel desperate enough to do whatever is necessary to stop the bleeding—even if it means getting a divorce.

If you are married to someone who has no business sense or wisdom about finances—who can't add, subtract, or count, and has no sense of financial discipline or responsibility in handling money—then I suggest you invest in knee pads for your frequent prayer vigils.

In any marriage where one person is working hard to make a living and conserve their finances wisely and the other is foolishly spending money faster than it is coming in, there will be major problems. If one person would rather save money for the future instead of spending on luxury items, and the other wants to buy everything they want the moment they want it without any thought for the future, there will be problems. If one person tells lies and manipulates in order to hide his (her) expenditures so the other one won't find out, there will be problems. If one person doesn't care what the other wants or thinks, there will be problems. If one person is responsible and the other isn't, there will be problems. The problems mentioned above are enough to ruin any marriage.

The stress caused by spending foolishly, making unwise investments, and accumulating debt with never enough money to pay it off is beyond what any marriage can tolerate. If two people are going to live together success-fully, they have to come to an agreement about how money is earned, spent, saved, given, and invested.

The Message says, "The one who stays on the job has food on the table; the witless chases whims and fancies" (Proverbs 12:11). That same verse in the New Century Version says, "Those who work their land will have plenty of food, but the one who chases empty dreams is not wise." Chasing whims, fancies, and empty dreams can ruin a person's life. When it comes to finances, some people are in dreamland. They can't put two and two together. That's why communication between a husband and wife about their finances is vital. You must have the same financial goals, the same mind about how money is handled, and be living in the same reality.

There has to be financial honesty in marriage. You and your spouse need to be upfront with one other about income and spending. You must always consider the other when buying anything. If your spouse is secretly spending money faster than either of you can earn it, then it feels as though he (she) has no consideration of your future and what you want. It puts up a wall of separation and kills love between you.

If you and your spouse have a bad habit of accumulating debt, ask God to open your eyes so you can clearly see the truth. Pray for discernment about what you don't really need and ask God to give you the strength to resist buying it. We have all bought things in our lives that were a waste of money and now wish we had the money back instead of those things. Pray that God will give you the wisdom to make sound financial decisions, and that He will help you to be wise about the things you buy. Ask Him to help you avoid getting into debt in the first place. If you are already in debt, ask God to show you how to pay it all off.

TEN THINGS TO ASK GOD FOR REGARDING YOUR FINANCES

1. To give you wisdom about your finances.

2. To help you make good decisions with regard to spending.

3. To enable you to get out of debt and stay debt free.

4. To eliminate any craving for unnecessary material possessions.

5. To help you plan ahead for future expenses.

6. To enable you to find good work that is secure.

7. To bless your employer so that you can be blessed as well.

8. To help you give to God as He has instructed.

9. To show you how to give to others according to His will.

10. To help you trust Him to meet all your needs.

Giving to God

One of the greatest keys to financial freedom is giving. The first and most important place to start is giving to God. This is a big part of getting your finances under control. Here are five things to remember about *giving to God:*

1. If you give God ten percent of what you bring in, He will pour great blessings on you. " 'Bring all the tithes into the storehouse, that there may be food in My house, and try Me now in this,' says the LORD of hosts, 'If I will not open for you the windows of heaven and pour out for you such blessing that there will not be room enough to receive it. And I will rebuke the devourer for your sakes, so that he will not destroy the fruit of your ground, nor shall the vine fail to bear fruit for you in the field,' says the LORD of hosts" (Malachi 3:10-11). God will not only bless your finances, but also He will not allow the enemy to steal from you. He will prosper the work you do.

But be sure you and your spouse are in unity on this. If your spouse is not a believer and he (she) objects to tithing, he (she) may not understand the principle of it and it won't make sense to him (her). In that case, ask what amount he (she) would feel comfortable giving and try to come to some agreement about it. Don't let this become a point of strife. Getting him (her) to come to know Jesus is more important than tithing his (her) money against his (her) will. I have seen great strife in marriages over this very thing. It's not right.

2. Don't work to build your own house and not contribute to building God's house, or it will seem as though you will never get ahead. " 'You have sown much, and bring in little; you eat, but do not have enough; you drink, but you are not filled with drink; you clothe yourselves, but no one is warm; and he who earns wages, earns wages to put into a bag with holes…You looked for much, but indeed it came to little; and when you brought it home, I blew it away. Why?' says the LORD of hosts. 'Because of My house that is in ruins, while every one of you runs to his own house' " (Haggai 1:6,9). If it ever seems as though you work hard and never get ahead, or that money is always slipping through your fingers, ask God if you are giving toward the building of His church and kingdom in the way He would have you to do.

3. You have to be faithful with what you have before God will bless you with more. In responding to a servant who wisely invested his money, the Lord said of the servant, "Well done, good and faithful servant; you were faithful over a few things, I will make you ruler over many things. Enter into the joy of your lord" (Matthew 25:21). If you are faithful to give a portion of your money to God, He will be faithful to trust you with more.

4. If you truly believe that everything you have belongs to God or came from God, you will want to be a good steward of the things He has given you. "Yours, O LORD, is the greatness, the power and the glory, the victory and the majesty; for all that is in heaven and in earth is Yours…Both riches and honor come from You, and You reign over all…For all things come from You, and of Your own we have given You" (1 Chronicles 29:11-12,14). When you believe that everything you have comes from God, it will cause you to want to give back to Him.

5. You will always receive from God far more than you give. "Give and it will be given to you: good measure, pressed down, shaken together, and running over will be put into your bosom. For with the same measure that you use, it will be measured back to you" (Luke 6:38). God's law is that you will reap a great blessing because of what you give to Him, and you can test Him on that.

Giving to Others

After giving to God, giving to others who have nothing, who can't help themselves, and who don't have enough food or clothes or a home is extremely important to God and crucial to your own financial peace and freedom. Don't give only to rich people's causes; give to those who can do nothing for you or for themselves. God sees you giving to others and considers that as something you are giving to Him. Jesus said that when He returned He would invite certain people to partake of what had been prepared for them from the foundation of the world. He will say, "I was hungry and you gave Me food; I was thirsty and you gave Me drink; I was a stranger and you took Me in; I was naked and you clothed Me." And we, the believers, will say, "When did we do that?"

And Jesus will answer, "Assuredly, I say to you, inasmuch as you did it to one of the least of these My brethren, you did it to Me" (Matthew 25:35-40). Anything we do for others, we have done it for the Lord, and that brings great rewards.

Here are some things to remember about *giving to others:*

1. Ask God to show you a person in need you can help in some way. You will be surprised at what will be revealed to you. There are always people around you who you may not even realize have great needs, and God is waiting to show you who they are. Be on the lookout for where God wants you to put your time, effort, and money.

2. Ask your husband (wife) to be a part of any giving you do, so he (she) can share in the blessing. Tell your husband (wife) what you're feeling about who you want to give to and why. If he (she) is reticent when it comes to giving, don't let that stop you from helping others. Just because your spouse doesn't understand how to open up the flow of God's blessings into his (her) life by giving doesn't mean you have to limit what God wants to do through you. There are things you can do or give that won't affect your mate.

For example, you can give food, clothes, furniture, and household items to people who can use them. Perhaps all you have to give someone at this moment is a ride, some kind of help or assistance, or an encouraging word. You can't imagine how much of a blessing doing something like these things can be to others. You never know what can bless someone else until you offer it to them.

3. Give from what you have. Even if you don't have much money to give, you may have other things that can help meet the needs of others. Do you have a talent you can use to bless someone? Ask God to show you. If you have a skill you have been using for 40 hours a week, it may be that this is the last thing you want to do when you get off work, but ask God to show you where there is a need for your skill or talent that would bless someone greatly. "Do not forget to do good and to share, for with such sacrifices God is well pleased" (Hebrews 13:16). *God doesn't require that you give money you don't have.* If you owe a debt to someone and when money comes in you give it to someone else instead of paying the person you owe, that is not right. Paying your debts is part of being a good steward. One of the greatest things about being out of debt is being able to give to others as God directs you.

4. Give to God, not to impress others. I know someone who was so into giving that he gave away practically everything at the expense of his wife and children. But his giving was not for God so much as it was to impress other people. It was giving to be admired. "Take heed that you do not do your charitable deeds before men, to be seen by them. Otherwise you have no reward from your Father in heaven" (Matthew 6:1). It's good to have a giving spirit, but when you are married you have to be considerate of your mate and come to an agreement together about giving.

5. You have to give in order to receive. If you are in need of financial blessing, give something of yourself to others today. Often, just the act of giving will break whatever has a hold on your finances. You will always have enough for what you need if you give to God and others. "This I say: He who sows sparingly will also reap sparingly, and he who sows bountifully will also reap bountifully. So let each one give as he purposes in his heart, not grudgingly or of necessity; for God loves a cheerful giver" (2 Corinthians 9:6-7). Give generously and you will receive generously from God.

Obtain Advice from Experts

If you and your spouse need financial help, seek the advice of an expert or professional. There are many good Christian financial advisers, plus excellent Christian books and seminars on the subject. If you and your husband (wife) can attend one of these seminars together, it will be greatly beneficial for you. Half the battle will be won if you can face all financial matters full force together.

One of the things financial experts advise is to not sustain credit card debt if you can avoid it. Instead, pay off your credit cards each month. I know there are times when you need to purchase something big that is a necessity and pay it off monthly, such as a new refrigerator, tires for your car, or repairs on your home. And you do need to put vacation expenses on a credit card because it is unwise to travel with large amounts of cash. But even then, be sure you can pay it all off within a few payments. Paying huge finance charges for credit card debt is like throwing your money down the drain. If buying things on credit puts you under a mountain of debt that you can't get out from under, it doesn't make you feel good about your life—or your spouse, if he (she) is the one causing the problem. A professional can help you see where you have gone wrong and how to change it.

SEVEN THINGS TO REMEMBER ABOUT MONEY

1. ***Keep in mind that all you have comes from God.*** "What do you have that you did not receive? Now if you did indeed receive it, why do you boast as if you had not received it?" (1 Corinthians 4:7).

2. ***Pray about every aspect of your finances.*** "Ask and it will be given to you; seek, and you will find; knock, and it will be opened to you. For everyone who asks receives, and he who seeks finds, and to him who knocks it will be opened" (Matthew 7:7-8).

3. ***Stay out of debt.*** "Owe no one anything except to love one another, for he who loves another has fulfilled the law" (Romans 13:8).

4. ***Be faithful with what God has given you.*** "He who is faithful

in what is least is faithful also in much; and he who is unjust in what is least is unjust also in much" (Luke 16:10).

5. *Spend wisely.* "Why do you spend money for what is not bread, and your wages for what does not satisfy? Listen carefully to Me, and eat what is good, and let your soul delight itself in abundance" (Isaiah 55:2).

6. *Give and you will be blessed.* "Remember the words of the Lord Jesus, that He said, 'It is more blessed to give than to receive'" (Acts 20:35).

7. *Love God, not money.* "The love of money is a root of all kinds of evil, for which some have strayed from the faith in their greediness, and pierced themselves through with many sorrows" (1 Timothy 6:10).

Learn to Simplify

Financial stress always takes a great toll on a marriage, but you can either let it tear you apart or make you stronger. One thing financial stress *can* do for you is force you to draw closer to God, to depend on Him to get you through and turn things around. It also encourages you to work more closely with your spouse so you will be on the same team financially.

Another thing a financial crunch will do is help you learn how to simplify. Learning to live more simply takes stress off your marriage and financial pressure off both of you. God will show you how to live without certain things and be wise about every purchase. I was raised extremely poor. And even after I was out on my own, I have been poor to the point that every penny, nickel, dime, and quarter counted. Sometimes it meant having food for dinner, being able to do a load of wash at the Laundromat, or paying the phone bill. This is not a good way to live, so ask God to keep you out of that kind of gut-wrenching poverty. He says He does not want His children begging bread, but He also doesn't want us to kill ourselves working for material possessions (Proverbs 23:4). We have to find that godly balance. And the way to find it, God says, is to understand that we don't have because we don't ask. He wants us to pray about the things we need.

Ask God to give you the wisdom to not purchase anything you don't need. Ask Him to help you establish an emergency savings account. Ask Him to guide you *before* you spend money on anything so you won't make a mistake you will regret. Remember that whatever you want to buy that your spouse *strongly* opposes will not be worth the toll it will take on your marriage. "Take heed and beware of covetousness, for one's life does not consist in the abundance of the things he possesses" (Luke 12:15).

You have to be able to enjoy your life, and unless you have lost all contact with reality, it is impossible to enjoy life if you are heavily burdened with debt or are struggling to just survive. You need to have money to live and also to do some things that are enjoyable, such as take a day off and go out to dinner together. Say no to things you don't absolutely have to have so that you can get out of debt and never be a slave to it again.

My husband and I try constantly to simplify our lives. We are not successful at it all the time, but when we can eliminate something we don't need—especially as we get older—our lives are richer for it. "Aspire to lead a quiet life, to mind your own business, and to work with your own hands" (1 Thessalonians 4:11). Ask God to show you ways you can work at what you love and simplify your lives together.

Gambling

There are many types of bad habits that have to do with finances, but none are as destructive as gambling. If one person is conserving and saving and denying themselves and doing all they can to stay out of debt, and their husband or wife is out gambling money away, the result is a heartbreaking sense of futility. And it is at epidemic proportions in families right now because of the easy access to gambling on the Internet and the numerous gambling places within driving distance from most cities.

If you gamble, remember you are gambling with the Lord's money. It's hard to think that God would want to bless you with riches so that they can be given to gambling casino owners. Actually, gambling casinos are betting on people losing, and they are successful because they are winning that bet. Gambling is one of the enemy's plans for your life and a pit he has prepared for you to fall into.

Some people try gambling a few times and when they win it is like an elixir, always drawing them back to experience the thrill of the win again. But the truth is they have a strong discontent with what they have, and an unwillingness to look to God to provide what they need. When God promises us that He will never leave or forsake us, He means that in the way He provides for us too. "Be content with such things as you have. For He Himself has said, 'I will never leave you nor forsake you'" (Hebrews 13:5).

Gambling may seem like the solution to a debt problem, but it never is. "There is a way that seems right to a man, but its end is the way of death" (Proverbs 14:12). Even if you win, you will eventually lose in every way. The money won't be blessed and will slip through your fingers, and you will have nothing lasting to show for it. Nothing good will come out of it.

Marriage is building a life together—a home, a family, and a future—and that cannot happen without financial security. When a husband or wife is foolishly gambling their money, a breakdown of trust happens that is extremely hard to repair. If you are trying to build a life and your spouse's out of control gambling problem is tearing down all you have built, you feel as though you have no future. No marriage can survive that.

I have seen this happen with a dear friend who started gambling to escape the emptiness in her marriage, and it became a terrible problem as she lost great amounts of money. But she has now surrendered her life completely to the Lord and is free of her gambling addiction. She has fallen back into it a couple times in the past two years and was quite discouraged each time, but I assured her that with any addiction everyone slips off the path at some point. It's to be expected that the enemy will not let you off easily. She has to remember that *falling into* the devil's trap is not sinful; *staying in it* is. Getting back up and on the right path again is where you find victory.

So don't feel discouraged if you have ever chosen a path of freedom only to find yourself slipping off of it. *There is a difference between slipping off the path you have chosen and choosing to go down the wrong path.* Declare the freedom in Christ that you have been given and get back on the path toward life and blessing.

If either you or your mate have a problem with gambling, stay in God's Word and fast and pray until you are set free. Jesus said, "If you abide in My word, you are My disciples indeed. And you shall know the truth, and the truth shall make you free" (John 8:31-32). You need a miracle from God, and when you lay all else aside and seek Him for that miracle, He will work one in your life. Determine to want God and all *He* has more than you want the fleeting and deceptive thrill of winning at gambling, and you will come to know the far greater thrill of winning in life and in your marriage.

Be Content and Work Hard While Waiting for Finances to Turn Around

Being content doesn't mean resigning yourself to thinking that this is as good as it gets and nothing will ever change. It means being content with what God has given you while you pray about your finances and wait patiently for His future blessings. "Godliness with contentment is great gain…And having food and clothing, with these we shall be content" (1 Timothy 6:6,8). Being content doesn't mean doing nothing, either. Working hard is one of the ways God blesses us.

When you work hard to provide for your family, that is not a sign of loving money. Putting the making of money *before* your family *is*.

SEVEN THINGS TO REMEMBER ABOUT THE WORK YOU DO

1. ***Begin all the work you do by seeking the Lord.*** "In every work that [Hezekiah] began in the service of the house of God, in the law and in the commandment, to seek his God, he did it with all his heart. So he prospered" (2 Chronicles 31:21).

2. ***Commit your work to God.*** "Whatever you do, do it heartily, as to the Lord and not to men" (Colossians 3:23).

3. ***Work hard and your work will be rewarded.*** "You, be strong and do not let your hands be weak, for your work shall be rewarded" (2 Chronicles 15:7).

4. ***Pray for God to establish your work.*** "Let the beauty of the Lord our God be upon us, and establish the work of our hands for us; yes, establish the work of our hands" (Psalm 90:17).

5. ***Work diligently and your wealth will increase.*** "He who has a slack hand becomes poor, but the hand of the diligent makes rich" (Proverbs 10:4-5).

6. ***Take a day to rest from your work each week.*** "Six days you shall labor and do all your work, but the seventh day is the

Sabbath of the LORD your God. In it you shall do no work" (Exodus 20:9-10).

7. ***Ask God for success in your work and He will lift you up.*** "Do you see a man who excels in his work? He will stand before kings; he will not stand before unknown men" (Proverbs 22:29).

Getting Out from Under

God is the one who supplies all your needs and keeps your life from being sucked dry with one disaster after another. Always recognize where your provision comes from. "My God shall supply all your need according to His riches in glory by Christ Jesus" (Philippians 4:19).

The devourer, by contrast, comes to steal and destroy all you have. The list of ways for him to gobble up your life is endless. You can have one disaster after another, such as the car breaks down, the house needs repair, you get sick and have to miss work, and you have unexpected medical expenses. But when you live God's way financially, He protects you from these things. It's not that these things will never happen, but He blesses you in ways you may not even realize. He hides you in the shadow of His wing and keeps you from disaster far more than you realize (Psalm 91:1).

Jesus said, "Do not lay up for yourselves treasures on earth, where moth and rust destroy and where thieves break in and steal; but lay up for yourselves treasures in heaven, where neither moth nor rust destroys and where thieves do not break in and steal. For where your treasure is, there your heart will be also" (Matthew 6:19-21). He is not saying you can never have anything, just that your heart must be with Him and not these things.

It was said of Uzziah, one of the kings of Judah, that "as he sought the LORD, God made him prosper" (2 Chronicles 26:5). It is the same for you and your spouse in your marriage. Seek God's guidance in your acquiring, giving, spending, saving, and investing. "If riches increase, do not set your heart on them" (Psalm 62:10). Set your heart on God, be in His Word, and live His way, and He will prosper you. "This Book of the Law shall not depart from your mouth, but you shall meditate in it day and night, that you may observe to do according to all that is written in it. For then you will make your way prosperous, and then you will have good success" (Joshua 1:8).

Pray that you and your husband (wife) will be able to think *God's* way about money. If you have any bad habits with finances, ask Him for a transformed heart so you can overcome them. Ask God to renew your mind about finances so that your finances can be renewed. Don't live like the world, always trying to get out of *yesterday's* debt. Live wisely *today* and plan for your *future*. Thank God that He promises to supply everything you need. And in time when you look back over your life, you will see how He has done that.

PRAYERS FOR MY MARRIAGE

Prayer for Protection

LORD, HELP MY HUSBAND (WIFE) and me to remember that it is You who gives us the ability to produce wealth (Deuteronomy 8:18). That the earth is Yours and everything in it belongs to You (Psalm 24:1). That You, Lord, own every animal and creature and "the cattle on a thousand hills" (Psalm 50:10-11). All silver and gold and all things valuable belong to You (Haggai 2:8). Everything we have comes from You, so help us to be good stewards of our finances. Help us to be calm and wise in handling money so that we may prosper and not make hasty, rash, or impulsive decisions (Proverbs 21:5).

Help us to work diligently, to be content with what we have, and to learn to give (Proverbs 21:25-26). Help us to always discern between the dream of something more or better that is in line with Your will for our lives, and the lusting greed for material possessions that is not Your will at all. Enable us to stay out of debt and pay off any debt we have quickly. Help us to not be drawn in by the ways of the world, but instead seek after what truly satisfies our soul (Romans 12:2).

I know that having good health, a loving and supportive family, a solid marriage, great friends, good and satisfying work, and a sense of purpose in helping others is the richest life of all. Help us to always put our sights on those clear priorities. Lord, I pray that You would bless us with provision and help us to always be wise in the decisions we make regarding our spending. Give us the wisdom and the courage to resist spending foolishly. Help us to tithe and give offerings to You, and show us how you would have us to give to others. Help my husband (wife) and me to completely agree on our spending as well as our giving. In Jesus' name I pray.

Prayer for Breakthrough in Me

LORD, I PRAY THAT YOU will give me wisdom with money. Help me to generate it and spend it wisely. Help me to give according to Your will and ways. Thank You that any charitable deed I do in secret, You will reward openly (Matthew 6:1-4). Show me when I am tempted to buy something I don't need or will regret later. Show me what is a waste of money and what is not. Help me to avoid certain places that are traps for me, where I will be tempted to spend foolishly. Help me not to be drawn toward things that will not add to our lives.

I submit our finances to You and ask that You would reveal to me all that I should know or do. I don't want to look back in regret but look forward to a secure future. Reveal to me anything I need to see in myself that are bad habits with regard to spending. Help me to glorify You with the money I spend. I acknowledge You as the Lord who gives us the power to gain wealth, and I thank You that You give no burden with it (Deuteronomy 8:18). I know that I must not trust in uncertain riches but in You, for it is You "who gives us richly all things to enjoy" (1 Timothy 6:17). "Oh, how great is Your goodness, which You have laid up for those who fear You, which You have prepared for those who trust in You" (Psalm 31:19). In Jesus' name I pray.

Prayer for Breakthrough in My Husband (Wife)

I THANK YOU, JESUS, THAT You are the power and wisdom of God (1 Corinthians 1:24). I pray that You would give my husband (wife) wisdom about our finances. Help him (her) to trust You with all his (her) heart and not depend on his (her) own understanding (Proverbs 3:5). Help him (her) to not be wise in his (her) own eyes, but to fear You and stay far from evil (Proverbs 3:7). Give him (her) a good business sense and the ability to be responsible with money. Show him (her) insight into Your truth and give him (her) the power to resist temptation when it comes to needless spending. Where he (she) has made mistakes with money, I pray that You would reveal Your truth to him (her).

Where he (she) is feeling financial strain, I pray You would take the stress of that burden away. Enable him (her) to get free of all debt and understand how to avoid it in the future. Help him (her) to know that "there is nothing too hard for You" (Jeremiah 32:17). Help him (her) to know that even though there are times when he (she) is not seeing the desired fruit of his (her) labor now, that he (she) can still rejoice and say, "The LORD God is my strength; He will make my feet like deer's feet, and He will make me walk on my high hills" (Habakkuk 3:19). Help him (her) to be anxious for nothing, but to pray about everything and be thankful (Philippians 4:6). Teach him (her) to trust in You and Your promise to provide for those who love You and look to You for everything.

Help my husband (wife) to excel in his (her) work and be recognized by many for the work he (she) does (Proverbs 22:29). Help him (her) to not be lacking in diligence, but to be fervent in spirit, serving You in everything he (she) does. Establish the work of his (her) hands (Psalm 90:17). In Jesus' name I pray.

Truth to Stand On

Set your mind on things above,
not on things on the earth.

Colossians 3:2

The Lord your God will make you abound
in all the work of your hand.

Deuteronomy 30:9

Prepare your outside work,
make it fit for yourself in the field;
and afterward build your house.

Proverbs 24:27

Oh, taste and see that the Lord is good;
blessed is the man who trusts in Him!

Psalm 34:8

The Lord will open to you His good treasure, the heavens,
to give the rain to your land in its season,
and to bless all the work of your hand.

Deuteronomy 28:12

7

If ADDICTIONS *or* OTHER DESTRUCTIVE BEHAVIORS MANIFEST

A marriage is for two people only and exclusively. Outside of including God in your relationship, any other third party breaks the relational bond. Drugs, alcohol, and any other destructive behavior will be a third party in any marriage. It will be an intruder in your relationship together.

There is a price to pay for everything we do that is not God's will for our lives. God says, "I, the LORD, search the heart, I test the mind, even to give every man according to his ways, according to the fruit of his doings" (Jeremiah 17:10). There is also a reward for every attempt we make to do the right thing. "He will reward each according to his works" (Matthew 16:27).

Destructive behavior—or simply behavior that constantly annoys your spouse to the point of desperation—is not right, and there will always be a serious consequence for it in your marriage and personal life. But every attempt you make to rid yourself of that behavior and do what's right will bring reward.

You may not have a single bad habit and neither does your spouse, but you still must pray about this issue. There are countless couples who are now divorced because in a weak moment in their lives, one of them resorted to some kind of destructive behavior that they couldn't get free of. And it became their downfall.

Why People Turn to Alcohol, Drugs, or Other Destructive Substances

Addictions and substance abuse are happening everywhere to all kinds of people—rich or poor, educated or not, young or old, and from every race. We have become a society where we can get anything we want, whenever we want it. Some destructive behaviors are not taken seriously and have even become socially acceptable. You don't have to have an addiction in order to play around with substances that have the potential to harm you. This is called risky living. This is gambling with your health, your work, your relationships, your marriage, your future, and your life.

Some people start taking drugs or drinking as a social experiment, just to follow the crowd. Some do it because they feel hopeless, insecure, or overwhelmed, and an intoxicant makes them feel better. Others want to be in *control* of their situation, and they feel as though they have control when they drink or take drugs. They let themselves get *out* of control doing something bad so that they can feel *in* control. "To a hungry soul every bitter thing is sweet" (Proverbs 27:7). People like that often say they feel something inside them compelling them to do it. I say it's the voice of the enemy of their soul luring them away from all God has for them.

People often use alcohol, drugs, or other harmful substances as a quick solution to their problems. When life becomes unbearable, this is the way they avoid facing it. They usually have a low opinion of themselves and feel inadequate. They want approval and are oversensitive to rejection. Their fear of rejection leads them to see rejection in every little thing that goes wrong, and this spurs them on to become more and more self-destructive. They develop destructive habits as a way of coping with stress, loneliness, and pain. They want to be *perfect* but feel powerless to even feel acceptable. Often the person feels as though there is an empty hole in them that needs to be filled. And actually this is true, but they are filling it with something that will destroy them instead of give them life. Using any kind of drug outside of prescriptions from a doctor is not only illegal, but there is a steep physical, mental, and emotional price to pay for every unnecessary thing a person puts into their body. This short-term pleasure always brings forth long-term misery.

The Truth About Eating Disorders and Other Compulsive Behaviors

We are not created by God to destroy ourselves. We are built to preserve our lives. We have a survival instinct in us. We don't willingly let ourselves drown, step in front of a train, jump off a high building, or put a gun to our head and pull the trigger unless we are not in our right mind or we are under the influence of something other than God.

Any kind of personality disorder involves choice. To deliberately choose something that will do damage to yourself or completely destroy your body is a disorder of the mind. People who have these kinds of disorders and practice any kind of self-destructive behavior don't fully understand who God made them to be and the purpose He has for their lives. Nor do they understand the power of God to set them free. If you or your husband (wife) struggles with any kind of personality disorder—for example, an eating disorder—pray that the *spirit* of wisdom and revelation will open your eyes to the truth. This is not just having wisdom about a few things, or having some things revealed, this is having *the Spirit* of *wisdom and revelation* so that you are able to understand *all things* needed in order to get free.

When you have a *true revelation from God* that eating disorders and any other self-destructive compulsion or behavior is a ploy of the enemy designed to keep you from realizing your purpose and becoming all God created you to be, those behaviors will fall away. Only in weak moments under enemy fire will you even consider giving place to them again. Ask God to show you what your calling is. You may not be able to understand it in full detail, but you will sense there is some great purpose God has for you, and you need to be completely available to Him in order to be in the right place at the right time.

When the Problem Is Your Spouse

Any kind of destructive behavior your spouse cannot seem to gain control over is addictive. Even if he (she) doesn't do it every day, if it is on any kind of regular basis, it is a problem that has to be addressed. When it affects the quality and success of his (her) work or physical health; when it causes him (her) to be unpleasant to others and have poor judgment or lack of control; when it does terrible things to you, your children, and other family members and friends, he (she) has a problem and needs help. If your spouse lives in denial that there *is* a problem, or thinks that what he (she) is doing is not really all that bad, ask God to reveal the truth to him (her) in the clearest way possible.

If your spouse cannot stop using drugs, alcohol, or being involved with any other addictive or destructive behavior, you have to seek *professional help* for him (her). This kind of serious addiction does not get better on its own. It is a sickness and must be treated as such. There are some people who are users but are not addicted and can stop on their own, and I have seen many success stories where reality hit and they were able to just lay it down completely and never look back. But for those who have the disease, they must have outside help.

Alcohol and drug addiction are considered diseases of the mind. Being addicted in any way is a form of mental illness. A person who drinks or does drugs and doesn't have control over the addiction cares more about himself (herself) and what *he (she)* wants than about what his (her) family's needs are. An alcoholic or drug addict may feel he (she) loves his (her) spouse and children, but actually he (she) doesn't have what it takes to *really* love them, which means getting rid of all self-destructive behavior for his (her) family's sake, as well as his (her) own. The addiction will always take priority over other people.

When you are around a spouse who is addicted to alcohol, drugs, or any other destructive behavior, their *insanity* affects your *sanity* and you can start to feel as though you are losing it. That's why you must get professional help for yourself too. Don't try to go through this alone. Your love for your troubled and sick spouse has to be strong enough to not accept what is unacceptable. You need the support and prayers of others so you can stand strong through this to complete freedom and victory for you both.

People don't change unless they want to. Pray for your spouse to *want* to change. The only changes that are lasting come when we surrender our lives completely to the Lord and give Him free rein. When we invite God to make changes in us, He makes us new.

When the Problem Is You

When I was in my twenties, before I became a believer, I used to drink and take drugs because doing so made me less timid. Drugs and alcohol seemed to release my spontaneity and sense of humor. Feeling inadequate and uncomfortable in a group of people made me afraid, and drinking took that fear away. I also wanted some relief from the pain and terrible insecurity I felt about myself and the anxiety and fear I felt about the future. Drugs and alcohol seemed to do that temporarily. And they were so readily available through the Hollywood circles I traveled in that they became like a spring that never ran dry. It's not that I felt all-powerful when I drank; I just felt *less powerless*. I did stupid and dangerous things while under the influence of those substances, and it's a miracle I lived through that period of my life. At least I had enough sense to not drink and drive. Nor did I drink when I was alone or when I was working. I was too professional and serious about my work to ever do something stupid to jeopardize it.

When I received the Lord and discovered God had a purpose for my life and a hope for my future, I did not drink like that again. That was it. I found in Jesus what I had been looking for in alcohol and drugs, and so those things instantly lost their appeal. I didn't want any part of something that was not God's will for me. I refused to find relief in the self-destructive behaviors that had nearly killed me so many times in the past. For the first time I had a sense that God had a purpose for my being born, and I wanted to stay alive and find out what that was.

It's possible to be a normal person and still fall into the trap of substance abuse and other destructive behaviors. You can even be a mature adult who has never had a problem before, and you try something once in a weak moment and find it comforting, empowering, or stress-relieving. Then every time you need comfort, relief from stress, or the feeling of empowerment, you try it again. Then you need to take more than before, because there is a tendency toward diminishing returns when it comes to this kind of behavior. Just as a gambler will place bigger and bigger bets in an attempt to regain what they've lost, an addict will take in more and more in order to gain that sense of euphoria, control, freedom, or whatever it was they experienced in the first place.

In some cases, there is an altering of chemistry in the brain, and eventually that person has a biochemical dependency. It may be that the connection between feeling good and the drugs or alcohol they consumed establishes some kind of a pattern in the brain. A person can also be predisposed to do something or inherit a tendency or a weakness from a family member.

It has been said that you can be addicted to more than one thing if you have an addictive personality. In other words, take away one addictive substance and you will find something else to be addicted to. That's why you need to pray that you will be addicted only to God's presence and His Word. That's where freedom comes from. Pray to not be a slave to this kind of behavior, but rather to be a slave to God (Romans 6:16).

People who do self-destructive things are often doing them to feel better about themselves, but the truth is, partaking in something that alters your mood and makes you think it's fulfilling you is actually luring you into a trap of delusions that keep you from experiencing the fulfillment *God* has for you. We all have a spiritual hunger. Whether we understand it as that or not, the truth is we can only be satisfied by God and nothing else.

Having a mother who is mentally ill is very similar to having a parent who is an alcoholic. My best friend in high school had an alcoholic mother, and we realized we shared the same struggles. For example, we both learned not to ever bring a friend home because we never knew what we would find. Her mother might be passed out on the floor, and mine might be having an insane rage. Our mothers were entirely unavailable to us, and we could never connect with them emotionally. We both had pacifistic fathers who worked hard to support the family, but they never rescued us from our mothers. Because of that, we felt doubtful about ourselves and fearful about the future. We felt insecure, unloved, and empty inside and didn't know how to fill that emptiness.

Our situations were swept under a rug at home. We didn't talk with our dads, families, or friends about what was happening. We only talked with each other. We felt unimportant, confused, and sad. We had little sense of purpose in life, and there was no hopeful expectation. I turned to drugs and alcohol, but she developed an eating disorder that eventually killed her. Since that time I've known countless people who had alcoholic parents, and every single one of them struggled desperately in their lives because of it.

If you have a problem stopping any kind of destructive behavior, you need to get help immediately because this will not only take its toll on you, but also on your entire family. Your bad behavior will always be an intruder in your relationships with your sons or daughters. It will make them feel abandoned because it doesn't seem as if you love them enough to quit. Next to abuse, this is the ultimate destroyer of children.

Drugs and alcohol have become your idol when it's something you love more than *God,* who has said not to do it, and more than your *husband* (*wife*), who has asked you not to do it, and more than your *children,* who are frightened by your doing it. The Bible says that those who practice drunkenness are "not wise" (Proverbs 20:1), do not "walk properly" (Romans 13:13), "will not inherit the kingdom of God" (Galatians 5:21), and will ultimately be the loser (Proverbs 23:31-32). Pray that this will not happen to you. If you can't stop this behavior by yourself, seek professional help immediately. Don't live with this problem one more day. It won't get better on its own. And don't try to handle it alone. You need all the love, support, and help from others you can get.

FIVE WAYS TO RISE ABOVE YOUR WEAKNESSES

1. *Invite the Holy Spirit to fill you afresh each day.* "[I pray] that He would grant you, according to the riches of His glory, to be strengthened with might through His Spirit in the inner man, that Christ may dwell in your hearts through faith" (Ephesians 3:16-17).

2. *Be in Christ and crucify your fleshly desires.* "Those who are Christ's have crucified the flesh with its passions and desires. If we live in the Spirit, let us also walk in the Spirit" (Galatians 5:24-25).

3. *Resist worldly temptation.* "Denying ungodliness and worldly lusts, we should live soberly, righteously, and godly in the present age" (Titus 2:12).

4. *Don't be intoxicated with anything other than the Holy Spirit.* "Do not be drunk with wine, in which is dissipation; but be filled with the Spirit" (Ephesians 5:18).

5. *Decide every day to sow to the Spirit and not the flesh.* "He who sows to his flesh will of the flesh reap corruption, but he who sows to the Spirit will of the Spirit reap everlasting life" (Galatians 6:8).

Pray for Freedom from Bad Behavior

Trying to get free of destructive habits of any kind can feel like an impossible task. The pull is so strong and your will-power seems so weak. But that is exacerbated by the enemy speaking to your mind, saying, "Do this. You deserve it after all you have been through." "You can't help it. It's just the way you are." "It's in your genes. It's in your family." "There is no power greater than this, and so you have to surrender to it." Identifying these lies and the source of them will help you see what you're facing from the proper perspective.

There is also the aspect of rebellion that can't be ignored in this. Any time *your* will is exerted over God's will, you are in rebellion against Him. You may not seem to be blatantly rebellious, but there is something that rises up within you that says, "*I* am in charge. I *will not* be told what to do. I *will* do *what* I *want* to do *when* I *want* to do it." I'm not saying you are necessarily being rebellious if you can't control your destructive habits, but I believe a rebellious spirit comes to everyone at some point as a child, and if a parent allows rebelliousness to have a place in that child's behavior instead of teaching and disciplining them away from it, this rebellious attitude or mind-set stays with them and influences their decisions and choices from then on. It causes them to say to themselves, without even consciously realizing they are doing it, "I will do what I want."

Whenever you *won't*—or *will not*—stop doing what you are doing, even though your spouse has asked you to repeatedly, you are in rebellion. You are not only in rebellion toward *him* (*her*), but most of all, you are in rebellion toward *God*. The first way to break down a stronghold of rebellion is to resist it in prayer.

If you and your husband (wife) have any uncontrollable habits, God has healing for you both. But in order to get free and move into all God has for you, you must believe that when you received Jesus as Savior, He became your Savior in *every way*. He even *saves* you from *yourself* when you ask Him to. You must believe that the Word of God has life and liberty for you. You need to believe that God hears your prayers and will answer them. You must have *faith* that the only limits to what God can do in your life are the limits *you* put on Him when you don't have *faith*. You have to understand that God has the power to set you free from whatever binds you, but you still have to *ask* for His power to manifest on your behalf.

When you realize the purpose God has for you, you won't allow any self-destructive behavior to control you. You will take whatever steps are necessary to get free of it. You will remember that Jesus is your *healer* and *deliverer* and you won't accept less than the freedom He has for you (Mark 16:17-18).

If your father or grandfather was an alcoholic, it doesn't mean *you* have to be, but it may mean there are consequences of his sins that you have had to deal with. Maybe you have struggled because those spirits were invited into your family by sins that happened before you were born. It may well be that any weakness you have was inherited. The good news is that Jesus has broken every curse in our lives, including any that came down through our family. But we still have to make an effort to stop doing anything that misses the mark God has for us.

Jesus gave His 12 disciples "power over unclean spirits, to cast them out, and to heal all kinds of sickness and all kinds of disease" (Matthew 10:1). The key words here are "all kinds." There wasn't a disease, sickness, or unclean spirit that was greater than the healing power of God. Jesus came as *your* healer and deliverer. He is the same yesterday, today, and tomorrow. Why would He bother coming as your healer or deliverer if you could be healed and delivered on your own?

What to Do When I Do the Things I Do Not Want to Do

Read these encouraging words the apostle Paul said that have been powerfully and beautifully translated by Eugene H. Peterson in The Message. See if this doesn't speak to anyone who has ever struggled with a behavior that they knew wasn't good:

> What I don't understand about myself is that I decide one way, but then I act another, doing things I absolutely despise. So if I can't be trusted to figure out what is best for myself and then do it, it becomes obvious that God's command is necessary. But I need something *more!* For if I know the law but still can't keep it, and if the power of sin within me keeps sabotaging my best intentions, I obviously need help! I realize that I don't have what it takes. I can will it, but I can't *do* it. I decide to do good, but I don't *really* do it; I decide not to do bad, but then

I do it anyway. My decisions, such as they are, don't result in actions. Something has gone wrong deep within me and gets the better of me every time. It happens so regularly that it's predictable. The moment I decide to do good, sin is there to trip me up. I truly delight in God's commands, but it's pretty obvious that not all of me joins in that delight. Parts of me covertly rebel, and just when I least expect it, they take charge. I've tried everything and nothing helps. I'm at the end of my rope. Is there no one who can do anything for me? Isn't that the real question? The answer, thank God, is that Jesus Christ can and does. He acted to set things right in this life of contradictions where I want to serve God with all my heart and mind, but am pulled by the influence of sin to do something totally different (Romans 7:15-25, emphasis added).

The point is, when you try to get free and do the right thing on your own, you can't. But with Jesus, you can do all the things you need to do because He will strengthen you and enable you to do them (Philippians 4:13). And if God is for you, who on earth can be against you? (Romans 8:31). Ask God to show you what steps to take to find all the healing, deliverance, and wholeness you and your spouse need.

PRAYERS FOR MY MARRIAGE

Prayer for Protection

LORD, I PRAY THAT YOU would protect my husband (wife) and me from any kind of self-destructive behavior. Open our eyes to see if we have allowed habits into our lives that have the potential to harm us. Bring to light all things, so that we will have nothing hidden from one another. Where we have opened ourselves up to bad or destructive habits, help us to get free. Give us the ability to cope with any frustration or anxiety we may have by taking all concerns to You and each other and not looking for relief from outside resources.

Lord, You have promised that "if we confess our sins" You are "faithful and just to forgive us our sins and to cleanse us from all unrighteousness" (1 John 1:9). Help us to confess any sin the moment we see it so that we will be cleansed from it before it can establish a hold on us. Thank You that we are "predestined to be conformed to the image" of Your Son (Romans 8:29). That's what we want. Help us to always be Your slaves and not slaves of sin (Romans 6:22). Help us to understand that the power that raised Jesus from the dead is the same power that will raise us above all that tempts us (Ephesians 1:19-20). Lift us above anything that would bring us down. In Jesus' name I pray.

Prayer for Breakthrough in Me

LORD, I PRAY THAT YOU would reveal to me any destructive habit I have embraced and help me to fully understand why I do it. Help me to truly see how it is not Your will for my life. Break any spirit of rebellion in me that causes me to feel that I can do what I want, when I want, without regard for the consequences. Enable me to see how what I do affects my husband (wife) and family. Where You or other people—especially my husband (wife) or children—have tried to warn me, give me ears to hear. Bring me to complete repentance before You and them for ever ignoring those warnings.

Help me not to hold resentment toward anyone who tries to confront me on any problem, especially my husband (wife). Enable me to remember that "open rebuke is better than love carefully concealed" and "faithful are the wounds of a friend" (Proverbs 27:5-6). I know that "You desire truth in the inward parts, and in the hidden part You will make me to know wisdom" (Psalm 51:6). Help me to become a person of truth who does not have a secret life.

Thank You, Jesus, that You are my healer. You are my refuge and strength, a very present help in times of trouble (Psalm 46:1). Thank You, God, that you are my Comforter and Helper. I cast my burden on You, Lord, knowing You will sustain me, for You have said that You will never permit the righteous to be moved (Psalm 55:22). Help me to get free of anything that influences me in a destructive way and to "stand fast therefore in the liberty by which" You have made me free, and keep me from being "entangled again with a yoke of bondage" (Galatians 5:1). I willingly present myself to You as a slave of righteousness and not uncleanness (Romans 6:19). I know that I am just flesh and I depend on the excellence of Your power to set me free (2 Corinthians 4:7).

Thank You that "I have been crucified with Christ; it is no longer I who live, but Christ lives in me; and the life which I now live in the flesh I live by faith in the Son of God, who loved me and gave Himself for me" (Galatians 2:20). So even though I may be weak in and of myself, Jesus in me is strong enough to set me free and help me to resist all temptation. Thank You that I can do what I need to do because You enable me to do it (Philippians 4:13). I pray You will restore all that has been stolen from my life by the enemy (Joel 2:25). I ask You to "build the old waste places" in me and "raise up the foundations of many generations" of my past (Isaiah 58:12). My soul waits quietly for You to save me from myself (Psalm 62:1). In Jesus' name I pray.

Prayer for Breakthrough in My Husband (Wife)

LORD, I PRAY THAT MY husband (wife) will have eyes to see the truth and ears to hear Your voice speaking to him (her). May Your will be done in his (her) life. I release him (her) to You and ask You to set him (her) free from any destructive habits. I fully realize that I can't control the situation, nor do I even want to. I give up any need to try and fix things or take control of the problem. I give up any desire to make my husband (wife) change. I release him (her) into Your hands and ask You to do what it takes to make the changes You want in him (her). I pray that You, "the God of our Lord Jesus Christ, the Father of glory," will give to my husband (wife) "the spirit of wisdom and revelation" in the knowledge of You, that the eyes of his (her) understanding would be enlightened, that he (she) would "know what is the hope of His calling, what are the riches of the glory of His inheritance" and "what is the exceeding greatness" of Your power toward him (her) who believes, according to the work of Your mighty power in his (her) life (Ephesians 1:18-19).

Help him (her) face all problems and view them as something that can be overcome and not something insurmountable. Enable him (her) to take responsibility for his (her) actions and not live in denial about them. Help him (her) to be able to evaluate his (her) work or progress without beating himself (herself) up. Help him (her) to take responsibility for his (her) own life and not blame others for things that have happened. I pray that he (she) will always be completely honest with me about everything he (she) is doing. Let there be no secrets. Tear down any walls that have been erected between us.

Help him (her) to understand his (her) worth in Your sight, and to see that his (her) life is too important to waste. Help him (her) to seek You as his (her) healer and deliverer, so he (she) can find total restoration in You. To my husband (wife) I say that "sin shall not have dominion over you, for you are not under law but under grace" (Romans 6:14). I say that God has deliverance and healing for your life. I say that "the God of peace will crush Satan under your feet shortly" (Romans 16:20). I say "stand fast therefore in the liberty by which Christ has made us free, and do not be entangled again with a yoke of bondage" (Galatians 5:1). In Jesus' name I pray.

TRUTH TO STAND ON

I can do all things through Christ
who strengthens me.

PHILIPPIANS 4:13

Do not be conformed to this world,
but be transformed by the renewing of your mind,
that you may prove what is that good and
acceptable and perfect will of God.

ROMANS 12:2

All things are lawful for me, but all things are not helpful.
All things are lawful for me, but I will not be brought
under the power of any.

1 CORINTHIANS 6:12

Being confident of this very thing,
that He who has begun a good work in you
will complete it until the day of Jesus Christ.

PHILIPPIANS 1:6

My brethren, be strong in the Lord and in the power of His might.
Put on the whole armor of God,
that you may be able to stand against the wiles of the devil.

EPHESIANS 6:10-11

8

If OUTSIDE INFLUENCES POLLUTE *Your* SEXUAL RELATIONSHIP

D on't think for a moment that you can skip this chapter just because your sex life with your husband (wife) is perfect and neither of you have ever had the slightest problem in that area. Don't think that because you have never viewed anything even bordering on pornography that your mind hasn't been polluted. The truth is that the enemy of your soul, your purpose, and your marriage is also the enemy of your marital intimacy. By injecting into your relationship outside influences that distract, sexual images that pollute, and worldly and self-centered attitudes that destroy, your life together sexually can easily become less than what it was intended to be.

Sex in marriage was intended by God to be more than a great way to spend an afternoon before you have kids. Or the means of escaping the tensions of a busy day. Or something you do to feel good about yourself and each other. Or a way to have children. It is also a means of unifying the two of you, joining your bodies, hearts, minds, and souls together in order to break down any strongholds erected by the enemy to destroy your marriage. Sex in marriage reaffirms the oneness, intimacy, and closeness you have as a couple. It always serves to rekindle life in the relationship, without which deadness can subtly set in.

The enemy despises your oneness with each other, and he will do all he can to undermine it. That's why everywhere you look there are sexual enticements to get you off track—if not in deed then at least in thought. Promiscuity is glorified. Temptation is justified. Casual sex is expected. Sex *outside* of marriage is exalted far above sex within marriage. You can see sexual images on something as innocuous as a billboard while you're driving down the street, or even in regular news magazines, popular TV shows, or what is supposed to be a decent film. These are all a setup by the enemy to water down the impact of your sex life with your spouse by making it less than what it should be. Or even worse, *more* than what it was ever intended to be. Sex was never intended to be an idol that we worship, but it has become that in our culture.

Sex can be exalted to the point that if you are not experiencing romantic, fulfilling, amazing sex every time you are with your husband (wife), something must be wrong with you or him (her). Because of the way our society is crazed over sex, our minds can be so completely messed up about it that we can end up with anxiety or uncertainty. Something that God meant to be meaningful and deeply enjoyable can become another added pressure, giving you doubts about yourself or your mate.

Keeping Your Eyes from Evil

What you see even innocently can affect your sexual relationship negatively. Have you ever been to a film that is supposed to have a decent rating and yet something indecent flashes suddenly in front of your eyes? And even if you close your eyes the moment you realize what it is, that scene will play over and over in your mind and infect your soul. You end up feeling shock, repulsion, stimulation, guilt, disgust, or attraction—all of which take up way too much space in your brain. You now have to spend time and energy dealing with these thoughts and feelings that you wouldn't have had to do if you had never seen those images in the first place. Now you have to seek God for cleansing so that this mental infection doesn't spread to your good sense. This kind of assault on our senses has become so widespread that we are growing increasingly used to it.

God warns us in His Word over and over that we are to flee such things. We are to turn away from it and not look at it. Change the channel the minute you see it. Get up and walk out of the theater. Close the magazine. Look away from the billboard. "A prudent man foresees evil and hides himself; the simple pass on and are punished" (Proverbs 27:12). God wants purity to reign in your sexual relationship. That means not allowing outside influences to pollute and infect it.

Any deviation from the path God has established for us—which is sex within marriage and only with your spouse—will set a snare for your soul, even if it's only happening in your own mind. Looking at any form of sex portrayed in photos and films is a snare that will have to be dealt with on a spiritual level in order to reestablish yourself on solid ground. Even if you don't realize at the time that you are in disobedience to God's laws, your soul will reap the consequences of that unintended violation.

FIVE THINGS YOU SHOULD NEVER LOOK AT

1. ***Don't look at anything that draws you away from obeying God.*** "If your eye causes you to sin, pluck it out and cast it from you. It is better for you to enter into life with one eye, rather than having two eyes, to be cast into hell fire" (Matthew 18:9).

2. ***Don't look at worthless things.*** "Turn away my eyes from looking at worthless things, and revive me in Your way" (Psalm 119:37).

3. ***Don't look at the world's attractions.*** "For all that is in the world—the lust of the flesh, the lust of the eyes, and the pride of life—is not of the Father but is of the world" (1 John 2:16).

4. ***Don't look at the dark side of life.*** "The lamp of the body is the eye. Therefore, when your eye is good, your whole body also is full of light. But when your eye is bad, your body also is full of darkness" (Luke 11:34).

5. ***Don't look away from the path God has for you.*** "Let your eyes look straight ahead, and your eyelids look right before you" (Proverbs 4:25).

There's No Comparison

One of the greatest threats to your sex life is having your mind filled with visions of perfect people having perfect sex. These images are an illusion, and they set up a dangerous trap of comparison you can fall into. When you compare your spouse or yourself to the images you see, it can make you think you either fall short of what you are supposed to be or that you are missing something great.

Let me tell you something about looking at others and feeling inadequate. When I was a teenager I used to look at pictures of beautiful people and feel ugly. But when I was in my twenties, I started working on television with some of the biggest stars at that time, and I saw how they really looked when they came in to the studio for makeup early in the morning. It was shocking. I quickly realized that anyone who has a good makeup artist, a great hair stylist and colorist, an expert to give facials, a personal trainer, a nutritionist, enough money to eat well, a great photographer who understands the necessity of good lighting, a wardrobe stylist, a good plastic surgeon (who can make you look rested and happy and not stretched and contorted), and a nanny for your children (who can watch your kids while you have all these things done) can look good. I guarantee that if you were to have all these things for a month, you would look fantastic too. How these "beautiful people" get into a position to have all these things is that they have good bone structure, charisma, and a talent of some kind.

I'm not saying there weren't any naturally beautiful people. There were. But they were far more rare than you might think. And even those people saw flaws in themselves. They, like the rest of us, always have something they don't like about their body, their face, or their abilities and talents. The point is, seeing how most people *really* look helped me to not be so hard on myself. It helped me to stop focusing on everything I saw that was wrong with me.

Don't set yourself up for negative comparisons by letting photos, films, magazines, and billboards influence your own self-image. Anything you dislike about your body, face, hair, personality, or talent can inhibit you sexually with your spouse. By all means do all you can to feel good about yourself, but don't hold yourself to a standard set forth in magazines, movies, and television. Don't put this kind of added pressure on yourself, because these images aren't real and will only undermine your sexual relationship with your husband (wife).

Consider One Another

Regarding your sexual relationship, the Bible says, "The wife does not have authority over her own body, but the husband does. And likewise the husband does not have authority over his own body, but the wife does" (1 Corinthians 7:4). That doesn't mean that you allow your husband (wife) to abuse you. Nor does it mean you can force your spouse to do something they don't want to do. And neither of you should require the other to practice abstinence far more than he (she) wants to, either. It means that if your spouse needs intimacy with you, you should provide it or have a really good reason why you can't. You have to consider your spouse's needs ahead of your own preoccupation.

Outside of the Lord's realm, sex is all about "*me* first." It's something that will make *me* feel better about *me*. But in the Lord, you always have to put one another first. So if you don't want to be intimate because you have been so hurt or disappointed by your spouse that you don't even want to be touched, then say so. Not saying anything and trying to force intimacy will surely make it go badly and do more damage than not doing anything at all. Tell him (her) you need to talk first and get things off your chest. On the other hand, just "not feeling like it" isn't a good enough excuse. Part of success in anything you do is doing what you need to do when you need to do it, whether you totally feel like it at the moment or not.

Of course, there are times when you don't feel good or you are exhausted, but that can't become the norm. The Bible says, "Do not deprive one another except with consent for a time, that you may give yourselves to fasting and prayer; and come together again so that Satan does not tempt you because of your lack of self-control" (1 Corinthians 7:5). That means when your spouse gives you signals that the time is right, you'd better be fasting and praying if you're not going to honor his (her) expressed wishes. The thing to be most concerned about with regard to abstinence is that if it goes on too long or happens too frequently in a marriage, you both are more susceptible to temptation.

Putting each other first in your sexual relationship will protect you both from temptations that arise. Whenever you refuse to have sex with your husband (wife), there is always the possibility that the enemy will place a snare right in front of him (her) the very next day. It may not be an actual person, but the sexual images that are everywhere could have a greater impact. However, if your husband (wife) has already had his (her) sexual needs fulfilled with you, he (she) won't be vulnerable to temptation when it presents itself.

The stresses of life, such as building a career, establishing a home, raising children, coping with sickness or injuries, financial struggles, disagreements, and arguments, can all affect your sex life. If a wife feels that the only time her husband is interested in her is when he wants to have sex, then she will be discouraged. If a husband feels that unless he does everything perfectly for his wife he will never have sex again, he will feel resentful. But if each of you puts the other first, an active sex life will keep your relationship alive. It will keep you feeling younger. It will clear your mind. It will balance things out between you. Forget about the bills, the disagreements, the kids, the problems at work, and concentrate on each other. If you always think in terms of *what can I do to make this good for him (her)?* instead of *what can I get out of this for me?* then your sex life will be good. You will fight off the enemy's plans for your demise every time you do.

Clear the Slate

It's important to bring any sexual encounter you had before marriage to the Lord and repent of it so that it won't affect your marriage now. Even if you never had sex before you got married, if there was anything you did with someone that you suspect was not God's will for your life, confess it before God. If it was something that was perpetrated upon you, ask God to cleanse you of the entire memory. If you don't do this, the memories of these encounters will come up like specters every time you make love to your husband (wife). They will be there with you in the bedroom. Don't allow the devil to have this stronghold. Sever those soul ties immediately. Ask God to bring them all to mind so you can confess them before Him and be free. If you were a virgin before marriage, thank God that you don't have to go through this graveyard of past memories and kick out each ghost one by one.

Pray to Resist Temptation

No matter how much you try to live a holy life, there will always come some kind of temptation. And you have to remember that when it comes, it is not God helping you to find greater fulfillment. It is the enemy trying to destroy you. But God will give you a way out. He says to *submit* to *Him* and *resist* the *devil,* and when you do, the enemy has to leave (James 4:7). If you ever find yourself being tempted, resist all inclination to act on it, humble yourself before God, and pray until the enemy is forced to exit.

The important thing in marriage is to guard your heart from any stray thoughts (Proverbs 4:23). Don't allow yourself to think of anyone else but your husband (wife) in a sexual way. The enemy will always try to capture your attention away from your spouse and then attempt to imprison you with paralyzing guilt. Don't let him get away with that. If you are ever with other people and you find a particular person attractive, force yourself to think of him or her only as your brother or sister in Christ. Ask God to help you and your spouse keep your eyes on each other and to make sexual intimacy between you a priority.

The Threat of Pornography

Of the countless people I have heard from regarding the trouble in their marriages, the two most common issues are infidelity and pornography. I have frankly been shocked at how epidemic these problems are among believers. Pornography is one of the most insidious tactics of the enemy to destroy lives and marriages today. And because it is just a few clicks away on the Internet, it is too easily accessible. A common complaint I have heard from women whose husbands are heavily into pornography is that they have watched it together as a couple hoping to enhance their sex life, but instead it destroyed their marriage.

This horrible habit starts a little at a time. Just seeing a suggestive magazine cover in an airport, gas station, or grocery store can plant a seed in the mind that grows into something insidious. The more one is exposed to it, the more seeds are planted and the deeper they grow. Then a person becomes drawn to it and starts to seek it out. They become secretive, not forthcoming, and not full-faced before the Lord. They don't have clear-eyed laughter anymore. Blindness covers their eyes so they cannot see the truth.

When I was young I received a wood-burning set. I plugged in the handheld wood burner, and whenever I pressed it to the wood it burned an image that was there permanently. Pornography is like that. It burns an image into the brain that stays there. It can cause a person to be obsessed with it to the point of insanity. It not only destroys the soul, it makes a person mentally unbalanced.

It doesn't matter how old or young you are, you can be susceptible to it at any age. When exposure to pornography happens to a young child, it plants a seed in his (her) heart that will keep growing long after the event has taken place. Somewhere down the road in adulthood it will surface. That's because behind every lustful thought is a seducing spirit that wants to draw its victim away from the things of God and toward the vile and evil that brings destruction. And it will continue silently waiting to surface in a moment of weakness. It comes straight from hell for the purpose of ensnaring you and destroying your life.

Even if you and your spouse are not tempted in the least by pornography, there are still countless sexual images everywhere that may be thrust before your eyes, and that alone can open the door to this problem. I have seen legitimate news magazines have images in an advertisement for some product that border on pornographic. There are TV shows, movies, and videos you can easily see that have suggestive material in them. I'm not talking about going to an adult bookstore and asking for the brown paper-wrapped magazines in the back room. I am not even talking about clicking on a pornographic sight on the Internet. I am talking about racy and explicit images in commercials, print ads, videos, and films. When we let our eyes see these images or hear suggestive dialogue, it pollutes our mind. When we become accustomed to it, we are susceptible to a hook of the enemy being planted in our soul. The more material like that we see, the deeper that hook will go.

Jesus said that sin happens just by looking (Matthew 5:28). But Jesus also gave the solution. "If your right eye causes you to sin, pluck it out and cast it from you; for it is more profitable for you that one of your members perish, than for your whole body to be cast into hell" (Matthew 5:29). That means if something comes on the TV that is sexual, turn it off. If it presents itself in a scene of a film, walk out. Don't even stare for a moment. Make it an instantaneous reaction. Don't let the enemy gain a stronghold in your soul. There is an evil spirit behind anything that is sexually explicit. That's why unless you have already become jaded, you will recoil whenever you see anything that even borders on pornography.

FIVE WARNINGS TO REMEMBER ABOUT LUST

1. *Lust is always against God's will.* "He no longer should live the rest of his time in the flesh for the lusts of men, but for the will of God" (1 Peter 4:2).

2. *Lust in your heart is adultery.* "I say to you that whoever looks

at a woman to lust for her has already committed adultery with her in his heart" (Matthew 5:28).

3. *Lust always destroys peace in your soul.* "Beloved, I beg you as sojourners and pilgrims, abstain from fleshly lusts which war against the soul" (1 Peter 2:11).

4. *Lust wars against your spirit.* "The flesh lusts against the Spirit, and the Spirit against the flesh; and these are contrary to one another, so that you do not do the things that you wish" (Galatians 5:17).

5. *Lust in your heart sets a trap for your soul.* "The righteousness of the upright will deliver them, but the unfaithful will be caught by their lust" (Proverbs 11:6).

If Your Spouse Has the Problem

It can be difficult to spot a problem with pornography in your spouse because your lives are busy and you give each other latitude and you believe for the best in each other. But if you ever sense that something is very wrong and you don't know what it is, trust the instincts God has given you and ask Him to show you what it is you are sensing. I know of situations where the wife could feel there was something wrong, even though she had no hard evidence. She only sensed the divided attentions of her husband and saw that the light had died in his eyes. Those were signs of a deeper issue.

So many times we don't see what's wrong because we don't *want* to see it. We want to see what's *right*. We want to see the *good*. We want to think the best. We don't want to see what we fear it might be because we can't bear for it to be that. We understand that everything in our life will be affected, and we can't face it. But the good news is that you are never alone when you have Jesus, who is Immanuel—the God who is with you. He has sent His Holy Spirit to come alongside of you to be your Helper and Comforter and to guide you in all things—even to face the threat of pornography in your marriage.

When a wife discovers that her husband is into pornography, it makes her feel betrayed, inadequate, unattractive, full of self-doubt, grieved, hurt, and a failure. But the truth is, it has nothing to do with her. It is not her fault in any way. No one forces someone else to become perverted. The enemy has planted a seed of lust in her husband's flesh—whether it happened to him as a child or he has allowed it as an adult—and it has trapped him.

So if your husband (wife) is into pornography, please know it is not your fault. It really has nothing to do with you. It affects you terribly, but you are not responsible. But don't desert your spouse if he (she) is willing to try to get free. The fact is, he (she) needs your support more than ever. That doesn't mean you have to suppress your feelings of anger and disappointment, but don't allow those feelings and any unforgiveness to get in the way of having your prayers answered.

You may become angry that you have to think about this problem at all, that your mind has to even be occupied with such depraved thoughts, and you will rightfully be upset about having to even wonder about whether or not the problem is really gone. There is nothing wrong with expecting human decency, and when you find a lack of it in your spouse, you grieve for the person you thought you married. Give yourself the right to grieve and be angry, but remember that it is your spouse who has the problem and you are part of the solution. Your prayers can help him (her) get free, and you can guide him (her) to get professional help. There are experts who know what to do, and your spouse has to be held accountable by someone besides you.

Once pornography has invaded your lives, you can't go back to the way you were. You have to commit to working through this and building a new life together. Seek godly counselors and prayer partners. Commit to praying through this together. No force of hell can stand against the power of God manifesting on behalf of a husband and wife who pray together.

If your husband (wife) is caught in a stronghold of the enemy, the power of your prayers for him (her) is greatly enhanced if you *fast* and pray. Even after a simple 24-hour fast where you only drink water and you pray every time you get a hunger pang, you will see God do miracles. God says that fasting is *"to loose the bonds of wickedness,* to *undo the heavy burdens,* to *let the oppressed go free,* and that you *break every yoke"* (Isaiah 58:6, emphasis added). That is exactly what you need to combat a problem of this magnitude.

If the Problem Is Yours

Every one of us has a point of weakness, a place in us where we are vulnerable, and the devil knows it. If you have an eye that wanders toward sexually charged images, every time you view one it will engrave itself deeper in your mind as well as your heart and soul. Even accidentally watching a moment of it can stay with you forever. The fantasies will one day turn to acting out in some way, and sex within your marriage will not be satisfying enough anymore.

Pornography is made up of a series of lies that a person buys into. Once planted, the seeds of pornography will spread like weeds with thorns that will choke out all other life or potential. If your mind dwells on things that are perverted, worthless, and vile, you will reap perverse, worthless, and vile things in your life.

When a spirit of lust controls you, the rest of your life begins to crumble because it destroys your soul and mind. If you look at that which is evil in the sight of God, you descend into darkness. You become a hollow person who is unable to connect in any other part of your life. "For by means of a harlot a man is reduced to a crust of bread; and an adulteress will prey upon his precious life. Can a man take fire to his bosom, and his clothes not be burned?" (Proverbs 6:26-27). It erodes the substance of who you are and who you can be. It kills healthy, fulfilling sex between a husband and wife. If you don't try to find what you need in each other, watching videos of other people having sex isn't going to make it better. In fact, it will make things worse. You can never appreciate the attractiveness of your spouse if you are seeking thrills from looking at other attractive people.

The Bible says, "I will set nothing wicked before my eyes" (Psalm 101:3). Pornography is wicked. It is an act of lust, not an act of love. Lust is all about "me" and what "I" want. It's not about sharing and building on a foundation of love. Lust is never satisfied. It always wants more.

Behind every sin is an evil spirit waiting to establish a stronghold. Every time a person gives place to that sin, the stronghold gets more established. Someone cannot be possessed by a demon if they have received Jesus as their Lord and Savior, but they can certainly invite evil into their lives by the things they do and allow, and that will keep them from realizing the good life God has for them. They can still get to heaven, but they're going to have to walk through a lot of hell here on earth before they do. God will allow the horrible condition of their soul to make them miserable because He wants them to stop worshipping at the altar of their lusts and start worshipping Him.

Any secret life of lust grieves the Holy Spirit. It makes a mockery out of a Savior who laid down His life so that we can escape sin and its consequences. It's as if He set you free in vain because you don't want what He died to give you. It offends God when His children choose to open up to that which separates them from Him.

Pornographic videos and images become branded on your mind and heart every time you see them, and they will pull you toward them like a magnet. You become stimulated more and more by pictures and images of others and less and less by your mate. There is freedom from it, but first of all you have to turn it off. You have to refuse to allow yourself to have any secret sin. The first step toward cleansing and deliverance is to recognize that this is a sin *against* God. Confession of your sin *before* God is the next step.

Jesus said, "If anyone desires to come after Me, let him deny himself, and take up his cross, and follow Me" (Matthew 16:24). Refusing to allow anything sexually explicit to come before your eyes is part of denying yourself and taking up *His* cross and following Him. Do whatever you have to do to avoid it. Whatever is tempting you, get rid of it. Throw out any videos or magazines that have any sexually explicit images and language on them. That includes the "F" word, which is sexually explicit language. This is also a snare, so do whatever you have to do in order to disconnect from it. Stop going to movies, get rid of the Internet, have your cable disconnected, disconnect your television if you are in a hotel room alone or have the "adult" channels blocked the minute you walk in the room. Get rid of anything that is not of God. Do what it takes. Cut off the source of whatever is causing you to sin.

The good news is that Jesus' death on the cross broke the power of the accuser in your life. The enemy will try to convince you otherwise and attempt to control you if you do not understand your God-given authority over him. That means you have access to the power that can set you free from anything that tries to poison your life and soul.

When you look totally to the Lord for everything, especially deliverance from things you don't even want to mention before God, you will be completely set free and no longer need to be ashamed. "They looked to Him and were radiant, and their faces were not ashamed" (Psalm 34:5). The Bible says people "should repent, turn to God, and do works befitting repentance" (Acts 26:20). Works befitting repentance means that you stop doing what you have repented of and live the way you are supposed to.

If you are in any kind of Christian leadership or place of influence, prominence, or work for the glory of God and His kingdom, you will be tempted in some way because of it. Don't try to face the temptation alone. Everyone needs two or more strong believers to stand with them ongoingly to resist the plans of the enemy for their destruction. The more the better. "Though one may be overpowered by another, two can withstand him. And a threefold cord is not quickly broken" (Ecclesiastes 4:12). Find strong believers who are in the Word, who live godly lives and who are not gossips, who will be prayer partners with you and your spouse. "Confess your trespasses to one another, and pray for one another, that you may be healed. The effective, fervent prayer of a righteous man avails much" (James 5:16).

You also need to be connected to the body of Christ through your local church (1 Corinthians 12:12). You are not fully under God's covering if you are not submitted to a godly body of believers. When you are not connected, you lose the power that comes in numbers. I am not talking about being mind-controlled; I am talking about letting your heart find a home in a church where you become part of the family there. Don't just go to church to watch what's going on. Go to be connected to what God is doing there. Make contact with the people and serve the church in some capacity. It will be a protection for you.

The Power of God's Word to Give Strength

I learned years ago that quoting Scripture, especially in your prayers, is powerful and the only thing strong enough to silence the voices of despair and desperation. The words of Scripture have power on their own, but when you speak them out loud, they increase your faith and give you strength. Scripture has the power to set us free from wherever we are stuck. Your mind can be renewed and transformed as you read God's Word because it lines your heart and mind up with God's. If you are *not* doing that, you are always drifting away from Him without even realizing it. And the drift will be subtle and almost imperceptible until one day you realize you fell and God wasn't there to catch you—because you fell far outside the parameters God has established for your life.

While outside counseling is extremely important and can make a tremendous difference, only God can fully heal the inside of us. Counseling can only help us change our behavior—which definitely needs to be changed—but it can't transform us into the people God created us to be. Only the Holy Spirit can do that. Along with counseling, you still have to establish and deepen your relationship with God. You have to stay in His Word and in communication with Him through prayer, praise, and worship. "Before I was afflicted I went astray, but now I keep Your word" (Psalm 119:67). Don't stop praying until you have the freedom you need.

PRAYERS FOR MY MARRIAGE

Prayer for Protection

LORD, I PRAY YOU WOULD BLESS our marriage in every way and specifically protect our sexual relationship. Help us to always put each other first and never sacrifice one another out of selfish disregard for the other's needs. Keep our eyes from looking at anything that would compromise our relationship. Keep our hearts from being enticed and drawn away from each other. Help us to walk properly and not in lust or strife (Romans 13:13). Enable us to always live in the Spirit so we don't fulfill the lust of the flesh (Galatians 5:16). Open our eyes to recognize ungodliness and worldliness so that we can reject those enticements and learn to live Your way.

Lord, help us to become so committed to You that nothing else matters to us more than living in obedience to Your ways. Enable us to see things from Your perspective. Help us to recognize in advance what will lead to temptation in us so that we always take steps to avoid it. Help us to stay away from anything that could tempt us to view something of an explicit nature. Expose all of our sins to Your light so that neither of us can have a secret life. Reveal everything in either of us that needs to be seen.

Where we are blind to the true nature of the things we allow ourselves to look at, open our eyes to see the truth. Where we have become imprisoned by ungodly desires, deliver us. Where we are in darkness about this, shine Your light on our attraction to disobedience (Isaiah 42:5-7). I know that "to be carnally minded is death, but to be spiritually minded is life and peace" (Romans 8:6). I know that if we live in the flesh we cannot please You (Romans 8:8). Help us to learn to live in a way that pleases You. In Jesus' name I pray.

Prayer for Breakthrough in Me

LORD, I PRAY THAT YOU would make me the wife (husband) You want me to be. Help me to fulfill my husband (wife) sexually. Teach me how to be attentive to his (her) needs and desires, and to put his (her) needs before my own. Cause us to always feel attracted to one another.

Lord, I pray that You would search my heart and reveal any evil thoughts, attractions, or fantasies I harbor so I can be free of them completely (Psalm 139:23-24). Show me the root of any kind of problem in me so that I can eliminate it absolutely. Where I have found another man (woman) attractive other than my husband (wife), I confess that as sin before You. Even if I only allowed it in my mind and never acted on it, I know it is still sin in Your eyes. Deliver me from that stronghold. Break any hold of the enemy on me (Romans 7:15-21). I love Your laws, Lord, and I don't want to have conflict in my mind that brings me into captivity to sin. Thank You, Jesus, that I can find freedom from my flesh, which serves the law of sin, so that I can serve Your laws instead (Romans 7:22-25).

Lord, I lift my eyes up to You in heaven and deliberately take them off the things of earth (Psalm 123:1). I take comfort in the fact that You are my refuge that I can go to any time I am tempted to look at anything ungodly, or see in my mind that which does not please You (Psalm 141:8). Take away all that is in me that holds the door open for sinful and lustful thoughts. Help me to be a wife (husband) who is faithful and true in thought and deed. "O Lord, You have searched me and known me...You understand my thought afar off" (Psalm 139:1-2). "Show me Your ways, O Lord...on You I wait all the day" (Psalm 25:4-5). In Jesus' name I pray.

Prayer for Breakthrough in My Husband (Wife)

Lord, I pray for my husband's (wife's) mind to be protected from the lies of Satan and open to Your truth. Take all blinders completely off of him (her) so that he (she) can see every pit of lust for what it is. Help him (her) to fully understand what damage any degree of lust does to our marriage when he (she) gives place to it in any way. Open his (her) eyes to danger and give him (her) strength to avoid situations and people that could draw him (her) into it again.

Enable him (her) to see pornography and any other sexually explicit images as wrong in Your eyes. Turn his (her) eyes away from worthless things (Psalm 119:37-39). Help him (her) understand the greatness of Your power on his (her) behalf (Ephesians 1:17-19). If he (she) fails in this area, help me to trust him (her) again. Help me to still want to be intimate with him (her) and not have resentment, suspicion, or jealousy because of his (her) misplaced affections. Help me to not feel betrayed. Show me all I can do to help him (her).

Lord, I surrender my husband (wife) to You completely. Do whatever it takes to get him (her) to see the truth about all that he (she) does. Put Your love in his (her) heart for me, and keep his (her) eyes, heart, and mind from finding others attractive. Expose every lie masquerading as truth to him (her). Help him (her) to put off all conduct that is not in alignment with Your will and reject all corruption that comes from "deceitful lusts" (Ephesians 4:22). Don't let him (her) be taken down a path that leads to death and hell (Proverbs 5:3-5). Deliver him (her) and we will say, "This was the LORD's doing, and it is marvelous in our eyes" (Mark 12:11). Help him (her) to resist all temptation. Give him (her) the "spirit of wisdom and revelation" so that the eyes of his (her) understanding will be enlightened and that he (she) will know the hope of his (her) calling (Ephesians 1:17-18). In Jesus' name I pray.

Truth to Stand On

Do not be conformed to this world,
but be transformed by the renewing of your mind,
that you may prove what is that good and acceptable
and perfect will of God.

ROMANS 12:2

How can a young man cleanse his way?
By taking heed according to Your Word.
With my whole heart I have sought You;
oh, let me not wander from Your commandments!
Your word I have hidden in my heart,
that I might not sin against You.

PSALM 119:9-11

When wisdom enters your heart,
and knowledge is pleasant to your soul,
discretion will preserve you; understanding will keep you,
to deliver you from the way of evil.

PROVERBS 2:10-12

Ponder the path of your feet,
and let all your ways be established.
Do not turn to the right or the left;
remove your foot from evil.

PROVERBS 4:26-27

Those who are of a perverse heart are an abomination to the LORD,
but the blameless in their ways are His delight.

PROVERBS 11:20

9

If HARDNESS *of* HEART CAUSES LOVE *to* DIE

I have to warn you about something. There can come a point in any marriage when you get fed up. You've lost patience with waiting to see some kind of change in your spouse. You've forgiven again and again and you're weary of the struggle. You're through with trying to make things better. You're tired of being hurt over and over and waiting for a breakthrough that never comes. Your heart begins to close a door that was once open between you. The years have taken their toll, and you subconsciously (or consciously) decide you are not going to try anymore. You no longer feel love for your husband (wife) the way you did, and you don't even care about getting it back.

This can happen in any marriage where one spouse is working to make things better and the other isn't trying at all. Your heart can grow cold and hard like a stone, and it will seem as if the love you once had has died. But the good news is that God has the power to completely turn things around. He is the God of miracles and restoration who makes all things new. Jesus—the ultimate source of resurrection power—can resurrect love that has died and soften your heart toward your spouse. He can bring your marriage to life again, and it can happen quickly.

Unlocking the Doors to the Home of Your Heart

When you get married, your heart has found a home. But your heart is also a home for whatever you allow into it. The home of your heart can be cold, uncomfortable, miserable, and barren. Or it can be full of warmth, light, love, and life. Sometimes that home is locked up because you have shut out the Lord or your spouse. But you can unlock the door if you have the right key. Jesus said, "I will give you the keys of the kingdom of heaven, and whatever you bind on earth will be bound in heaven, and whatever you loose on earth will be loosed in heaven" (Matthew 16:19). God has given us keys of authority and the power to change things—even our hearts.

It is imperative that you remind yourself often that when something goes wrong in your marriage—no matter what it is—Jesus has given you the power and authority to take charge of it in the spirit realm through prayer. That doesn't mean you attempt to dominate your spouse or get heavy-handed and make ultimatums. It means you recognize the enemy's footprint and take charge of what is happening by praying for God to break through the atmosphere of your marriage and the condition of your heart with His love and power. By praying, you open the door and welcome in His healing, deliverance, transformation, and restoration.

If there is strife, anger, anxiety, sadness, despair, hopelessness, resentment, or bitterness in your marriage relationship, you can take authority over the spirits behind those negative emotions and tell the enemy that your heart and your home are established for God's glory, and he doesn't have the right to be there because you have full authority over him. If he torments you with suggestions that your authority has been compromised because you haven't been to church lately, haven't read your Bible, or haven't obeyed all of God's laws, then declare, "Those are issues between me and my heavenly Father, and my authority comes from what *Jesus* did, not what *I* do." Then invite God's Spirit of love, joy, peace, forgiveness, and hope to be the guest of honor who is poured out in your heart and your marriage relationship.

It is up to you to do everything within your power to see that hardness does not find a way to move into your heart, because bad things are sure to happen if you don't. "Happy is the man who is always reverent, but he who hardens his heart will fall into calamity" (Proverbs 28:14). When you harden your heart toward your spouse, you have hardened it toward God as well. This is dangerous ground to be standing on.

Don't trust your heart, because it can grow hard over something you believe is completely justified. "He who trusts in his own heart is a fool, but whoever walks wisely will be delivered" (Proverbs 28:26). God sees hardness of heart as never being justified. That's because when you receive the Lord, He sends the Holy Spirit to live in your heart and soften it. "Then I will give them one heart, and I will put a new spirit within them, and take the stony heart out of their flesh, and give them a heart of flesh" (Ezekiel 11:19). Allowing your heart to become like stone means you have not given the Holy Spirit free reign in it. When you invite the Holy Spirit to flow freely through you, all others around you will be watered—especially your spouse and your children.

Repentance and Forgiveness Are Fabric-of-the-Heart Softeners

Remember the amazingly forgiving Amish people who instantly forgave the murderer who killed their children in a schoolhouse? How loving they were to even be able to say the words "I forgive you" after such a senseless and horrific tragedy. But surely there will need to be layers of forgiveness in the years to come as the extent of those violations unfold over time. Perhaps forgiveness has to be extended on every birthday that this child never celebrated, at the family gatherings this child never attended, for this child's wedding that the family never got to witness, the grandchildren that were never born, and the dreams for this child that would never be realized. Surely all that has to be forgiven over time. And I am certain with the deep faith and purity of the Amish people, they will do that.

The point is that forgiveness isn't always a onetime thing. There are layers of it that need to be recognized in any situation—especially in a marriage. Sometimes we think we have forgiven, but we don't realize how many layers there are. And if we don't deal with each layer, hardness of heart can set in and build up to monumental proportions.

King David spoke of his heart often, saying such things as, "My heart pants" (Psalm 38:10), "my heart fails me" (Psalm 40:12), "my heart is severely pained" (Psalm 55:4), "my heart is overwhelmed" (Psalm 61:2), "my heart is wounded within me" (Psalm 109:22), "my heart within me is distressed" (Psalm 143:4), and "reproach has broken my heart" (Psalm 69:20). When we have suffering in our heart like that in a prolonged and unresolved way, our heart can grow hard. But David's heart didn't grow hard, and the reason is that his heart was filled with *repentance* and *worship* of God. Those two heartfelt attitudes will always soften a heart or keep it from getting hard in the first place.

A hard heart doesn't happen overnight. It happens little by little, as layer upon layer of crustiness builds up in your heart, and then becomes covered with a seemingly impenetrable coat of armor that is designed by necessity to protect it from being shot through or broken again. Sometimes hardness of heart doesn't fully manifest until later in life. Sometimes your heart can get broken so many times that forgiveness stops flowing and there is thick scar tissue that forms around the heart, making it hard.

The good news is that no matter how long those scars have been there, they can be completely removed by being in the presence of God. "The LORD is near to those who have a broken heart, and saves such as have a contrite spirit" (Psalm 34:18). Sometimes you have to go through layers of forgiveness to strip away the layers of unforgiveness that have built up, but it can be done with a heart of repentance and forgiveness that says, "I confess where I have not had a perfect heart toward You, Lord, or my husband (wife) either, and I repent of all that. Because You have forgiven me, I can do nothing less than forgive him (her) too."

Your Heart Is Not Too Hard for God to Soften

God asked Abraham, "Is there anything too hard for the LORD?" (Genesis 18:14). He wanted to know if Abraham doubted what God could do. Our heart can get hard because we doubt that God will actually do what seems impossible to us when it comes to our marriage. When we start believing that God can't change the situation, or our spouse, or us, we lose heart and hardness sets in.

The Bible talks about Rachel laboring in childbirth, saying that she had "hard labor" (Genesis 35:16). Sometimes we have hard labor trying to bring forth new life in our marriage, and year after year it feels as though nothing ever changes. Our heart becomes hard when we have hard labor and we don't see the birth of anything. But Rachel did give birth to something great. His name was Benjamin, and he would eventually be the head of one of the 12 tribes of Israel. The bad news is that she died in the process. Often we have to die in the process of giving birth to something great. We don't have to die physically because Jesus already did that, but our selfishness and pride do have to die.

The Israelites became bitter because of the hard bondage they were under. All their work was difficult and fruitless and caused them to feel defeated. They saw no hope for the future. Perhaps you feel as though you have worked so hard in so many ways to try to make your marriage what you know it could be and what God wants it to be, and yet you feel defeated because you don't see results. Even though you may be justified in having those thoughts, God says you are not to entertain them. Your heart was not designed to carry loads of discouragement or bitterness. That will not only cause your heart to grow hard, but also it will make you sick.

If God can make heaven and earth by the power of His outstretched arm, then He can stretch His arm toward you and soften your heart in an instant. When you become discouraged, say to the Lord, "There is nothing too hard for You" and ask Him to soften your heart (Jeremiah 32:17).

How Do I Keep My Heart Soft?

1. Every day ask God to speak to you through His Word. You can become hard of hearing when it comes to God's Word, and when that happens, your heart will grow hard as well. When you shut off yourself to God's truth, you lose understanding. When you don't open your heart to hear God speak to you through His Word, you lose the opportunities He has for your blessing and healing. God's Word also reveals what is in your heart. "The word of God is living and powerful, and sharper than any two-edged sword, piercing even to the division of soul and spirit, and of joints and marrow, and is a discerner of the thoughts and intents of the heart" (Hebrews 4:12). You can be blind to what is really happening in your heart if you don't allow the Word of God to reveal it to you.

2. Prepare your heart by seeking after God each morning. The Bible says of King Rehoboam, one of the kings of Judah, that "he did evil, because he did not prepare his heart to seek the Lord" (2 Chronicles 12:14). God looks for the person who will seek Him faithfully so He can show Himself strong on their behalf. "The eyes of the Lord run to and fro throughout the whole earth, to show Himself strong on behalf of those whose heart is loyal to Him" (2 Chronicles 16:9). Prepare your heart by inviting Him to reign powerfully in you every day. When you seek after God with all that is in you, you will find Him and He will change your heart (Deuteronomy 4:29).

3. Ask God for a wise and understanding heart (1 Kings 3:12). God put wisdom in Solomon's heart because he asked for it (2 Chronicles 9:23). If you want a heart of love, compassion, wisdom, and understanding, He will give you all that when you ask Him for it. He can take away any hardness of heart and replace it with a soft heart toward your spouse. That means no matter what condition your heart is in, God can fix it (1 Chronicles 29:18).

4. Ask God to give you a repentant heart so that you are quick to see your own sin. David did some terrible things—adultery and murder being the worst. But he said, "I acknowledge my transgressions, and my sin is always before me. Against You, You only, have I sinned and done this evil in Your sight—that You may be found just when You speak, and blameless when You judge" (Psalm 51:3-4). As a result, God looked upon his heart of repentance and forgave him and blessed him. God always looks at our heart, even when we do wrong things accidentally or stupid things on purpose. "The LORD does not see as man sees; for man looks at the outward appearance, but the LORD looks at the heart" (1 Samuel 16:7). If you don't want God to see a stone when He looks at your heart, have a repentant heart that is always willing to say, "I see where I have missed the mark for the way You want me to live, and I ask You to forgive me."

5. Ask God to remove all sorrow from your heart. When your foundation is shaken and you are afraid for the future, fear melts your heart. "I am poured out like water, and all My bones are out of joint; my heart is like wax; it has melted within Me" (Psalm 22:14). But "the LORD is near to those who have a broken heart, and saves such as have a contrite spirit" (Psalm 34:18). When your heart is broken by sorrow, it breaks your very spirit. If you allow bitterness in, you become hard-hearted (Ecclesiastes 7:3-4). But if you turn to the Lord, sorrow can be taken away and your heart made purer and stronger. Pray that God will take away all sorrow from your life.

6. Ask God to instruct you even as you sleep. If you ask Him to, God will teach you in the night and you will wake up in the morning with a different heart (Psalm 16:7-9). I have seen it happen many times in my own life where I have gone to bed feeling a hardness creeping into my heart toward my husband, and I have confessed it to God and asked Him to take it away. Each time I have awakened in the morning feeling totally the opposite. Only God can change a heart that way. The Bible says that

God gave Saul another heart (1 Samuel 10:9). If you ask God, He can give you a new heart too.

7. Praise God throughout the day no matter what is happening. When you worship God, you invite His presence in greater measure into your life. In His presence your heart is changed. Always! The hardness melts away. "The sacrifices of God are a broken spirit, a broken and a contrite heart—these, O God, You will not despise" (Psalm 51:17). When we have a pure heart toward God, we can stand in His presence and receive a new heart from Him (Psalm 24:3-5).

TEN WAYS TO HAVE A CHANGE OF HEART

1. **Believe in God.** "He who believes in Me, as the Scripture has said, out of his heart will flow rivers of living water" (John 7:38).

2. **Draw near to God with your whole heart.** "These people draw near to Me with their mouth, and honor Me with their lips, but their heart is far from Me" (Matthew 15:8).

3. **Confess all sin before the Lord.** "If our heart condemns us, God is greater than our heart, and knows all things. Beloved, if our heart does not condemn us, we have confidence toward God" (1 John 3:20-21).

4. **Seek God with all your heart.** "Blessed are those who keep His testimonies, who seek Him with the whole heart!" (Psalm 119:2).

5. **Pray about everything.** "He spoke a parable to them, that men always ought to pray and not lose heart" (Luke 18:1).

6. **Trust in God more than your feelings.** "Trust in the LORD with all your heart, and lean not on your own understanding" (Proverbs 3:5).

7. **Value the Lord above all else.** "Where your treasure is, there your heart will be also" (Matthew 6:21).

8. **Pour out your heart before the Lord.** "Trust in Him at all times, you people; pour out your heart before Him; God is a refuge for us" (Psalm 62:8).

9. ***Praise God with your whole heart.*** "I will praise You, O LORD, with my whole heart; I will tell of all Your marvelous works" (Psalm 9:1).

10. ***Tell God that you love Him with all that is in you.*** "Jesus said to him, 'You shall love the LORD your God with all your heart, with all your soul, and with all your mind'" (Matthew 22:37).

Prayer Can Soften Your Heart

You know how bad you start to feel when your heart is not right toward your spouse. That's because "a sound heart is life to the body" (Proverbs 14:30). If your heart is not sound, it will harden and drain life away from you. When your heart is hard and unrepentant, you can sense that something bad will happen if you don't straighten it out (Romans 2:5).

We mistakenly believe our thoughts are harmless, but they're not. We think we can have our thoughts to ourselves and no one will know the bitterness sheltered there. But our thoughts are viable and a deep well from which we either draw life or from which we are poisoned. "Both the inward thought and the heart of man are deep" (Psalm 64:6). God knows the deep secrets of your heart (Psalm 44:21). The truth is that you will become what you think. "As he thinks in his heart, so is he" (Proverbs 23:7). If you think bitter thoughts, you will become bitter. Your thoughts affect who you are.

Whenever you want to break through any kind of hardness in your heart, fasting and prayer always does it. Fasting unleashes the power of God to break the strongholds that keep your heart captive. God says, "Turn to Me with all your heart, with fasting, with weeping, and with mourning. So rend your heart, and not your garments; return to the LORD your God, for He is gracious and merciful, slow to anger, and of great kindness; and He relents from doing harm" (Joel 2:12-13). Your heart always changes when you fast. It's amazing how something so simple can be so powerful.

When you try to make yourself stop caring about your spouse so that your heart won't hurt every time you feel rejected, you toughen up and steel yourself for the next offense. Your hard heart becomes a place of safety, an impenetrable security blanket, your coat of armor to protect you from inevitable arrows. This makes your heart harder over time until there is nothing that will soften it except a touch of the Holy Spirit.

When we become hard-hearted, we extend no grace or mercy. We become righteous in our own eyes. We think we know the truth. We not only put up an impenetrable wall between ourself and our spouse, but also between us and God. In fact, we blame God, which is a foolish and twisted way to live. "The foolishness of a man twists his way, and his heart frets against the LORD" (Proverbs 19:3). We no longer move from a place of love. You can't love God and resent your husband (wife). That's sin. If you have sin in your life that is not confessed and repented of, the Lord will not hear your prayers. "If I regard iniquity in my heart, the Lord will not hear" (Psalm 66:18). You absolutely must have your prayers heard.

When you've been hurt, it takes great courage to want to feel again, to possibly set yourself up to be hurt again. But when you let go of any hardness in your heart and confess it as sin, God can change it. We are the clay; God is the potter, and He will mold us however He wants if we fully submit to Him (Isaiah 64:8). Jesus rebuked His disciples for "their unbelief and hardness of heart" (Mark 16:14). You don't want Him to rebuke you for yours. Pray that you will never be able to hang on to a hard heart.

Ask God to show you what is in your heart that shouldn't be there, and what isn't in your heart that should be. And then ask Him to make the home of your heart a showplace for His love.

PRAYERS FOR MY MARRIAGE

Prayer for Protection

LORD, I THANK YOU THAT You are "a sun and a shield" to us and because of Your grace and glory there is no good thing that You will withhold from us when we live Your way (Psalm 84:11). I pray that You would protect my marriage from any hard-heartedness that could develop between us. I pray our hearts will never grow hard toward one another.

Help us to not be stubborn or rebellious, refusing to set our hearts right before You (Psalm 78:8). Teach us both to "number our days"—to value the time you have given us together—so that we may gain a heart of wisdom as you have promised in Your Word (Psalm 90:12). Take away any perversity in our hearts, so there is never any wrong attitude taking root in either of us (Psalm 101:4). Take away any pride or bitterness in us so that we will not displease You.

Where our hearts have become hard, soften them toward one another. I ask that rivers of Your living water will flow in and through us at all times to soften, mend, and restore our hearts (John 7:37-38). Heal any brokenness so that the damage is not irreparable, and take away any scars that form. I ask that we will always feel love for one another in our hearts. In Jesus' name I pray.

Prayer for Breakthrough in Me

LORD, I CONFESS ANY HARDNESS of my heart toward my husband (wife) as sin. Melt it like ice in the presence of the hot sun. Burn any solid, heavy, frosty lump within me until it pours out like water before You. Take my heart of stone and give me a heart of love and compassion. Break up the fallow ground where nothing good can grow and life gets choked out. I confess to any sin of anger, resentment, unforgiveness, or criticism of my husband (wife). Forgive me and cleanse my heart completely.

Lord, I pray that You would give me a pure heart toward You so that I may stand in Your holy place. Give me clean hands so that I may rise above my situation. Help me to not lift my soul toward an idol or speak words that are not true in light of Your Word so that I can receive all You have for me (Psalm 24:3-5). You know what is in my heart (Psalm 44:21). Take away all negative thoughts and feelings, and overflow my heart with good things (Psalm 45:1). May the good thoughts in my heart cause my mouth to speak wisdom and not harshness (Psalm 49:3). Create in me a clean heart, and make my spirit right before You (Psalm 51:10). I want to bring to You the sacrifice of a broken spirit and a humble heart (Psalm 51:17).

Don't let me succumb to being stubborn in my heart. I want to walk in Your counsel and not my own. Take away any disappointment in me with regard to my marriage and show me if I have blamed my husband (wife) without seeking to know what my part is in it. Remove all pride so that I can escape the consequences of sin and better hear from You. Change me by the power of Your Spirit. Cut away from my heart all that is not of You. Help me to love You and serve You with all my heart and soul (Joshua 22:5). Show me how to keep my heart with diligence (Proverbs 4:23).

Give me the wisdom to do what's right so that I will walk in my house with a perfect heart (Psalm 101:2). Break down any hardness of heart in me, and I will repent of it. Restore love in my heart for my husband (wife) if ever I don't feel it anymore. With my whole heart I seek You, and I ask that You would help me hide Your Word in my heart and keep all of Your commandments (Psalm 119:11). Help me to understand and keep Your law (Psalm 119:34). Enable me to trust You with all my heart and not depend on my own limited understanding of things.

I believe that I will see Your goodness in my life and therefore I will not lose heart. I will wait on You, Lord, and I will stand strong in all I understand of You, knowing that you will strengthen my heart (Psalm 27:13-14). Thank You that You are a God of new beginnings. Help me to take steps that signify a new beginning in me today. In Jesus' name I pray.

Prayer for Breakthrough in My Husband (Wife)

LORD, I PRAY THAT YOU would give my husband (wife) a heart to know You better so that his (her) heart will be soft toward both You and me. Where his (her) heart has already become hard, I pray that he (she) will turn to You with all of his (her) heart and find Your presence waiting for him (Jeremiah 29:13). Open his (her) heart to hear what You are speaking to him (her) (Acts 16:14).

Lord, I pray that You would help him (her) to have a heart filled with truth and not one that is open to the lies of the enemy. Keep him (her) from having a rebellious spirit and a stubborn heart, and make his (her) heart right before You (Psalm 81:12). Give him (her) a heart that is strong in faith so that he (she) doesn't have to be afraid of the future (Psalm 112:7). Give him (her) a heart of love for me. Resurrect it if it feels to him (her) as if it has died.

Lord, I know that pride is an abomination to You, so I pray that You would do whatever it takes to remove all pride from my husband's (wife's) heart so there is no need to suffer the punishment that comes with it (Proverbs 16:5). I know that "he who is of a proud heart stirs up strife, but he who trusts in the LORD will be prospered" (Proverbs 28:25). Don't let pride in either of us stir up strife in our marriage. Help our relationship to prosper because we look to You.

Lord, help me to be sensitive to heaviness in my husband's (wife's) heart. Show me what his (her) burdens are and how I can help ease them. Help me to encourage and support his (her) decisions. I pray that the heart of my husband (wife) will trust me so that our marriage will be blessed (Proverbs 31:11). In Jesus' name I pray.

TRUTH TO STAND ON

A good man out of the good treasure of his heart
brings forth good things, and an evil man out of the
evil treasure brings forth evil things...The heart is deceitful
above all things, and desperately wicked; who can know it?

JEREMIAH 17:9

Keep your heart with all diligence,
for out of it spring the issues of life.

PROVERBS 4:23

Wait on the LORD; be of good courage,
and He shall strengthen your heart;
wait, I say, on the LORD!

PSALM 27:14

I will give you a new heart and put a new spirit within you;
I will take the heart of stone out of your flesh
and give you a heart of flesh.

EZEKIEL 36:26

Let us not grow weary while doing good,
for in due season we shall reap if we do not lose heart.

GALATIANS 6:9

10

If YOU *Are* NO LONGER EACH OTHER'S TOP PRIORITY

When it comes to priorities, Jesus made it crystal clear what ours should be. He said we should love God first and love others second (Matthew 22:37-40). Putting God first doesn't mean you neglect your spouse and children. It doesn't mean you abandon your family and spend all your time in church. It doesn't mean you yell at your family and tell them to fend for themselves because you're going to the mission field. Jesus said, "If you love Me, keep My commandments" (John 14:15). Putting God first means you love Him enough to always do what He says. Next to loving Him, the most important thing He says He wants you to do is to love others (1 John 3:10-18).

There have to be priorities within the "love others" command too. First of all, you have to love your husband (wife) first and your children second. The reason for that is if you don't put your spouse before your children, you may end up not having a spouse, and that is not good for your children.

You will find it amazing, however, that when you love God and put Him first in your heart, all the other priorities fall into place. Loving God doesn't mean just having occasional loving feelings for God. It means loving Him with all that is within you. It means your heart is always with Him.

Even Delilah knew it isn't really love if your heart is not in it. When Samson wouldn't tell her what she wanted to know, she said, "How can you say, 'I love you,' when your heart is not with me? You have mocked me these three times, and have not told me where your great strength lies" (Judges 16:15). Of course, he was living in sin and wasn't married to her, and he should not have even put himself in the position of being pressured to tell her in the first place. And it was his ultimate downfall that he did. But the point is, she knew that his whole heart had to be with *her* or it wasn't love. The same is true for you. Your whole heart has to be with God. And it has to be with your spouse as well. You cannot be halfhearted when it comes to your marriage being your greatest priority under God, or you will get completely off track in your life. But when you love God with all your heart, loving your spouse the way you are supposed to will be easy.

Keeping your priorities straight is not that hard until children come along, and then it becomes a lot more complex. Perhaps both of you have to work to support the family, and there is so much time needed to raise children and keep a home clean and running. Plus all the other things you need to do in order to stay healthy, be in church, and have contact with friends and family. How can you do all of this without violating what your top priorities should be? It seems you are always going to be neglecting something or someone. And most likely you will be neglecting your spouse in favor of your children. Or neglecting your family in favor of your work. But it doesn't have to be that way.

Jesus told a religious scholar who understood this principle of loving God and loving others that he was not far from the kingdom of God (Mark 12:32-34). We will be as close as possible to God's kingdom on earth when we understand this principle too.

It All Has to Flow from Love

We will feel good if we can obey some of God's "most important" laws and only neglect a few. But we are not supposed to show partiality by favoring one law over another (Malachi 2:9). We can't say, "I'll obey this law but not that one." God says He wants them all obeyed, and the only way we can do that is to love Him first and then love others.

Every law of God is fulfilled by love. Love is what leads us to obey God in the first place. The Bible says, "Love does no harm to a neighbor; therefore love is the fulfillment of the law" (Romans 13:10). We were created by *love* to *love* and be *loved*. But our love and affection must be directed toward

God first of all. We are to love nothing *more* than Him. The first of the Ten Commandments says we are to have no other God but our God. He wants us to love Him with *all* our heart, soul, and mind, and acknowledge Him as everything. That means we love Him with our whole being and not just with the words we say. That means praising Him *with all that we are* because we love Him *with all that is in us.*

Loving God will cause you to resist any kind of temptation that comes into your life to draw you away from what is most important. When God is your first priority, you are not going to allow anything to dilute or pollute your relationship with Him. You will refuse to let less important things scream for your attention.

This demand for attention is similar to when commercials come on TV that are so much louder than the regular program that you are forced to reach for the remote to adjust the sound. I don't know about you, but if I have to reach for the remote to adjust the sound because of a commercial that is too loud, then I will change the channel or turn the TV off completely. I'm amazed that some TV programmers don't yet realize we have remotes and seem to think we are going to just sit and take their volume abuse. It's the same if the program is offensive. I'm not going to allow pollution of any kind to invade my life. I will turn it off.

When you love God and you see the enemy trying to pollute your life in any way, you can grab your holy remote and turn him off completely. You don't have to listen to his abuse because you have the power to change the channel. You can turn down the volume on the voice of your flesh that screams "I want what I want." You can put God first because you love God most. If your heart is divided—in other words, you are pulled in different directions by your love for something other than God—your love for the Lord is weakened.

If you are a woman, for example, you can put God first when you go shopping. Say, "God, show me what to buy and what not to buy. I don't want to waste the money You have given me by buying something I don't need or won't wear, and I especially don't want to purchase anything that is not glorifying to You. Make me sensitive to Your will regarding this right now." Once I started praying like that, I made far fewer mistakes or unnecessary purchases. If you keep your love of God first and the love of your mate second, you can't go wrong.

If you are a man who loves sports, for example, ask God to help you not put sports' schedules before God's schedules and God's people. If you want to go to a game or watch a game on TV, don't scream at your wife, "I'm watching the game. Don't talk to me for the rest of the afternoon!" Instead, a few days earlier say, "There is a game on Sunday afternoon. Let's go to the earlier service at church and have lunch on the way home. Let me know if there is anything I can do for you before it starts." That way you make sure everything you are doing flows from love of God and the love of your spouse. This demonstrates right priorities.

I'm not saying that these simple examples I have just given you mean that you can't shop or watch sports events. I am just saying that you should ask yourself, "Do the things I am doing have a higher place in my heart than God or my spouse? Do they spring from a heart that loves God and my family?" Everything you do has to flow from your love for God.

Showing love for your husband (wife) is one of the ways you demonstrate your love for God. "If someone says, 'I love God,' and hates his brother, he is a liar; for he who does not love his brother whom he has seen, how can he love God whom he has not seen?" (1 John 4:20). Jesus said we should love others as we *love ourselves*. But there is a self-love that is selfish, prideful, and greedy, and is not born out of love for God and others. That kind of self-love is corrupt and is the root of sin. The kind of self-love Jesus is talking about appreciates your own God-given gifts, talents, uniqueness, and the wonderful way He has made you. And it motivates you to be a good steward of your body, mind, soul, and life. You will be better able to love others as yourself if you learn to love yourself the way God wants you to.

Nothing is more important than loving God and your neighbor—your brother and sister in the Lord—and your spouse is the closest neighbor you will ever have. If you love your spouse the way you love yourself, you will never do to him (her) what you would not want done to you.

Where Your Treasure Is

The way you live out those two most important commandments that fulfill all the laws of God is to seek God every day so you can be led by the Spirit. If you can't hear God guiding you, you will end up having misplaced priorities. Only God can tell you what your priorities should be in the way you live out each day. He says to seek Him and His kingdom first, and all the things you need shall be added to you (Luke 12:31). When you seek Him first, everything falls into place. Everything you need will come to you.

Our priorities can get off track when we pursue other things before God. Jesus said, "Do not worry about your life...for it is your Father's good pleasure to give you the kingdom" (Luke 12:22,32). He says to store up treasures in heaven because they don't fail. He also says that your heart will be with whatever you treasure (Luke 12:34). If your heart is with God and your spouse, you will store up treasures in heaven. If you see your marriage as being your greatest treasure next to your relationship to God—a treasure in which you will invest your whole heart—it will transform your marriage. When you put your spouse first under God, you will keep your marriage strong, free of strife, and more pleasant in every way. And that in turn will be the greatest blessing for your children.

In order to stop being prideful, selfish, and sinfully oversensitive, you have to ask God to help you be humble, selfless, and kind. That means you must be able to exhibit the fruit of the Spirit. And you can't do that unless you are walking *in* the Spirit every day. Each morning you have to wake up and say, "Fill me afresh with Your Holy Spirit, Lord, and help me to be led by Your Holy Spirit today. Help me to exhibit the fruit of Your Spirit in everything I say and do."

NINE WAYS TO DISPLAY THE FRUIT OF THE SPIRIT IN MY MARRIAGE

The Fruit of the Spirit Is:	With Regard to My Marriage:
1. Love	I will show love to my spouse every day.
2. Joy	I will invite the joy of the Lord to rise in me continually.
3. Peace	I will walk in peace and not stress.
4. Patience	I will be patient with my spouse and not lose my temper.
5. Kindness	I will show kindness to my spouse no matter what.

6. Goodness	I will do good for my spouse in every way.
7. Faithfulness	I will be faithful to my spouse in all I do.
8. Gentleness	I will be gentle and not harsh with my spouse.
9. Self-Control	I will not allow myself to get out of control.

GALATIANS 5:22-23 NCV

When You Feel You Are No Longer Your Spouse's Priority

If you feel your commitment to the marriage has remained strong but your husband's (wife's) has not, it is a terribly hurtful and disappointing situation, but don't let yourself become resentful. That only makes matters worse, and it will hurt you more than it does your spouse. It may cause you to blurt out words you will regret and further distance you from one another.

Instead, ask God to show you what the real problem is. Is your husband (wife) just too busy with work, establishing a career, raising children, or being active in the church or community? Is he (she) too preoccupied with outside interests, sports, people, or hobbies? Is it a sign of someone who is *careless* or *clueless?* Is it truly that he (she) doesn't care, or is it actually that he (she) just can't see it or figure it out on his (her) own?

Talk it out together and establish where each of you think your priorities *are right now* and where you think they *should be.* Determine what needs changing. Come to a complete understanding about the situation you're in. The most important thing is to come to an agreement. For example, there are seasons in business that are more demanding than others, and perhaps you both can agree that during this busy season a lot more time has to be put into work. Decide how you can best compensate for that loss of time together. If you are in total agreement about this, then no damage will be done.

Another example is when you have young children at home who haven't started school yet. The smaller they are, the more moment by moment attention they need. Talk to your spouse and agree that this is a season where there is not as much free time for the two of you, and so you really have to make a concentrated effort to find time for the two of you to be alone and make it count.

Still another example is when you have an important project or assignment due and you need to complete it as successfully as possible. Or when there are seasons of special interests happening, and it's either do it now or not do it at all. Talk it out and say something like, "I have to work hard on this project, but it will be completed in eight weeks and then I'll be home more." Or if you are worried about your spouse's time away from home, say something like, "Until the children start school, let's be home together as much as possible for their sake." If you can communicate and come to an understanding about these things, it will become clear that your greatest priority is still God, spouse, and children. It will set the record straight in your hearts and minds.

Another thing that will always cause us to lose track of our right priority is pride. It causes us to end up making wrong choices. Pride in either of you will always cause strife between you (Proverbs 13:10). "Pride goes before destruction, and a haughty spirit before a fall" (Proverbs 16:18). God doesn't want us to think or act as though we are better than anyone, especially our spouse. That's because pride always causes a person to think that he (she) is right, and so it's not necessary to listen to their spouse's input. This is dangerous ground to be walking on. "Be of the same mind toward one another...Do not be wise in your own opinion" (Romans 12:16).

When we get "puffed up with pride," we become like the enemy (1 Timothy 3:6). If you see pride in yourself or your spouse, pray that it will be broken. If priorities are out of order in your marriage—whether it is you, your spouse, or both of you—"come boldly to the throne of grace" that you "may obtain mercy and find grace to help in time of need" (Hebrews 4:16). Then say, "Lord, take away any pride in me so that I can see what is most important."

When the Pressure at Work Affects Your Relationship

Everyone wants to feel significant—as if what they do matters and that they can make a difference in the world in some good way. That's why the work we do is important to us. A man's work is especially important to him, in some ways more than it is for a woman. That's because a man's identity and feelings about himself are wrapped up in his work to the extreme. He throws himself into it because he continually senses the pressure to be successful. And he senses it even more when he is *not* working. A man out of work feels as though his entire life is on the brink of disaster. He feels discouraged, angry, sad, depressed, hopeless, irritable, oversensitive, and like a failure. This tremendous stress he carries can't help but spill over into his marriage.

A woman, on the other hand, seems to have a greater sense of herself as a person of value aside from her work. Her work is very important to her, and she absolutely wants to excel and succeed, but her sense of identity and personal value does not rise and fall with the success of her work.

The pressure a man feels about his work adds to the pressure in his home. If he works too long, too hard, too focused, or too obsessed, his wife feels that she is being replaced by a faceless mistress. Because the pressure a man senses about work is something he feels all the time and is such a big part of him, he may not be able to see it in himself. That's why it is crucial for a wife to pray that her husband will find fulfillment in his work. And also that he will be able to use his talents and gifts according to God's will, and that his work will be blessed. A husband should pray for his wife's work to be successful as well, and that she will find favor with the people she works with and for.

Practical Ways to Restore Your Priorities

1. Ask God to help you show love and commitment to your spouse in some tangible way every day. Be affectionate with one another in ways that aren't always about leading to sex. Showing affection to your spouse should be high on your priority list. Your spouse needs to know that he (she) is loved for who he (she) is at that moment without having to perform. Do things for him (her) that will make him (her) miss you whenever you are gone. Jesus said, "Greater love has no one than this, than to lay down one's life for his friends" (John 15:13). Ask God to show you how to lay down your life—selfish desires—for your husband (wife) in some way every day.

2. Say no to certain things whenever possible in order to spend time alone with your spouse. Try getting away together, even if it is just overnight. Drive somewhere that will take an hour or two in the car so that you can have time alone without interruption. If you are married to a workaholic, try to convince him (her) that time away alone would be the best thing for *him (her)*. Time alone together can make a major difference in your relationship.

Michael and I have been to a number of marriage retreats, and during a particular one not long ago we found that even after 34 years of marriage we were still learning new things. Not that we had never heard these things before, but this time there was actual breakthrough. My husband likes to stay home, so we used to have two semiannual dates a year outside of birthdays. What my husband took away from this retreat was that he needed to take me out on a date night once a week. I had stopped hoping for that years ago, but something clicked with him, and now we go to dinner and sometimes to a film almost every week—although it is a lot harder to find a decent film than it is to find a good restaurant. Doing this has made all the difference in our relationship. We try to make time for that, and it's something we look forward to. It seems like such a simple thing, but it is an impactful way to put each other first. So no matter how busy we are during the rest of the week, we know we will have that time alone for a few hours.

3. Have a devotional time together with your spouse as often as you can. If you can't do it every day, then try for at least once a week. If your husband (wife) is resistant to that, ask if you can just read a verse or two of Scripture to him (her) periodically and see if he (she) will let you pray for him (her). Praying together is one of the most life-changing things you can do for each other—even if only one of you does the praying.

Priority equals time. We all have to put aside some things to make time for what is most important. If something comes up that takes up all of your time—a sick child, an injured elderly parent, the finishing of a big project—communicate with your spouse that this is just temporary and you will be back spending quality time together as soon as the situation is under control.

Don't Drink the Enemy's Kool-Aid

"Drinking the Kool-Aid" is a phrase that comes from the 1978 Jonestown massacre in Guyana, in which some members of the Peoples Temple cult committed suicide by drinking cyanide-laced Kool-Aid. For those of you too young to remember this incident, in the 1970s there rose up a guru named Jim Jones. I was aware of him early on because of my housekeeper, Rosetta, who worked for me every Saturday for about five years. She was a Christian, but somehow she and her church got into following Jim Jones. She started talking about him frequently and how great he was, and I sensed right away that she had an unhealthy esteem for this "spiritual leader." When she started wearing a long necklace attached to a 2"x4" plastic photo holder with a photo of Jim Jones encased in it, I told her in detail about my reservations regarding her allegiance to him. In our conversation she told me that Jim Jones had acquired land in Guyana and was asking his followers to go there and work the land, and he would take care of their needs. She was seriously considering going.

I had a terrible feeling about that for her sake, and so I prayed fervently for her to come to her senses. The more I prayed, the more strongly I felt that this was the enemy's doing. Thanks be to God, the next time I talked to her about it I succeeded in convincing her not to go. I persuaded her on the grounds that it was a big mistake for her to leave her son. I knew she'd had a hard life, and she wanted someone to take care of her and allow her to serve the Lord at the same time. And she thought that her son at age 19 was old enough to be on his own.

"But he still needs you," I said. "You can't just leave him. Besides, I don't believe this is what God wants you to do."

She finally decided not to go, and it wasn't many months after that when Jim Jones gave his followers in Guyana the poisoned Kool-Aid. Except for a very few who escaped, Jim Jones' followers died. It was sad beyond belief.

The point is, the devil always has some kind of poison waiting for us that he hopes we will drink. Don't partake of the enemy's drink of death and destruction—especially with regard to your priorities and your marriage. Remember that the devil "is a liar and the father of it" (John 8:44). The enemy will tell you that everything in your life is more important than your marriage—your work is more important, and so are your dreams, your children, your friends, your relatives, your recreation, your interests, your career, or even what you do with your own time. Don't drink in those lies. They are poison to you and will prove to be your downfall. Instead, drink the "same spiritual drink" from "that spiritual Rock" which is Christ (1 Corinthians 10:4). Overcome the enemy's lies with God's truth, because God "who is in you is greater than [the enemy] who is in the world" (1 John 4:4).

After the incident happened, my housekeeper grieved terribly for all of her friends who died in Guyana. It was an unbearable disaster that shook her life tremendously, but she might have been one of them. Had I not taken a strong stand against her going, I would have regretted that for the rest of my life. I am taking a strong stand against the devil's plans for you too. I don't want you to buy into the trap he has set for you and your marriage by enticing you to let your priorities get out of order. Love God and love your husband (wife), and all else will fall into place.

PRAYERS FOR MY MARRIAGE

Prayer for Protection

LORD, I PRAY YOU WOULD HELP my husband (wife) and me to always make You our top priority, and to make each other our priority under You. Enable us to live in Your love so that we can learn to love each other the way You want us to. Make us to be vessels through which Your love flows. Show us how to establish right priorities in our marriage and in our family.

I pray that we will not do anything "through selfish ambition or conceit, but in lowliness of mind" may we esteem each other better than ourselves (Philippians 2:3). Help us to always find time for one another to be a help, support, encourager, uplifter, lover, companion, and sharer of good things. Enable us to always bear the burden of the other concerning the difficult things that happen in life. Help us to choose each other over the other seemingly important things that vie for our attention. Teach us to set aside time to be together alone and to reaffirm each other as our top priority under You. In our seasons of necessary busyness, help us to be understanding of one another and in agreement as to how to handle those times successfully. Thank You that You have chosen us to be people for Yourself, "a special treasure" for Your glory (Deuteronomy 7:6). Help us to always find our treasure in You above all else. In Jesus' name I pray.

Prayer for Breakthrough in Me

LORD, HELP ME TO ALWAYS put You first in my life and to put my husband (wife) next above everything else. Show me how to do that and how to let him (her) clearly know that this is what I am doing. I look to You to teach me the way I should walk and what I should do (Psalm 143:8). Reveal to me any place where my priorities are off. Show me where I have put other things, people, or activities before You or my husband (wife). If I have made my husband (wife) feel as though he (she) is less than a top priority in my life, help me to apologize to him (her) and make amends for it. Where damage has been done to our relationship because of it, I pray You would heal those wounds. Restore us to the place where we should be. Help me to put our children in highest priority, just under You, Lord, and my husband (wife), for I know that the greatest blessing for them is that we stay together.

Thank You that Your love for me is everlasting, and that in Your lovingkindness You are always drawing me closer to You (Jeremiah 31:3). Help me to seek You first in all things, to keep Your commandments, and to abide in Your love (John 15:9-10). Thank You that before I chose You, You chose me that I "should be holy and without blame" before You in love (Ephesians 1:3-6). I know my holiness and blamelessness comes from all that Jesus *is,* being attributed to me. I am forever grateful, and I long to please You in every way—especially in the way I prioritize my life. In Jesus' name I pray.

Prayer for Breakthrough in My Husband (Wife)

LORD, I PRAY THAT YOU would penetrate my husband's (wife's) heart with Your love. Help him (her) to understand the greatness of it. Deliver him (her) from any lies of the enemy that have caused him (her) to doubt Your love for him (her). Jesus, You have said, "God is love, and he who abides in love abides in God, and God in him" (1 John 4:16). Help my husband (wife) learn to love You above all else. Let everything he (she) does be done in love (1 Corinthians 16:14).

Where his (her) priorities are out of order, I pray You would help him (her) to realize he (she) needs to put You first, me second, and our children next before everything else. Help him (her) to see where he (she) must make necessary changes in the way he (she) spends time. Help him (her) to not feel so pressured by his (her) work that it overtakes his (her) life and our family suffers. Bless his (her) work so that he (she) can accomplish more in less time. Enable him (her) to say no to the things which do not please You and are not to be high on the priority list. Don't let him (her) be led astray by delusion, and don't let his (her) fears come upon him (her) (Isaiah 66:4). Help him (her) to clearly see what is most important in life and what is not. Help him (her) to choose the path of humility and righteousness. Thank You that whatever we ask in Your name, You will give us (John 15:16). In Jesus' name I pray.

Truth to Stand On

Seek first the kingdom of God and His righteousness,
and all these things shall be added to you.

Matthew 6:33

Humble yourselves under the mighty hand of God,
that He may exalt you in due time,
casting all your care upon Him, for He cares for you.

1 Peter 5:6-7

I call heaven and earth as witnesses today against you,
that I have set before you life and death, blessing and cursing; therefore
choose life, that both you and your descendants may live.

Deuteronomy 30:19

If it seems evil to you to serve the Lord,
choose for yourselves this day whom you will serve…
But as for me and my house, we will serve the Lord.

Joshua 24:15

Cause me to hear Your lovingkindness in the morning,
for in You do I trust; cause me to know the way in which I should walk,
for I lift up my soul to You.

Psalm 143:8

IF *the* "D" WORD BECOMES *an* OPTION

A marriage—just like the people in it—is either growing deeper and more solid, or it is breaking down and becoming more vulnerable. It never stays in just one place, although it may feel as though it does sometimes. Marriage actually has a life of its own and can move forward or backward. It can breathe deeply when given fresh air, or it can suffocate if it is deprived of spiritual oxygen. Each spouse has a great influence on which direction their marriage will go by the words they speak, the way they act, and the fervency of their prayers. Fresh air or suffocation. It's their choice.

The good news in all this is that even when you have made mistakes in your marriage and should have done things differently, God is a God of second chances. That's something not all couples are willing to give each other, but God always gives us another opportunity to make things right. That means if your marriage is headed in the wrong direction, it's never too late to turn things around.

Most people get married with the intention of staying married in a wonderful relationship for the rest of their lives. You're in love with each other, and you both have an idea of what you think life together is going to be like. But it is impossible to know exactly what you are getting into before you're married, no matter how long you have dated or known each other. We don't even know *ourselves* completely before we're married, let alone the person we are marrying.

Marriage reveals everything we are because there is no place to hide—not even from ourselves. The marriage contract changes things. The relationship is now *really* up close and personal, and the ways we formerly disguised ourselves no longer work. The truth comes out. That's why a marriage requires commitment and work. A 50-50 partnership doesn't cut it. Each person has to give 100 percent of themselves to the other. And that's not easy to do when we are all selfish enough to want to hold back.

One person can be so wrapped up in themselves or their work that they are completely unaware that their spouse is feeling neglected and lonely. They believe that everything is great, but their spouse is miserable. Because there is no communication, it's going to come as a surprise when the lonely spouse leaves or has an affair. The point is, if *one* person in a marriage doesn't think everything is great, then the marriage is not great.

Marriage has to be worked on all the time so it can grow stronger and deeper. If it doesn't grow, it is deteriorating. It may feel as though it is maintaining, but in unseen places it is breaking down. It's like putting a pin in an egg and letting the contents inside slowly drain out. You don't see that happening. The egg looks the same. But then one day pressure is put on the egg and it cracks to the point of destruction. When everything cracks in a marriage, divorce can seem like the only way to save your own life in an impossible situation. Didn't we all learn that Humpty Dumpty could never be put back together again?

A Violent Sin

God hates divorce, "for it covers one's garment with violence" (Malachi 2:16). He uses the words "hate" and "violence" to describe His feelings about divorce. After He said this to His people at the end of the Old Testament, He didn't speak to them again for about 400 years. That's an even longer silence than what happens between warring couples. I think He means it.

God says "a husband is not to divorce his wife" (1 Corinthians 7:11). That "what God has joined together, let not man separate" (Mark 10:9). It was because of our hard-heartedness that divorce came about, but God never intended for it to be that way (Matthew 19:7-8). Divorce was never supposed to happen. But our hard hearts made room for it, even knowing that God hates it.

The reason the divorce rate is so high is because divorce is considered an *option* in the minds of at least half of the people getting divorced. It is spoken of as the *solution.* It appears to be the *only way out* of a miserable situation. If you have the mind-set that you don't want that option, that solution, or that way out, it forces you to have to find *another* option, a better solution, and a way *through* your seemingly impossible situation.

God is a witness to your marriage, viewing it as a covenant, which means *enduring commitment and faithfulness to one another.* When two people get divorced, it is a violent shattering of that covenant and of God's order for their lives. But when you keep your marriage vows, God stands behind your marriage. That's why your prayers for the preservation and strengthening of your relationship have such power. They are already God's will before you even speak them. Praying puts God's will into action. It means God's power will stand against any enemy you face—whether the enemy comes from the outside or it is actually one or both of you.

Refuse to Use the "D" Word

As I mentioned earlier, I was married before I became a believer to someone who also was not a believer. That marriage was doomed from the start because I went into it knowing it wouldn't last. I just wanted to have a home and some kind of companionship, even if those things were only temporary. Divorce was always at the back of my mind. I didn't expect my marriage to last two years, and we never even made it to the second anniversary. As miserable as that marriage was—and *I* was the one who left *him*—the divorce was awful. It felt as though my life were ripping apart. I didn't know about covenants and God's ways, but even so I felt the violence God speaks of with regard to divorce. I can't imagine how painful a divorce is when you don't want it and your spouse does.

Ideally, this issue of divorce is best decided once and for all *before* you get married. But whether you are recently married or you've been married a long time, you can decide today to not let the word "divorce" become an option in your thoughts or words. Even if you and your spouse have talked about divorce in the past, agree to not think of it as an option and to never speak of it as a threat to each other again. Instead, agree to talk things out and listen to each other's feelings and thoughts. Agree that you will do whatever it takes to get beyond every impasse or problem that arises, because above all you don't want this relationship to fail. You don't want to divide up the property, the children, the income, and start all over again. You definitely don't want the things that have been bothering you for a long time to continue, but you do want to find a way to make some changes and work it out.

You have to remember that your words always have power. When you say the word "divorce" as a solution or a threat, there is a spirit of divorce that gets into your mind and heart—or your husband's (wife's) mind and heart—and the enemy waits at the door you have just opened to use it against you. You may have merely used the word as an idle threat, perhaps to bring about an awakening as to the seriousness of the situation, but not meaning to actually follow through on it, but now you have planted that thought in your husband's (wife's) mind. You have put it out there in your relationship, and the enemy will feed the idea so it can grow like a cancer.

God thinks of divorce as treachery. "The LORD has been witness between you and the wife of your youth, with whom you have dealt treacherously; yet she is your companion and your wife by covenant. But did He not make them one, having a remnant of the Spirit? And why one? He seeks godly offspring. Therefore take heed to your spirit, and let none deal treacherously with the wife of his youth" (Malachi 2:14-15). God wants us to have a strong commitment to love and take care of each other. He likes unconditional love because He invented it. That's who *He is*. God has joined you together in a covenant, not only with each other but with Him as well. If you deal treacherously with each other by divorcing, it grieves His Holy Spirit.

Don't Offend God by the Way You Treat Each Other

Marriage is supposed to be a manifestation of the relationship between Christ and the church. Christ doesn't walk out on, get fed up with, leave, desert, or divorce the church. He also doesn't get rude, abusive, mean, inconsiderate, selfish, unaffectionate, arrogant, or angry with the church, either. All problems in a marriage could be solved if each person were to become more Christlike, especially with one another. A relationship disintegrates slowly with each careless word or insensitive action and every opportunity missed to comfort and support the other. It breaks down gradually with every criticism or complaint voiced to the other without any affirmation and love. If one of you treats the other with disregard, abuse, or dishonor, you are shutting off blessings God has for your life.

God says He wants you to have the kind of love for one another that is patient, not arrogant or prideful, not rude or selfish, and not easily provoked. He wants you to be the kind of people who don't think about evil things, don't enjoy lawlessness, are willing to put up with imperfection, and who believe for the best in each other. He wants you to have the kind of love that never loses hope and believes that with God, everything will turn out right. He wants you to have the kind of love that embraces the truth and is willing to endure whatever is necessary in order to do the right thing (1 Corinthians 13:4-7). God says that kind of love never fails, even though all else will (1 Corinthians 13:8). This kind of love comes from God and can only be developed by spending time with God. That's because being in the presence of God changes us.

Transformation is found in the presence of God.

God can transform us from someone who doesn't know how to love into someone who loves the way that He does. All we have to do is ask Him to work that in us and then do what He says.

Of course, it's impossible to be perfect for each other. There are no two people who can live up to one another's expectations all the time. At some point there are going to be disagreements. The things that one person does are going to get on the other's nerves. Each one is going to disappoint the other sometime. But it's what happens during those times that sets the marriage on one path or the other. One path with the fresh air leads to growing deeper and better together; the other path of suffocation leads to a breaking down of the bond of love and commitment.

When offenses happen—and they will in even the best of circumstances because of the differences in male and female perspectives—these things have to be talked out. When you try to come to a mutual understanding and you never can because one of you *refuses* to work it out, you can become so discouraged and hopeless that you withdraw and stop trying. But when you invite God to help you communicate and be of one mind and one spirit, things work out. You can grow through the difficult times when you walk through them together with God.

Emotional Divorce

You become divorced in your heart first. That's why even though a couple may be committed to staying married, their hearts can still be divorced from one another. That sucks the oxygen out of a marriage, and it becomes lifeless. The Lord does not like that. And neither do we. Living in a dead and miserable marriage is hell on earth. And it doesn't glorify God in the least.

Whenever one spouse starts to feel *unloved,* and the other spouse is *unloving,* they are in dangerous territory. They can then become strangers living in the same house but never making contact. And this is far more common than most people care to admit. At that point, the relationship is dying. If one or both of them then become involved in the activities of life and never include the other, they are headed for emotional divorce. They will grow completely apart if they don't take immediate steps to stop it. They have to start saying no to everything and everyone else and yes to each other. They have to decide if those activities and people are going to be that important to them if their marriage fails. Don't settle for an emotional divorce. Don't settle for less than what God has for you in your marriage. And what He has for you cannot come about if you have a big "D" branded on your heart that represents the divorce you are always considering and leaving open as an option. Once that gets into your heart, it will start to burn an imprint. If you let it stay there long enough, it gives you a way out and keeps your relationship from growing deeper and more committed.

The more you give place to divorce as an option, the deeper the imprint burns, the greater the distance that grows between you, and the more disconnected you will feel from one another until you have a spirit of divorce. Then it becomes a tearing of the heart. It becomes not about *if* you will divorce, but *when.* Once the "D" word takes hold in your mind, it almost has a life of its own. The spirit of divorce takes over and gets the process rolling. It's as though a divorce demon says, "I'll take it from here." Then you stop making plans for a future together and you only make plans for a future alone. Things will get worse between you, and one day when you have constant strife, arguments, and discord, divorce will seem like a pleasant relief.

If you are in a dead marriage relationship where there is no joy, no pleasure, no communication, no common interests or goals, nothing to look forward to, and no hope for the future—in other words, no fresh air—then you must do something immediately. Get before the Lord and confess every thought you have had of divorce so the spirit of divorce won't establish a stronghold in your heart. Pray for God to renew a right spirit in you and in your spouse. If your husband (wife) won't sit down and work things out, then find a good Christian marriage counselor. Counseling is much cheaper than a divorce. And often it takes a wise third party who knows what they're doing to wake up people who are drifting apart.

Twelve Reasons Why Divorce Is Bad for You

1. It's something God hates.
2. It destroys what was once your dream.
3. You have to divide up your children between you.
4. Your children will suffer more than you know.
5. Many friends will desert you.
6. You won't feel as comfortable in church.
7. You may lose your home.
8. There will be loss of income.
9. Family gatherings will never be the same.
10. It takes a big toll on your health.
11. You will have to divide up all your belongings.
12. You will always have a sense of failure about it.

Leaving a Legacy of Divorce

Children always suffer in a divorce. If that isn't true, then why are there so many books for the hurting adult children of divorced parents? And why are they selling so well? It's because these people struggle terribly. They know what it's like to have their worst fears come upon them. They have seen their prayers that Mom and Dad won't get divorced not be answered by God. (That is, if they were not made to understand that their prayers weren't answered because of the strong will of one or both of their parents.) They blame themselves for the divorce. They have trouble in school because they are hurt, depressed, anxious, confused, and unable to concentrate. They frequently seek alcohol, drugs, and promiscuity as a way out of their pain.

For your children, divorce is like experiencing a death, only without the sympathy one receives from others when there is a real death. In a physical death there is a mourning period, a period of recovery, and then you eventually grieve less. With a divorce, however, they are not afforded a mourning period with sympathy cards. There is no period of recovery. And they never seem to grieve less. They may *appear* as though they do, but they carry the ramifications of the divorce into their own relationships. They have fear and insecurity in their own marriage later on. I know there are exceptions to that, but they are not the majority. The majority are hurting. Keeping your children from all that pain is worth whatever effort it takes to stay married.

If you have children and you are already divorced, pray they won't blame themselves. Ask God to heal them of any guilt they carry for thinking that if they had been a better kid, this divorce wouldn't have happened. And pray they won't blame you or your spouse, either. Everything that goes wrong in their life after the divorce might be seen as their parents' fault. They will have a harder time honoring you if they are blaming you for their miserable life. Pray that they will forgive you and be free of anger so they won't get into trouble and grow up to take their anger out on the person they marry.

TWELVE GOOD REASONS TO STAY MARRIED

1. It pleases God.
2. Married people live longer.
3. You will be healthier.
4. You don't have to divide up your income.
5. You don't have to divide up your children.
6. You will be more protected.
7. You don't have to live alone.
8. You can build something together.
9. You won't leave a legacy of divorce for your family.
10. You don't have to move into a smaller place.
11. You will be able to lift up one another when you fall.
12. Your prayers together are more powerful.

How to Avoid a Divorce

Pray often that you and your spouse will always take a strong stand against divorce. Declare that you are building your marriage on the Word of God, and therefore you will not allow the enemy to break apart what God has joined together. Declare that your marriage is God's plan, and you will not leave a legacy of divorce and brokenness for your children.

Every marriage is vulnerable. Every husband-and-wife relationship takes work. In the best of situations the marriage can still deteriorate and fall apart. I have seen what appears to be the greatest relationships disintegrate. Nothing surprises me in that regard anymore. No one knows what really goes on in a marriage except the two people who are in it. But you have to do whatever it takes to turn your marriage in the right direction and away from divorce. And that means not letting divorce stay in your heart. You have to guard your heart and not allow into it what God says is evil (Proverbs 4:23). You have to say, "I will not let divorce be an option for me. I will not seek divorce as the solution to my marriage problems."

Pray that you will not put other things or people before God or your spouse. Ask God to help you see where work or activities have taken over your life. Be brave and ask your spouse to share how *he (she)* feels. He (she) will be more than happy to tell you. But the thing is, you have to *listen* to what he (she) says and *not ignore* it. You have to *show interest* in his (her) *perspective*. Get rid of all anger, resentment, unforgiveness, and bitterness *before* you come together to talk. These emotions have absolutely no place in a marriage that lasts.

No marriage is too far gone to save if both partners want to save it. But if you are married to someone who is determined to divorce, there are still things you can do and ways you can pray that can also save it. I've seen marriages that have gone through divorce court be saved when the wife or husband started to pray fervently. However, if you have done all that you can do and your spouse is still determined to leave, release him (her) into God's hands. Let God deal with him (her), and you get on with doing what God has called you to do.

I am not saying there are no grounds for divorce. Some marriages are a disaster from the beginning, and allowing yourself to be destroyed in a marriage is not glorifying to God, either. When I was married the first time, I told someone I would rather be dead than stay married and I meant it. I didn't want to live another day in the hell I was in. I know many people have that same feeling, and my heart goes out to them. The person they are married to may be too mean, abusive, angry, godless, or evil to ever be able to work things out, and they need to save their own lives. People have to do what they have to do in order to survive, and God won't strike them with lightning. Marriage was never designed by God to destroy you. He has a better life for you than that.

I by no means want to bring condemnation on anyone who has been divorced in the past. I myself am a member of that group, but there is healing from the effects of it: restoration of your heart and a new beginning given to you by the Lord. God either makes all things new or He doesn't. If you choose to believe the Bible, then you are a candidate for complete renewal. But it is a mistake to remarry until you have found that place of restoration and wholeness God has for you. You also need an understanding and knowledge of why your marriage didn't work the first time and why you think it will this time. Seek good counsel and much prayer through this process.

There has to be something to look forward to in your marriage. If you're married to someone who is getting meaner and more inconsiderate with each passing year and seems to enjoy being that way, all you will see for your future is being alone with someone like that. You can either become resigned to that joyless life or choose to not lose the dream in your heart for the future. Ask God for a miracle. I have seen Him do a miracle for me in our marriage. It took years of praying, but I am glad I didn't give up.

We sometimes believe our heart is a private domain and we can think whatever we want, but it's not true. Whenever you entertain a thought that isn't of the Lord, you are inviting trouble. If you are struggling with thoughts of divorce, draw near to God and let Him fight the battle for you. "Do not be afraid. Stand still, and see the salvation of the LORD, which He will accomplish for you today...The LORD will fight for you, and you shall hold your peace" (Exodus 14:13-14). Put a protective guard over your heart, and don't let the "D" word in. You will be glad you stood your ground in the battle and won.

PRAYERS FOR MY MARRIAGE

Prayer for Protection

LORD, I PRAY YOU WOULD HELP my husband (wife) and me to rise far above any thoughts of divorce as a solution to our problems or a way out of our marriage. Take away any desire in our hearts for it. Keep our hearts so close to You and each other that we never even speak the word "divorce" in regard to each other and never harbor the idea of divorce in our minds. God, help us to always be affectionate to one another, "in honor giving preference to one another" (Romans 12:10). Show us where we are doing things that are breaking our marriage down instead of building it up. Help us both to grow stronger in You and learn to treat each other in a way that pleases You.

Help us to stand strong together through every problem and to not be afraid to seek outside help when we need it. Keep us from ever falling into denial about what is going on in our relationship so that we are blinded to what the enemy is doing. Help us to confess as sin before You any time we think about divorce as a solution to the problems in our marriage. In Jesus' name I pray.

Prayer for Breakthrough in Me

LORD, I CONFESS ANY TIME that I have ever considered divorce in my mind or have uttered that word to my husband (wife), friends, or family members in regard to my marriage. Whenever I have thought of divorce as an option or a way out of our problems, I ask You to forgive me, for I know it displeases You. I know You hate divorce and it grieves Your Spirit, so I pray that You would help me to never do that again from this day forward.

I reject any spirit of divorce that I have invited into my heart and our marriage by the careless words I have spoken or thoughts I have had. I repent of any time I have even thought about what it would be like to be married to someone else. I recognize these thoughts as evil and adulterous, and I repent of them before You. I turn to You to find solutions to any problems in my marriage. Give me wisdom to do things Your way. In Jesus' name I pray.

Prayer for Breakthrough in My Husband (Wife)

LORD, I ASK THAT YOU would take any thoughts of divorce out of my husband's (wife's) mind and heart. Where he (she) has entertained those kinds of thoughts, I ask that You open his (her) eyes to see how far away that is from Your best for his (her) life and our lives together. For any time we have discussed divorce or he (she) has used the word "divorce" as a way out of our problems, I come before You on my husband's (wife's) behalf and ask for Your forgiveness. Forgive him (her) for that sin so that a spirit of divorce cannot find a home in his (her) heart. If it already has, I ask that You would break that stronghold by the power of Your Spirit. Destroy that lie of the enemy so that it can never rise up again. Show him (her) a better way, which is Your way for our lives. Let there be no divorce in our future. In Jesus' name I pray.

TRUTH TO STAND ON

The LORD God of Israel says that He hates divorce,
for it covers one's garment with violence.

MALACHI 2:16

I say to you that whoever divorces his wife for any reason
except sexual immorality causes her to commit adultery;
and whoever marries a woman who is divorced commits adultery.

MATTHEW 5:32

If any brother has a wife who does not believe,
and she is willing to live with him, let him not divorce her.
And a woman who has a husband who does not believe,
if he is willing to live with her, let her not divorce him.

1 CORINTHIANS 7:12-13

Therefore, what God has joined together,
let not man separate.

MATTHEW 19:6

If two lie down together,
they will keep warm;
but how can one be warm alone?

ECCLESIASTES 4:11

If INFIDELITY
SHAKES *Your*
FOUNDATION

God is so grieved by infidelity in marriage that, as much as He hates divorce, He allows infidelity to be grounds enough to justify it. If your husband (wife) committed adultery, you could get a divorce if you wanted to because God understands the devastation of infidelity in our souls. Sex was God's idea, and He had a specific plan for the way it should be so that the greatest fulfillment could happen in our lives. Adultery violates that plan, and the consequences for it are severe.

Sexual sin does the greatest damage of all sins, besides murder, because its consequences are so far-reaching. One of the reasons for that is because you become one with whomever you have sex. Your soul is tied to them. "Do you not know that your bodies are members of Christ? Shall I then take the members of Christ and make them members of a harlot? Certainly not! Or do you not know that he who is joined to a harlot is one body with her? For 'the two,' He says, 'shall become one flesh'" (1 Corinthians 6:15-16).

Sexual sin not only violates a trust and a covenant made before God, but it hurts your soul and body. Every other sin a person does is outside the body, but sexual immorality is a sin against your own body (1 Corinthians 6:18). Our bodies belong to God and His Spirit dwells in them. Whatever you do with your body you are doing with the temple of the Holy Spirit (1 Corinthians 3:16-17).

If we commit one sin, we are guilty of all sins in God's eyes (James 2:10). But some sins do more damage in our lives than others. Pastor Jack Hayford says, "Sex sins are not harder for God to forgive, but they are more *damaging* at a personal and social dimension than other sins. Sexual sin assaults the fountainhead of every great thing that God intended for our lives on this earth, and it leaves in its wake a destructive fallout that can permeate generations."*

Adultery begins with the eyes and in the heart long before the physical act actually happens. Jesus said that "whoever looks at a woman to lust for her has already committed adultery with her in his heart" (Matthew 5:28). Adultery, even in the heart, destroys the soul (Proverbs 6:32).

What Do I Do if It Happens to Me?

I have talked with more people whose marriages were devastated by infidelity than for any other reason. It is epidemic because of our culture. You may not realize how prevalent it is because few people let it be known to others. It's embarrassing for everyone involved, and not many want to disclose it. The way I see it, if your spouse commits adultery, you have two choices:

1. Stay and do whatever it takes to find healing and restoration for both of you and your marriage.
2. Leave and move on with your life.

There is a third possibility, which is to stay and make his (her) life as miserable as he (she) has made yours by letting your anger, unforgiveness, and bitterness make him (her) pay for what happened for the rest of your lives. But that's not really a choice; it's a cop out.

As far as the "stay and do whatever it takes" choice, there is one particular couple who recovered from infidelity better than any couple I have ever known. They were both believers who were faithful in their church. They were excellent parents who volunteered in the schools their children attended. They seemed to have a wonderful marriage and family. However, the husband discovered that his wife had been having an affair with another man. When he confronted her, she admitted it was true.

---

* Jack Hayford, *Fatal Attractions* (Ventura, CA: Regal Books, 2004), p.11.

The husband came to our house to tell us that he had discovered this affair and to share how angry and devastated he felt. He asked us for our prayer support as he dealt with the aftermath of it all. However, as he sought the Lord, he realized that he wanted to save his marriage more than he wanted revenge. So he took time off from work and spent uninterrupted quality time with his wife, listening to her tell him everything that had been going on inside of her through the years that led up to the affair. I also went to his wife and talked with her and prayed for her, and I gained some understanding of how this had happened. It appeared that neither one of them wanted a divorce, so Michael and I both prayed that they could survive this.

Just a few weeks later, the husband brought his wife to our house on a Saturday morning saying he wanted to tell us something. The four of us sat together in a private room where no one else in the house could hear and he said he wanted to take the blame for what happened. He told us that God had opened his eyes to how insensitive he had been to his wife's needs and requests for years, and he wanted to apologize in front of us for his part in this and for his anger and disappointment in her when he came to our house the first time.

I have never heard anything so amazing as this tender and heartfelt apology by this husband. He knew he had set up a condition in his marriage that led to his wife's downfall and he took *full* responsibility. His wife was so touched by his declaration of unconditional love, and his commitment to do whatever it took to save their marriage, that she was completely broken and repentant.

After that, he took time off from his business and traveled with her to places she had longed to go, and he did things with her that she had asked him to do for years and years. They went to counseling together as well as separately. They stayed in the church, and they stayed with each other. Their marriage survived this terrible disaster, and it is still strong today. Their children are now grown and married with children of their own, and there has been no legacy of divorce for their family to inherit.

They survived what would have destroyed most people. And in the years since this began, the husband's business has been thriving beyond anyone's wildest dreams. I believe it was due to his willingness to examine himself and let God show him where he could have been a better husband. And he was humble enough to not only receive what God showed him, but also he was willing to expose his failings in front of his wife and his friends so that she could be healed and their marriage restored. He is the perfect example of what it means to have a repentant heart.

I will never forget the amazing generosity of spirit of that husband or the beauty of his wife's restoration. He wasn't living in denial or letting his wife off the hook. He was placing himself *on* the hook the way Jesus did. And I think only someone completely sold out to the Lord could do what that husband did. He certainly had the heart of the Lord, and he refused to receive any accolades for it. He admitted that God had to deal with him to get him to that point because that was not his initial reaction. But I applaud him for listening to what God was saying, and I applaud her for truly repenting, and I applaud them both for turning what could have been their greatest disaster into God's greatest blessing for their marriage and family.

On the other hand, I know another couple where the wife had an affair, but the husband was insistent on her paying retribution for what she had done. There was no recognition on his part that he was in any way responsible. His young wife had been emotionally damaged in her childhood and had grown up insecure and hurting. Not long after they married, they moved to a city a thousand miles away from all friends and family so he could go to a particular school. The problem was he also worked full-time as well as went to school full-time, so he was never home. She was extremely lonely and felt abandoned and was insecure enough to fall into an affair with someone at her workplace.

Of course, she was wrong to do it, and there were great consequences for it, but she was completely repentant and wanted to keep her marriage together. He, on the other hand, left her immediately and moved back home to his family. He refused to see her except with a counselor he had chosen, and she had to drive hundreds of miles alone to get there and back. He did not let her forget that this was her failure and he had every right to make these demands on her. He refused to handle the situation any other way, and he had nothing remotely resembling a repentant heart. This couple, as you might suspect, are divorced now.

They might have had a different outcome if that husband would have said to his unfaithful wife, "What you have done has devastated me, but I love you no matter what. I have sought the Lord, and I see how I have been complicit in this. He showed me how I abandoned you to work and go to school when you needed me most. Even though I was doing that for us and I thought you understood that, as the head of the house I did not serve you well. I want us to stay together and work this out. Let's go to counseling and let's seek God together, and let Him change us both so that our marriage will last."

I know this is extremely hard to do. And it's easy for me to say because I have never had anything at all like that happen to me. And I'm sure it takes more forgiveness and courage than I have on my own. But I have seen the results of laying down all pride and selfishness to save your marriage, and I know that the outcome is good.

God gives us a *way out* because this kind of betrayal is so devastating. But He also gives us a way to *rise above* and find His total restoration. Some people are willing to give up their God-given option of divorce in order to save their marriage and see it become all that God wants it to be. Those people are the heroes among us.

If Your Spouse Has Already Committed Adultery

If infidelity has already happened with your spouse, God has given you a way out. No questions asked. You are free to go. God understands that the pain of your husband's (wife's) adultery can be too hard to bear. He doesn't require you to endure it. However, if you choose to stay and work it out, and are willing to humble yourself before Him and hear what He is saying to you about how to proceed, God can work a miracle. You, as the violated spouse, have two choices:

1. *Forgive* and move on.
2. *Forgive* and stay.

Either way forgiveness is a must, because the alternative will kill you. Don't even think of trying to pay your spouse back for all the pain he (she) has caused you. That never works, and it will always hurt you more than it hurts him (her). Plus, it makes you look bad, and then he (she) feels justified in finding someone else. Instead, let him (her) fully know your pain and get to a counselor immediately—either on your own or with him (her). Preferably both. Write him (her) a nasty letter putting the worst of all your feelings down on paper, but don't send it. Shred it instead. Then write a letter to God telling Him what you're feeling and what you want Him to do in you and your spouse. Keep that one in a special place where you can read it again and perhaps show it to your husband (wife) if the time seems right. Above all, ask God to work complete forgiveness in your heart, because He is the only one who can. God knows you can't do it fully on your own.

There are, however, people who are adulterers without repentance. There is a difference between someone who commits an act of infidelity and feels remorse and repents and does whatever is necessary to make things right with God and their spouse, and the other extreme of a person who commits acts of infidelity over and over again without repentance. You can only take so much. That's the way God feels too. That's why He gives you a way out.

One woman I know forgave her husband at least three times that I'm aware of for his adulterous affairs with three different women. She mistakenly thought each time that her love and forgiveness would be enough. But it wasn't, because he continued to be entirely selfish and unrepentant. His next affair was with her best friend, for whom he left his wife so they could marry. About a year after he had married this second wife, he called his first wife and begged her to take him back. She said simply, "It's too late." She had forgiven him, but she knew he had not changed and it would happen again.

I advise anyone who has a spouse who commits sexual infidelity over and over and you cannot live with it anymore to release him (her) and let God deal with him (her) while you recover and move on. Don't torture yourself another minute. God has a better life for you than that.

Adulterers who refuse to change their ways will not inherit the kingdom of God or anything the Lord has for them (1 Corinthians 6:9-10). That particular adulterous husband I just mentioned had an extremely successful career, but his star stopped rising soon after all this occurred. In fact, a major tragedy happened to him and his star completely fell from the sky. I have seen more up-and-coming people with great futures ahead of them lose it all because they couldn't keep themselves from adultery. They didn't see that this was the enemy's plan to destroy the great future God had for them, and so they went with their flesh instead of submitting themselves to the Spirit of God.

Don't be afraid to let an adulterous spouse come to the end of himself (herself). "Blows that hurt cleanse away evil, as do stripes the inner depths of the heart" (Proverbs 20:30). Be strong enough to let him (her) suffer the natural consequences for what was done, because it can wake a person up to their own sin and cleanse their heart of evil. That being said, you also have to examine yourself to see where you are complicit in any way.

The Bible says that a wise person builds their house, but a foolish person pulls it down with their hands (Proverbs 14:1). You have to ask God, *Have I done anything to pull down my house? Is there something more I could have done to build it up?* We can all think of things we should have done differently in our marriages. I'm not saying this to make you feel guilty, especially if your spouse has committed adultery. Adultery is always wrong. It is never justified under any circumstances. And the adulterer is always guilty. But remember what I said earlier about having a repentant heart? In order for healing to come in a marriage for any reason, there always has to be an examining of your own heart, soul, and mind before the Lord. You always have to tell God that you are willing to see any place in you where you have fallen short of His will for your life.

Did you treat your spouse with disrespect? Were you inconsiderate of his (her) needs? Did you deny him (her) sexual gratification? These things are not justification for him (her) to commit adultery, but sometimes we set the stage for those things to happen because we weren't careful to guard the marriage in thought, word, deed, and prayer.

When a husband or wife feels lonely, disconnected, distanced, disappointed, or abandoned emotionally by their spouse, all it takes is being around someone who gives them a strong sense of being understood, acknowledged, or cared about. They are vulnerable, and this can establish a connection with that person. Even if it doesn't turn into physical infidelity, there is an infidelity of the heart that occurs, and that is not pleasing to God, either (Matthew 15:19).

Do you realize, *husbands,* that every time you are rude, critical, demeaning, verbally abusive, cruel, neglectful, or abandoning of your wife that you create in her a fertile ground into which seeds of unfaithfulness can be planted? Unless she is extremely strong in the Lord, deep longings and thoughts will come to her heart and mind, and she can become ripe for an affair of the heart, if not the body. It's amazing how attractive someone else can look to you when the person who is supposed to love you no longer acts as though he (she) does (2 Timothy 2:22). If you have set your wife up for that kind of fall, then you are partly to blame for what happens.

Do you realize, *wives,* that every time you criticize your husband in a demeaning way, put him down in front of others, neglect to compliment him and let him know that he is valuable to you, or refuse to have sex with him that you make it much more difficult for him to resist the temptations that are everywhere around him? You set him up for infidelity. He is more susceptible to flattery and unholy attention than he would have been otherwise.

Of course, there are certain husbands and wives who have already determined in their heart that they are open to the slightest advance from someone and will welcome any opportunity to commit adultery. There is nothing you can do with these people because they have a "self-sickness" and are wired for sin. They will not change without a professional counselor in their face confronting them, and even then that may not work. So don't blame yourself if you feel you have done your best to be a good husband or wife and your spouse still cheats. It is not your fault, and there is nothing you could have done to stop it. Tell him (her) "Goodbye and good luck!" and move on to better things.

SEVEN THINGS THAT ARE TRUE ABOUT ADULTERY

1. *God told us not to do it in His Ten Commandments.* "You shall not commit adultery" (Exodus 20:14).

2. *Jesus said don't do it.* "Jesus said, 'you shall not murder,' 'you shall not commit adultery,' 'you shall not steal'" (Matthew 19:18).

3. *Adultery brings judgment upon you.* "Marriage is honorable among all, and the bed undefiled; but fornicators and adulterers God will judge" (Hebrews 13:4).

4. *Adultery happens in the heart as well as the body.* "I say to you that whoever looks at a woman to lust for her has already committed adultery with her in his heart" (Matthew 5:28).

5. *Adultery will cause you to lose out on all God has for you.* "Do you not know that the unrighteous will not inherit the kingdom of God? Do not be deceived. Neither fornicators, nor idolaters, nor adulterers, nor homosexuals, nor sodomites" (1 Corinthians 6:9).

6. ***Adultery is entirely a work of the flesh, and as such it will reap death in your life.*** "The works of the flesh are evident, which are: adultery, fornication, uncleanness, lewdness" (Galatians 5:19).

7. ***Adultery will destroy you.*** "Whoever commits adultery with a woman lacks understanding; he who does so destroys his own soul" (Proverbs 6:32).

The Devil's Favorite Target

The devil's most prized target, as far as tempting someone toward infidelity, are the leaders in the body of Christ—and especially pastors and their wives. That's because these people are on the front lines and are doing the most to lead people in the kingdom of God. The enemy will come in like a tsunami to their hearts and emotions, especially after he has bombarded them with discouragement on one end of the spectrum and pride on the other. It is such an all-out spiritual assault on them that we in the body of Christ have to surround our pastors and spiritual leaders and their families with prayer. If we don't, they will suffer. When *they* suffer, so do *we* (1 Corinthians 12:14,26).

We must pray that they are able to be honest with the people closest to them, whom they trust, about the temptations they face. And we must pray against the rising up of a spirit of gossip. One of the sorriest sins is gossip. When someone confides a struggle to another in confidence asking for prayer, and the person who was told the confidence then goes and tells others, their sin of gossiping is as great as the sin they are gossiping about. Gossip in the church is a sin that keeps leaders and their families from sharing what needs to be shared in order for healing and renewal to come. It keeps them from seeking the prayer support they need. Do all you can to stop gossip.

If You Are Ever Attracted to Someone Else

Infidelity begins in the mind before any action ever takes place. And that is where it has to stop as well. "From within, out of the heart of men, proceed evil thoughts, adulteries, fornications...all these evil things come from within and defile a man" (Mark 7:21,23). You have to carefully monitor your thoughts. If you ever find yourself thinking about someone else besides your husband (wife), and wondering if they might be the perfect mate for you, this is adultery of the mind. And the consequences will be serious.

If you ever find you can't stop thinking about a certain person in that way, go before God immediately and confess it and pray for deliverance from those thoughts. Stay before the Lord until this obsession is gone. There is no good that will come out of it and the consequences for pursuing it, or allowing it to overtake you, could ruin your life. Ask someone to pray with you about this. It's possible that you could tell your husband (wife), but then after your attraction is gone—which it will be if you stay before the Lord long enough—then your poor husband (wife) is left having to sort through all the rejection and hurt feelings. It's not worth it. I say, go to the Lord and prostrate yourself on the ground. Fast and pray. Stay there before Him until this thing is broken. Every time the feeling comes back, humble yourself before God. If all that doesn't work, and this attraction becomes an obsession, call in a close friend who doesn't gossip to stand with you in prayer and break this stronghold of the enemy. If even that fails, then tell your husband (wife) and go to counseling together. You're going to need it.

If you are attracted to someone, by all means don't tell that person. It only opens up feelings in him (her) of being appreciated in the wrong way. It inspires an intimacy between the two of you because of a secret you now share. At the first sign of an attraction, don't fool yourself with fancy words like "attraction" and "affair" that make it sound like flowers in spring. Call it what it is—adultery of the heart and fornication of the mind. Don't create a sexual tension or inspire an attraction in the other person, or force that person to have to fight one off. Leave them out of it. This is between you and God. Tell God, a counselor, or your spouse, or all three.

An adulterous spirit is a strong spirit. It's heady and will try to make you think you have finally found the one you have been waiting for and the fulfillment of a perfect life is ahead. But it is all an illusion. The one you have been waiting for is actually at home waiting for *you*. And you need to go back and give your marriage all your efforts to make it work. You need to give God a chance to do a miracle.

I know a young pastor's wife who was having a strong attraction toward someone other than her husband in her church. She had come to the point where she felt her marriage was not anything like what she thought it would be. She came to me for help, and I suggested she call two other women she trusted to pray with her as well. Between the three of us we stood by her, talking with her and praying with and for her, until we saw that thing completely broken.

We are all vulnerable to being attracted in our mind to people around us, but I was convinced beyond any doubt that for her this was a ploy of the enemy to destroy the great ministry she and her husband would one day have. We prayed that this work of hell in her life be broken completely. It took months to finally break through this, but we did. And she and her husband went on to have a great marriage and many years together in a highly successful ministry. They raised a wonderful family with children and grandchildren. No one else ever knew about it, not even her husband, and definitely not the person she was attracted to. This was entirely a battle in the spirit, and the enemy lost.

If you find yourself attracted to another person other than your husband (wife), ask God to break that attraction like severing the head off of a snake so that there is no way it can ever regenerate. Ask Him to put a guard over your heart to protect it from any further sinful intrusion. You have authority over evil in your life. "Sin lies at the door. And its desire is for you, but you should rule over it" (Genesis 4:7). The enemy wants to entice you away from the life God has for you, but God has given you the power to put a stop to it.

You will be able to tell if there is still a residue in your heart with regard to any ungodly attraction if you are sad when you don't see that person. Or if you have excitement when you do. You will know you are free when you see that person one day and you thank God with all your heart that you didn't act on your attraction. That you didn't sacrifice your marriage, your children, or your life for it. You will wonder, *What in the world was I thinking?* And you will thank God that He rescued you from your own foolishness.

It Can Happen to Anyone, but It Doesn't Have To

Don't think for a moment that you could never fall into an adulterous trap. It is a strong, heady thing that can wrap around you like an invisible python, and when the time is right it will constrict your good sense until you can't breathe. And it can happen with someone you never dreamed it could. Or it might happen suddenly with someone you just met. It's insidious, treacherous, and devious, a deceitful entrapment that can sweep you away and entice you to do things you will regret. That's why you can never entertain any infatuation, or any soul connection, or even a flirtation with another person of the opposite sex. (Or of the same sex, for that matter.)

There were two important things I prayed for in a marriage partner. One was that he must have a strong personal relationship with God through Jesus Christ. It was out of the question for me to think of sharing my life with someone who didn't share my love for the Lord. I couldn't imagine how to make a marriage work without it. The other important thing I prayed for in a husband was that he would be faithful to me. I knew I could never tolerate sexual sin in marriage. I wouldn't be able to live with it. God answered my prayers and gave me a husband who loves Him and has always been faithful. Michael's faithfulness to me and to the Lord is his most admirable quality in my mind, and he has never given me any reason to doubt it. Even so, I have prayed throughout all of our 34 years of marriage that the enemy would never be able to destroy us with any kind of temptation to sexual sin. I believe that has not only kept us strong but also away from danger.

Seduction is subtle and opportunities are everywhere, and you may be approached by someone somewhere, sometime. We've all heard of people who get themselves into an adulterous situation and say, "I wasn't looking to fall in love or have an affair; it just happened." It just happened because they let thoughts of an adulterous affair get into their mind. They didn't have to look *for* it. They needed to stop looking *at* it when it presented itself. We all have enough insecurity in us to be attracted to flattery or admiration. We all have enough pride that we can be puffed up from someone's attention. We all are vulnerable to inappropriate feelings. We can be strong, humble, and secure 99.99 percent of the time, but in a moment of weakness or overconfidence, we can fall.

It can happen to anyone, but it won't happen to everyone. It won't happen to those who have learned to keep their heart with all diligence, who understand the ploy of the enemy, and who know how to stand against it.

In *The Anatomy of Seduction*, Jack Hayford lists four "steps of an advancing seduction." These are danger signs that should sound a major alarm in each of us if any one of them ever occurs:

1. Mental preoccupation about the other person
2. An unusual desire to be near or around the person

3. A growing desire to give frequent compliments

4. The supposition that an "innocent" fling or flirtation can be indulged*

If you sense any of these four warnings happening in you, run as fast as you can to God, get on your face before Him, confess your unholy attraction as sin, ask Him to take it away completely, and stay there until it is gone. If even for the briefest of moments there is a temptation that you give in to, a hook will lodge itself in your heart and bring you pain one way or another. It's not worth sacrificing your marriage and the future God has for you.

You know how it is when you entertain someone in your home. You *invite* them *in*. You give them a *place* to sit. You provide something of sustenance to *sustain* them. It is the same with lustful images or thoughts. They come across your mind, but you are the one who *invites them in*. You are the one who gives them a *place to reside* in your heart. You are the one who *sustains them with unholy longings*.

What you must do is command these thoughts to leave. That might seem rude to a guest in your home, yet if your guest was doing something that would destroy your life or close the door to God's best for you, you would demand that this person leave immediately. And so you must do with adulterous thoughts that try to stay in your mind. Throw them out, close the door to your heart, and lock it behind them. The Bible warns us about being enraptured by immorality, saying that the adulterer "did not know it would cost him his life" (Proverbs 7:20,22-23). Lust seduces us away from the life God has for us and into the pit the enemy has set as a snare.

An adulterous spirit is everywhere. It's in the workplace, in the neighborhood, sadly in some churches—nearly every place you go. It is impossible to avoid contact with it completely. You have to be clear in your understanding of what it is—which is a trap to ensnare and destroy you and your marriage. And what it is *not*—a means of achieving true happiness and fulfillment.

Remember that no matter how strong the temptation is, God will not allow you to be tempted beyond what you are able to resist. He will give you a way out and give you the strength and the ability to successfully resist it (1 Corinthians 10:13). Cling to God and embrace Him as your way out of all temptation, especially infidelity.

---

* Jack Hayford, *Fatal Attractions* (Ventura, CA: Regal Books, 2004), pp. 42-44.

PRAYERS FOR MY MARRIAGE

Prayer for Protection

LORD, I PRAY YOU WOULD protect my marriage from any kind of infidelity. May adultery be far from us and never find a place in either of our minds or hearts. Pour Your wisdom and knowledge into us so that we are too wise and too smart to allow the enemy to sneak up on our blind side and throw temptation in our path. I pray You would not allow temptation to even come near us. Keep us far from anyone who would try to lead us into anything evil. Remove anyone from our lives who would ever tempt us with adulterous thoughts.

Lord, I know that in You "are hidden all the treasures of wisdom and knowledge" (Colossians 2:3). Give us the ability to see danger in advance and the wisdom to not do anything stupid. "Let us walk properly" (Romans 13:13). Keep us from ever "having eyes full of adultery and that cannot cease from sin" (2 Peter 2:14). Help us to live in integrity before You and each other so that we will walk securely (Proverbs 10:9). Establish us in our faith. Keep us from being deceived by the world and the enemy (Colossians 2:6-8). Thank You, Lord, that we are complete in You and need not seek anything outside of what You have given us in each other and in You (Colossians 2:10). In Jesus' name I pray.

Prayer for Breakthrough in Me

LORD, HELP ME TO LOVE You with all my heart, soul, mind, and strength, and help me to love my husband (wife) the same way (Mark 12:30). Keep me far from the broad way that leads to destruction, and help me to always choose the narrow gate that leads to life (Matthew 7:13-14). Thank You for my husband (wife) and for the marriage You have given us. I smash down any dream I have entertained of being loved by someone else. Help me to see this as a false god I have set up to worship in place of You.

Lord, show me anything in me that has given place to infidelity in my heart. Wherever I have thought of another man (woman) and how it would be to be married to him (her) instead of my husband (wife), I confess that as sin. Where I have found myself attracted to someone of the opposite sex who is not my spouse, I also confess that before You as sin. Take all sinful and lustful thoughts out of my heart. I refuse to listen to the lies of the enemy telling me that anything would be better for me than what I have in my husband (wife).

I rebuke the devourer, who would come to destroy me with temptation, and say that I will serve only You, Lord. Thank You, Jesus, that You understand temptation and are able to help me when I am tempted (Hebrews 2:18). Lord, I ask that my desire would always be only for my husband (wife) and no one else. Help me to be so sold out to You that nothing and no one can buy my affections away from my husband (wife). In Jesus' name I pray.

Prayer for Breakthrough in My Husband (Wife)

LORD, I PRAY YOU WOULD fill my husband's (wife's) heart with Your Spirit so that it does not wander from me and our marriage to anyone else. Remove from him (her) all opportunities for anything inappropriate or anything that crosses the line of decency. Take away all lust and attraction from his (her) heart and replace it with Your love. Show me all I can do to build him (her) up and be the wife (husband) he (she) needs me to be. Help him (her) to flee all adulterous thoughts and be able to glorify You in his (her) body, soul, and spirit (1 Corinthians 6:18-20).

Where he (she) has crossed that line and succumbed to temptation in his (her) thoughts or deeds, restore him (her) to You. Help him (her) confess every transgression because his (her) sin will always be with him (her) until that happens (Psalm 51:1-3). Wash him (her) thoroughly from his (her) iniquity. I pray that if he (she) sins against You or me in any way, that his (her) sins will find him (her) out (Numbers 32:23). Deliver him (her) from all immorality. Do what it takes to bring him (her) to his (her) knees before You in repentance so that he (she) can be restored and cleansed to become "a vessel for honor" for Your glory prepared for every good work (2 Timothy 2:20-22). In Jesus' name I pray.

TRUTH TO STAND ON

Each one is tempted when he is drawn away by his own desires and
enticed. Then, when desire has conceived, it gives birth to sin;
and sin, when it is full-grown, brings forth death.

JAMES 1:14-15

No temptation has overtaken you except such as is common to man;
but God is faithful, who will not allow you to be tempted
beyond what you are able, but with the temptation will also make the
way of escape, that you may be able to bear it.

1 CORINTHIANS 10:13

This is the will of God, your sanctification:
that you should abstain from sexual immorality; that each of you should
know how to possess his own vessel in sanctification and honor.

1 THESSALONIANS 4:3-4

Nevertheless, because of sexual immorality, let each man have his own
wife, and let each woman have her own husband.

1 CORINTHIANS 7:2

Watch and pray, lest you enter into temptation.
The spirit indeed is willing, but the flesh is weak.

MATTHEW 26:41

13

If ONE *of* YOU DECIDES *to* LEAVE HOME

Separation begins in the heart long before anyone ever decides to move out of their home. It first starts when communication breaks down and the husband or wife no longer understands what the other is thinking, feeling, going through, or planning. It is reinforced by anger, rudeness, abuse, unforgiveness, or negative emotions. It intensifies when arguments happen over such things as the children, financial problems, one person's destructive behavior, or an unsatisfying to nonexistent sex life. The separation of heart grows wider if either the husband or the wife develops a hardness of heart, or it becomes obvious that they are no longer each other's top priority. Not long after that, divorce begins to be thought of as a way out of the marriage, and the separation process is nearly complete. All it will take is an act of infidelity or some other action that brings great hurt, and an overwhelming sense of hopelessness will push it all over the edge. At that point, leaving the marriage will seem like a relief.

The good news is that this process can be *stopped* at any point and totally *reversed* if there is *repentance* of heart and *forgiveness* flowing from *both* husband and wife to one another. All it takes is one person saying, "I don't want to go on like this. I want to make some changes. I want to seek the Lord and have Him make changes in you and me and in us together. Let's talk about the things that are bothering each of us and get counseling if we need to. I am willing to confess before you and before God anything I have done or not done that was wrong. I want to ask for your forgiveness. I am willing to do what it takes to turn things around and renew our marriage so it will last."

I guarantee that if a man or woman would say those words to their spouse and mean them, and if their spouse would receive them and agree to say the same thing in return, they could not only save their marriage, but they would make it better than they ever thought it could be. Sadly, too many people don't recognize the signs until it's too late. They are clueless to what is happening in themselves, and blind to all that is going on in their spouse.

How many stories have we heard about a husband who comes home to find that his wife has suddenly moved out? He is shocked and baffled, but this was not a quick decision for her. She had been contemplating this for a very long time. No woman decides to leave her home and marriage on a whim. And a woman with children will not leave her home without thinking long and hard about it. It is way too traumatic and difficult to uproot children, deprive them of their parent, and start all over while trying to support them and find child care. There has to be an emotional separation happening long before any physical separation occurs. If the husband was surprised, it's probably because he had not been listening for a very long time. Once a woman finally makes that decision, she is not going to come back unless there are some major changes made.

We've also heard countless stories of a wife who was suddenly left by her husband. Again, there were surely signs of emotional separation long before the physical separation occurred. There had to have been communication problems, sexual problems, or just plain compatibility problems. And she may not have been really listening to him for a long time, either. Of course, there are men who can be easily seduced by another woman and way too many women who will go after a married man. But the wife always has home field advantage if she makes herself and their home a place he doesn't want to leave. The reason a man can "suddenly" leave a marriage and do something impulsive, as in go off with his secretary, is because at that point he doubts if things will ever get any better at home.

Is There Ever a Right Time to Leave?

In regard to having a separation with the intent of working things out, you need to be led by the Holy Spirit. The case for a husband or wife leaving and separating from their spouse has to be made on the grounds that they care enough about the person they are leaving—as well as themselves and their children—to do what's best. The motivation must be to save and not to punish. They do it because staying would be worse. Sometimes extreme measures are needed in extreme situations.

There are some believers who think that separation is the best thing you can do for someone who needs a wake-up call. Sometimes it takes a major shock to force a person to face the truth about themselves and what they are doing. It is definitely a wake-up call when your spouse moves out of the home, but I have seen this tactic completely backfire and have the opposite effect. In one case, a husband moved out and separated from his wife over something relatively trivial, and this drove her into the arms and comfort of another man because of her tremendous fear of abandonment and rejection. That's why much prayer has to go into a decision like this. You have to have the mind of God. It is not a "one size fits all." There are no guarantees. "A man's heart plans his way, but the Lord directs his steps" (Proverbs 16:9). Make plans for your life, but not without the leading of the Holy Spirit.

One wife moved out and said she wouldn't come back if her husband didn't make major changes. But after much time passed and a great deal of effort had gone into counseling that did not prove productive, it was easy to just go ahead and file the divorce papers. If you are separated too long, it can seem more convenient to just stay separated. Of course, the best reason to separate is if there is abuse in the home directed at either a spouse or a child. You have to get away from a violent spouse and a volatile home situation until you both are calm enough to work things out. Also, if there is adultery, separation may be necessary before there can be restoration.

One young woman I know had just been married a couple years to a young man she had met in church. They had an adorable baby who was about a year old when she found out that her husband had been having an affair with someone at work. The young wife was devastated and immediately took the baby and moved in with her parents. She went for counseling at her church, and she, her parents, the counselor, and her pastor agreed that she should stay separated from him until he was willing to come in for counseling on a regular basis and do whatever it took to turn his life around.

The husband was so devastated that his wife and child were gone, and so disgusted with himself for what he had done, that he agreed to do whatever it took to restore his family. He started going regularly to counseling and to church, and he became so completely broken and repentant that he was able to experience a major deliverance from a longtime problem with sexual addiction. He had never faced his problem before, and his wife was unaware of it. His life was completely transformed, and his wife was totally forgiving. Only God can do that. She and the baby eventually moved back home with him, and the two of them started a business together that is thriving today. This was one of the greatest success stories I have heard with regard to separation as a solution. It is a perfect example of how a devastating situation can be turned around for the glory of God.

God says a woman is not to leave her husband, but if she does she is to remain unmarried or try to be reconciled to him (1 Corinthians 7:10-11). That means you don't just leave because you get a better offer. It means leaving is done with the intention of reconciling, if possible, or of protecting yourself or your children from a situation that is destroying you—whether physically, mentally, or emotionally.

If Separation Has Already Happened

If your spouse left you, or you have left him (her), there has to be a very good reason why there is so much unhappiness in your marriage. No one in a great marriage leaves their home and family. Ask God to show you what the true reasons are. Along with that, find a counselor and mature believers who can help you sort through your past, present, and future, and pray with you. Don't try to go through this alone. You need the support of others. You need to be candid about what is happening in your life and be able to ask for prayer concerning it.

Whenever you get a chance to meet your spouse face-to-face, if even for a moment, look your best. Don't wear the same thing he (she) has seen you in every day for the past five years. Be clean, fresh smelling, and put together well. Do something to enhance your attractiveness. Your competition for his (her) affection is out there doing all that and more. Give your spouse every reason to want to be with you again. Make yourself desirable, like you were when he (she) fell in love with you. When you have the opportunity to speak to your husband (wife), say words that are kind, loving, and appreciative. Ask God to flow His love through you to your husband (wife).

Ask God to bring your husband (wife) home and give you patience to wait for His timing. Praise God that in this waiting time you will have an opportunity to become more like the Lord. Thank Him that He has joy waiting for both of you in the midst of this trial.

Without sidestepping or minimizing what sins your spouse has committed that led to this separation, be willing to admit anything you have done or not done that has contributed as well. Tell your spouse that you want to work with him (her) to build a good life, and you are willing to do whatever it takes. Listen to his (her) complaints about whatever you've done wrong with an open and receptive heart. Even if your spouse says it's over and you are through, continue to pray. Many a heart has been changed because a husband and wife refused to stop praying.

While you are waiting for God to restore your marriage, go on a self-improvement marathon. Do whatever you need to do to improve yourself both spiritually, physically, emotionally, or mentally. Become appealing and magnetic. Grow your soul and your mind. Become interesting and interested.

Wives, a husband needs a wife, not a mother. Even if he has needed a mother that he didn't have at one time in his life, you are not the one to fill that role. So first of all, don't look like his mother. Fix yourself up so that you don't make him feel old because you look unatractive and dowdy. And don't act like his mother by nagging him about picking up his socks.

Husbands, a wife doesn't need a son; she needs a husband. So don't try to make her into your mother. You are the husband, so take charge of things that need to be done around the house and don't make her have to ask you over and over to do them. Treat her with honor, and she will honor you. Treat her like the best thing that ever happened to you, and she will be. And pick up your socks so she doesn't have to trip over them every day and be annoyed.

Remember that separation is not divorce. And it doesn't have to end in divorce. Not if you pray that it won't. With God, things can change. People can change. But they have to at least *want* to. They have to at least have some degree of love and appreciation for their spouse and want to see that fire rekindled and the marriage restored.

Deepening your relationship with God is one of the best things you can do for your marriage. Get close to God and ask Him to show you the truth about yourself, about your spouse, about your marriage, and about His ways.

God asks you to come to Him in your struggle and lay your problems at His feet, and He will give you a place of rest from them. Do that and you will have peace in your heart, no matter what is going on in your marriage.

TEN THINGS GOD SAYS
ABOUT FINDING A PLACE OF REST

1. *God has promised you rest.* "Therefore, since a promise remains of entering His rest, let us fear lest any of you seem to have come short of it" (Hebrews 4:1).

2. *You will find rest in God's presence.* "He said, 'My Presence will go with you, and I will give you rest'" (Exodus 33:14).

3. *God is with you to give you rest in every situation.* "Is not the LORD your God with you? And has He not given you rest on every side?" (1 Chronicles 22:18).

4. *God has rest and refreshing for you if you will listen to Him.* "He said, 'This is the rest with which You may cause the weary to rest,' and, 'This is the refreshing;' yet they would not hear" (Isaiah 28:12).

5. *God's rest is complete and all-encompassing.* "Now the LORD my God has given me rest on every side; there is neither adversary nor evil occurrence" (1 Kings 5:4).

6. *Because you are God's child, He has rest for your soul.* "There remains therefore a rest for the people of God" (Hebrews 4:9).

7. *When you are burdened, God will give you rest.* "Come to Me, all you who labor and are heavy laden, and I will give you rest" (Matthew 11:28).

8. *When you turn to God, you will find rest.* "In returning and rest you shall be saved; in quietness and confidence shall be your strength" (Isaiah 30:15).

9. *When you yoke up with God, He will give your soul rest.* "Take My yoke upon you and learn from Me, for I am gentle and lowly in heart, and you will find rest for your souls" (Matthew 11:29).

10. *When you obey God, you will find rest.* "To whom did He swear that they would not enter His rest, but to those who did not obey?" (Hebrews 3:18).

Time to Let Go

With all that being said about learning to find God's rest and not giving up hope when you are separated, there is a time when you need to let go. Of course, you need to release your spouse into God's hands right from the beginning of the separation, but I am talking about *really* letting go.

One lady I know tried to get her husband back for years after he left her. She was still trying to get him back even after he was married to someone else and had two children with his new wife. During her marriage to him, she never made any effort to look nice, smell nice, or keep the house clean. She never wore makeup or perfume, never fixed her hair to be in any way attractive, never wore clothes that had the least bit of flattering style to them, and never used a breath mint. A husband (wife) has to feel somewhat attracted to the person they are married to.

Her husband complained often about these things, but she paid no attention. She was child-obsessed, and that's where all her efforts went. Everything was for their children, and no attempt was made to please him. She was determined to homeschool all four of their children full-time, over the strong objections of her husband. He wanted to have some kind of companion in his wife, but she would not take any time away from her children, not even for a couple hours to go out to dinner with him. I'm all for homeschooling; I did it myself for a while. But if it becomes an issue in a marriage to the point of destroying the relationship, I don't see how that is ultimately benefiting the children.

When he first left her, she still made no effort whatsoever to clean up the house or fix herself up when he came to pick up their children for the day. She had a great opportunity right then to win him back, but she didn't use it to any advantage whatsoever. They ended up divorced, and she had to put the children in school full-time anyway and go to work. It would have taken so little effort to listen to her husband and see how strongly he felt and take the necessary steps to do what he needed. He needed a companion, a wife, and a sex partner, but she was so devoted to her children that she didn't have time to be any of the above. She never saw that if she really cared about her children, she would have made sure they had a happy father. Her children would have had an easier time in school than they did living through the divorce of their parents.

That's why it is important to listen carefully to your spouse. What are the comments, observations, or opinions he (she) has made in the past? Think back. Have any of them been repeated, even subtly? Try to understand the signs. Do you remember the example of Wrigley and the praying paws in the communication chapter? His wants were expressed so subtly, and we knew that if we didn't read him right, there might be an unpleasant mess to clean up. Do you get my analogy here? Ask God to show you what is really going on in your mate's heart and life. You may *think* you know, but no one really knows the heart of another without being told. Only God sees the inner workings of the heart. Ask Him to show you what your spouse won't reveal.

I used to wonder why people could be married for 35 years and then get a divorce. I thought if you stuck it out that long, why wouldn't you stay with it the rest of the way? But I realize that the older you get, the harder it is to take abuse of any kind. You come to a point where you realize you don't have that many years left, and you absolutely cannot spend them being miserable the way you have been. Don't let that happen to you. If you are miserable now, do something about it. It is not going to get better on its own. Talk to your spouse and make him (her) listen to how you feel. Ask him (her) to talk to you about what is going on inside of him (her). Go to counseling if you need to.

If you and your spouse have never even considered moving out, thank God and ask Him what each of you can do to make sure that neither of you would ever want to. Pray that God will help you do whatever it takes to see that you never become separated in your hearts. Pray for wisdom so you can be the best wife (husband) possible. "If any of you lacks wisdom, let him ask of God, who gives to all liberally and without reproach, and it will be given to him" (James 1:5). Ask God to make you both so wise that you will have enough sense to never get separated in your hearts in the first place.

PRAYERS FOR MY MARRIAGE

Prayer for Protection

LORD, I PRAY YOU WOULD protect my marriage from the separation of heart that can happen when two people stop communicating. Help us to always be in close contact and emotionally current with one another. Help us to learn to do what pleases the other and not be neglectful of each other's needs. Teach us to be kind when we could be stern, merciful when we could be judgmental, and forgiving when we could take offense. Open our eyes whenever either of us is blind to what is going on inside the other. Show us where we have been preoccupied with other things and other people. Give us revelation so that we can see the truth and stay on the path You have for us (Proverbs 29:18).

Lord, Your Word says that You allow calamity because of sin when people forsake You and worship other gods (Jeremiah 1:16). I pray that my husband (wife) and I will never depart from Your ways and get so wrapped up in other things that we begin to serve those things instead of You. Keep us on track and on the path You have for us so that calamity never comes near us. One of the greatest calamities would be to separate from one another. I pray that it would never happen to us in any way. Help us to always pray and be watchful about this. If You are *for* us, who can be *against* us? (Romans 8:31). In Jesus' name I pray.

Prayer for Breakthrough in Me

LORD, I CONFESS ANY PLACE where I have separated myself in my heart from my husband (wife). I break that hardness in me that has kept me distanced—whether as a self-protective measure or just by being preoccupied with other things. I know any kind of distance between two people, especially whom You have made to be one, goes against Your will. I recognize this state of mind as an offense against You. Thank You that because of Your love for me, I am more than a conqueror, and I can conquer this. Thank You that nothing can ever separate me from Your love (Romans 8:37-39).

I refuse to let myself become anxious about any sense of distance I feel between my husband (wife) and me. Instead, I come to You with thanksgiving for who You are and all that You have done for us, and I let my requests be made known to You. Thank You that Your peace which passes all understanding will keep my heart and mind in Christ Jesus (Philippians 4:6-7). I will not let my heart be troubled, but I will trust in You instead (John 14:1). I know that Your grace is sufficient for me and Your strength is made perfect in my weakness. I can trust that when I am weak You will make me strong, because I depend on You (2 Corinthians 12:9-10). Even if I am deserted, You are still here for me and will be to me what my husband (wife) can't or doesn't want to be (Isaiah 54:4-5). If it ever does come to a separation between us, I pray that You would help us to be reconciled to one another again. Bring forth any changes in both of us that are needed. In Jesus' name I pray.

Prayer for Breakthrough in My Husband (Wife)

LORD, WHERE MY HUSBAND (WIFE) has separated from me in any way—whether physically, emotionally, or mentally—I pray You would bring him (her) back. Thank You, Lord, that even though he (she) may leave me, You have promised that You never will (Deuteronomy 31:6). Lord, I pray for restoration of any emotional and physical separation between us. Change our hearts and help me to be everything he (she) needs me to be. Restore us emotionally together again. Give me courage and strength to fight for our relationship until it is the way You want it to be.

I pray that he (she) will not be lured into any trap or enticement by the enemy. Open his (her) eyes to see that if You are for us, no one can be against us and succeed (Romans 8:31). Help him (her) to understand that separation, except for the purpose of working things out, is not Your perfect will for our lives. I trust that anything we go through will be for Your glory (Romans 8:18). Enable him (her) to "taste and see that" You are a good God and that he (she) will find the greatest blessings by following You and trusting in Your ways. (Psalm 34:8).

Help him (her) to hear Your voice and follow You (John 10:27). Draw us both closer to You and closer to each other. Where our love for one another has failed, help us to fall in love all over again in even greater measure than ever before. Just as no one can "separate us from the love of Christ," I pray that nothing will be able to separate us from our love for each other (Romans 8:35). In Jesus' name I pray.

TRUTH TO STAND ON

I consider that the sufferings of this present time
are not worthy to be compared with the glory
which shall be revealed in us.

ROMANS 8:18

Count it all joy when you fall into various trials,
knowing that the testing of your faith produces patience.
But let patience have its perfect work,
that you may be perfect and complete, lacking nothing.

JAMES 1:3-4

Two are better than one, because they have a good
reward for their labor. For if they fall,
one will lift up his companion.
But woe to him who is alone when he falls,
for he has no one to help him up.

ECCLESIASTES 4:9-10

The LORD will perfect that which concerns me;
Your mercy, O LORD, endures forever;
do not forsake the works of Your hands.

PSALM 138:8

He Himself has said, "I will never leave you nor forsake you."
So we may boldly say: "The LORD is my helper;
I will not fear. What can man do to me?"

HEBREWS 13:5-6

14

If HOPE SEEMS LOST *and* YOU NEED *a* MIRACLE

There are seasons in every marriage. First there is the romantic-in-love-exciting-passionate-fun-getting-to-know-each-other period. This is when love is so heady you can't see clearly, which means you can't clearly see what you've gotten into. The intensity of that period will fade no matter how you try to keep it from happening, and although that feeling is great, it is entirely exhausting. The next stage is the busy-making-a-home-establishing-a-career time. When the children come there is the too-little-sleep-never-a-moment-when-something-doesn't-need-to-be-done-and-there-is-not-enough-time-in-a-day period. Later comes the children-are-gone-and-you-have-to-remember-why-you-got-married-and-get-to-know-each-other-and-fall-in-love-all-over-again period. Then it's the I'm-too-old-to-put-up-with-this-anymore-and-I-don't-want-to-spend-what-little-time-I-have-left-with-this-kind-of-misery-so-there-have-to-be-some-changes-made season. And that's where a lot of marriages end. But if you can work hard and both be willing to make changes and get past that, you will have the I-hope-we-grow-old-together-because-I-don't-want-to-be-with-anyone-else-and-I-know-we-will-take-care-of-each-other-until-the-end period to look forward to.

Things can go wrong in a marriage in any one of these seasons, but if you know these times are coming, and you know they will end, it makes getting through them a lot easier. It gives you hope in each season.

You may feel full of hope about your marriage today, and if so, I pray that it will always be that way for you. May you both be prisoners of hope no matter what happens in your lives together (Zechariah 9:12). However, if you ever do start to feel hopeless about any particular aspect of your marriage, let this chapter be an encouragement to you. And if you ever get to the point where you feel that all hope is lost for your marriage and it would take nothing less than a miracle to save it, then I have good news for you. God is in the miracle business. That means even if it got so bad that you were in divorce proceedings, and the divorce papers had already been signed and the ink is completely dry, there is still hope.

Over the years I have heard from countless couples who had come to that point in the divorce proceedings and one of them started to pray for the other and things turned around to the point of total reconciliation. They canceled all plans to be divorced and got completely back together. Some had to get remarried because the divorce was final.

One particular couple is precious to me because their story is so touching and miraculous. They waited for more than two hours while I signed books, and they came up to me at the end of the line. They told me they had experienced great strife in their marriage and had separated. While they were separated, he was put in prison for a year, and she eventually filed for divorce. He received the Lord while in prison, and the day before he was to be released, someone gave him a copy of *The Power of a Praying Husband*. He read the entire book the day and night before he was to be freed from prison, and he said he knew in those moments as he was reading that his life would never be the same. He called his wife when he got out and told her what had happened and that God had revealed to him what kind of husband he was supposed to be and how he needed to be praying for her every day. He asked her to take him back, and he promised to do whatever it took to be the husband she needed.

His part of the story was amazing enough, but then his wife continued, saying that she too had been given a book just a few days before he was to be released called *The Power of a Praying Wife*. When she read it, she said her eyes were opened as to how she needed to be praying for her husband. As they were relating this story to me, their eyes filled with tears and they struggled to get out the words without choking up. They told me that they had driven hundreds of miles just to tell me their story and to thank me in person for writing the books and saving their marriage. They had canceled their divorce and were back together, and their marriage was strong and their lives had been set on a totally different path than they had ever been on before. They showed me their worn books and asked if I would sign a special message to them. I told them that meeting them and hearing their story was one of the best gifts I have ever received, and I will always remember them and keep them in my prayers. They were in a hopeless situation, but when they started to pray for one another, God did a miracle.

Our God is a God of hope. He is the all-powerful God of the universe, and nothing is too hard for Him. What He did for them, He can do for you if you will commit to pray for your husband (wife). He will be with you to guide and help you every step of the way. God's will is to save, restore, and preserve your marriage, and if you seek Him for that, He will give you everything you need to do it.

Waiting for Your Miracle

You may not feel hopeless about your entire marriage, but perhaps just one aspect of it. Maybe your spouse has a habit that drives you crazy. Or maybe you have a problem your spouse has no patience with, and without his (her) support you feel you cannot overcome it. You may feel hopeless because you can't see how your situation can ever be any different. But take comfort in knowing that as long as you walk close to God, your sorrow will end. "Weeping may endure for a night, but joy comes in the morning" (Psalm 30:5). There are no guarantees that your spouse will change, but it is certain that *you* will. And if *you* do, it's a good possibility that *he (she)* will eventually too. Your trouble will be gone one way or another.

Because God is a God of miracles, He can bring back what has been lost or resurrect what has died. When you turn to God as your only hope for a miracle, you are in the best position to receive one. But you must come to the point where you give up—not on the marriage, but on trying to make a miracle happen yourself. Humble yourself before God like a child and tell Him you can't do this without Him (Matthew 18:4). Tell Him you have to come to the point where your hope is entirely in Him, and you trust that because of His great love for you, you will never be disappointed by the hope that is in you. The hope that is in you reflects your faith in God. And all things are possible to him who believes (Romans 5:5).

Hope in the Lord means that anything can happen because God is in charge, and He is the God of the impossible. He can turn anything around in an instant. You can be in despair one moment, and suddenly there can be a change of heart and you are headed in the direction of joy. The greatest thing you can do while waiting for your miracle is to let the joy of the Lord rise in your heart.

Hope allows you to keep making plans for your future. Hopelessness keeps you from seeing a future at all.

Jesus said, "By your patience possess your souls" (Luke 21:19). At first glance this verse seems as if you almost have to be passive and wait around for things to happen and someday maybe they will get under control. But Jack Hayford says, "In this verse, the Greek word for 'patience' *(hupomone)* means 'to bear up under pressure.' That is the call of the hour as the pressure of seducing spirits linked to the last days are loose and at work" (*The Anatomy of Seduction*, p. 45).

With this perspective and dimension of understanding, the word "patience" becomes very active. Being patient—or bearing up under pressure—is how we win. Sometimes victory comes simply because we are not giving up—even if we have to fight one battle after another. Too many people give up way too early. I could have given up in my marriage a long time before I started to see changes in my husband—and in me. But both of us have truly changed. And I believe these changes are lasting because God did a miracle in our lives. I feel Michael and I communicate far better, and he doesn't let anger control him as before. It took a lot of prayer, and bearing up under pressure (patience), but it happened. We made it, and we are in that last stage now where we know we will always be together, and whatever happens we will work it out. There is great peace in that.

That's why you can't view losing hope as the end of the world. It is actually a setup for God to do a miracle. We win by standing strong to the end. We say, "God, help me to be at peace where I am right now in the situation I am in, knowing You won't leave me there forever. Help me to say as Paul did that, " 'I have learned in whatever state I am, to be content' " (Philippians 4:11).

As long as you are walking with God, and you have not turned your back on the Holy Spirit, then you are going from glory to glory and strength to strength, whether it feels like it or not. "We all, with unveiled face, beholding as in a mirror the glory of the Lord, are being transformed into the same image from glory to glory, just as by the Spirit of the Lord" (2 Corinthians 3:18). You are becoming more like Him. So once you pray, believe that God has heard and move into the peace that He has for you while you bear up under pressure. It's not the kind of peace you can get from anything in the world, because there is no earthly reason for it (John 14:27).

TEN THINGS TO REMEMBER ABOUT GOD'S PEACE

1. *Knowing God brings peace and strength.* "The LORD will give strength to His people; the LORD will bless His people with peace" (Psalm 29:11).

2. *Seeing that the Lord fights for you brings peace.* "The LORD will fight for you, and you shall hold your peace" (Exodus 14:14).

3. *Humility brings peace.* "The meek shall inherit the earth, and shall delight themselves in the abundance of peace" (Psalm 37:11).

4. *Obedience brings peace.* "Oh, that you had heeded My commandments! Then your peace would have been like a river" (Isaiah 48:18).

5. *Faith brings peace.* "Your faith has saved you. Go in peace" (Luke 7:50).

6. *Knowing Jesus brings us His peace.* "Peace I leave with you, My peace I give to you; not as the world gives do I give to you. Let not your heart be troubled, neither let it be afraid" (John 14:27).

7. *Life in the Spirit brings peace.* "To be carnally minded is death, but to be spiritually minded is life and peace" (Romans 8:6).

8. *Living God's way brings peace.* "The work of righteousness will be peace, and the effect of righteousness, quietness and assurance forever" (Isaiah 32:17).

9. *Loving God's laws brings peace and protection.* "Great peace

have those who love Your law, and nothing causes them to stumble" (Psalm 119:165).

10. **Pursuing peace with others brings the peace of God.** "Pursue peace with all people, and holiness, without which no one will see the Lord" (Hebrews 12:14).

If You Have Lost All Hope

Even if you or your husband (wife) has given up hope on the marriage, if just *one of you* wants your marriage transformed, and *God* wants your marriage transformed, that's two out of three. And that is a powerful enough majority to sway the last third of the equation. Pray that God will give you and your husband (wife) the ability to see the situation from the Lord's perspective. Pray that you both will be able to lift your eyes up to the hills where your help comes from (Psalm 121:1).

If you are truly wanting to see your marriage restored to wholeness or made to be all it is supposed to be, don't be around people who tell you you are crazy to even consider being together. (Unless, of course, you are in an abusive situation and they are trying to tell you something for your own good.) Pray that any pain, disappointment, or discouragement you or your spouse experience will drive you closer to God and not further away. Find people who are supportive of what you are trying to do and believe for in your marriage.

If you've been married long enough to experience more than a few trials, know that prayer to the almighty God of the universe, who invented marriage in the first place, unleashes His power to restore it. God says, "When you pass through the waters, I will be with you; and through the rivers, they shall not overflow you. When you walk through the fire, you shall not be burned, nor shall the flame scorch you. For I am the LORD your God, the Holy One of Israel, your Savior" (Isaiah 43:2-3).

Remember that hopelessness doesn't happen overnight, although things can happen suddenly that thrust you into a hopeless state. Hopelessness usually happens little by little, as each offense, each disappointment, each hurt builds up until discouragement sets in and covers those things like cement, solidifying the wall that has been built. Hopelessness usually happens when your prayers have not yet been answered and you don't believe they ever will be.

You may feel as though you and your marriage are in a free fall and only the hand of God can reach out and save you before you crash at the bottom, but your prayers can influence the hand of God at any moment. That's why you always have hope. When you have given up hope that *anything* will ever be any different, know that God's will is to change *everything* in your life. Know that you can reject hopelessness and put your hope in a miracle-working God.

When you put your hope in God, you will not be disappointed (Isaiah 49:23), good things will happen to you (Lamentations 3:25), you will please God (Psalm 147:11), you won't need to be sad (Psalm 42:11), and you will find rest (Psalm 62:5).

TEN GOOD REASONS TO NOT LOSE HOPE

1. *You have hope because of Jesus.* "Blessed be the God and Father of our Lord Jesus Christ, who according to His abundant mercy has begotten us again to a living hope through the resurrection of Jesus Christ from the dead" (1 Peter 1:3).

2. *God's plan is to give you hope.* " 'I know the thoughts that I think toward you,' says the LORD, 'thoughts of peace and not of evil, to give you a future and a hope' " (Jeremiah 29:11).

3. *God's Word gives you hope.* "For whatever things were written before were written for our learning, that we through the patience and comfort of the Scriptures might have hope" (Romans 15:4).

4. *God is pleased when you put your hope in Him.* "The Lord takes pleasure in those who fear Him, in those who hope in His mercy" (Psalm 147:11).

5. *When you put your hope in God, He keeps His eye on you.* "But the eyes of the LORD are on those who fear him, on those whose hope is in his unfailing love" (Psalm 33:18 NIV).

6. *There is always hope for your future.* "There is surely a future hope for you, and your hope will not be cut off" (Proverbs 23:18 NIV).

7. ***God fills you with hope as you put your trust in Him.*** "May the God of hope fill you with all joy and peace as you trust in him, so that you may overflow with hope by the power of the Holy Spirit" (Romans 15:13 NIV).

8. ***You always have hope that God will deliver you.*** "He has delivered us from such a deadly peril, and he will deliver us. On him we have set our hope that He will continue to deliver us" (2 Corinthians 1:10 NIV).

9. ***We have hope because God is faithful to keep His promise.*** "Let us hold fast the confession of our hope without wavering, for He who promised is faithful" (Hebrews 10:23).

10. ***True hope is when you don't give up, even when you see every reason to.*** "We were saved in this hope, but hope that is seen is not hope; for why does one still hope for what he sees?" (Romans 8:24).

The love and respect that is commanded in the Bible between husband and wife is not based on "if you feel like it" or "if your spouse deserves it." It's based on doing what God says to do because He has poured love into your heart. God loves us even when we do something wrong and disappoint Him. He loves us even when we forget to love Him back and neglect to spend time with Him. He says we are to love others even when they don't seem to love us. "If you love those who love you, what reward have you?" (Matthew 5:46). The reason we can love at all times is because of the unconditional love of God poured into our hearts.

That's why you have to keep loving your spouse, even when hope seems lost. Don't allow negative thoughts about yourself, your spouse, or your marriage to dominate your mind. Demand of your thoughts that they be positive and good. Cast down every argument that "exalts itself against the knowledge of God, bringing every thought into captivity to the obedience of Christ" (2 Corinthians 10:5). Require of yourself to be loving to others the way the Lord is toward you. Set your heart as Daniel did to understand the Lord and His ways, and humble yourself before Him. The angel said to Daniel, "Do not fear, Daniel, for from the first day that you set your heart to understand, and to humble yourself before your God, your words were heard; and I have come because of your words" (Daniel 10:12). That means your prayers are being heard too. And there will come a day when you will say, "I am so glad I put my hope in the Lord, because He did not disappoint me." The Lord will bring change when you cry out to Him with a pure heart and ask Him to move in power in your life and in the life of your husband or wife. Refuse to give up hope.

PRAYERS FOR MY MARRIAGE

Prayer for Protection

LORD, I COMMIT MY MARRIAGE to You. May it become all You want it to be. Even in times where we may suffer hurt or misunderstanding, I believe You are able to keep all I have committed to You (2 Timothy 1:12). I pray You would help my husband (wife) and me to never fall into hopelessness, especially with regard to our relationship and marriage. Help us to grow strong in faith—faith in You and in each other. Help us to put our hope in You, for You are our helper and protector (Psalm 33:20). May Your unfailing love and favor rest on us (Psalm 33:22). Enable us to inherit all You have for us because we have hope in our hearts (Psalm 37:9).

Lord, I pray we will always have patience to wait for You to work in our lives and our marriage. Thank You that because You were crucified and resurrected from the dead, we can have hope that You will resurrect anything in our lives no matter how dead and hopeless it may seem (1 Peter 1:3). Help us to not give up on each other, but rather to "let patience have its perfect work" in us so that we "may be perfect and complete, lacking nothing" (James 1:4). Help us to "lay aside every weight, and the sin which so easily ensnares us, and let us run with endurance the race that is set before us, looking unto Jesus, the author and finisher of our faith, who for the joy that was set before Him endured the cross" (Hebrews 12:1-2). Help us to keep our eyes on You. In Jesus' name I pray.

Prayer for Breakthrough in Me

LORD, I COME BEFORE YOU and cast all my cares at Your feet, knowing that You care for me (1 Peter 5:7). I thank You that Your plans for me are for a good future filled with peace and hope (Jeremiah 29:11). Help me to remember that no matter what is happening in my life and in my marriage, You will never leave me or forsake me.

Lord, I confess as sin any time I have felt hopeless about my situation and especially about important aspects of my marriage. Your Word says that "hope deferred makes the heart sick, but when desire comes, it is a tree of life" (Proverbs 13:12). When time passes for so long and I see no change, I feel heartsick and hopeless. But I confess any hopelessness I have to You, for You have said that whatever doesn't come from faith is sin (Romans 14:23). It reveals that my faith in Your power to change things is weak. I pray that You would help me to not hesitate to hope again out of fear that I will be disappointed. I commit to trusting in You at all times. I pour out my heart before You, knowing You are my God of refuge (Psalm 62:8).

Help me to become like a child—entirely dependent upon You, for I know that this is the safest place I can be. I pray that You would "search me, O God, and know my heart; try me, and know my anxieties; and see if there is any wicked way in me, and lead me in the way everlasting" (Psalm 139:23-24). Enable me to become all I need to be. In the midst of challenges in my marriage I say, "Be merciful to me, O God, be merciful to me! For my soul trusts in You; and in the shadow of Your wings I will make my refuge, until these calamities have passed by" (Psalm 57:1).

Even though we may suffer at times in this marriage because of things one of us has done or not done, I know that You are "able to do exceedingly abundantly above all that we ask or think, according to the power that works in us" (Ephesians 3:20-21). I will be strong and take heart because my hope is in You (Psalm 31:24). Thank You that You put my tears in Your bottle (Psalm 56:8). I pray that You, Holy Spirit, would give me "beauty for ashes, the oil of joy for mourning, and the garment of praise for the spirit of heaviness" (Isaiah 61:1-3). Make me to be a pillar of righteousness for Your glory. Help me to not cease my "work of faith, labor of love, and patience of hope in our Lord Jesus Christ" for I know You can change everything in my life (1 Thessalonians 1:3). In Jesus' name I pray.

Prayer for Breakthrough in My Husband (Wife)

LORD, I COMMIT MY HUSBAND (WIFE) into Your hands. I pray that any hopelessness he (she) has felt about himself (herself) will be taken out of his (her) heart. Make him (her) all You created him (her) to be. Break down any strongholds in his (her) mind where hopelessness has been allowed to reign. Help him (her) to put his (her) hope in You and understand that it is not by our might or power, but by Your Spirit that our relationship can be transformed to become all it was made to be. Take away any hopelessness he (she) feels about me, our marriage, and our life together. Thank You that You are the God of hope, and You are "the same yesterday, today, and forever" (Hebrews 13:8).

Holy Spirit, help my husband (wife) to understand that because of You our situation is never hopeless (John 14:26). Even though we may have difficulties, we are not crushed because You sustain us. We don't have to live with despair because our hope is in You. "We are hard pressed on every side, yet not crushed; we are perplexed, but not in despair" (2 Corinthians 4:8). I pray that the eyes of his (her) understanding will be opened so that he (she) may know the hope of Your calling on his (her) life, and come to understand "what is the exceeding greatness" of Your power toward those who believe (Ephesians 1:18-19). Give him (her) unfailing hope and faith in You. In Jesus' name I pray.

Truth to Stand On

Those who wait on the Lord shall renew their strength;
they shall mount up with wings like eagles,
they shall run and not be weary,
they shall walk and not faint.

Isaiah 40:31

For everyone who asks receives, and he who seeks finds,
and to him who knocks it will be opened.

Matthew 7:8

The righteous cry out, and the Lord hears,
and delivers them out of all their troubles.

Psalm 34:17 niv

O Israel, put your hope in the Lord,
for with the Lord is unfailing love and
with him is full redemption.

Psalm 130:7 niv

Being confident of this very thing,
that He who has begun a good work in you
will complete it until the day of Jesus Christ.

Philippians 1:6

PLAN *to* BE *a* SUCCESS STORY

Just last week I heard of another couple close to us who are getting a divorce. They are Christian parents of two and are well known in our community. They always seemed like the perfect family, so talented and funny. Everyone loves them. Their family is being *ripped apart* now, and all the people around them are *deeply saddened*.

Today I talked with a single mom who was married for 25 years but has been divorced for five, and she is still hurting over the divorce. She works very hard to support herself and her two children, and she always struggles with guilt over the time she has to be away from them in order to do that. Her entire extended family has been *negatively impacted* by this.

Recently a well-respected pastor divorced his wife because she resumed an unholy relationship with an old boyfriend. There had been tremendous loneliness in their marriage for some time. The congregation and the community are *shaken*, as well as their children.

Days ago a wonderful young couple severed their relationship completely because of a terrible misunderstanding on both their parts. Their families are *devastated and grieved,* and the *fallout* seems to be without end.

I know all of these fine people personally, and it breaks my heart to see their *sadness and pain*—especially when I know that it all could have been avoided because God has a better way. I don't judge them. I know how hard it is to make a marriage work. But I also know that it is worth every effort to rise above the problems and hurt and see that your marriage not only survives, but becomes good and solid. That's what happened in my marriage, and it was worth the years it took of praying and learning to live God's way, even in the face of hopelessness. It was worth having my heart reconstructed by God until repentance, forgiveness, and love flowed through it every day no matter what. This is something God did because I was willing to do what it takes. That's why my prayer for you is that you too will find the strength, faith, and courage to do whatever it takes to see your marriage become one of the success stories. And I will be pulling for you all the way.

Michael & Stormie

have been married for more than three decades
and have three grown children.

The Power of a
PRAYING®
WIFE

STORMIE OMARTIAN

HARVEST HOUSE PUBLISHERS

EUGENE, OREGON

THE POWER OF A PRAYING® WIFE

Copyright © 1997 by Stormie Omartian
Published by Harvest House Publishers
Eugene, Oregon 97402
www.harvesthousepublishers.com

The Library of Congress has cataloged the edition as follows:

Omartian, Stormie.
  The power of a praying wife / Stormie Omartian.
    p.   cm.

Trade Edition	Deluxe Edition
ISBN 978-0-7369-1924-1	ISBN 978-0-7369-0600-5

  1. Wives—Religious life.   2. Intercessory prayer—Christianity.
I. Title.
BV4527.043 1997   97-7436
248.8'435—dc21   CIP

This book is dedicated with love to my husband, Michael, who has consistently given me more than I ever wanted to pray about. You and I both know that prayer works.

Contents

Acknowledgments

With special thanks:

- To my secretary, Susan Martinez, for bearing the load of another book deadline. Your love as a sister, faithfulness as a friend, and richness as a prayer partner can only be equaled by your efficiency and dedication as my highly treasured and irreplaceable assistant.

- To my prayer partners and fellow praying wives, Sally Anderson, Susan Martinez, Donna Summer, Katie Stewart, Roz Thompson, and Jan Williamson, who have experienced along with me what gut-level, crying-out-to-God intercession for our husbands really means. Without your deep and faithful commitment to God and to prayer, this book might never have been written. You are eternal treasures in my heart.

- To my daughter, Mandy, and my son, Chris, for loving your dad and me, even through the times we didn't model for you the best way to run a marriage. I regret any time we argued in front of you, before we learned that prayer is more powerful than contention. I pray that you will carry all the good we have learned into your own marriages.

- To my new son, John David Kendrick, for letting me be your mom on earth now that your dad is in heaven with your mom. You are what our family has been missing all these years and we didn't know it until you came to be with us.

- To Pastor Jack and Anna Hayford, and Pastor Dale and Joan Evrist for teaching me how to pray and showing me the way a good marriage works.

- To my Harvest House family, Bob Hawkins Sr., Bob Hawkins Jr., Bill Jensen, Julie McKinney, Teresa Evenson, Betty Fletcher, and LaRae Weikert for your enthusiasm about the book and your consistently positive input. You are all a delight. And to Editorial Director Carolyn McCready for being such a joy. Thank you for your encouragement.

- To my editor, Holly Halverson, for your good eye and sharp mind.

- To Tom and Patti Brussat, Michael and Terry Harriton, Jan and Dave Williamson, and Dave and Priscilla Navarro for sharing your lives and experiences in order to give me good examples of the power of a praying wife.

Foreword

There is a joke in our household when I refer to the number of years Stormie and I have been married. I always say, "It's been twenty-five wonderful years for me and twenty-five miserable years for her." After twenty-five years of marriage to Stormie, there aren't any phases of my complex personality left for her to discover. She has seen me triumph, fail, struggle, be fearful and depressed, and doubt my competency as a husband, father, and musician. She has seen me angry at God because He wouldn't jump when I asked Him to. She has witnessed miracles, as God redeemed something from the ashes to gold. Every step of the way has been accompanied by her prayers and this book was written from her experience over the years. I cannot imagine what my life would be without her praying for me. It gives me comfort and security, and also fulfills the mission the Lord has for us to pray for each other and bear one another's burdens. I can think of no better way to truly love your husband than by lifting him up in prayer on a consistent basis. It is a priceless gift that helps him experience God's blessings and grace.

Stormie, I love you.

Your covered-in-prayer husband,
Michael

Who can find a virtuous wife? For her worth is far above rubies. The heart of her husband safely trusts her; so he will have no lack of gain. She does him good and not evil all the days of her life.

PROVERBS 31:10-12

The Power

First of all, let me make it perfectly clear that the power of a praying wife is not a means of gaining control over your husband, so don't get your hopes up! In fact, it is quite the opposite. It's laying down all claim to power in and of yourself, and relying on *God's* power to transform you, your husband, your circumstances, and your marriage. This power is not given to wield like a weapon in order to beat back an unruly beast. It's a gentle tool of restoration appropriated through the prayers of a wife who longs to *do* right more than *be* right, and to *give life* more than *get even*. It's a way to invite God's power into your husband's life for his greatest blessing, which is ultimately yours, too.

When my husband, Michael, and I were first married and differences arose between us, praying was definitely not my first thought. In fact, it was closer to a last resort. I tried other methods first such as arguing, pleading, ignoring, avoiding, confronting, debating, and of course the ever-popular silent treatment, all with far less than satisfying results. It took some time to realize that by praying *first*, these unpleasant methods of operation could be avoided.

By the time you read this book, Michael and I will have been married over a quarter of a century. This is nothing less than miraculous. It's certainly not a testimony to our greatness, but to God's faithfulness to answer prayer. I confess that even after all these years, I am still learning about this and it doesn't come easy. While I may not have as much practice doing it right as I have had doing it wrong, I can say without reservation that *prayer works*.

Unfortunately, I didn't learn how to *really* pray for my husband until I started praying for my children. As I saw profound answers to prayer for them, I decided to try being just as detailed and fervent in praying for him. But I found that praying for children is far easier. From the first moment we lay eyes on them, we want the best for their lives—unconditionally, wholeheartedly, without question. But with a husband, it's often not that simple—especially for someone who's been married awhile. A husband can hurt your feelings, be inconsiderate, uncaring, abusive, irritating, or negligent. He can say or do things that pierce your heart like a sliver. And every time you start to pray for him, you find the sliver festering. It's obvious you can't give yourself to praying the way God wants you to until you are rid of it.

Praying for your husband is not the same as praying for a child (even though it may seem similar), because you are not your husband's mother. We have authority over our children that is given to us by the Lord. We *don't* have authority over our husbands. However, we have been given authority "over all the power of the enemy" (Luke 10:19) and can do great damage to the enemy's plans when we pray. Many difficult things that happen in a marriage relationship are actually part of the enemy's plan set up for its demise. But we can say, "I will not allow anything to destroy my marriage."

"I will not stand by and watch my husband be wearied, beaten down, or destroyed."

"I will not sit idle while an invisible wall goes up between us."

"I will not allow confusion, miscommunication, wrong attitudes, and bad choices to erode what we are trying to build together."

"I will not tolerate hurt and unforgiveness leading us to divorce." We can take a stand against any negative influences in our marriage relationship and know that God has given us authority in His name to back it up.

You have the means to establish a hedge of protection around your marriage because Jesus said, "Whatever you bind on earth will be bound in heaven, and whatever you loose on earth will be loosed in heaven" (Matthew 18:18). You have authority in the name of Jesus to *stop evil* and *permit good*. You can submit to God in prayer whatever controls your husband—alcoholism, workaholism, laziness, depression, infirmity, abusiveness, anxiety, fear, or failure— and pray for him to be released from it.

Wait! Before You Write Off the Marriage . . . . .

I confess right now that there was a time when I considered separation or divorce. This is an embarrassing disclosure because I don't believe either of those options is the best answer to a troubled marriage. I believe in God's position on divorce. He says it's not right and it grieves Him. The last thing I want to do is grieve God. But I know what it's like to feel the kind of despair that paralyzes good decision making. I've experienced the degree of hopelessness that causes a person to give up on trying to do what's right. I understand the torture of loneliness that leaves you longing for anyone who will look into your soul and see *you*.

I've felt pain so bad that the fear of dying from it propelled me to seek out the only immediately foreseeable means of survival: escape from the source of agony. I know what it's like to contemplate acts of desperation because you see no future. I've experienced such a buildup of negative emotions day after day that separation and divorce seemed like nothing more than the promise of pleasant relief.

The biggest problem I faced in our marriage was my husband's temper. The only ones who were ever the object of his anger were me and the children. He used words like weapons that left me crippled or paralyzed. I'm not saying that I was without fault—quite the contrary. I was sure I was as much to blame as he, but I didn't know what to do about it. I pleaded with God on a regular basis to make my husband more sensitive, less angry, more pleasant, less irritable. But I saw few changes. Was God not listening? Or did He favor the husband over the wife, as I suspected?

After a number of years, with little change, I cried out to the Lord one day in despair, saying, "God, I can't live this way anymore. I know what You've said about divorce, but I can't live in the same house with him. Help me, Lord." I sat on the bed holding my Bible for hours as I struggled with the strongest desire to take the children and leave. I believe that because I came to God in total honesty about what I felt, He allowed me to thoroughly and clearly envision what life would be like if I left: Where I would live, how I would support myself and care for the children, who would still be my friends, and worst of all, how a heritage of divorce would affect my son and daughter. It was the most horrible and unspeakably sad picture. If I left I would find some relief, but at the price of everything dear to me. I knew it wasn't God's plan for us.

As I sat there, God also impressed upon my heart that if I would deliberately lay down my life before His throne, die to the desire to leave, and give my needs to Him, He would teach me how to lay down my life in prayer for Michael. He would show me how to really intercede for him as a son of God, and in the process He would revive my marriage and pour His blessings out on both of us. We would be better together, if we could get past this, than we could ever be separated and alone. He showed me that Michael was caught in a web from his past that rendered him incapable of being different from what he was at that moment, but God would use me as an instrument of His deliverance if I would consent to it. It hurt to say yes to this and I cried a lot. But when I did, I felt hopeful for the first time in years.

I began to pray every day for Michael, like I had never prayed before. Each time, though, I had to confess my own hardness of heart. I saw how deeply hurt and unforgiving of him I was. *I don't want to pray for him. I don't want to ask God to bless him. I only want God to strike his heart with lightning and convict him of how cruel he has been,* I thought. I had to say over and over, "God, I confess my unforgiveness toward my husband. Deliver me from all of it."

Little by little, I began to see changes occur in both of us. When Michael became angry, instead of reacting negatively, I prayed for him. I asked God to give me insight into what was causing his rage. He did. I asked Him what I could do to make things better. He showed me. My husband's anger became less frequent and more quickly soothed. Every day, prayer built something positive. We're still not perfected, but we've come a long way. It hasn't been easy, yet I'm convinced that God's way is worth the effort it takes to walk in it. It's the only way to save a marriage.

A wife's prayers for her husband have a far greater effect on him than anyone else's, even his mother's. (Sorry, Mom.) A mother's prayers for her child are certainly fervent. But when a man marries, he leaves his father and mother and becomes one with his wife (Matthew 19:5). They are a team, one unit, unified in spirit. The strength of a man and wife joined together in God's sight is *far* greater than the sum of the strengths of each of the two individuals. That's because the Holy Spirit unites them and gives added power to their prayers.

That's also why there is so much at stake if we *don't* pray. Can you imagine praying for the right side of your body and not the left? If the right side is not sustained and protected and it falls, it's going to bring down the left side with it. The same is true of you and your husband. If you pray for yourself and not him, you will never find the blessings and fulfillment you want. What happens to him happens to you and you can't get around it.

This oneness gives us a power that the enemy doesn't like. That's why he devises ways to weaken it. He gives us whatever we will fall for, whether it be low self-esteem, pride, the need to be right, miscommunication, or the bowing to our own selfish desires. He will tell you lies like, "Nothing will ever change." "Your failures are irreparable." "There's no hope for reconciliation." "You'd be happier with someone else." He'll tell you whatever you will believe, because he knows if he can get you to believe it, there is no future for your marriage. If you believe enough lies, your heart will eventually be hardened against God's truth.

In every broken marriage, there is at least one person whose heart is hard against God. When a heart becomes hard, there is no vision from God's perspective. When we're miserable in a marriage, we feel that anything will be an improvement over what we're experiencing. But we don't see the whole picture. We only see the way it is, not the way God wants it to become. When we pray, however, our hearts become *soft* toward God and we get a vision. We see there is hope. We have faith that He will restore all that has been devoured, destroyed, and eaten away from the marriage. "I will restore to you the years that the swarming locust has eaten" (Joel 2:25). We can trust Him to take away the pain, hopelessness, hardness, and unforgiveness. We are able to envision His ability to resurrect love and life from the deadest of places.

Imagine Mary Magdalene's joy when she went to Jesus' tomb the third day after He had been crucified and found that He was not dead after all, but had been raised up by the power of God. The joy of seeing something hopelessly dead brought to life is the greatest joy we can know. The power that resurrected Jesus is the very same power that will resurrect the dead places of your marriage and put life back into it. "God both raised up the Lord and will also raise us up by His power" (1 Corinthians 6:14). It's the only power that can. But it doesn't happen without a heart for God that is willing to gut it out in prayer, grow through tough times, and wait for love to be resurrected. We have to go through the pain to get to the joy.

You have to decide if you want your marriage to work, and if you want it badly enough to do whatever is necessary, within healthy parameters, to see it happen. *You* have to believe the part of your relationship that has been eaten away by pain, indifference, and selfishness can be restored. *You* have to trust that what has swarmed over you, such as abuse, death of a child, infidelity, poverty, loss, catastrophic illness, or accident, can be relieved of its death grip. *You* have to determine that everything consuming you and your husband, such as workaholism, alcoholism, drug abuse, or depression, can be destroyed. *You* have to know that whatever has crept into your relationship so silently and stealthily as to not even be perceived as a threat until it is clearly present— such as making idols of your career, your dreams, your kids, or your selfish desires—can be removed. You have to trust that God is big enough to accomplish all this and more.

If you wake up one morning with a stranger in your bed and it's your husband, if you experience a silent withdrawal from one another's lives that severs all emotional connection, if you sense a relentless draining away of love and hope, if your relationship is in so bottomless a pit of hurt and anger that every day sends you deeper into despair, if every word spoken drives a wedge further between you until it becomes an impenetrable barrier keeping you miles apart, be assured that none of the above is God's will for your marriage. God's will is to break down all these barriers and lift you out of that pit. He can heal the wounds and put love back in your heart. Nothing and no one else can.

But you have to rise up and say, "Lord, I pray for an end to this conflict and a breaking of the hold strife has on us. Take away the hurt and the armor we've put up to protect ourselves. Lift us out of the pit of unforgiveness. Speak through us so that our words reflect Your love, peace, and reconciliation. Tear down this wall between us and teach us how to walk through it. Enable us to rise up from this paralysis and move into the healing and wholeness You have for us."

Don't write off the marriage. Ask God to give you a new husband. He is able to take the one you have and make him a new creation in Christ. Husbands and wives are not destined to fight, emotionally disconnect, live in marital deadness, be miserable, or divorce. We have God's power on our side. We don't have to leave our marriages to chance. We can fight for them in prayer and not give up, because as long as we are praying, there is hope. With God, nothing is ever as dead as it seems. Not even your own feelings.

What About Me? I Need Prayer, Too.

It's natural to enter into this prayer venture wondering if your husband will ever be praying for you in the same way you're praying for him. While that would certainly be great, don't count on it. Praying for your husband will be an act of unselfish, unconditional love and sacrifice on your part. You must be willing to make this commitment knowing it is quite possible—even highly probable—that he will never pray for you in the same way. In some cases, he may not pray for you at all. You can ask him to, and you can pray for him to pray for you, but you can't demand it of him. Regardless, whether he does or doesn't is not your concern, it's God's. So release him from that obligation. If he doesn't pray for you, it's *his* loss more than yours anyway. Your happiness and fulfillment will not ride on whether he prays, it will depend on your own relationship with the Lord. Yes, wives need prayer, too. But I'm convinced we should not depend on our husbands to be the sole providers of it. In fact, looking to your husband to be your dedicated prayer partner could be a setup for failure and disappointment for both of you.

I learned that the best thing for our marriage was for me to have women prayer partners with whom I prayed every week. I now believe this is vital for any marriage. If you can find two or more strong, faith-filled women whom you thoroughly trust, and with whom you can share the longings of your heart, set up a weekly prayer time. It will change your life. This doesn't mean you have to tell your prayer partners everything about your husband or expose the private details of his life. The purpose is to ask God to make *your* heart right, show *you* how to be a good wife, share the burdens of *your* soul, and seek God's blessing on your husband.

Of course, if there is an issue with serious consequences, and you can trust your prayer partners with the confidential nature of your request, by all means share it. I've seen many marriages end in separation or divorce because people were too prideful or afraid to share their problems with someone who could pray for them. They go along putting up a good front and suddenly one day the marriage is over. Be sure to stress the confidential nature of what you're sharing with your prayer partners, but don't throw away the marriage because you're hesitant to pray about it with others. If you have a prayer partner who can't keep a confidence, find someone else with more wisdom, sensitivity, and spiritual maturity.

Even without prayer partners or a praying husband, when you pray fervently you'll see things happen. *Before* your prayers are answered there will be blessings from God that will come to you simply because you are praying. That's because you will have spent time in the presence of God, where all lasting transformation begins.

One Prayer at a Time

Don't be overwhelmed by the many ways there are to pray for your husband. It's not necessary to do it all in one day, one week, or even a month. Let the suggestions in this book be a guide and then pray as the Holy Spirit leads you. Where there are tough issues and you need a dynamic breakthrough, fasting will make your prayers more effective. Also, praying Scripture over your husband is powerful. That's what I have done in the prayers at the end of each chapter, wherever you see a Scripture reference.

Above all, don't give place to impatience. Seeing answers to your prayers can take time, especially if your marriage is deeply wounded or strained. Be patient to persevere and wait for God to heal. Keep in mind that you are both imperfect people. Only the Lord is perfect. Look to God as the source of all you want to see happen in your marriage, and don't worry about *how* it will happen. It's your responsibility to pray. It's God's job to answer. Leave it in *His* hands.

CHAPTER ONE

His Wife

The hard part about being a praying wife, other than the sacrifice of time, is maintaining a pure heart. It must be clean before God in order for you to see good results. That's why praying for a husband must begin with praying for his wife. If you have resentment, anger, unforgiveness, or an ungodly attitude, even if there's good reason for it, you'll have a difficult time seeing answers to your prayers. But if you can release those feelings to God in total honesty and then move into prayer, there is nothing that can change a marriage more dramatically. Sometimes wives sabotage their own prayers because they don't pray them from a right heart. It took me awhile to figure that out.

My Favorite Three-word Prayer

I wish I could say that I've been regularly praying for my husband from the beginning of our marriage until now. I haven't. At least not like I'm suggesting in this book. Oh, I prayed. The prayers were short: "Protect him, Lord." They were to the point: "Save our marriage." But most commonly they were my favorite three-word prayer: "Change him, Lord."

When we were first married, I was a new believer coming out of a life of great bondage and error and had much to learn about the delivering and restoring power of God. I thought I had married a man who was close to perfect, and what wasn't perfect was cute. As time went on, cute became irritating and perfect became driving perfectionism. I decided that what irritated me most about him had to be changed and then everything would be fine.

It took a number of years for me to realize my husband was never going to conform to my image. It took a few years beyond that to understand I couldn't make him change in *any* way. In fact, it wasn't until I started going to God with what bothered me that I began to see any difference at all. And then it didn't happen the way I thought it would. *I* was the one God worked on first. *I* was the one who began to change. My heart had to be softened, humbled, pummeled, molded, and reconstructed before He even started working on my husband. *I* had to learn to see things according to the way God saw them—not how I thought they should be.

Gradually I realized it's impossible to truly give yourself in prayer for your husband without first examining your own heart. I couldn't go to God and expect answers to prayer if I harbored unforgiveness, bitterness, or resentment. I couldn't pray *my* favorite three-word prayer without knowing in the deepest recesses of my soul that I had to first pray *God's* favorite three-word prayer: "Change me, Lord."

Who, Me? . . . Change?

Don't say I didn't warn you. When you pray for your husband, especially in the hopes of changing him, you can surely expect some changes. But the first changes won't be in *him*. They'll be in *you*. If this makes you as mad as it made me, you'll say, "Wait a minute! I'm not the one that needs changing here!" But God sees things we don't. He knows where we have room for improvement. He doesn't have to search long to uncover attitudes and habits that are outside His perfect will for us. He requires us to not sin in our hearts because sin separates us from Him and we don't get our prayers answered. "If I regard iniquity in my heart, the Lord will not hear" (Psalm 66:18). God wants our hearts to be right so the answers to our prayers are not compromised.

This whole requirement is especially hard when you feel your husband has sinned against you with unkindness, lack of respect, indifference, irresponsibility, infidelity, abandonment, cruelty, or abuse. But God considers the sins of unforgiveness, anger, hatred, self-pity, lovelessness, and revenge to be just as bad as any others. Confess them and ask God to set you free from anything that is not of Him. One of the greatest gifts you can give your husband is your own wholeness. The most effective tool in transforming him may be your own transformation.

Don't worry, I struggled with all this, too. In fact, every time my husband and I came to an impasse, God and I had a conversation that went something like this:

"Do you see the way he is, Lord?"

"Do you see the way *you* are?"

"Lord, are You saying there are things you want to change in me?"

"Many things. Are you ready to hear them?"

"Well, I guess so."

"Tell me when you're really ready."

"Why me, God? *He's* the one that needs to change."

"The point is not who *needs* to change. The point is who is *willing* to change."

"But God, this isn't fair."

"I never said life is fair, I said *I* am fair."

"But I . . ."

"Someone has to be willing to start."

"But. . . ."

"How important is preserving your marriage?"

"Very important. The other options are unacceptable."

"I rest my case. Let's get on with changing you."

"Help me to have a good attitude about this, Lord."

"That's up to you."

"Do I have to pray for my husband even if he's not praying for me?"

"Precisely."

"But that's not . . . okay, okay, I remember. Life's not fair. *You're* fair!"

(Silent nodding from heaven)

"I give up. Go ahead. Oh, this is going to be painful! Cha . . . change. . . . I can't believe I'm saying this."

(Deep breath) "Change me, Lord."

Painful? Yes! Dying to yourself is always painful. Especially when you are convinced that the other person needs more changing than you. But this kind of pain leads to *life*. The other alternative is just as painful and its ultimate end is the death of a dream, a relationship, a marriage, and a family.

God can resurrect the deadest of marriages, but it takes humbling ourselves before Him and desiring to live His way— forgiveness, kindness, and love. It means letting go of the past and all hurt associated with it and being willing to lose the argument in order to win the battle. I'm not saying you have to become a person void of personality, feelings, or thoughts of your own, or be the whipping post for a husband's whim. God doesn't require that of you. (In fact, if you are in any kind of physical or emotional danger, remove yourself immediately from the situation to a place of safety and get help. You can pray from there while your husband receives the counseling he needs.) Submission is something you give from your heart, not something demanded of you. Jesus said, "He who loses his life for My sake will find it" (Matthew 10:39). But laying down your life is something you willingly do, *not* something that is forcefully taken from you. What I'm saying is that your attitude must be, "Whatever You want, Lord. Show me and I'll do it." It means being willing to die to yourself and say, "Change me, Lord."

The Ultimate Love Language

Something amazing happens to our hearts when we pray for another person. The hardness melts. We become able to get beyond the hurts, and forgive. We even end up loving the person we are praying for. It's miraculous! It happens because when we pray we enter into the presence of God and He fills us with His Spirit of love. When you pray for your husband, the love of God will grow in your heart for him. Not only that, you'll find love growing in *his* heart for *you*, without him even knowing you are praying. That's because prayer is the ultimate love language. It communicates in ways we can't. I've seen women with no feelings of love for their husbands find that as they prayed, over time, those feelings came. Sometimes they felt differently even after the first heartfelt prayer.

Talking to God about your husband is an act of love. Prayer gives rise to love, love begets more prayer, which in turn gives rise to more love. Even if your praying is not born out of completely selfless motives, your motives will become more unselfish as prayer continues. You'll find yourself more loving in your responses. You'll notice that issues which formerly caused strife between you will no longer do that. You'll be able to come to mutual agreements without a fight. This unity is vital.

When we are not united, everything falls apart. Jesus said, "Every kingdom divided against itself is brought to desolation, and every city or house divided against itself will not stand" (Matthew 12:25). Prayer brings unity even if you aren't praying together. I've seen great tension relieved between my husband and me simply by praying for him. Also, asking him, "How can I pray for you?" brings an aspect of love and care into the situation. My husband will usually stop and answer that question in great detail when he might otherwise not say anything. I know of even nonbelieving husbands who respond positively to that question from their wives.

The point in all this is that as husband and wife we don't want to be taking separate roads. We want to be on the same path together. We want to be deeply compatible, lifelong companions, and have the love that lasts a lifetime. Prayer, as the ultimate love language, can make that happen.

I Don't Even Like Him—How Can I Pray for Him?

Have you ever been so mad at your husband that the last thing you wanted to do was pray for him? So have I. It's hard to pray for someone when you're angry or he's hurt you. But that's exactly what God wants us to do. If He asks us to pray for our *enemies*, how much more should we be praying for the person with whom we have become one and are supposed to love? But how do we get past the unforgiveness and critical attitude?

The first thing to do is be completely honest with God. In order to break down the walls in our hearts and smash the barriers that stop communication, we have to be totally up front with the Lord about our feelings. We don't have to "pretty it up" for Him. He already knows the truth. He just wants to see if we're willing to admit it and confess it as disobedience to His ways. If so, He then has a heart with which He can work.

If you are angry at your husband, tell God. Don't let it become a cancer that grows with each passing day. Don't say, "I'm going to live my life and let him live his." There's a price to pay when we act entirely independently of one another. "Neither is man independent of woman, nor woman independent of man, in the Lord" (1 Corinthians 11:11).

Instead say, "Lord, nothing in me wants to pray for this man. I confess my anger, hurt, unforgiveness, disappointment, resentment, and hardness of heart toward him. Forgive me and create in me a clean heart and right spirit before You. Give me a new, positive, joyful, loving, forgiving attitude toward him. Where he has erred, reveal it to him and convict his heart about it. Lead him through the paths of repentance and deliverance. Help me not to hold myself apart from him emotionally, mentally, or physically because of unforgiveness. Where either of us needs to ask forgiveness of the other, help us to do so. If there is something I'm not seeing that is adding to this problem, reveal it to me and help me to understand it. Remove any wedge of confusion that has created misunderstanding or miscommunication. Where there is behavior that needs to change in either of us, I pray You would enable that change to happen. As much as I want to hang on to my anger toward him because I feel it is justified, I want to do what *You* want. I release all those feelings to You. Give me a renewed sense of love for him and words to heal this situation."

If you feel you are able, try this little experiment and see what happens. Pray for your husband every day for a month using each one of the thirty areas of prayer focus I have included in this book. Pray a chapter a day. Ask God to pour out His blessings on him and fill you both with His love. See if your heart doesn't soften toward him. Notice if his attitude toward you doesn't change as well. Observe whether your relationship isn't running more smoothly. If you have trouble making that kind of prayer commitment, think of it from the Lord's perspective. Seeing your husband through God's eyes—not just as your husband, but as God's child, a son whom the Lord loves—can be a great revelation. If someone called and asked you to pray for his or her son, you would do it, wouldn't you? Well, God is asking.

"Shut Up and Pray"

There is a time for everything, it says in the Bible. And it is never more true than in a marriage, especially when it comes to the words we say. There is a time to speak and a time *not* to speak, and happy is the man whose wife can discern between the two. Anyone who has been married for any length of time realizes that there are things that are better left unsaid. A wife has the ability to hurt her husband more deeply than anyone else can, and he can do the same to her. No matter how much apology, the words can not be erased. They can only be forgiven and that is not always easy. Sometimes anything we say will only hinder the flow of what God wants to do, so it's best to, well, shut up and pray.

When Michael and I were first married, I didn't say much if I felt something was wrong. I stuffed my feelings inside. After our first child was born, I became increasingly vocal. But the more I voiced my objections and opinions, the more he resisted and the more we would argue. Whatever I said not only accomplished nothing in the area I wanted it to, it had the opposite effect. It took me a number of years to learn what millions of women have learned over the centuries. *Nagging doesn't work!* Criticizing doesn't work. Sometimes, just plain talking doesn't accomplish anything either. I've found that prayer is the only thing that *always* works. The safeguard you have with prayer is that you have to go through God to do it. This means you can't get away with a bad attitude, wrong thinking, or incorrect motives. When you pray, God reveals anything in your personality that is resistant to His order of things.

My husband will not do something he doesn't want to do. And if he ends up doing something he doesn't want to do, his immediate family members will pay for it. If there is anything I really want him to do, I've learned to pray about it until I have God's peace in my heart *before* I ask. Sometimes God changes my heart about it, or shows me a different way so I don't have to say anything. If I do need to say something, I try not to just blurt it out. I pray first for God's leading.

It took me a long time to figure this out, however. It happened one day when I came across the Proverb, "Better to dwell in the wilderness, than with a contentious and angry woman" (Proverbs 21:19). For *some reason* it struck a nerve.

"But, Lord," I questioned, "what about 'Open rebuke is better than love carefully concealed' [Proverbs 27:5]? Don't we wives have to tell our husbands when something is wrong?"

He replied, "There is . . . a time for every purpose under heaven . . . a time to keep silence and a time to speak" (Ecclesiastes 3:1,7). "The problem is you don't know when to do either. And you don't know how to do it in love."

"Okay, Lord," I said. "Show me when to speak and when to just keep quiet and pray."

The first opportunity for this came right away. I had started a new weekly women's prayer group in my home, and it was so life-changing I suggested to my husband that he start a similar group for men. But he wouldn't hear of it.

"I don't have time," was his not-too-pleased-at-the-idea answer.

The more I talked about it, the more irritated Michael became. After getting my "Be quiet and pray" directions from God, I decided to try that approach. I stopped talking about it and started praying. I also asked my prayer group to pray along with me. It was more than two years after I stopped mentioning it to him and started praying that Michael abruptly announced one day he was organizing a weekly men's prayer group. It has been going ever since, and he still doesn't know I prayed. Even though it took longer than I would have liked, it did happen. And there was peace in the waiting, which I wouldn't have had if I had not kept quiet.

Queen Esther in the Bible prayed, fasted, and sought God's timing before she approached her husband, the king, about a very important matter. There was a lot at stake and she knew it. She didn't run in and scream, "Your hoodlum friends are going to ruin our lives!" Rather she prayed first and then ministered to him in love, while God prepared his heart. The Lord will always give us words to say, and show us when to say them if we ask Him. Timing is everything.

I've known people who use the excuse of "just being honest" to devastate others with their words. The Bible says, "A fool vents all his feelings, but a wise man holds them back" (Proverbs 29:11). In other words, it's foolish to share every feeling and thought. Being honest doesn't mean you have to be completely frank in your every comment. That hurts people. While honesty is a requirement for a successful marriage, telling your husband everything that is wrong with him is not only ill-advised, it probably doesn't reveal the complete truth. The total truth is from God's perspective and He, undoubtedly, doesn't have the same problem with some of your husband's actions as you do. Our goal must not be to get our husbands to do what *we* want, but rather to release them to God so He can get them to do what *He* wants.

Distinguish carefully between what is truly right and wrong. If it doesn't fall clearly into either of those categories, keep your personal opinions to yourself. Or pray about them and then, as the Lord leads, reveal them for calm discussion. The Bible says, "Do not be rash with your mouth, and let not your heart utter anything hastily before God. For God is in heaven, and you on earth; therefore let your words be few" (Ecclesiastes 5:2). There are times when we are just to listen and not offer advice, to support and not offer constructive criticism.

I'm not for a moment suggesting that you become a timid doormat who doesn't ever confront your husband with the truth—especially when it's for his greater good. By all means you must clearly communicate your thoughts and feelings. But once he has heard them, don't continue to press him until it becomes a point of contention and strife.

If you *do* have to say words that are hard to hear, ask God to help you discern when your husband would be most open to hearing them. Pray for the right words and for his heart to be totally receptive. I know that's difficult to do if you have a few choice words you're dying to let loose. But hard as it may seem, it's best to let God hear them first so He can temper them with His Spirit. This is especially true when talking has ceased altogether and every word only brings more pain. I wish I had learned earlier to pray before I spoke. My words too often set up a defensive reaction in my husband that produced harsh words we both regret. He received my suggestions as pressure to do or be something, even though I always had his best interests at heart. It had to come to him from God.

When we live by the power of God rather than our flesh, we don't have to strive for power with our words. "For the kingdom of God is not in word but in power" (1 Corinthians 4:20). It's not the words we speak that make a difference, it is the power of God accompanying them. You'll be amazed at how much power your words have when you pray before you speak them. You'll be even more amazed at what can happen when you shut up and let God work.

Believer or Not

If your husband is not a believer, you probably already know how much good it does to keep talking to him about the Lord if he didn't respond the first number of times. It's not that you can't ever say anything to him, but if what you say is always met with indifference or irritation, the next step is to keep silent and pray. The Bible says a wife can win over her husband without saying anything, because what he *observes* in his wife speaks more loudly than what she tells him. "They, without a word, may be won by the conduct of their wives" (1 Peter 3:1,2).

God says He speaks of things that are not as though they were. You can do that, too. You can say, "I'm not going to pretend, but I'm going to speak of things that are *not* part of my husband's life as though they *were* a part of it. Even though he doesn't have faith, I'm going to pray for him as if he does." Of course you can't force him to do something he doesn't want to do, but you can access God's power through praying for His voice to penetrate your husband's soul. No matter how long you have to pray for your husband to come to know the Lord, even if it takes his whole life, the time will not be wasted. In the meantime, whether your husband is a believer or not, you can still pray all the prayers in this book for him and expect to see significant answers to them.

Creating a Home

I don't care how liberated you are, when you are married there will always be two areas that will ultimately be your responsibility: home and children. Even if you are the only one working and your husband stays home to keep the house and tend the kids, you will still be expected to see that the heart of your home is a peaceful sanctuary—a source of contentment, acceptance, rejuvenation, nurturing, rest, and love for your family. On top of this, you will also be expected to be sexually appealing, a good cook, a great mother, and physically, emotionally, and spiritually fit. It's overwhelming to most women, but the good news is that you don't have to do it all on your own. You can seek God's help.

Ask the Lord to show you how to make your home a safe haven that builds up your family—a place where creativity flows and communication is ongoing. Ask God to help you keep the house clean, the laundry done, the kitchen in order, the pantry and the refrigerator full, and the beds made. These are basic things a man may not compliment his wife on every day (or ever), but he will notice if they are *not* done. My husband may not look in the cupboard for a light bulb or a battery for months. But when he does, he wants it to be there. Nor does he want to come home late from work one night and find that there is no bread for a sandwich. I do my best to make sure it is there. I ask God to help me maintain a house that my husband is pleased to come home to and bring his friends. It's not necessary to have expensive furniture or a decorator in order to do all that. My first home was small and had second-hand furniture I bought from yard sales. I painted the entire place myself (with the help of a girlfriend) and made it look attractive. It just takes some thought and a little care.

Part of making a house a home is allowing your husband to be the head so you can be the heart. Trying to be both is too much. God placed the husband as the head over the family, whether he deserves it or not and whether he rises up to take his position or not. It's God's order of things. This doesn't mean that one position is more important than the other. They work together. If your husband is to be the head of the house, you must allow him that headship. If you are to be the heart of the home, you still must take the steps necessary to do so, even if you are a major contributor to the financial support. Trying to reverse that keeps a constant struggle going.

This doesn't mean that the wife can't work and the husband can't care for the home; it's the attitudes of the heart and head that makes the difference. There were weeks of time during the finishing of each book I've written when my husband took care of the house and the children so I could meet the deadline. It never minimized his headship or caused me to usurp his position. It was something he did for me. There were times he needed me to work so he could rest. It's what I did for him. It's a delicate balance for most people, so it's best to pray that the integrity of the two positions in the home—head and heart—are not compromised.

Keeping order in the home doesn't mean it has to be perfect, but it shouldn't be out of control. If you are working as hard as he is to bring home a paycheck, the responsibilities should be shared in the home. If he doesn't want to share them, spending a certain amount of money for someone to help you a few hours a week is a lot cheaper than a divorce, a chiropractor, a therapist, a medical doctor, or a funeral. Ask God to show you about that.

Everything I've said about the home goes for your body, soul, and spirit as well. Some effort must be put into maintaining them. I once heard a radio talk show where a woman called in to complain to a popular psychologist that her husband told her he no longer found her attractive. The host said, "What are you doing to make yourself attractive?" The caller had no answer. The point is, being attractive doesn't just happen. Even the most gorgeous women in the world do much to maintain their attractiveness. Queen Esther was one of the most beautiful women in her country and she still spent a year beautifying herself before she met the king.

We have to ask ourselves the same question. "What am I doing to make myself attractive to my husband?" Do I keep myself clean and smelling good? Do I see that my internal self is cleansed and rejuvenated with regular exercise? Do I preserve my strength and vitality with a healthful diet? Do I dress attractively? And most important: Do I spend time alone with God every day? I guarantee that the more time you spend with the Lord, the more radiant you will become. "Charm is deceitful and beauty is passing, but a woman who fears the LORD, she shall be praised" (Proverbs 31:30).

You can't afford not to make this investment in yourself, your health, and your future. It's not selfish to do it. It's selfish *not* to do it. Pray for God to show you what steps to take and then enable you to take them. Invite the Holy Spirit to dwell in you *and* your home.

Letting Go of Expectations

Shortly after we were married, my husband called from work and said he wanted me to prepare a certain chicken dish for dinner. I went to the store, got the food, prepared the dish, and when he came home, he walked in the door and said bluntly, "I don't feel like chicken tonight, I want lamb chops." I needn't tell you the thoughts that went through my mind because I'm sure you already know them. This was not an isolated incident. Similar ones happened far too frequently. I can't count the number of times Michael promised to be home for dinner and called ten minutes *after* dinner was ready to say he was going to work late and would eat out with his coworkers. I finally learned that it did no good to be angry, hurt, or resentful. That only made matters worse. It made him defensive because he thought I didn't understand his situation. I realized it was healthier for both of us if I rearranged my expectations. From then on, I prepared meals as if only I and the children would be eating them. If Michael was able to join us, it was a pleasant surprise. If he didn't, I could live with it.

I've learned that when disappointing things happen, it's best to remind myself of my husband's good qualities. I recount how he sometimes helps with the household chores and the cooking. He is faithful and does not give me reason to doubt it. He is a believer who goes to church, reads his Bible, prays, and has high moral standards. He loves me and our children. He uses his talents for God's glory. He is a good and generous provider. Things could be a lot worse, so I won't complain about whether he's home for dinner or not.

I think if I could help a new wife in any area, it would be to discourage her from coming into her marriage with a big list of expectations and then being upset when her husband doesn't live up to them. Of course there are some basics that should be agreed upon before the wedding date, such as fidelity, financial support, honesty, kindness, basic decency, high moral standards, physical and emotional love, and protection. When you don't get those things, you can ask for them. When you still don't get them, you can pray.

But when it comes to specifics, you can't require one pe
to meet all of your needs. The pressure to do that and fu
your dreams at the same time can be overwhelming to
man. Instead, take your needs to God in prayer and look to
Him for the answers. If we try to control our husbands by
having a big list for them to live up to and then are angry
and disappointed when they can't, *we* are the ones in error.
The biggest problems in my marriage occurred when my expectations of what I thought Michael should be or do didn't
coincide with the reality of who he was.

Let go of as many expectations as possible. The changes
you try to make happen in your husband, or that your husband tries to make in himself to please you, are doomed to
failure and will bring disappointment for you both. Instead,
ask God to make any necessary changes. He will do a far
better job because "whatever God does, it shall be forever.
Nothing can be added to it, and nothing taken from it" (Ecclesiastes 3:14). Accept your husband the way he is and
pray for him to grow. Then when change happens, it will be
because God has worked it in him and it will be lasting. "My
soul, wait silently for God alone, for my expectation is from
Him" (Psalm 62:5). Your greatest expectations must be from
God, not your husband.

With All Due Respect

It's interesting that God requires the husband to *love* his
wife, but the wife is required to have *respect* for her husband.
"Let each one of you in particular so love his own wife as himself, and let the wife see that she respects her husband" (Ephesians 5:33). I assume no woman would marry a man she didn't
love, but too often a wife loses respect for her husband after
they've been married awhile. Loss of respect seems to precede
loss of love and is more hurtful to a man than we realize.

s of losing respect for your husband can
David's wife, Michal, watched her hus-
joy before the Lord in front of the people,
kingly clothing and in his undergarments, as
of the covenant was being brought into the city.
al not only didn't share his joy, she had contempt for him
(2 Samuel 6:16). She was critical instead of trying to understand the situation from God's perspective. She paid a dear price for her lack of respect; God's judgment caused her to be unable to ever bear children. I believe we not only bring defeat into our marriages and our husbands when we don't have respect for them, but it shuts the door to new life in us as well.

In another example, Queen Vashti refused to go to the king at his command. The king was giving a feast for his friends, he was in a party mood, and he wanted to show off his beautiful wife. All he asked of her was that she put on her royal clothes, don her royal crown, and make a royal appearance to the people he was entertaining. She declined, knowing full well it would be humiliating for him. "Queen Vashti refused to come at the king's command brought by his eunuchs; therefore the king was furious, and his anger burned within him" (Esther 1:12). The result was that Vashti lost her position as queen. She not only wronged her husband, the king, but the people as well. Unless a wife wants to lose her position as queen of her husband's heart, and hurt her family and friends besides, she mustn't humiliate her husband no matter how much she thinks he deserves it. The price is too high.

If this has already happened to you, and you know you've shown disrespect for your husband, confess it to God right now. Say, "Lord, I confess I do not esteem my husband the way Your Word says to. There is a wall in my heart that I know was erected as a protection against being hurt. But I am ready to let it come down so that my heart can heal. I confess the times I have shown a lack of respect for him. I confess my disrespectful attitude and words as sin against You. Show me how to dismantle this barrier over my emotions that keeps me from having the unconditional love You want me to have. Tear down the wall of hardness around my heart and show me how to respect my husband the way You want me to. Give me *Your* heart for him, Lord, and help me to see him the way You see him."

Praying like this will free you to see your man's potential for greatness, as opposed to his flaws. It will enable you to say something positive that will encourage, build up, give life, and make the marriage better. Love is diminished if we dwell on the negatives. Love grows if we focus on the positive. When you have God's heart for your husband, you will be able to see through new eyes. There are times when you can't understand where your husband is coming from, what he is feeling, and why he is doing the things he does, unless you have the discernment of God. Ask God to give it to you.

When you are praying for yourself—his wife—remember this model of a good wife from the Bible. It says she takes care of her home and runs it well. She knows how to buy and sell and make wise investments. She keeps herself healthy and strong and dresses attractively. She works diligently and has skills which are marketable. She is giving and conscientiously prepares for the future. She contributes to her husband's good reputation. She is strong, solid, honorable, and not afraid of growing older. She speaks wisely and kindly. She doesn't sit around doing nothing, but carefully watches what goes on in her home. Her children and her husband praise her. She doesn't rely on charm and beauty but knows that the fear of the Lord is what is most attractive. She supports her husband and still has a fruitful life of her own which speaks loudly for itself (Proverbs 31).

This is an amazing woman, the kind of woman we can become only through God's enablement and our own surrendering. The bottom line is that she is a woman whose husband trusts her because "she does him good and not evil all the days of her life." I believe the most important "good" a wife can do for her husband is pray. Shall we?

Prayer

Lord, Help me to be a good wife. I fully realize that I don't have what it takes to be one without Your help. Take my selfishness, impatience, and irritability and turn them into kindness, long-suffering, and the willingness to bear all things. Take my old emotional habits, mindsets, automatic reactions, rude assumptions, and self-protective stance, and make me patient, kind, good, faithful, gentle, and self-controlled. Take the hardness of my heart and break down the walls with Your battering ram of revelation. Give me a new heart and work in me Your love, peace, and joy (Galatians 5:22,23). I am not able to rise above who I am at this moment. Only You can transform me.

Show me where there is sin in my heart, especially with regard to my husband. I confess the times I've been unloving, critical, angry, resentful, disrespectful, or unforgiving toward him. Help me to put aside any hurt, anger, or disappointment I feel and forgive him the way You do—totally and completely, no looking back. Make me a tool of reconciliation, peace, and healing in this marriage. Enable us to communicate well and rescue us from the threshold of separation where the realities of divorce begin.

Make me my husband's helpmate, companion, champion, friend, and support. Help me to create a peaceful, restful, safe place for him to come home to. Teach me how to take care of myself and stay attractive to him. Grow me into a creative and confident woman who is rich in mind, soul, and spirit. Make me the kind of woman he can be proud to say is his wife.

I lay all my expectations at Your cross. I release my husband from the burden of fulfilling me in areas where I should be looking to You. Help me to accept him the way he is and not try to change him. I realize that in some ways he may never change, but at the same time, I release him to change in ways I never thought he could. I leave any changing that needs to be done in Your hands, fully accepting that neither of us is perfect and never will be. Only You, Lord, are perfect and I look to You to perfect us.

Teach me how to pray for my husband and make my prayers a true language of love. Where love has died, create new love between us. Show me what unconditional love really is and how to communicate it in a way he can clearly perceive. Bring unity between us so that we can be in agreement about everything (Amos 3:3). May the God of patience and comfort grant us to be like-minded toward one another, according to Christ Jesus (Romans 15:5). Make us a team, not pursuing separate, competitive, or independent lives, but working together, overlooking each other's faults and weaknesses for the greater good of the marriage. Help us to pursue the things which make for peace and the things by which one may edify another (Romans 14:19). May we be "perfectly joined together in the same mind and in the same judgment" (1 Corinthians 1:10).

I pray that our commitment to You and to one another will grow stronger and more passionate every day. Enable him to be the head of the home as You made him to be, and show me how to support and respect him as he rises to that place of leadership. Help me to understand his dreams and see things from his perspective. Reveal to me what he wants and needs and show me potential problems before they arise. Breathe Your life into this marriage.

Make me a new person, Lord. Give me a fresh perspective, a positive outlook, and a renewed relationship with the man You've given me. Help me see him with new eyes, new appreciation, new love, new compassion, and new acceptance. Give my husband a new wife, and let it be me.

POWER TOOLS

Whatever things you ask when you pray, believe that you receive them, and you will have them. And whenever you stand praying, if you have anything against anyone, forgive him, that your Father in heaven may also forgive you your trespasses.

MARK 11:24,25

Be kind to one another, tenderhearted, forgiving one another, even as God in Christ forgave you.

EPHESIANS 4:32

Ask, and it will be given to you; seek, and you will
find; knock, and it will be opened to you. For
everyone who asks receives, and he who seeks finds,
and to him who knocks it will be opened.
MATTHEW 7:7,8

Through wisdom a house is built, and by
understanding it is established; by knowledge
the rooms are filled with all precious
and pleasant riches.
PROVERBS 24:3,4

Let us not grow weary while doing good, for in due
season we shall reap if we do not lose heart.
GALATIANS 6:9

CHAPTER TWO

His Work

*B*ill seldom works. He's willing to let his wife, Kim, support the family while he pursues his dream. The problem is that Kim is not content to bear the entire burden of supporting the family on her shoulders indefinitely, and Bill has been pursuing his dream for seventeen years with nothing to show for it. I believe the root of Bill's inactivity is fear. He's afraid that if he doesn't get the job of his dreams, he will end up in a job he hates and be stuck there forever.

Steven is working himself to death. He can never rest and enjoy the success of his labor. He seldom spends time with his family, and his teenagers are fast approaching adulthood. He doesn't work that hard because he has to, but because he is afraid. He fears that if he ever stops, he will be worth nothing in everyone's eyes, including his own.

These are extreme examples of how a man can relate to his work. On one hand is laziness—avoiding work out of selfishness, fear, lack of confidence, depression, or apprehension about the future. Of the lazy, God says, "As a door turns on its hinges, so does the lazy man on his bed" (Proverbs 26:14). "Drowsiness will clothe a man with rags" (Proverbs 23:21). "The way of the lazy man is like a hedge of thorns" (Proverbs 15:19). "The desire of the lazy man kills him, for his hands refuse to labor" (Proverbs 21:25). In other words, a lazy man will never get anywhere, he will never have anything, he will have a rough road ahead, and it will ultimately destroy him.

The opposite extreme is workaholism—obsessing over work to the exclusion of all else and losing one's life in the process. Of the workaholic, God says, "So are the ways of everyone who is greedy for gain; it takes away the life of its owners" (Proverbs 1:19). "I looked on all the works that my hands had done and on the labor in which I had toiled; and indeed all was vanity and grasping for the wind. There was no profit under the sun" (Ecclesiastes 2:11). In other words, workaholism is draining and pointless.

Neither extreme promotes happiness and fulfillment. Only a perfect balance between the two, which God can help a man find, will ever bring that quality of life.

What causes a man to go to either extreme can be, oddly enough, the same reason: fear. That's because a man's identity is often very tied up in his work. He needs to be appreciated and he needs to win, and his work is often a means of seeing both happen. It frightens him to think he may never experience either. If he is doing work that is demeaning to him, he feels devalued as a person. If his work is not successful, he feels like a loser.

God recognizes that a man's work is a source of fulfillment to him. He says there is nothing better than for a man to "enjoy the good of all his labor—it is the gift of God" (Ecclesiastes 3:13). The fact that many men are not fulfilled in their work has less to do with what their work is than with whether or not they have a sense of purpose. A man who doesn't have that can eventually come to a place where he has worked hard and long for so little reward that he no longer sees a future for himself—at least not one worth living. If there's also the specter of age creeping up on him, he may hear words in his head like, "You're not valuable to anyone." "You're replaceable." "You can't do what you used to." "You're too old to learn new things." "You don't have it." "You have no purpose." This is a dangerous place for a man to be.

Gary, his father, and his grandfather all had difficulty making a living. In fact, it was very late in each of their lives before they were even able to discern what they were supposed to be doing. They went from job to job without any clear leading. They struggled financially. None of them had parents who prayed for them to have their gifts and talents revealed, to know the calling of God on their lives, to have doors opened to them, and to become all they were created to be. History tends to repeat itself without the intervention of God.

I've observed that people who have had actively praying parents seem to find their life's work early. Their careers may not take off immediately, but they have a sense of purpose and destiny that propels them in the right direction. They don't live with the frustration and aimlessness that the others do. While many parents have an agenda for their children, not enough of them seek out *God's* plan for their lives. When a child's life is left to chance that way, a kind of vocational wandering can result. There is needless floundering, disappointment, doubt, and despair as he tries to carve out a place for himself. If your husband had that kind of start, your prayers can change his life.

If your husband didn't have praying parents, you can step in the gap. You can pray for his eyes to be opened to see what God wants him to do, and where God is leading. Your prayers can help him feel appreciated and encouraged enough to recognize he has worth no matter what he does. You can assure him that God has uniquely gifted him with ability and talent and has something good ahead for him. Then pray for God to reveal it and open a door of opportunity which no man can shut. Your prayers can pave a path for him.

Even if your husband already has a successful career, it's still good to pray that he is where God wants him to be and that everything will continue to go smoothly. My husband, who is a songwriter and record producer, said he felt my prayers have prevented him from working with the wrong clients. He has never worked with anyone who is difficult, weird, evil, or unsuitable, which is nothing less than a miracle in his business. He knew I always prayed that God would lead him to the right people and remove from his path those who would be trouble. While our prayers cannot ensure a trouble-free road for our husbands, they can certainly steer them clear of many problems.

If your husband is a hard worker, make sure he has times of rest and enjoyment—to do things that entertain him and give him a reprieve from the weight of a lifetime of supporting a family. Men need periods of refreshing. If they don't have them, they are prone to burnout and temptation of all kinds. Your prayers can help your husband understand that the true meaning of life doesn't come from work, it comes from following God. Let's pray for our husbands to find that perfect balance.

Prayer

Lord, I pray that You would bless the work of my husband's hands. May his labor bring not only favor, success, and prosperity, but great fulfillment as well. If the work he is doing is not in line with Your perfect will for his life, reveal it to him. Show him what he should do differently and guide him down the right path. Give him strength, faith, and a vision for the future so he can rise above any propensity for laziness. May he never run from work out of fear, selfishness, or a desire to avoid responsibility. On the other hand, help him to see that he doesn't have to work himself to death for man's approval, or grasp for gain beyond what is a gift from You. Give him the ability to enjoy his success without striving for more. Help him to excel, but free him from the pressure to do so.

I pray that You will be Lord over his work, and may he bring You into every aspect of it. Give him enough confidence in the gifts You've placed in him to be able to seek, find, and do good work. Open up doors of opportunity for him that no man can close. Develop his skills so that they grow more valuable with each passing year. Show me what I can do to encourage him.

I pray that his work will be established, secure, successful, satisfying, and financially rewarding. May he not be "lagging in diligence, [but] fervent in spirit, serving the Lord" (Romans 12:11). Let him be like a tree planted by the stream of Your living water, which brings forth fruit in due season. May he never wither under pressure, but grow strong and prosper (Psalm 1:3).

POWER TOOLS

Do you see a man who excels in his work?
He will stand before kings; he will not stand
before unknown men.
PROVERBS 22:29

Do not overwork to be rich; because of your own understanding, cease! Will you set your eyes on that
which is not? For riches certainly make themselves
wings; they fly away like an eagle toward heaven.
PROVERBS 23:4,5

For what profit is it to a man if he gains the whole
world, and loses his own soul? Or what will a man
give in exchange for his soul?
MATTHEW 16:26

Because of laziness the building decays, and through
idleness of hands the house leaks.
ECCLESIASTES 10:18

Let the beauty of the LORD our God be upon us, and
establish the work of our hands for us; yes, establish
the work of our hands.
PSALM 90:17

CHAPTER THREE

His Finances

*M*uch of who your husband is and what he experiences in life is wrapped up in how he relates to his finances. Is he giving or miserly? Is he thankful or envious of others? Is money a blessing or a curse? Is he wise or reckless with what he has? Is he in agreement with you as to how it is to be spent, or does your marriage exhibit financial strife? Nothing puts more pressure on a marriage than financial irresponsibility, lack of money, and huge debt. Only when we recognize that all we have comes from God and seek to make Him Lord over it can we avoid the pitfalls that money, or the lack of it, brings.

Although my husband has always made a good living, the nature of his business is "feast or famine" with regard to when and how much money comes in. One year there was a recession in the music business and everybody felt it. Even the companies who owed us money withheld payment because of their own lack of cash flow. It was a frightening time, but it would have been much worse if we hadn't had faith in the Lord and committed our finances to Him. Our comfort came in knowing that we had obeyed God in tithing our money to the church. "Bring all the tithes into the storehouse" and see if He "will not open for you the windows of heaven and pour out for you such blessing that there will not be room enough to receive it" (Malachi 3:10). We had also been faithful to give to the poor and those in need. "Blessed is he who considers the poor; the LORD will deliver him in time of trouble. The LORD will preserve him and keep him alive, and he will be blessed on the earth" (Psalm 41:1,2). We also knew the Bible promises that "those who seek the LORD shall not lack any good thing" (Psalm 34:10). We certainly were seeking the Lord. We believed that by looking to God as our source and living in obedience to His ways, He would provide for us and we would have everything we need. He did and we do.

So many money problems can be solved by putting all finances under God's covering and doing what He says to do with them. That means giving when He says to give. When you do, God promises to deliver you, protect you, bless you, heal you, and keep you alive. When you don't, you will experience the same desolation the poor do. "Whoever shuts his ears to the cry of the poor will also cry himself and not be heard" (Proverbs 21:13). Not giving cuts off your own ability to enjoy what you have and leads to lifelong difficulties.

To be sure, there are wealthy people who do not give. But if you were to check closely into their lives, you'd find that they are missing many of the Lord's blessings. The blessings of wholeness, protection, love, peace, health, and fulfillment continually elude them and they don't know why. They gain wealth but lose the ability to enjoy it, all because they don't know that the key to life is knowing the Lord and living His way. This means giving time, energy, love, talent, and finances according to His direction.

Pray that your husband gets hold of this key to life and understands God's will for his finances. Pray that he becomes a giving person who is content to live within his means and not always strive for more. I'm not saying he should never try to increase his earnings—quite the contrary. A man deserves to earn what his work is worth and his wife should pray he does. Backbreaking drudgery that leads to gut-wrenching poverty and with it bitterness, anguish, sickness, and envy should not be accepted as a way of life. By all means pray that the storehouses of blessing will be opened upon him, but pray that it all comes from the hand of God. "The blessing of the LORD makes one rich, and He adds no sorrow with it" (Proverbs 10:22).

It may not be possible to use prayer to avoid every financial problem because God sometimes uses finances to get our attention and teach us things. But your prayers will certainly help protect your husband from unnecessary struggle and loss. God's desire is to bless those who have obedient, grateful, and giving hearts, whose true treasure is in the Lord. "Where your treasure is, there your heart will be also" (Matthew 6:21). God wants your husband to find his treasure in Him, not in his finances.

Prayer

Lord, I commit our finances to You. Be in charge of them and use them for Your purposes. May we both be good stewards of all that You give us, and walk in total agreement as to how it is to be dispersed. I pray that we will learn to live free of burdensome debt. Where we have not been wise, bring restoration and give us guidance. Show me how I can help increase our finances and not decrease them unwisely. Help us to remember that all we have belongs to You, and to be grateful for it.

I pray that (husband's name) will find it easy to give to You and to others as You have instructed in Your Word. Give him wisdom to handle money wisely. Help him make good decisions as to how he spends. Show him how to plan for the future. I pray that he will find the perfect balance between spending needlessly and being miserly. May he always be paid well for the work he does, and may his money not be stolen, lost, devoured, destroyed, or wasted. Multiply it so that what he makes will go a long way. I pray that he will not be anxious about finances, but will seek Your kingdom first, knowing that as he does, we will have all we need (Luke 12:31).

POWER TOOLS

Do not seek what you should eat or what you
should drink, nor have an anxious mind. For all
these things the nations of the world seek after,
and your Father knows that you need these things.
But seek the kingdom of God, and all these
things shall be added to you.

LUKE 12:29-31

As for every man to whom God has given riches and
wealth, and given him power to eat of it, to
receive his heritage and rejoice in his labor;
this is the gift of God.

ECCLESIASTES 5:19

He who gives to the poor will not lack, but he
who hides his eyes will have many curses.
PROVERBS 28:27

I have been young, and now am old; yet I have not
seen the righteous forsaken, nor his descendants
begging bread.
PSALM 37:25

My God shall supply all your need according to
His riches in glory by Christ Jesus.
PHILIPPIANS 4:19

CHAPTER FOUR

His Sexuality

e're hitting the top priorities in a man's life right away in this book. I feel if we can contribute to our husbands' happiness in these areas most dear to their hearts, we will have greater success making inroads in other areas that are crucial to their well-being.

After twenty years of praying with women about their failing, struggling, unfulfilling, or dead marriages, I've observed that frequently the sexual relationship is a low priority in their minds. It isn't that the wife cares nothing about that part of her life. It's that there are so many other things screaming for her attention, such as raising children, work, finances, managing a home, emotional stress, exhaustion, sickness, and marital strife. In the wife's juggling of priorities, sex can end up on the bottom of her list. Some women allow week after week, month after month, six months, a year, or even more to go by without having sexual relations with their husbands for one reason or another. When disaster hits, they are surprised. Even though the wife may have felt fine about this arrangement, her husband was being neglected in an important part of his being.

For a wife, sex comes out of affection. She doesn't want to be affectionate with a man who makes her feel angry, hurt, lonely, disappointed, overworked, unsupported, uncared for, or abandoned. But for a husband, sex is pure need. His eyes, ears, brain, and emotions get clouded if he doesn't have that release. He has trouble hearing anything his wife says or seeing what she needs when that area of his being is neglected. Wives sometimes have it backwards. They think, *We can have sex after we get these other issues settled*. But actually there is a far greater chance of settling the other issues if sex comes first.

That's why it's important to make sex a matter of priority in your marriage. Whether all conditions are perfect or whether you feel like it or not isn't the point. The point is meeting the needs of your husband and keeping communication lines open. A man can easily be made to feel insignificant, beaten down, discouraged, destroyed, or tempted in this area of his being. There is probably no more important means of fulfillment for a man, and no area where he is more vulnerable.

Sexual problems are quite common because many women don't have a clear grasp of what God's view is on the subject. But the Bible is crystal clear. "The wife does not have authority over her own body but the husband does. And likewise the husband does not have authority over his own body but the wife does. Do not deprive one another except with consent for a time, that you may give yourselves to fasting and prayer; and come together again so that Satan does not tempt you because of your lack of self-control" (1 Corinthians 7:4,5). Sex between a husband and wife is God's idea. Unless we're fasting and praying for weeks at a time, or are experiencing physical infirmity or separation, there is no excuse not to engage in it regularly.

When we're married, our bodies are not our own. We *owe* each other physical attention and we're not to deprive one another. The frequency of sex depends on the *other person's* need, not ours alone. If your attitude about having sex comes down to only what *you* need or what *you* don't want, then you don't have God's perspective. He says our body is to be used to comfort and complete the *other* person. Something is built up in the man and the marriage when this need is met by his wife. Something is diminished when it is not. You leave yourselves open for temptation, and far more destruction than you can imagine, when this area of intimate communication is neglected. It can happen to anyone, and that's why the sexual aspect of your marriage and your husband's sexuality need to be covered in prayer. And it's best to start praying about it *before* you have to.

If your husband desires sex more frequently and you are the one keeping it from happening, pray for God to help you change your ways. I've found that the most difficult time to deal with the issue of sex is when the children are small and can't do much for themselves. By the time you get them in bed, you are exhausted and ready to drop. You're thinking about getting to sleep as soon as possible, while your husband has been making other plans for you. Your options are to totally shut him down and say, "Forget about it. I'm tired," or communicate how exhausted you are and hope *he'll* say, "No problem. You get some rest," or proceed with a bad attitude and make him feel guilty or angry. But I've found a fourth option which works much better. Try this and see if it doesn't work for you.

When your husband communicates to you what he has in mind, as only a husband can do, don't roll your eyes and sigh deeply. Instead, say, "Okay, give me fifteen minutes." (Or ten or twenty, or whatever you need.) During that time, do something to make yourself feel attractive. For example, take a shower or a relaxing bath. Put on scented body lotion or his favorite perfume. (Have perfume you wear only for these times alone with him.) Comb your hair. Wash your face and prepare it with products that make your skin look dewy and fresh. Put on lip gloss and blush. Slip into lingerie you know he finds irresistible. Don't worry about your imperfections; he's not thinking about them. If you feel self-conscious, wear a beautiful nightgown that covers areas that bother you. While you're doing this, pray for God to give you renewed energy, strength, vitality, and a good attitude. Hopefully, when you're ready, your husband will find you were worth the wait. You'll be surprised at how much better a sex partner you are when you feel good about yourself. He'll be happier and you'll both sleep better. This is a small investment of time to see great rewards in your marriage.

Sometimes there is the opposite situation, where the wife is sexually neglected by her husband. His lack of interest can happen for many reasons—physical, mental, or emotional. But if he is content to go month after month without sex, then something is wrong. If there is no physical problem hindering him, maybe he's having deep feelings of failure, disappointment, depression, or hopelessness that need to be addressed. Prayer can help reveal what the problem is and how to solve it. Get professional help if you need to. It's cheaper than a divorce or the physical, emotional, and mental ravages of a dead marriage. Don't let negative emotions like resentment, bitterness, self-pity, and unforgiveness build up in you. Keep yourself healthy and attractive. If you don't think highly enough of yourself to take care of your body, do it as an act of kindness for *him*. Have special lingerie that *he* likes and put it on when you're with him. Get a new hairstyle. Surprise him with a new attitude. Keep your mind refreshed and growing. Basically, *don't do nothing*.

Bad things develop when the sexual part of a marriage is neglected. Don't let that happen to you. Keep an eye on the calendar and refuse to allow much time to go by without coming together physically. If it has been too long, ask God to show you why and help you remedy the situation. And remember, it's never too late to pray for sexual purity, no matter what has occurred in either of your pasts. Sometimes sexual problems in a marriage happen as a result of sexual experiences before the marriage. Pray to be set free and healed of those memories. Purity happens the moment it takes root in the heart. Prayer is where it starts. Don't jeopardize or forfeit what God has for your marriage by neglecting to pray for this vital area of your life.

Prayer

Lord, bless my husband's sexuality and make it an area of great fulfillment for him. Restore what needs to be restored, balance what needs to be balanced. Protect us from apathy, disappointment, criticism, busyness, unforgiveness, deadness, or disinterest. I pray that we make time for one another, communicate our true feelings openly, and remain sensitive to what each other needs.

Keep us sexually pure in mind and body, and close the door to anything lustful or illicit that seeks to encroach upon us. Deliver us from the bondage of past mistakes. Remove from our midst the effects of any sexual experience—in thought or deed—that happened outside of our relationship. Take away anyone or anything from our lives that would inspire temptation to infidelity. Help us to "abstain from sexual immorality" so that each of us will know "how to possess his own vessel in sanctification and honor" (1 Thessalonians 4:3-5). I pray that we will desire each other and no one else. Show me how to make myself attractive and desirable to him and be the kind of partner he needs. I pray that neither of us will ever be tempted to think about seeking fulfillment elsewhere.

I realize that an important part of my ministry to my husband is sexual. Help me to never use it as a weapon or a means of manipulation by giving and withholding it for selfish reasons. I commit this area of our lives to You, Lord. May it be continually new and alive. Make it all that You created it to be.

POWER TOOLS

Flee sexual immorality. Every sin that a man does
is outside the body, but he who commits sexual
immorality sins against his own body. Or do you
not know that your body is the temple of the
Holy Spirit who is in you, whom you have from
God, and you are not your own? For you were
bought at a price; therefore glorify God in
your body and in your spirit, which are God's.

1 CORINTHIANS 6:18-20

The body is not for sexual immorality but for the
Lord, and the Lord for the body.
1 CORINTHIANS 6:13

Drink water from your own cistern, and running
water from your own well. Should your fountains be
dispersed abroad, streams of water in the streets? Let
them be only your own, and not for strangers with
you. Let your fountain be blessed, and rejoice with
the wife of your youth. As a loving deer and a
graceful doe, let her breasts satisfy you at all times;
and always be enraptured with her love.
PROVERBS 5:15-19

CHAPTER FIVE

His Affection

om and Patti had been married a number of
years before she actually had a serious talk
with him about his lack of affection. Tom
was a wonderful husband in every other way and their
sexual relationship was good, but apart from the sexual act
there was no affection. It wasn't because Tom didn't love
Patti—he adored her. It was because affection was something he grew up without as a child. Patti felt guilty about
the way she was feeling and didn't want to criticize or hurt
Tom, but she had not known affection as a child, either,
and that's why she needed it so in her marriage. Each time
Patti confronted Tom about this problem he would try to
change, but soon things were back to the way they had
been. This led to great frustration and hurt in both of
them. Eventually Patti became hopeless and felt like she
was dying inside. She didn't see how she could live the rest
of her life without affection, but she saw no hope of Tom's
ever being any different.

Finally, Patti's misery forced her to take the problem to
her prayer partners. They diligently covered it in prayer

every week and as they prayed, God worked on Patti. He spoke to her about obeying Him in the area of eating right and getting proper exercise—an area where she had always been in rebellion. When she totally submitted to God regarding this and started doing the things He had been telling her to do, she began to feel better about herself and realized that she *deserved* to be treated affectionately by her husband. She didn't have to feel guilty about wanting affection because the Lord wanted that for her, too. Soon she felt the leading of God to confront Tom about it again. This time it would be different because she was now led by the Holy Spirit, and she and her prayer partners had been praying for a miraculous transformation in Tom.

"It took courage for me to even speak of this again," she told me. "I was afraid it could lead to divorce because we were both so hurt and saw no hope in each other. But God gave me the ability to speak in love the words that needed to be said, and this time the conversation brought immediate breakthrough."

"The turning point came," Tom recalled, "when Patti said to me, 'Honey, how can someone as wonderful as you, with all your attributes, someone I love and trust so much, not be able to be affectionate?'"

"Because I said words that affirmed him," Patti explained further, "it gave him hope that it was worth trying again."

Tom proceeded differently this time. He took the problem to his own prayer group of men, who instantly rallied around him. They decided not only to support him daily in prayer, but also to keep him accountable to show some form of affection to Patti each day.

"This was something I welcomed, because I wanted to change," Tom said. "I love Patti and hated that I was hurting her. I wanted to be different and I knew that true transformation can only happen by the power of the Holy Spirit."

Every day for a number of weeks, one of the men from the group called Tom and said, "What have you done to show affection to Patti today?" They also suggested *ways* to show affection and affirm her. They told Tom to check in regularly with Patti and say, "How am I doing?" For someone whose heart had not been prepared by the Holy Spirit, this could have been extremely annoying. But because Tom welcomed the Lord's working in him, it brought no burden.

"Now the first thing he does when he comes home is give me a hug and a kiss," Patti said with a radiant smile. "I felt like a new person after five hugs."

Tom and Patti's situation is not a rare one. Many people, even godly men and women, live in marriages that are dead because there is no affection. And women endure it because their husbands are good in other ways, or they don't feel worthy enough to ask for affection. But this is not the way God designed the marital relationship. "Let the husband render to his wife the affection due her, and likewise also the wife to her husband" (1 Corinthians 7:3). There is "a time to embrace," the Bible says (Ecclesiastes 3:5). When you're married, it's definitely the time. Affection isn't at the top of a man's priority list because men often see sex and affection as being the same. A woman's greatest need is for affection. If you are in a marriage that lacks it, pray for the Holy Spirit's transformation.

Prayer

Lord, I pray for open physical affection between my husband and me. Enable each of us to lay aside self-consciousness or apathy and be effusive in our display of love. Help us to demonstrate how much we care for and value each other. Remind us throughout each day to affectionately touch one another in some way. Help us to not be cold, undemonstrative, uninterested, or remote. Enable us to be warm, tender, compassionate, loving, and adoring. Break through any hardheadedness on our part that refuses to change and grow. If one of us is less affectionate to the other's detriment, bring us into balance.

Where any lack of affection has planted a negative view of marriage in our children, or taught them an incorrect way of relating to a marriage partner, help us to model the right way so that they can observe it. Show us how to openly confess our errors to them and demonstrate our commitment to live differently.

Change our habits of indifference or busyness. May we not so take each other for granted that we don't make the effort to reach out and touch one another with affection. Help us not to weaken the marriage through neglect of this vital means of communication. I pray that we always "greet one another with a kiss of love" (1 Peter 5:14). I know that only the transforming power of the Holy Spirit can make changes that last. I trust You to transform us and make us the husband and wife You called us to be.

POWER TOOLS

If there is any consolation in Christ, if any comfort of love, if any fellowship of the Spirit, if any affection and mercy, fulfill my joy by being like-minded, having the same love, being of one accord, of one mind.
PHILIPPIANS 2:1,2

So husbands ought to love their own wives as their own bodies; he who loves his wife loves himself. For no one ever hated his own flesh, but nourishes and cherishes it, just as the Lord does the church.
EPHESIANS 5:28,29

Let each of you look out not only for his own interests, but also for the interests of others.
PHILIPPIANS 2:4

His left hand is under my head, and his right hand embraces me.
SONG OF SOLOMON 2:6

Let no one seek his own, but each one the other's well-being.
1 CORINTHIANS 10:24

CHAPTER SIX

His Temptations

F rom the time Michael and I were married, I
prayed for God to remove temptation from
our lives. I don't know if it has been the result of prayer or the fact that we both guard ourselves
against such things, but we've never given each other a
single moment of concern. I'm sure it's due more to the
hand of God than the strength of human restraint, but both
are important.

I know several couples who experienced adultery in
their marriages, but because in each case there was a wife
who was willing to pray and a husband open to allowing
God to change and restore him, the marriages are still intact
and successful today. Only prayer, a submitted heart, and
the transforming power of the Holy Spirit can work those
kinds of miracles.

I have another friend whose husband had numerous
affairs before they finally divorced. Each time it was with
one of her best friends. I questioned her choice of "friends,"
but I never questioned her godliness or commitment to
pray. She prayed. But a heart that refuses to listen to the

promptings of the Holy Spirit will not change, no matter how hard you pray.

Temptation is everywhere today and we're fools if we think we or our husbands can't be lured by it in some form or another. The Bible says, "The eyes of man are never satisfied" (Proverbs 27:20). If that's true, temptation is always a possibility and we must be ever watchful. Certain people are tempted by alcohol and drugs; others have a lust for money and power. Still others find food addictions, pornography, or sexual immorality to be irresistible lures. The enemy of our souls knows where our flesh is the weakest and he will put temptations in our paths at our most vulnerable points. The question is not whether there will be temptations, it's how we will handle them when they arise. I recommend praying through them. While prayer may not be able to stop a man from doing something he is determined to do, it *can* diminish the voices of temptation and strengthen his resolve. It can pave the way for him to make right choices.

The Bible says that God does not tempt us. It is our *desires* that draw us away to what entices us. It is our *desires* that cause us to sin and bring death into our lives. But "blessed is the man who endures temptation; for when he has been approved, he will receive the crown of life which the Lord has promised to those who love Him" (James 1:12). God wants us to get through temptation because He wants to bless us. But He needs to see if we can be trusted to chose His ways over our fleshly desires. He'll always give us a way out if we want it badly enough to seek Him for it.

The best time to start praying about this is *before* anything happens. Jesus instructed His disciples to "pray that you may not enter into temptation" (Luke 22:40). He said to be watchful because "the spirit indeed is willing, but the flesh is weak" (Mark 14:38). If your husband struggles in a certain area, pray that he will want to have godly prayer partners with whom he can share openly, be accountable, and receive prayer. Open confession before God and other believers does more to minimize the power of the tempter than anything else. Unfortunately, many men are reticent to reveal what tempts them most and so they shut off to the very thing that could protect them.

If after all your praying, your husband still falls into the hands of temptation, do not blame yourself. The decision is ultimately his. He has chosen to walk in the flesh and not in the Spirit. "Walk in the Spirit, and you shall not fulfill the lust of the flesh. For the flesh lusts against the Spirit, and the Spirit against the flesh; and these are contrary to one another, so that you do not do the things that you wish" (Galatians 5:16,17). Don't stop praying for him. No matter how hopeless it seems when you see him being tempted again and again, know that God has provided a means of escape and you may be the instrument He will use to help him find it. If there is no temptation problem in your marriage, be thankful and pray that it stays that way.

Prayer

Lord, I pray that You would strengthen my husband to resist any temptation that comes his way. Stamp it out of his mind before it ever reaches his heart or personal experience. Lead him not into temptation, but deliver him from evils such as adultery, pornography, drugs, alcohol, food addiction, gambling, and perversion. Remove temptation especially in the area of <u>(name specific temptation)</u>. Make him strong where he is weak. Help him to rise above anything that erects itself as a stronghold in his life. May he say, "I will set nothing wicked before my eyes; I hate the work of those who fall away; it shall not cling to me" (Psalm 101:3).

Lord, You've said that "Whoever has no rule over his own spirit is like a city broken down, without walls" (Proverbs 25:28). I pray that <u>(husband's name)</u> will not be broken down by the power of evil, but raised up by the power of God. Establish a wall of protection around him. Fill him with Your Spirit and flush out all that is not of You. Help him to take charge over his own spirit and have self-control to resist anything and anyone who becomes a lure. May he "abhor what is evil. Cling to what is good" (Romans 12:9). I pray that he will be repulsed by tempting situations. Give him courage to reject them. Teach him to walk in the Spirit so he will not fulfill the lust of the flesh.

POWER TOOLS

Let no one say when he is tempted, "I am tempted by God"; for God cannot be tempted by evil, nor does He Himself tempt anyone. But each one is tempted when he is drawn away by his own desires and enticed. Then, when desire has conceived, it gives birth to sin; and sin, when it is full-grown, brings forth death.

JAMES 1:13-15

No temptation has overtaken you except such as is common to man; but God is faithful, who will not allow you to be tempted beyond what you are able, but with the temptation will also make the way of escape, that you may be able to bear it.

1 CORINTHIANS 10:13

Let us walk properly, as in the day, not in revelry and drunkenness, not in lewdness and lust, not in strife and envy. But put on the Lord Jesus Christ, and make no provision for the flesh, to fulfill its lusts.

ROMANS 13:13,14

Those who desire to be rich fall into temptation and a snare, and into many foolish and harmful lusts which drown men in destruction and perdition.

1 TIMOTHY 6:9

The works of the flesh are evident, which are: adultery, fornication, uncleanness, lewdness, idolatry, sorcery, hatred, contentions, jealousies, outbursts of wrath, selfish ambitions, dissensions, heresies, envy, murders, drunkenness, revelries, and the like; of which I tell you beforehand, just as I also told you in time past, that those who practice such things will not inherit the kingdom of God.

GALATIANS 5:19-21

CHAPTER SEVEN

His Mind

I used to attribute my husband's mind struggles to his musical genius. You know the artistic temperament—bright and brilliant on one hand, dark and moody on the other. When he would get down, the words in his mind told him he was going to fail, be worth nothing, that he was incapable of doing what he needed to do. It had no basis in reality because he had those kinds of thoughts even in the midst of his most productive and successful work. I didn't realize for a long time that the mind battles he endured did not have to be written off as "just the way he is." Nor did he have to fight them alone. If he and I were one, then an assault on his mind was an assault on me as well. I could stand with him in the battle by declaring, "This is not *God* speaking into my husband's life, it's the voice of the enemy. I'm not going to stand by and watch deadly games being played with his mind and our lives."

I decided to try my own experiment and "stand against the wiles of the devil" on his behalf (Ephesians 6:11). After all, the Bible talks about "praying always with all prayer and supplication in the Spirit, being watchful to this end with all perseverance and supplication for all the saints" (Ephesians 6:18). Surely "all the saints" is a category, even if it's not a description, which includes my husband. As I persevered in prayer for him over the next few months, I was amazed at the results. Not only did he become better able to control the thoughts in his mind, but eventually I could even see the onslaught coming and attack it in prayer before it gained a foothold. The more he saw my prayers answered, the more he realized where the lies were coming from and the less willing he was to believe them.

As I have traveled the country with my speaking engagements and talked with women from all walks of life, I have been amazed to see how universal this problem is. In fact, it didn't seem to matter what temperaments or backgrounds their husbands had, they experienced the same kind of lies in their mind. I finally realized that all men have an enemy who wants to undermine what God desires to do in their lives. Women have that same enemy, but men seem to be more vulnerable to his attacks in certain areas. Even the strongest man can get exhausted, overwhelmed, burdened, desperate, or caught up in things that keep him away from the presence of God. He doesn't always see the traps of an enemy who wants him to believe that what he faces is insurmountable. His mind fills with words like "hopeless," "no good," "failure," "impossible," "it's over," and "why try?" A wife can pray that her husband will discern the lies and hear instead words like "hope," "prosperity," "possibility," "success," and "new beginning," and know that they're from God.

The two most powerful weapons against the attack of lies upon your husband's mind are the *Word of God* and *praise*. "The Word of God is living and powerful, and sharper than any two-edged sword, piercing even to the division of soul and spirit, and of joints and marrow, and is a *discerner of the thoughts and intents of the heart*" (Hebrews 4:12). By speaking God's Word, you can reveal wrong thinking and it will lose its power. If your husband won't do it for himself, you can speak the Word of God over him, either in his presence or alone in prayer, and see positive results. I've done that for my husband countless times and he will attest to the power of it. I remind him that God has not given him a spirit of fear, but of power and of love and of a *sound mind* (2 Timothy 1:7). I tell him I'm praying for him to lay claim to that sound mind at all times.

Praise is also a powerful tool because God's presence comes to dwell in our midst when we worship Him. In His presence we find healing and transformation for our lives. "Although they knew God, they did not glorify Him as God, nor were thankful, but became futile in their thoughts, and their foolish hearts were darkened" (Romans 1:21). You don't want futile thoughts to darken your husband's heart. Speak praise to God for your husband's sound mind, and he'll be able to think more clearly about what he will and will not allow into it.

Depression, bitterness, anger, fear, rejection, hopelessness, loneliness, rebellion, temptation, evil, and many diseases all begin in the mind. These things can control your life unless you take control of your mind first. That's why God instructs us not to accept as truth everything we think. "I have stretched out My hands all day long to a rebellious people, who walk in a way that is not good, according to their own thoughts" (Isaiah 65:2). He wants us to share *His* thoughts. "We [who believe] have the mind of Christ" (1 Corinthians 2:16). Let's pray for our husbands to receive the mind of Christ and bring every thought captive under God's control. Who doesn't need that?

Prayer

Lord, I pray for Your protection on my husband's mind. Shield him from the lies of the enemy. Help him to clearly discern between Your voice and any other, and show him how to take every thought captive as You have instructed us to do. May he thirst for Your Word and hunger for Your truth so that he can recognize wrong thinking. Give him strength to resist lying thoughts. Remind him that he has the mind of Christ. Where the enemy's lies have already invaded his thoughts, I push them back by inviting the power of the Holy Spirit to cleanse his mind. Lord, You have given me authority "over all the power of the enemy" (Luke 10:19). By that authority given to me in Jesus Christ, I command all lying spirits away from my husband's mind. I proclaim that God has given (husband's name) a sound mind. He will not entertain confusion, but live in clarity. He will not be tormented with impure, evil, negative, or sinful thoughts, but be transformed by the renewing of his mind, that he may prove what is that good and acceptable and perfect will of God (Romans 12:2).

Enable him to "be strong in the Lord and in the power of His might" (Ephesians 6:10). Help him to be anxious for nothing, but in everything by prayer and supplication, with thanksgiving, let his requests be made known to You; and may Your peace, which surpasses all understanding, guard his heart and mind through Christ Jesus (Philippians 4:6,7). And finally, whatever things are true, noble, just, pure, lovely, of good report, having virtue, or anything praiseworthy, let him think on these things (Philippians 4:8).

POWER TOOLS

Though we walk in the flesh, we do not war
according to the flesh. For the weapons of our
warfare are not carnal but mighty in God for pulling
down strongholds, casting down arguments and every
high thing that exalts itself against the knowledge of
God, bringing every thought into captivity to the
obedience of Christ.
2 CORINTHIANS 10:3-5

To be carnally minded is death, but to be
spiritually minded is life and peace.
ROMANS 8:6

I see another law in my members, warring against the
law of my mind, and bringing me into captivity to
the law of sin which is in my members.
ROMANS 7:23

With the mind I myself serve the law of God,
but with the flesh the law of sin.
ROMANS 7:25

You shall love the LORD your God with all your
heart, with all your soul, with all your mind,
and with all your strength.
MARK 12:30

CHAPTER EIGHT

His Fears

There are many things in this world to be afraid of; only a fool would say otherwise. But when fear seizes us, tormenting and ruling our lives, we have become captive to it. Men are often susceptible to that because without even realizing it, they get attacked by the "what if's." "What if I can't make enough money?" "What if something happens to my wife and children?" "What if I get a terrible disease?" "What if my business fails?" "What if I can't be a good father?" "What if I become disabled and can't work to support my family?" "What if I'm overpowered or threatened?" "What if I can't perform sexually?" "What if no one respects me?" "What if I'm in an accident?" "What if I die?" Fear can take hold of a man (Psalm 48:6) and cause his life to be wasted (Psalm 78:33). If he is "seized with great fear" (Luke 8:37), it can keep him from all God has for him.

The second year we were married, Michael and I took a trip to Italy, Greece, and Israel with our pastor, Jack Hayford, and his wife, Anna, and some people from our church. Michael had always been a very anxious traveler, so by the time we arrived in Greece, he was stressed. One night, after an exhausting few days, he said, "This is miserable for me. I can't stay on the tour."

"What exactly are you afraid of?" I questioned him.

"I'm not sure," he answered. "But it feels like everything in my life is going to fall apart if I don't go back home right away."

Even though it was late in the evening, I called Pastor Jack's room to tell him we were leaving in the morning. I'm sure he must have been in bed by that time, but he said, "I'll be right there."

He came to our room immediately and Michael shared with him what he was experiencing. Pastor Jack put a compassionate arm around his shoulder and talked about the love his heavenly Father had toward him.

"God has adopted you as His son," he said. "When you're in the presence of a strong and loving Father, there's no need to be afraid."

Pastor Jack prayed for Michael to clearly perceive the love of his heavenly Father, and he also demonstrated a father's love to him. It was a simple act of Holy Spirit-inspired kindness but a powerful revelation to Michael. Because of it, he was able to rise above his fear and we stayed on the tour until the end. And it was a good thing we did. I became pregnant in Jerusalem and nine months later our son, Christopher, was born on Pastor Jack's birthday. Significant things happen in our lives when we don't allow fear to rule the situation.

There is a difference between a fearful thought that comes to mind as a prompting to pray for a particular thing, and a tormenting spirit of fear that paralyzes. You don't want to undermine the promptings of the Holy Spirit to your husband's heart, but you do want to support him as he battles destructive fear. Jesus said, "I will show you whom you should fear: Fear Him who, after He has killed, has power to cast into hell" (Luke 12:5). The only kind of fear we are supposed to have is the fear of the Lord.

When you have the fear of the Lord, God promises to deliver you from your enemies (2 Kings 17:39), protect you from evil (Proverbs 16:6), keep His eye on you (Psalm 33:18), show you His mercy (Luke 1:50), give you riches and honor (Proverbs 22:4), supply everything you need (Psalm 34:9), reveal all you need to know (Psalm 25:14), bless your children and grandchildren (Psalm 103:17), give you confidence (Proverbs 14:26), a satisfying life (Proverbs 19:23), longevity (Proverbs 10:27), and the desires of your heart (Psalm 145:19). What more could you ask? Pray for the comforting, securing, perfect love of the Lord to surround your husband and deliver him from all his fears.

Prayer

Lord, You've said in Your Word that "there is no fear in love; but perfect love casts out fear, because fear involves torment. But he who fears has not been made perfect in love" (1 John 4:18). I pray You will perfect my husband in Your love so that tormenting fear finds no place in him. I know You have not given him a spirit of fear. You've given him power, love, and a sound mind (2 Timothy 1:7). I pray in the name of Jesus that fear will not rule over my husband. Instead, may Your Word penetrate every fiber of his being, convincing him that Your love for him is far greater than anything he faces and nothing can separate him from it.

I pray that he will acknowledge You as a Father whose love is unfailing, whose strength is without equal, and in whose presence there is nothing to fear. Deliver him this day from fear that destroys and replace it with godly fear (Jeremiah 32:40). Teach him Your way, O Lord. Help him to walk in Your truth. Unite his heart to fear Your name (Psalm 86:11). May he have no fear of men, but rise up and boldly say, "The LORD is my helper; I will not fear. What can man do to me?" (Hebrews 13:6) "How great is Your goodness, which You have laid up for those who fear You" (Psalm 31:19).

I say to you (husband's name), "Be strong, do not fear! Behold, your God will come with vengeance, with the recompense of God; He will come and save you" (Isaiah 35:4). "In righteousness you shall be established; you shall be far from oppression, for you shall not fear" (Isaiah 54:14). "You shall not be afraid of the terror by night, nor of the arrow that flies by day, nor of the pestilence that walks in darkness, nor of the destruction that lays waste at noonday" (Psalm 91:5,6). May the Spirit of the Lord rest upon you, "the Spirit of wisdom and understanding, the Spirit of counsel and might, the Spirit of knowledge and of the fear of the LORD" (Isaiah 11:2).

POWER TOOLS

The angel of the LORD encamps all around those
who fear Him, and delivers them.
PSALM 34:7

I sought the LORD, and He heard me, and
delivered me from all my fears.
PSALM 34:4

Yea, though I walk through the valley of the
shadow of death, I will fear no evil; for You
are with me; Your rod and Your staff,
they comfort me.
PSALM 23:4

Fear not, for I am with you; be not dismayed,
for I am your God. I will strengthen you, yes,
I will help you, I will uphold you with
My righteous right hand.
ISAIAH 41:10

The LORD is my light and my salvation;
whom shall I fear? The LORD is the strength
of my life; of whom shall I be afraid?
PSALM 27:1

CHAPTER NINE

His Purpose

*E*veryone has a purpose. It's the reason we exist. It's our life's mission, objective, or plan. Generally, we're here to glorify God and do His will. How that specifically translates in our lives is unique to each of us. Your husband needs to know the reason *he* exists. He needs to be sure his life is not just an accident, but that he's here by design. He must be certain he was created for a great purpose. When he discovers that purpose, and is doing what he was created to do, becoming what he was created to be, he will find fulfillment. This can only contribute to *your* happiness as well.

If I've learned anything being married two and one half decades, it's that a wife can't put pressure on her husband to *be* something, but she can pray for him to become it. She can pray that he be molded according to God's plan and not anyone else's. Then, who he becomes will be determined by whether he hears God's call on his life or not. For God has "called us with a holy calling, not according to our works, but according to His own purpose and grace which was given to us in Christ Jesus before time began" (2 Timothy 1:9). Your husband is "predestined according to the purpose of Him who works all things according to the counsel of His will" (Ephesians 1:11,12). But you still need to pray that he hears God's call, so that who he is and what he does lines up with *God's* purpose for his life.

You can always tell when a man is not living in the purpose for which God created him. You sense his unrest. You get a feeling something is not quite right, even if you can't put your finger on what it is. When you're around a man who is fulfilling his calling and doing what he was created to do, you're aware of his inner direction, confidence, and deep security. How do you feel about what your husband is doing with his life? Do you lack peace about it because he is on a path that's unfulfilling, beating him down, or going nowhere? If so, then pray, "Lord, take my husband from this place, reveal to him what You've called him to be, and open doors to what he should be doing."

Praying that way doesn't mean your husband will be pulled out of what he's doing and dropped into something else. It *can* happen that way, but often what takes place is a change in the man's perspective. I have a friend named David, who has worked for years in a factory, making airplanes. When he heard the call of God on his life, he knew he was to help troubled teenagers in low-income families. He also knew he wasn't to leave his job to do it. As it turned out, his work provided enough money to support his family while it afforded him exactly the kind of hours he needed to do what he had to do. He has organized food distribution to needy families, free concerts for underprivileged teens, Christian outreaches for the unsaved, and peace talks between rival gangs. He has done as much to bring restoration to his strife-torn city as any one man could possibly do. His is by no means an easy job, but it is fulfilling. And he has a sense of purpose that is unmistakable when you're around him. Physically, he is not a large man, but he is a spiritual giant and you know it when you're in his presence. His wife, Priscilla, also hears God's call on his life and she supports it in every way she can.

Whatever God has called your husband to be or do, He has also called you to support it and be a part of it, if in no other way than to pray, encourage, and help in whatever way possible. For some women that means creating a good home, raising the children, being there for him, and offering prayer support. Other women may take an active role by becoming a partner or helper. In either case, God does not ask you to deny your own personhood in the process. God has called *you* to something, too. But it will fit in with whatever your husband's calling is, it will not be in conflict with it. God is not the author of confusion, strife, or unworkable situations. He is a God of perfect timing. There is a time for everything, the Bible says. The timing to do what God has called *each* of you to do will work out perfectly, if it's submitted to God.

If your husband is already moving in the purpose for which God has called him, you can count on the enemy of his soul coming to cast doubt—especially if he hasn't yet seen anything close to the finished picture or realized the success he had envisioned. Your prayers can help cast away discouragement and keep it from taking hold. It can help your husband to hear and cling to God's revelation. It can cause him to live his life on purpose.

Prayer

Lord, I pray that __(husband's name)__ will clearly hear the call You have on his life. Help him to realize who he is in Christ and give him certainty that he was created for a high purpose. May the eyes of his understanding be enlightened so that he will know what is the hope of Your calling (Ephesians 1:18).

Lord, when You call us, You also enable us. Enable him to walk worthy of his calling and become the man of God You made him to be. Continue to remind him of what You've called him to and don't let him get sidetracked with things that are unessential to Your purpose. Strike down discouragement so that it will not defeat him. Lift his eyes above the circumstances of the moment so he can see the purpose for which You created him. Give him patience to wait for Your perfect timing. I pray that the desires of his heart will not be in conflict with the desires of Yours. May he seek You for direction, and hear when You speak to his soul.

POWER TOOLS

Each one has his own gift from God, one in
this manner and another in that.
1 CORINTHIANS 7:7

As God has distributed to each one, as the Lord
has called each one, so let him walk.
1 CORINTHIANS 7:17

We also pray always for you that our God
would count you worthy of this calling, and fulfill
all the good pleasure of His goodness and the
work of faith with power.
2 THESSALONIANS 1:11

The God of our Lord Jesus Christ, the Father of
glory, . . . give to you the spirit of wisdom and
revelation in the knowledge of Him, the eyes of
your understanding being enlightened; that you
may know what is the hope of His calling, what are
the riches of the glory of His inheritance in the
saints, and what is the exceeding greatness of His
power toward us who believe, according to the
working of His mighty power.
EPHESIANS 1:17-19

May He grant you according to your heart's
desire, and fulfill all your purpose.
PSALM 20:4

CHAPTER TEN

His Choices

There was a business deal my husband entered into that he did not mention to me until it was already in motion. From the moment I learned of it I did not have a good feeling. I thought the idea was great and his vision for it was excellent, but I couldn't escape the distinct lack of peace I had about it. In fact, the more I prayed, the stronger I felt. When I mentioned it to him he said defensively, "You don't trust me to make the right decision." He made clear this was something he wanted and he was not about to hear any opposition.

The only recourse I had was to pray, which I did. Time and again I said to God, "Show me if I'm wrong about this. I would love for it to work out because it's a great idea. But if what I'm sensing is correct, reveal it to him in time to stop the process. Show him the truth and close the door."

At the eleventh hour, just before contracts were to be signed, Michael's eyes were suddenly opened to a number of incidents that called into question the true intentions of the other parties involved. The revelation of God exposed everything to him and the entire deal was called off. As hard as it was for him to accept at the time, he is grateful to have been spared much grief.

Sometime later, while I was writing this book, I asked my husband what has meant the most about my praying for him. One of the things he mentioned was that it helped him to make good choices. "When major decisions came up and I was offered certain things, your prayers opened my eyes and kept me from entering into contractual agreements that would have been bad," he explained.

We have to remember that all men think they are doing the right thing. "Every way of a man is right in his own eyes" (Proverbs 21:2). But God is the only one who can give true discernment. He can give us wisdom when we ask for it. Wisdom brings success (Ecclesiastes 10:10), and it enables us to learn from experience (Proverbs 15:31). We want our husbands to be wise men.

The opposite of a wise man is a fool. The Bible describes a fool as someone who only "trusts in his own heart" (Proverbs 28:26). He despises wisdom (Proverbs 23:9). He only wants to talk and doesn't want to listen (Proverbs 18:2). In other words, you can't tell him anything. He is quarrelsome (Proverbs 20:3), and he rages and is arrogant when you try to reason with him (Proverbs 14:16). A fool is someone who is incapable of weighing thoroughly the consequences of his actions. As a result, he doesn't make wise choices. If you have a husband like that, pray for him to have wisdom.

If your husband is not a full-time fool, so to speak, but he does occasionally engage in foolish behavior, don't try to fix him. God is the only one who can do that. Your job is to love and pray for him. The Bible says, "The fear of the LORD is the beginning of wisdom, and the knowledge of the Holy One is understanding" (Proverbs 9:10). This means you start by praying for the fear of the Lord to overtake him. Then pray for him to have godly counsel: "Blessed is the man who walks not in the counsel of the ungodly" (Psalm 1:1). If you keep praying for your husband to have wisdom and godly counsel, then even if he does make a bad decision, you can enjoy the comfort of knowing you did your part and God will bring good out of it.

So much of our lives is affected by decisions our husbands make. We are wise to pray that they make good ones.

Prayer

Lord, fill my husband with the fear of the Lord and give him wisdom for every decision he makes. May he reverence You and Your ways and seek to know Your truth. Give him discernment to make decisions based on Your revelation. Help him to make godly choices and keep him from doing anything foolish. Take foolishness out of his heart and enable him to quickly recognize error and avoid it. Open his eyes to clearly see the consequences of any anticipated behavior.

I pray that he will listen to godly counselors and not be a man who is unteachable. Give him strength to reject the counsel of the ungodly and hear Your counsel above all others. I declare that although "there are many plans in a man's heart, nevertheless the LORD's counsel—that will stand" (Proverbs 19:21). Instruct him even as he is sleeping (Psalm 16:7), and in the morning, I pray he will do what's right rather than follow the leading of his own flesh. I know the wisdom of this world is foolishness with You, Lord (1 Corinthians 3:19). May he not buy into it, but keep his eyes on You and have ears to hear Your voice.

POWER TOOLS

A wise man will hear and increase learning, and a
man of understanding will attain wise counsel.
PROVERBS 1:5

Do not be wise in your own eyes; fear the
LORD and depart from evil.
PROVERBS 3:7

The fear of the LORD is the beginning of knowledge,
but fools despise wisdom and instruction.
PROVERBS 1:7

They will call on me, but I will not answer; they will
seek me diligently, but they will not find me. Because
they hated knowledge and did not choose the fear of
the LORD, they would have none of my counsel and
despised my every rebuke.
PROVERBS 1:28-30

A man who wanders from the way of understanding
will rest in the assembly of the dead.
PROVERBS 21:16

CHAPTER ELEVEN

His Health

For years my husband cared little about exercise. I would give lectures and meaningful talks, leave magazine articles in his path, and plead and cry about how I didn't want to be a widow, but it all fell on glazed eyes and deaf ears. Then one day I got the brilliant idea that if praying worked for other parts of his life, it might work for this, too. I decided to employ my "shut up and pray" method and ask God to give him the desire and motivation to exercise regularly. I prayed for a number of months without any results, but then one morning I heard an unfamiliar noise coming from another room. I followed the sound and much to my amazement, it was my husband on the treadmill. I didn't say a word. He has been using the treadmill and lifting weights about three days a week ever since. When he later remarked how much better he was feeling and wished he had started doing it sooner, I exercised admirable restraint and didn't even allow the words "I told you so" to be formed with my mouth. To this day he doesn't know I prayed.

Your husband's health is not something to take for granted, no matter what his age or condition. Pray for him to learn to take proper care of himself, and if he becomes ill, pray for him to be healed. I've seen too many answers to prayers for healing in my life and the lives of others to doubt that the God who healed in the Bible is the same yesterday, today, and tomorrow. I believe that when God said, "I am the LORD who heals You," He meant it (Exodus 15:26). I have the same faith as Jeremiah who prayed, "Heal me, O Lord, and I shall be healed" (Jeremiah 17:14). I trust His Word when it promises "I will restore health to you and heal you of your wounds" (Jeremiah 30:17).

Jesus "took our infirmities and bore our sicknesses" (Matthew 8:17). He gave His disciples power to "heal all kinds of sickness and all kinds of disease" (Matthew 10:1). He said "These signs will follow those who believe. . . . They will lay hands on the sick, and they will recover" (Mark 16:17,18). It seems to me that God is interested in healing, and He didn't put a time limit on it; only a faith limit (Matthew 9:22).

My husband told me that my prayers for his healing had the biggest impact on him in the mid-eighties when he discovered several lumps on his body and the doctor believed they were cancerous. A second doctor also suspected it was cancer, so a biopsy was taken. During those days of waiting to find out the results, Michael was tempted to worry. He said my prayers for his good health and peace sustained him until he found out it wasn't cancer at all. He had the lumps removed and there has never been a problem since.

Remember, however, that even though we pray and have faith, the outcome and timing are *God's* decisions. He says there is "a time to heal" (Ecclesiastes 3:3). If you pray for healing and nothing happens, don't beat yourself up for it. God sometimes uses a man's physical ailments to get his attention so He can speak to him. Keep praying, but know God's decision is the bottom line.

The same is true when praying that God will save someone's life. We don't have the final say over anyone's hour of death. The Bible says there is "a time to die" (Ecclesiastes 3:2), and we are not the ones who decide that, God does. And we must accept it. We can pray, but *He* determines the outcome. We have to give Him that privilege without resenting, faulting, or getting angry at Him. Pray for your husband's health, but leave it in God's hands.

Prayer

Lord, I pray for Your healing touch on (husband's name). Make every part of his body function the way You designed it to. Wherever there is anything out of balance, set it in perfect working order. Heal him of any disease, illness, injury, infirmity, or weakness. Strengthen his body to successfully endure his workload, and when he sleeps may he wake up completely rested, rejuvenated and refreshed. Give him a strong heart that doesn't fail. I don't want him to have heart failure at any time.

I pray that he will have the desire to take care of his body, to eat the kind of food that brings health, to get regular exercise, and avoid anything that would be harmful to him. Help him to understand that his body is Your temple and he should care for it as such (1 Corinthians 3:16). I pray that he will present it as a living sacrifice, holy and acceptable to You (Romans 12:1).

When he is ill, I pray You will sustain him and heal him. Fill him with your joy to give him strength. Specifically, I pray for (mention any area of concern). Give him faith to say. "'O Lord my God, I cried out to You, and You healed me' [Psalm 30:2]. Thank You, Lord, that You are my Healer." I pray that my husband will live a long and healthy life and when death does come, may it be accompanied by peace and not unbearable suffering and agony. Thank You, Lord, that You will be there to welcome him into Your presence, and not a moment before Your appointed hour.

POWER TOOLS

Bless the Lord, O my soul, and forget not all His
benefits: who forgives all your iniquities,
who heals all your diseases.
Psalm 103:2,3

They cried out to the Lord in their trouble, and
He saved them out of their distresses. He sent His
word and healed them, and delivered them
from their destructions.
Psalm 107:19,20

I have heard your prayer, I have seen your
tears; surely I will heal you.
2 Kings 20:5

Your light shall break forth like the morning,
your healing shall spring forth speedily, and your
righteousness shall go before you; the glory of the
Lord shall be your rear guard.
Isaiah 58:8

I will heal them and reveal to them the
abundance of peace and truth.
Jeremiah 33:6

CHAPTER TWELVE

His Protection

*H*ow many times have we heard stories about men who were on the battlefield and at the very moment when they were in the greatest danger, they experienced miraculous deliverance, only to learn later that someone back home was praying at that same moment? Our husbands are on the battlefield every day. There are dangers everywhere. Only God knows what traps the enemy has laid to bring accidents, diseases, evil, violence, and destruction into our lives. Few places are completely safe anymore, including your own home. But God has said that even though "the wicked watches the righteous, and seeks to slay him, the LORD will not leave him in his hand" (Psalm 37:32,33). He promises that He will be "a shield to those who put their trust in Him" (Proverbs 30:5). He can even be a shield to someone we pray about because of *our* faith.

I have always prayed for my husband and children to be safe while traveling in cars. But one morning I got a call from Michael shortly after he left the house to take our young son to school.

"We've just had an accident," he said, "but Christopher and I are fine."

I drove immediately to where they were, thanking God all the way for protecting them just as I had prayed for years. When I arrived and saw the condition of the car, I completely fell apart. Michael's little sports car, which I was never thrilled about his driving, had been broadsided by a much larger car and pushed into a concrete barrier at the side of the road. There was so much destruction to the little car that it was later considered a total loss by the insurance company. The only way to explain why neither of them were hurt had to be the protecting hand of God. They did have bruises on their chests and shoulders from the seat belts, but they could have been injured far worse or even killed. I firmly believe that the Lord answered my prayers for protection on my family. (I'm still waiting for Him to answer the ones about my husband not buying any more sports cars.)

My prayer group and I regularly pray for our husbands to be safe in planes, cars, the workplace, or walking down the street. We don't even have to think of all the specific dangers, we just ask the Lord to protect them from harm. God promises to "give His angels charge over you, to keep you in all your ways. In their hands they shall bear you up, lest you dash your foot against a stone" (Psalm 91:11,12). But accidents do happen, even to godly people, and when they do they are sudden and unexpected. That's why prayer for your husband's protection needs to be frequent and ongoing. You never know when it might be needed in the battlefield. And if something happens, you'll have the comfort of knowing you've invited God's presence and power into the midst of it.

Prayer

Lord, I pray that You would protect (husband's name) from any accidents, diseases, dangers, or evil influences. Keep him safe, especially in cars and planes. Hide him from violence and the plans of evil people. Wherever he walks, secure his steps. Keep him on Your path so that his feet don't slip (Psalm 17:5). If his foot does slip, hold him up by Your mercy (Psalm 94:18). Give him the wisdom and discretion that will help him walk safely and not fall into danger (Proverbs 3:21-23). Be his fortress, strength, shield, and stronghold (Psalm 18:2,3). Make him to dwell in the shadow of Your wings (Psalm 91:1-2). Be his rock, salvation, and defense, so that he will not be moved or shaken (Psalm 62:6). I pray that even though bad things may be happening all around him, they will not come near him (Psalm 91:7). Save him from any plans of the enemy that seek to destroy his life (Psalm 103:4). Preserve his going out and his coming in from this time forth and even forevermore (Psalm 121:8).

POWER TOOLS

He who dwells in the secret place of the Most High shall abide under the shadow of the Almighty. I will say of the LORD, "He is my refuge and my fortress; my God, in Him I will trust."

PSALM 91:1-2

In the time of trouble He shall hide me in His pavilion; in the secret place of His tabernacle He shall hide me; He shall set me high upon a rock.

PSALM 27:5

Yea, though I walk through the valley of the shadow of death, I will fear no evil; for You are with me; Your rod and Your staff, they comfort me.

PSALM 23:4

The LORD is my rock and my fortress and my deliverer; my God, my strength, in whom I will trust; my shield and the horn of my salvation, my stronghold. I will call upon the LORD, who is worthy to be praised; so shall I be saved from my enemies.

PSALM 18:2,3

Show Your marvelous lovingkindness by Your right hand, O You who save those who trust in You from those who rise up against them. Keep me as the apple of Your eye; hide me under the shadow of Your wings.

PSALM 17:7,8

CHAPTER THIRTEEN

His Trials

*E*veryone goes through hard times. It's nothing to be ashamed of. Sometimes our prayers help us to avoid them. Sometimes not. It's the attitude we have when we go through them that matters most. If we are filled with anger and bitterness, or insist on complaining and blaming God, things tend to turn out badly. If we go through them with thankfulness and praise to God, He promises to bring good things despite them. He says to "count it all joy when you fall into various trials, knowing that the testing of your faith produces patience" (James 1:2,3).

A wife's prayers for her husband during these times may not change some of the things he must go through. After all, if we never suffered anything, what kind of shallow, compassionless, impatient people would we be? But prayer can help him maintain a positive outlook of gratitude, hope, patience, and peace in the midst of it, and keep him from reaping the penalty of a wrong response.

My friend, Jan, watched her husband, Dave, hover near death as a result of being bitten by a poisonous spider. It was a terrifying time for both of them and the trial lasted for well over a year as he struggled to rise above each new physical problem that happened as a result. On top of that they had just moved to a new state, away from family, friends, and church, and they suffered financially because of the enormous medical bills. There was every reason to be angry and bitter, but they never allowed themselves to stop praying, praising God, and looking to Him as their source.

Through countless tears and fears of her own, Jan fervently prayed that Dave would not get discouraged in the battle, but be able to stand strong through it. God sustained them, Dave did recover, and they have become two of the richest people in the Lord one could ever hope to meet. Not only that, but their three children are all strong believers who use their enormous talents to glorify God. Dave became a music pastor at a church where he and Jan now have a highly successful ministry. Their lives are a testimony to the goodness of the Lord, and I believe that the manner in which they went through this trial has a lot to do with where they are today.

Whether it feels like it or not, when we serve God, His love attends every moment of our lives—even the toughest, loneliest, most painful and desperate. He is always there in our midst, working things out for good when we pray and look to Him to do so. "We know that all things work together for good to those who love God, to those who are the called according to His purpose" (Romans 8:28). His purpose for our trials is often to bring us humbly before Him to experience a breaking in our inner, independent, self-sufficient selves, and grow us up into compassionate, patient, spiritually strong, God-glorifying people. He uses these situations to teach us how to trust that He loves and cares for us enough to get us through the tough times.

I can't think of any trial that my husband or I have gone through that didn't grow us deeper in the things of God, even though it was miserable to endure at the time and we had little appreciation of where we were headed. But as we prayed through every rough spot, we found our faith growing and our walk with God deepening. And when our attitudes were right, so did our love for one another.

If your husband is going through a difficult time, carry it in prayer, but don't carry the burden. Even though you may want to, don't try to take away his load and make it yours. That will ultimately leave him feeling weak or like a failure. Besides, God doesn't want you doing *His* job. He doesn't want you trying to be the Holy Spirit to your husband. Even though it hurts to see him struggle and you want to fix it, you can't. You can pray, encourage, and support, but God uses trials for His purpose and you must stay out of His way.

If your husband feels crushed under the weight of such things as financial strain, illness, disability, loss of work, problems with the children, marital strife, catastrophes, disasters in the home, or strained relationships, invite the Holy Spirit to move into his circumstances and transform them. Remind your husband of the bigger picture: our suffering will seem like nothing compared to the glory of God worked in us, if we have the right reactions in the midst of the struggle. "For I consider that the sufferings of this present time are not worthy to be compared with the glory which shall be revealed in us" (Romans 8:18). Encourage him to say, "I can do all things through Christ who strengthens me" (Philippians 4:13).

Pray that your husband will be able to press in closer to God until he knows that nothing can separate him from His love—not what he is going through now and not what will happen in the future. "For I am persuaded that neither death nor life, nor angels nor principalities nor powers, nor things present nor things to come, nor height nor depth, nor any other created thing, shall be able to separate us from the love of God which is in Christ Jesus our Lord" (Romans 8:38,39). If nothing can separate him from the love of God, then no matter how bad it gets, he always has hope.

Trials can be a purifying fire and a cleansing water. You don't want your husband to get burned or drowned; you want him to get refined and renewed. God has promised that "in all these things we are more than conquerors through Him who loved us" (Romans 8:37). "He who endures to the end shall be saved" (Matthew 24:13). It's the determination of your husband to stand strong in faith and wait for God to answer his prayers that will save him from the heat and keep him afloat.

Prayer

Lord, You alone know the depth of the burden my husband carries. I may understand the specifics, but You have measured the weight of it on his shoulders. I've not come to minimize what You are doing in his life, for I know You work great things in the midst of trials. Nor am I trying to protect him from what he must face. I only want to support him so that he will get through this battle as the winner.

God, You are our refuge and strength, a very present help in trouble (Psalm 46:1). You have invited us to "come boldly to the throne of grace, that we may obtain mercy and find grace to help in time of need" (Hebrews 4:16). I come before Your throne and ask for grace for my husband. Strengthen his heart for this battle and give him patience to wait on You (Psalm 27:1-4). Build him up so that no matter what happens he will be able to stand strong through it. Help him to be always "rejoicing in hope, patient in tribulation, continuing steadfastly in prayer" (Romans 12:12). Give him endurance to run the race and not give up, for You have said that "a righteous man may fall seven times and rise again" (Proverbs 24:16). Help him to remember that "the steps of a good man are ordered by the LORD, and He delights in his way. Though he fall, he shall not be utterly cast down; for the LORD upholds him with His hand" (Psalm 37:23,24).

I pray he will look to You to be his "refuge until these calamities have passed by" (Psalm 57:1). May he learn to wait on You because "those who wait on the LORD shall renew their strength; they shall mount up with wings like eagles, they shall run and not be weary, they shall walk and not faint" (Isaiah 40:31). I pray that he will find his strength in You and as he cries out to You, You will hear him and save him out of all his troubles (Psalm 34:6).

POWER TOOLS

You have been grieved by various trials, that the genuineness of your faith, being much more precious than gold that perishes, though it is tested by fire, may be found to praise, honor, and glory at the revelation of Jesus Christ.

1 PETER 1:6,7

Cast your burden on the LORD, and He shall
sustain you; He shall never permit the
righteous to be moved.

PSALM 55:22

As for me, I will call upon God, and the LORD shall
save me. Evening and morning and at noon I will
pray, and cry aloud, and He shall hear my voice. He
has redeemed my soul in peace from the battle
that was against me.

PSALM 55:16-18

You, who have shown me great and severe troubles,
shall revive me again, and bring me up again from
the depths of the earth. You shall increase my greatness, and comfort me on every side.

PSALM 71:20,21

CHAPTER FOURTEEN

His Integrity

*I*ntegrity is not what you *appear* to be when all eyes are on you. It's who you *are* when no one is looking. It's a level of morality below which you never fall, no matter what's happening around you. It's a high standard of honesty, truthfulness, decency, and honor that is never breached. It's doing for others the way you would want them to do for you.

A man of integrity says something and means it. He doesn't play verbal games so you never really know where he stands. He knows to let his "Yes" be "Yes" and his "No" be "No." "For whatever is more than these is from the evil one" (Matthew 5:37). He will not play both sides of the fence to please everyone. His goal is to please God and do what is right. A man can be highly esteemed among men but an abomination to God (Luke 16:15).

A man of integrity "swears to his own hurt and does not change" (Psalm 15:4). He will keep his word even if it costs him something to do so. When placed in a possibly compromising situation, he will continue to stand strong in what he believes. Above all, he is a man of truth; you can depend on his solid honesty. A man "who walks with integrity walks securely" (Proverbs 10:9), because his integrity guides him and brings him into the presence of God (Psalm 41:12).

My husband is a man of integrity who has had to take a stand a number of times against things he believed were wrong. It often cost him a great deal. I've always prayed for him to do the right thing, but not because he wouldn't have done it without me. He surely would have. However, my prayers supported him as he faced opposition and helped him to stand strong through it. The Bible says, "The righteous man walks in his integrity; his children are blessed after him" (Proverbs 20:7). Whether my children fully recognize it or not, they will receive a heritage from their father's adherence to the principles of high moral integrity. There are blessings they will enjoy because of the kind of man he is. I pray they will pass those on to *their* children.

Integrity happens in the heart. Therefore, being a man of integrity is something your husband must *choose* to do on his own. But you can prayerfully help him fight the enemy that seeks to snare him, blind him, and keep him from making that decision. Even when he makes the right choice, there will be a negative reaction to it in the realm of evil. Your prayers can help shield him from anything that causes him to doubt and waver, and give him strength to do what's right—even when no one's looking.

Prayer

Lord, I pray that You would make my husband a man of integrity, according to Your standards. Give him strength to say "Yes" when he should say "Yes," and courage to say "No" when he should say "No." Enable him to stand for what he knows is right and not waver under pressure from the world. Don't let him be a man who is "always learning and never able to come to a knowledge of the truth" (2 Timothy 3:7). Give him, instead, a teachable spirit that is willing to listen to the voice of wisdom and grow in Your ways.

Make him a man who lives by truth. Help him to walk with Your Spirit of truth at all times (John 16:13). Be with him to bear witness to the truth so that in times of pressure he will act on it with confidence (1 John 1:8,9). Where he has erred in this and other matters, give him a heart that is quick to confess his mistakes. For You have said in Your Word, "If we say that we have no sin, we deceive ourselves, and the truth is not in us. If we confess our sins, He is faithful and just to forgive us our sins and to cleanse us from all unrighteousness" (1 John 1:8,9). Don't let him be deceived. Don't let him live a lie in any way. Bind mercy and truth around his neck and write them on the tablet of his heart so he will find favor and high esteem in the sight of God and man (Proverbs 3:3,4).

POWER TOOLS

Better is the poor who walks in his integrity than one perverse in his ways, though he be rich.
PROVERBS 28:6

The integrity of the upright will guide them, but the perversity of the unfaithful will destroy them.
PROVERBS 11:3

Judge me, O LORD, according to my righteousness,
and according to my integrity within me.
PSALM 7:8

Vindicate me, O LORD, for I have walked in my
integrity. I have also trusted in the LORD;
I shall not slip.
PSALM 26:1

Let integrity and uprightness preserve me,
for I wait for You.
PSALM 25:21

CHAPTER FIFTEEN

His Reputation

A good reputation is a fragile thing, especially in this day of rapid communication and mass media. Just being in the wrong place at the wrong time can ruin a person's life.

A reputation is not something to be taken lightly. A good name is to be chosen over great riches (Proverbs 22:1) and is better than the "precious ointment" (Ecclesiastes 7:1). It's something to value and protect. A person who doesn't value his reputation may someday desire credibility and not find it. Our reputations can be ruined by wrong things we do, by the people with whom we are associated, or by disparaging words spoken about us. In all three cases, evil is involved. One unfortunate court case, a significant round of gossip, an evil influence, an unflattering newspaper article, or fifteen minutes of notoriety can destroy everything a man has worked for all his life. Prayer is our only defense.

The times my husband was most concerned about his reputation was when he or someone else had been misquoted in a newspaper article as saying something that wasn't true. Because we knew how damaging these kinds of things can be, we always called people we thought would be most affected by any misquotes and told them what the truth was. Of course we couldn't possibly call everyone, so we prayed that those we did call would be enough and that God would put an end to it. As it turned out, what could have been wildfires totally burned themselves out within a day or two. It could easily have gone the other way and consumed us. I am certain it was the power of God in response to prayer that kept us protected.

A virtuous wife, the Bible says, has a husband who is respected. He is "known in the gates, when he sits among the elders of the land" (Proverbs 31:23). Does that just happen? Is every virtuous wife guaranteed a husband with a good reputation? Or does she have something to do with that? It's true that a man gets a certain amount of respect for having a good wife, but I believe one of the good things she does is pray for him and his reputation.

Prayer for your husband's reputation should be an ongoing process. However, keep in mind that he has a free will. If he is not sensitive to the leading of the Holy Spirit, he may still choose to go his own way and get into trouble. If something like that happens or has already happened to tarnish his reputation, pray for God to redeem the situation and bring good out of it. He can do that, too.

Prayer

Lord, I pray that (husband's name) will have a reputation that is untarnished. I know that a man is often valued "by what others say of him" (Proverbs 27:21), so I pray that he will be respected in our town and people will speak highly of him.

You've said in Your Word that "a curse without cause shall not alight" (Proverbs 26:2). I pray that there would never be any reason for bad things to be said of him. Keep him out of legal entanglements. Protect us from lawsuits and criminal proceedings. Deliver him from his enemies, O God. Defend him from those who rise up to do him harm (Psalm 59:1). Fight against those who fight against him (Psalm 35:1). In You, O Lord, we put our trust. Let us never be put to shame (Psalm 71:1). If You are for us, who can be against us (Romans 8:31)?

Your Word says that "a good tree cannot bear bad fruit, nor can a bad tree bear good fruit. Every tree that does not bear good fruit is cut down and thrown into the fire" (Matthew 7:18,19). I pray that my husband will bear good fruit out of the goodness that is within him, and that he will be known by the good that he does. May the fruits of honesty, trustworthiness, and humility sweeten all his dealings so that his reputation will never be spoiled.

Preserve his life from the enemy, hide him from the secret counsel of the wicked. Pull him out of any net which has been laid for him (Psalm 31:4). Keep him safe from the evil of gossiping mouths. Where there has been ill spoken of him, touch the lips of those who speak it with Your refining fire. Let the responsibility of those involved be revealed. Let them be ashamed and brought to confusion who seek to destroy his life; let them be driven backward and brought to dishonor who wish him evil (Psalm 40:14). May he trust in You and not be afraid of what man can do to him (Psalm 56:11). For You have said whoever be-lieves in You will not be put to shame (Romans 10:11). Lead him, guide him, and be his mighty fortress and hiding place. May his light so shine before men that they see his good works and glorify You, Lord (Matthew 5:16).

POWER TOOLS

Hide me from the secret plots of the wicked, from the rebellion of the workers of iniquity, who sharpen their tongue like a sword, and bend their bows to shoot their arrows—bitter words.

PSALM 64:2,3

Do not let me be ashamed, O LORD, for I have called upon You; let the wicked be ashamed; let them be silent in the grave. Let the lying lips be put to silence, which speak insolent things proudly and contemptuously against the righteous.

PSALM 31:17,18

Blessed are you when they revile and persecute you, and say all kinds of evil against you falsely for My sake. Rejoice and be exceedingly glad, for great is your reward in heaven, for so they persecuted the prophets who were before you.

MATTHEW 5:11,12

Do not go hastily to court; for what will you do in the end, when your neighbor has put you to shame? Debate your case with your neighbor, and do not dis-close the secret to another; lest he who hears it expose your shame, and your reputation be ruined.

PROVERBS 25:8-10

Who shall bring a charge against God's elect? It is
God who justifies. Who is he who condemns?
It is Christ who died, and furthermore is also risen,
who is even at the right hand of God, who also
makes intercession for us.

ROMANS 8:33,34

CHAPTER SIXTEEN

His Priorities

*M*en have many different ideas about what their priorities should be. But every wife feels she should be at the top of her husband's list—right there under God. I've found, however, that if a wife wants her husband's priorities to be in that kind of order, she has to make sure *hers* are in that order as well. In other words, if you want your husband to place you as a priority over work, children, friends, and activities, you need to do the same for him. If God and spouse aren't clearly top priorities in *your* life, your husband will have less incentive to make them so in his.

I know very well about the struggle to keep a right order of priorities, especially if there are little ones in the picture. Children's needs are immediate and urgent and you're the one to take care of them. A husband, after all, is an adult and hopefully can take care of himself. Even if there are no children, it's possible to be consumed by work, home, friends, projects, interests, and activities. It's hard, in the midst of everything that occupies your time and attention, not to allow your husband to fall down on the list—or at least feel as though he has.

Fortunately, priorities don't always have to do with the total amount of time spent on them, otherwise anyone with a forty-hour work week would be putting God second to their job unless he or she was praying at least eight hours a day. And there is no way a wife can give as much time to her husband as she does to a young child without neglecting the child. When it comes to your husband, it's not so much a matter of how much time you take, but that you *do* take time to make him feel like he is a priority.

Just greeting him first thing in the morning with a smile and a hug can make him feel he's important to you. So is asking him, "Is there anything you want me to do for you today?" (And then when he tells you, remember to do it.) Also, let him know you are praying for him and ask what he specifically wants you to pray about. Even checking in with him periodically in the midst of the many other things you are doing assures him he's still at the top of your list.

Priorities have to do with the position in the heart. Planning times for just the two of you—a date, a night or two away, a dinner alone, time in the home without any children or friends—communicates to him that he is a priority in your heart. If you want your husband to love *you* more, you need to love *him* more. It always works, especially if you're praying about it as well.

If you feel that you just don't have the time and energy to put your husband first and still do all that's expected of you, ask God for a fresh filling of His Holy Spirit. Seek Him first and He will help you get your priorities in order. If your schedule doesn't allow time to be with God and draw on His strength, then rework your priorities and make a new schedule. The old one is not working.

In the business my husband is in, we often see people experience success quickly. The problem with that is a spirit of lust for *more* success, *more* power, and *more* wealth usually comes along with it. When these people don't make a special effort to keep their priorities in order, their pride guides them, and they buy into its lure. They slip into overdrive, leaving God, family, church, and friends in their dust. When these shooting stars come back to earth, the landing is often hard. We don't want that to happen, even on a small scale, to our husbands. Pray for your husband to always put God first, you second, and children third. Then, no matter what else is going on in his life, his priorities will be in order and there will be greater peace and happiness ahead for both of you.

Prayer

God, I proclaim You Lord over my life. Help me to seek You first every day and set my priorities in perfect order. Reveal to me how to properly put my husband before children, work, family, friends, activities, and interests. Show me what I can do right now to demonstrate to him that he has this position in my heart. Mend the times I have caused him to doubt that. Tell me how to prioritize everything so that whatever steals life away, or has no lasting purpose, will not occupy my time.

I pray for my husband's priorities to be in perfect order as well. Be Lord and Ruler over his heart. Help him to choose a simplicity of life that will allow him to have time alone with You, Lord, a place to be quiet in Your presence every day. Speak to him about making Your Word, prayer, and praise a priority. Enable him to place me and our children in greater prominence in his heart than career, friends, and activities. I pray he will seek You first and submit his all to You, for when he does I know the other pieces of his life will fit together perfectly.

POWER TOOLS

Seek first the kingdom of God and His
righteousness, and all these things shall
be added to you.
MATTHEW 6:33

Let each of you look out not only for his own
interests, but also for the interests of others.
PHILIPPIANS 2:4

No one can serve two masters; for either he will hate
the one and love the other, or else he will be loyal to
the one and despise the other.
MATTHEW 6:24

The kingdom of heaven is like a merchant seeking
beautiful pearls, who, when he had found one
pearl of great price, went and sold all that he
had and bought it.
MATTHEW 13:45,46

You shall worship the LORD your God, and Him
only you shall serve.
MATTHEW 4:10

Chapter Seventeen

His Relationships

*I*solation is not healthy. We all need the influence of good people to keep us on the right path. Every married couple should have at least two strong believing couples with whom they can share encouragement, strength, and the richness of their lives. Being around such people is edifying, enriching, balancing, and fulfilling, and it helps us keep perspective when things seem to grow out of proportion. Having the positive qualities of other people rub off on us is the best thing for a marriage.

I remember one time when Michael and I had an argument just before we were to be at another couple's house for dinner. On the drive there we sat in stiffened silence, and all I could think about was how we could possibly get through the evening gracefully without making the other couple very uncomfortable. When we arrived, the warmth, love, and rich godliness we felt from them infected our thoughts and emotions. Soon we were laughing and talking and having a great time, forgetting about what had transpired previously. What those two people had was not just a "let the good times roll" party spirit. It was the joy of the Lord, and it wore off on us.

We've witnessed the exact same thing happen in reverse. There have been numerous instances when a couple in the midst of marital strife came to our house for dinner and went away with peace in their hearts. One particular couple even called just before they were to arrive—when the dinner was completely ready—to say that they'd just had a bad argument and couldn't possibly be enjoyable guests. I told them we completely understood, having experienced the same thing ourselves, but that we wanted them to come, even if they sat in silence all night. "Besides, you do need to eat," I said. "If necessary you can sit at opposite ends of the table." It took some persuading, but they came and it turned out to be a highly enjoyable evening for all. We even ended up laughing about what transpired earlier and they left hand in hand.

Being good friends with godly people who love the Lord doesn't just happen by chance. We must pray that such people will come into our lives. And then when we find them, we should continue to cover the relationships in prayer. We should also pray the bad influences away. The Bible says we must "not be unequally yoked together with unbelievers" (2 Corinthians 6:14). This doesn't mean we can never be around anyone who isn't a Christian, but our closest, most influential relationships should be with people who know and love the Lord, or there will be consequences. "The righteous should choose his friends carefully, for the way of the wicked leads them astray" (Proverbs 12:26). That's why it's very important to have a church home where it's possible to meet the kind of people you need. Choose to be around the highest quality people you can, the ones whose hearts are aimed toward God.

Pray also for your husband to have godly male friends. And when he finds them, give him time to be with them without criticism. Those friends will refine him. "As iron sharpens iron, so a man sharpens the countenance of his friend" (Proverbs 27:17). They will be a good influence. "Ointment and perfume delight the heart, and the sweetness of a man's friend does so by hearty counsel" (Proverbs 27:9). Of course if it becomes obsessive, pray for balance.

After we had children, Michael worked every day and night during the week and on the weekends he spent all his spare time on the golf course or at baseball and football games with his friends. There were many bitter arguments about that, but no changes happened until I started praying that *God* would convict him and turn his heart toward home. God did a much better job than I ever could have.

Often men have fewer close friends than women because of the way their time is consumed with establishing their careers. They don't take the necessary steps to develop close friendships like we do. That's where prayer can make a difference. Even if your husband is not a believer, you can still pray for him to have godly friends. A close friend of mine has a husband who doesn't know the Lord and we have prayed many times for him to have godly friends and be in contact with believers where he works. God has now brought so many strong Christians into his life that we laugh about how the Lord has him surrounded.

Pray about *all* of your husband's relationships. He needs to have good relationships with his parents, brothers, sisters, aunts, uncles, cousins, coworkers, and neighbors. Pray that none of his relationships be marred by his inability to forgive. A husband who is tortured with unforgiveness is not a pretty sight.

Prayer

Lord, I pray for (husband's name) to have good, godly male friends with whom he can openly share his heart. May they be trustworthy men of wisdom who will speak truth into his life and not just say what he wants to hear (Proverbs 28:23). Give him the discernment to separate himself from anyone who will not be a good influence (1 Corinthians 5:13). Show him the importance of godly friendships and help me encourage him to sustain them. Give us believing married couples with whom we can feel comfortable sharing our lives.

I pray for strong, peaceful relationships with each of his family members, neighbors, acquaintances, and coworkers. Today I specifically pray for his relationship with (name of person). Inspire open communication and mutual acceptance between them. Let there be reconciliation where there has been estrangement. Work peace into anything that needs to be worked out.

I pray that in his heart he will honor his father and mother so that he will live long and be blessed in his life (Exodus 20:12). Enable him to be a forgiving person and not carry grudges or hold things in his heart against others. Lord, You've said in Your Word that "he who hates his brother is in darkness and walks in darkness, and does not know where he is going, because the darkness has blinded his eyes" (1 John 2:11). I pray that my husband would never be blinded by the darkness of unforgiveness, but continually walk in the light of forgiveness. May he not judge or show contempt for anyone but remember that "we shall all stand before the judgment seat of Christ" (Romans 14:10). Enable him to love his enemies, bless those who curse him, do good to those who hate him, and pray for those who spitefully use him and persecute him (Matthew 5:44). I pray that I will be counted as his best friend and that our friendship with one another will continue to grow. Show him what it means to be a true friend and enable him to be one.

POWER TOOLS

Let us consider one another in order to stir up love and good works, not forsaking the assembling of ourselves together, as is the manner of some, but exhorting one another.
HEBREWS 10:24,25

If you bring your gift to the altar, and there remember that your brother has something against you, leave your gift there before the altar, and go your way. First be reconciled to your brother, and then come and offer your gift.
MATTHEW 5:23,24

If we walk in the light as He is in the light, we have fellowship with one another.
1 JOHN 1:7

Take heed to yourselves. If your brother sins against you, rebuke him; and if he repents, forgive him. And if he sins against you seven times in a day, and seven times in a day returns to you, saying, "I repent," you shall forgive him.
LUKE 17:3,4

A new commandment I give to you, that you love
one another; as I have loved you, that you also love
one another. By this all will know that you are My
disciples, if you have love for one another.

JOHN 13:34,35

CHAPTER EIGHTEEN

His Fatherhood

*W*hen I asked my husband to share with me his deepest fears, one of the things he mentioned was the fear of not being a good father. "I believe it's something men in general tend to fear," he said. "We get so caught up in doing what we do in our work that we're afraid we haven't done enough with our children. Or we're afraid we haven't done it *well* enough, or we're missing something. It becomes even more of a problem with teenagers. We fear we can't communicate with them because we'll be perceived as old and irrelevant."

I was touched by his perspective and resolved to pray for him to be a good father. I believe my prayers made a difference because I saw him become more patient with our children and less insecure about his own parenting skills. He grew increasingly relaxed and able to enjoy them. He became less guilt-ridden or angry when it was necessary to discipline them and more able to speak wisdom powerfully into their lives. He now sees that any flaw in our children is not necessarily a reflection of his value as a father.

Thoughts of failure and inadequacy are what cause so many fathers to give up, leave, become overbearing from trying too hard, or develop a passive attitude and fade into the background of their children's lives. It can be especially overwhelming to a man who already feels like a failure in other areas. Mothers get overwhelmed with feelings of inadequacy, too, but only the most deeply disturbed ever abandon, ignore, or hurt their children. That's because we have the opportunity from the moment of conception to pour so much of ourselves into our children's lives. We carry them in the womb, we nurse and nurture them as newborns, we guide and teach and love them so much that we have a full sense of bonding from the start. Fathers don't have that privilege and often feel they are starting on the outside, trying to work their way in. If they are also spending a great amount of time and energy trying to establish their careers, they can easily feel hopelessly removed and ineffectual. Our prayers can help redeem this situation.

Have you ever had someone pray for you when you couldn't think straight, and after they prayed you had complete clarity and vision? I've experienced that countless times. I believe this is what can happen for our husbands when we pray about their parenting. If they are tortured with doubt and burdened by a sense of responsibility, we can minimize these feelings with our prayers. Prayer can help them gain a clear perspective of what it means to be a good father, and open the door to Holy Spirit guidance on how to handle the parenting challenges that arise.

My husband recalled a specific incident where he knew my prayers for him regarding his fatherhood had made a big difference. It happened when our son, Christopher, was about seven and we had caught him in a lie. We knew we had to deal with it, but we wanted a full confession from him along with a repentant heart. Neither was forthcoming at that moment. Michael wanted to teach him a lesson but didn't know what to do, so he asked me to pray. While I was praying, it became very clear to him. As Chris watched, Michael drew a triangle and a picture of Satan, God, and Christopher, one at each of the points. He then described Satan's plan for Chris, and God's plan for Chris. He illustrated how lying was part of Satan's plan that Chris was going along with. He described in detail the ultimate consequences of going along with Satan's plans—which meant traveling on a spectrum away from God—and it shook Christopher up so badly that he broke down and confessed the lie with a completely repentant heart. Michael said he knew that without that clear picture from God he would not have been able to get through to his son with the depth he needed to.

The best way for a man to be a good father is to get to know his heavenly Father and learn to imitate Him. The more time he spends in the Lord's presence, being transformed into His likeness, the better influence he will be when he spends time with his children. He will have a father's heart because he understands *The Father's* heart. This can be difficult if your husband didn't have a good relationship with his earthly father. The way a man relates to his dad will often affect how he relates to his Father God. If he was abandoned by him, he may fear being abandoned by God. If his father was distant or uncaring, he may see God as distant and uncaring. If he doubted his father's love, he may doubt his heavenly Father's love. If he is angry with his father, he may be angry with his Father God as well. Events of the past with regard to his own dad can serve as a barrier that keeps him from truly knowing the Father's love. This will carry over into his relationship with his children.

Pray that your husband grows into a greater understanding of his heavenly Father's love and be healed of any misconceptions he has in his heart and mind about it. Where his father has failed him and he has blamed God, ask the Lord to heal that enormous hurt. The Bible says, "Whoever curses his father or his mother, his lamp will be put out in deep darkness" (Proverbs 20:20). Unless forgiveness happens in his heart for his dad, he will be in the dark as to how to be the best father for his children. His father doesn't have to be alive in order to right that relationship, because it's what is in his own heart regarding his dad that matters. Pray that he will gain a right attitude toward his earthly father so nothing will stand in the way of his relationship with his Father God.

Men don't always realize how important they are to their children. They sometimes feel they are only there to provide materially for them. But the importance of a father's influence can never be underestimated. How he relates to his children will shape their lives for bad or for good. It will change *his* life forever, too. For if he fails as a father, he will always carry that sense of failure with him. If he succeeds, there will be no greater measure of success in his life.

Prayer

Lord, teach __(husband's name)__ to be a good father. Where it was not modeled to him according to Your ways, heal those areas and help him to forgive his dad. Give him revelation of You and a hunger in his heart to really know You as his heavenly Father. Draw him close to spend time in Your presence so he can become more like You, and fully understand Your Father's heart of compassion and love toward him. Grow that same heart in him for his children. Help him to balance mercy, judgment, and instruction the way You do. Though You require obedience, You are quick to acknowledge a repentant heart. Make him that way, too. Show him when to discipline and how. Help him to see that he who loves his child disciplines him promptly (Proverbs 13:24). May he never provoke his "children to wrath, but bring them up in the training and admonition of the Lord" (Ephesians 6:4). I pray we will be united in the rules we set for our children and be in full agreement as to how they are raised. I pray that there will be no strife or argument over how to handle them and the issues that surround their lives.

Give him skills of communication with his children. I pray he will not be stern, hard, cruel, cold, abusive, noncommunicative, passive, critical, weak, uninterested, neglectful, undependable, or uninvolved. Help him instead to be kind, loving, softhearted, warm, interested, affirming, affectionate, involved, strong, consistent, dependable, verbally communicative, understanding, and patient. May he require and inspire his children to honor him as their father so that their lives will be long and blessed.

Lord, I know we pass a spiritual inheritance to our children. Let the heritage he passes on be one rich in the fullness of Your Holy Spirit. Enable him to model clearly a walk of submission to Your laws. May he delight in his children and long to grow them up Your way. Being a good father is something he wants very much. I pray that You would give him the desire of his heart.

POWER TOOLS

Children's children are the crown of old men, and
the glory of children is their father.
PROVERBS 17:6

For whom the LORD loves He corrects, just as a father the son in whom he delights.
PROVERBS 3:12

The father of the righteous will greatly rejoice, and
he who begets a wise child will delight in him.
PROVERBS 23:24

Correct your son, and he will give you rest; yes, he
will give delight to your soul.
PROVERBS 29:17

I will be a Father to you, and you shall be My sons
and daughters, says the LORD Almighty.
2 CORINTHIANS 6:18

CHAPTER NINETEEN

His Past

M ichael was nineteen when he collapsed from nervous exhaustion. He was attending college full time during the day and writing, arranging, playing piano and drums in local clubs in the afternoons and evenings. He had high stress, little sleep, and was rapidly working himself to death. The family doctor suggested he be placed in a nearby mental hospital where he could get the rest he needed. His mother later told me that she *and* the doctor regretted that decision, but at the time they didn't know what else to do. Michael described his two weeks of "rest" there as the most frightening experience of his life. He observed so much strange and horrifying behavior in the other patients that it traumatized him with fear that he might never get out. He went back to college with a less-stressful work schedule, but also great fear.

Throughout the years we've been married, there have been times when he was so overworked and pressured that he experienced that same kind of exhaustion. It always reminded him of what had happened when he was a teenager.

The past would come upon him like a specter and threaten him with the thought, *You're going to end up in a mental hospital again.* It's been at those times, he said, that my prayers for him have meant the most. I always prayed that he would know the truth, and the truth would set him free (John 8:32). I prayed for God to deliver him from his past. This has been a gradual process, but I saw strides forward every time I prayed.

The past should not be a place where we live, but something from which we learn. We are to forget "those things which are behind" and reach "forward to those things which are ahead," and we're to "press toward the goal for the prize of the upward call of God in Christ Jesus" (Philippians 3:13,14). God is a redeemer and a restorer. We need to allow Him to be both. He can redeem the past and restore what was lost. He can make up for the bad things that have happened (Psalm 90:15). We must trust Him to do those things. We can never move out of the present into the future of what God has for us if we cling to and live in the past.

Your husband's past not only affects him, it affects your offspring as well. More is passed down to your children and grandchildren than just the color of your hair and eyes. We can leave a legacy as painful and damaging as the one we experienced ourselves. We can bequeath a heritage of divorce, anger, anxiety, depression, and fear, to name a few. Whatever you and your husband can free yourselves from will mean more freedom for them. As long as you dwell in the past, you not only lose some of what God has for your future, but for your children's future as well.

The events of your husband's past that most affect his life today probably occurred in his childhood. Bad things that happened or good things that *didn't* happen with family members are the most significant. Being labeled in a certain way by a relative or peer carries over into adulthood. Such words as "fat," "stupid," "uncoordinated," "failure," "poor," "loser," "slob," "four-eyes," "slow," or "idiot" take their toll and imprint themselves into the mind and emotions well into adulthood. While no one can pretend the past didn't happen, it's possible to pray that all the effects of it are removed. No one is destined to live with them forever.

God says we are to cry out for deliverance, walk in His ways, proclaim His truth, and then we will find freedom from our past. But sometimes there are *levels* of freedom to go through. Your husband may think he's gotten free of something and it will rear its head again, leaving him feeling like he's right back where he started. Tell him not to be discouraged by that. If he has been walking with the Lord, he is probably moving into a deeper level of liberty that God wants to work in his life. Your prayers will surely gird him for the journey to greater freedom.

Being set free from the past can happen quickly or it can be a step-by-step process, depending on what God is teaching. The problem is, you can't make it happen on your timetable. You have to be patient and pray for as long as it takes to keep the voices of the past at bay so that your husband can make the decision to not listen to them.

Prayer

Lord, I pray that You would enable (husband's name) to let go of his past completely. Deliver him from any hold it has on him. Help him to put off his former conduct and habitual ways of thinking about it and be renewed in his mind

(Ephesians 4:22,23). Enlarge his understanding to know that You make all things new (Revelation 21:5). Show him a fresh, Holy Spirit-inspired way of relating to negative things that have happened. Give him the mind of Christ so that he can clearly discern Your voice from the voices of the past. When he hears those old voices, enable him to rise up and shut them down with the truth of Your Word. Where he has formerly experienced rejection or pain, I pray he not allow them to color what he sees and hears now. Pour forgiveness into his heart so that bitterness, resentment, revenge, and unforgiveness will have no place there. May he regard the past as only a history lesson and not a guide for his daily life. Wherever his past has become an unpleasant memory, I pray You would redeem it and bring life out of it. Bind up his wounds (Psalm 147:3). Restore his soul (Psalm 23:3). Help him to release the past so that he will not live in it, but learn from it, break out of it, and move into the future You have for him.

POWER TOOLS

Do not remember the former things, nor consider
the things of old. Behold, I will do a new thing, now it
shall spring forth; shall you not know it? I will even
make a road in the wilderness and rivers in the desert.

ISAIAH 43:18,19

If anyone is in Christ, he is a new creation;
old things have passed away; behold,
all things have become new.

2 CORINTHIANS 5:17

Put off, concerning your former conduct, the
old man which grows corrupt according to the
deceitful lusts, and be renewed in the spirit of
your mind, and . . . put on the new man
which was created according to God,
in true righteousness and holiness.
EPHESIANS 4:22-24

Even though our outward man is perishing, yet the
inward man is being renewed day by day.
2 CORINTHIANS 4:16

God will wipe away every tear from their eyes;
there shall be no more death, nor sorrow, nor crying;
and there shall be no more pain, for the former
things have passed away.
REVELATION 21:4

CHAPTER TWENTY

His Attitude

No one wants to be around a person with a bad attitude. Life is hard enough without listening to someone constantly complaining in your ear. I know a man who is so in the habit of being angry and miserable that it is his first reaction to everything—even good news. When great things happen, he finds something to be upset about. Unfortunately, this was modeled to him as a child, so it was probably a learned response. Perhaps no one ever showed him how to enjoy life. But allowing the past to control today is still a choice he makes. Because of that, not only will he never be happy, but neither will those around him. We don't want to be that kind of person, nor do we want to live with one.

Without naming names, let me assure you that I am an expert when it comes to praying for someone with a bad attitude. It took me a long time, however, to stop reacting to the negativity and start praying about it instead. It has paid off, but I'm still perfecting this mode of operation. Every time I prayed for a spirit of joy to arise in this person's heart, I saw visible changes and my reaction was better as well.

An angry, dour, unforgiving, negative person can get that way for various reasons. He *stays* that way because of a stubborn will that refuses to receive God's love. The Bible says we have a choice as to what we will allow into our heart (Psalm 101:4), and whether we will harden it to the love of God or not (Proverbs 28:14). We choose our attitude. We choose to receive the love of the Lord. We permit an attitude of thankfulness to rise in us.

If your husband allows himself to wallow in a consistently bad attitude, it will make a good marriage miserable, and a shaky marriage intolerable. A habit of responding negatively will adversely affect every aspect of his life. Of course you can't rule over your husband's will, but you can pray that his will lines up with God's. Pray that his heart becomes pure, because the Bible promises a person who has a pure heart will see God (Matthew 5:8) and have a cheerful countenance (Proverbs 15:13). (Who doesn't wish her husband could see God and have a cheerful countenance?) Pray for his heart to be filled with praise, thanksgiving, love, and joy, because "a good man out of the good treasure of his heart brings forth good things" (Matthew 12:35). Even if there are no major changes immediately, he is certain to be softened by your prayers. And that, at least, can give *you* a better attitude while you wait for his to improve.

Prayer

Lord, fill (husband's name) with Your love and peace today. May there be a calmness, serenity, and sense of well-being established in him because his life is God-controlled, rather than flesh-controlled. Enable him to walk in his house with a clean and perfect heart before You (Psalm 101:2). Shine the light of Your Spirit upon him and fill him with Your love.

I pray that he will be kind and patient, not selfish or easily provoked. Enable him to bear all things, believe all things, hope all things, and endure all things (1 Corinthians 13:7). Release him from anger, unrest, anxiety, concerns, inner turmoil, strife, and pressure. May he not be broken in spirit because of sorrow (Proverbs 15:13), but enjoy the continual feast of a merry heart (Proverbs 15:15). Give him a spirit of joy and keep him from growing into a grumpy old man. Help him to be anxious for nothing, but give thanks in all things so he can know the peace that passes all understanding. May he come to the point of saying, "I have learned in whatever state I am, to be content" (Philippians 4:11). I say to <u>(husband's name)</u> this day, "The LORD bless you and keep you; the LORD make His face shine upon you, and be gracious to you; the LORD lift up His countenance upon you, and give you peace" (Numbers 6:24-26).

POWER TOOLS

Be anxious for nothing, but in everything by prayer and supplication, with thanksgiving, let your requests be made known to God; and the peace of God, which surpasses all understanding, will guard your hearts and minds through Christ Jesus.

PHILIPPIANS 4:6,7

Cast away from you all the transgressions which you have committed, and get yourselves a new heart and a new spirit.

EZEKIEL 18:31

Whoever has no rule over his own spirit is
like a city broken down, without walls.
PROVERBS 25:28

Though I have the gift of prophecy, and understand
all mysteries and all knowledge, and though I have
all faith, so that I could remove mountains,
but have not love, I am nothing.
1 CORINTHIANS 13:2

Enter into His gates with thanksgiving,
and into His courts with praise.
Be thankful to Him, and bless His name.
PSALM 100:4

CHAPTER TWENTY-ONE

His Marriage

*B*efore I was married, one of the traits I knew I wanted in a husband was an avid disinterest in sports. I detested the thought of being with someone the rest of my life who spent every spare moment on a couch with remote in hand, watching football, baseball, basketball, and golf. One of the things I admired most about Michael when we first started dating was that he never mentioned sports when we were together. In fact, he claimed to be completely bored with them. You can imagine how shocked I was when, several years after we were married, he became not merely interested in sports, but obsessed. If the Chicago Bears lost, so, ultimately, did the rest of the family. When the Cubs won, everyone around him went deaf from his screaming. He wasn't content to see an occasional game; he had to see *every* game. He wasn't a passive observer. He dressed up in Bear T-shirts and Cub hats and jumped up and down. I tried going to games with him, but I found more intrigue in the hot dogs. I tried watching sports with him on TV, but the boredom was excruciating. I gave in to resentment over the fact that it seemed he would rather watch a sporting event than spend time with his family.

It wasn't until years later, when I really started praying about our marriage, that things changed. For some reason unfathomable to me, God didn't take away my husband's interest in sports like I prayed. Instead, He gave me peace and a new perspective on it. We worked out a compromise where I wouldn't pressure him to deny himself sports, if he wouldn't put pressure on me to feign interest. I would not accuse him of tactical deception before we were married, if he would allow me the same courtesy. This may seem like a minor concern in a marriage, but these kinds of things add up and can become pivotal in determining whether a marriage stays together or falls apart.

Praying about all aspects of a marriage keeps the concept of divorce from gaining any hold. So we mustn't neglect the major issues, even if we think they don't apply to us. From the day we were married, I prayed that there would be no divorce or adultery in our future. Although there was no history of either of those in our family backgrounds, divorce and adultery had so saturated our culture and the business we were in that they were almost expected in some circles. I prayed that God would preserve our marriage from any such destruction. He has been faithful to answer those prayers.

Marriage is great when two people enter into it with a mutual commitment to keep it strong no matter what. But often a couple will have preconceived ideas about who the other is and how married life is supposed to be, and then reality hits. That's when their kingdom can become divided. You have to continually pray that any unreal expectations be exposed and all incompatibilities be smoothed out so that you grow together in a spirit of unity, commitment, and a bond of intimacy. Pray that your marriage is a place where two agree so God will be in the midst of it (Matthew 18:19,20). If either of you has been married before, pray that you do not bring any residue from that into your marriage now. Break any ties—good or bad, emotional or spiritual—with any former relationships. You can't move forward into the future if you have a foot stuck in the past.

Don't take your marriage for granted, no matter how great it is. "Let him who thinks he stands take heed lest he fall" (1 Corinthians 10:12). Pray for your marriage to be protected from any person or situation that could destroy it. Ask the Lord to do whatever it takes to keep the marriage intact, even if it means striking one of you with lightning when you think about giving it all up! Pray that God will make your marriage a source of joy and life to both of you, and not a drudgery, a thorn, a dread, an irritation, or a temporary condition.

Prayer

Lord, I pray You would protect our marriage from anything that would harm or destroy it. Shield it from our own selfishness and neglect, from the evil plans and desires of others, and from unhealthy or dangerous situations. May there be no thoughts of divorce or infidelity in our hearts, and none in our future. Set us free from past hurts, memories, and ties from previous relationships, and unrealistic expectations of one another. I pray that there be no jealousy in either of us, or the low self-esteem that precedes that. Let nothing come into our hearts and habits that would threaten the marriage in any way, especially influences like alcohol, drugs, gambling, pornography, lust, or obsessions.

Unite us in a bond of friendship, commitment, generosity, and understanding. Eliminate our immaturity, hostility, or feelings of inadequacy. Help us to make time for one another alone, to nurture and renew the marriage and remind ourselves of the reasons we were married in the first place. I pray that <u>(husband's name)</u> will be so committed to You, Lord, that his commitment to me will not waiver, no matter what storms come. I pray that our love for each other will grow stronger every day, so that we will never leave a legacy of divorce to our children.

POWER TOOLS

Two are better than one, because they have a good reward for their labor. For if they fall, one will lift up his companion. But woe to him who is alone when he falls, for he has no one to help him up.

ECCLESIASTES 4:9,10

Take heed to your spirit, and let none deal treacherously with the wife of his youth. For the LORD God of Israel says that He hates divorce, "for it covers one's garment with violence," says the LORD of hosts. Therefore take heed to your spirit, that you do not deal treacherously.

MALACHI 2:15,16

Marriage is honorable among all, and the bed undefiled; but fornicators and adulterers God will judge.

HEBREWS 13:4

If two lie down together, they will keep warm;
but how can one be warm alone?
ECCLESIASTES 4:11

Now to the married I command, yet not I but the
Lord: A wife is not to depart from her husband. But
even if she does depart, let her remain unmarried or
be reconciled to her husband. And a husband is not
to divorce his wife.
1 CORINTHIANS 7:10,11

CHAPTER TWENTY-TWO

His Emotions

*D*on used anger to control his family. Each family member was so concerned about his temper that they lived their lives on tiptoe, doing his bidding out of fear rather than love. When his wife, Jenny, learned she not only didn't have to tolerate his anger, but going along with it was disobedient to God, things began to change: "Make no friendship with an angry man, and with a furious man do not go, lest you learn his ways and set a snare for your soul" (Proverbs 22:24,25).

Jenny realized she could still love the man but not approve of his sin, so she began praying fervently for him on a regular basis, both alone and with a group of prayer partners. She prayed he would stop being controlled by his emotions, and instead be controlled by the Holy Spirit. Her prayers not only helped to clear his mind enough for him to see how he had been acting, but they paved the way for him to find strength and courage to alter his behavior. "A gift in secret pacifies anger" (Proverbs 21:14). The best gift a wife can give in secret to calm her husband's anger is to pray for him.

Chad was tormented for years by chronic depression. Although his wife, Marilyn, was an upbeat person, his negative emotions brought her down and made her feel hopeless and depressed just like he was. Then she read about King David's experiences and recognized they described exactly what her husband had been feeling. "My soul is full of troubles, and my life draws near to the grave. I am counted with those who go down to the pit; I am like a man who has no strength" (Psalm 88:3,4). "I am troubled, I am bowed down greatly; I go mourning all the day long". . . . "I am feeble and severely broken; I groan because of the turmoil of my heart" (Psalm 38:6,8).

Marilyn saw that in spite of such deep despair, David found his hope in the Lord and rose above it. "O LORD, You have brought my soul up from the grave; You have kept me alive, that I should not go down to the pit" (Psalm 30:3). "I will be glad and rejoice in Your mercy, for You have considered my trouble; You have known my soul in adversities" (Psalm 31:7). "Draw near to my soul, and redeem it" (Psalm 69:18). She felt God surely had compassion for Chad and it sparked hope in her that prayer was the key to his freedom from the grips of depression.

She told Chad she had committed to pray for him every day and wanted him to keep her informed as to how he was feeling. From the first day, they both noticed that every time she prayed, his spirit lifted. Soon he could no longer deny the power of prayer and he began to pray along with her. He has been steadily improving ever since. His depressions are less frequent now and he is able to rise above them far more quickly. The two of them are committed to seek God for Chad's total freedom.

Anger and depression are but two of the many negative emotions that can torment a man's soul. Often they are only an habitual way of thinking that has been given place over time. Men tend to believe it's part of their character that can't be altered, but these patterns can be broken. Don't stand by and watch your husband be manipulated by his emotions. Freedom may be just a prayer away.

Prayer

Lord, You have said in Your Word that You redeem our souls when we put our trust in You (Psalm 34:22). I pray that <u>(husband's name)</u> would have faith in You to redeem his soul from negative emotions. May he never be controlled by depression, anger, anxiety, jealousy, hopelessness, fear, or suicidal thoughts. Specifically I pray about <u>(area of concern)</u>. Deliver him from this and all other controlling emotions (Psalm 40:17). I know that only You can deliver and heal, but use me as Your instrument of restoration. Help me not to be pulled down with him when he struggles. Enable me instead to understand and have words to say that will bring life.

Free him to share his deepest feelings with me and others who can help. Liberate him to cry when he needs to and not bottle his emotions inside. At the same time, give him the gift of laughter and ability to find humor in even serious situations. Teach him to take his eyes off his circumstances and trust in You, regardless of how he is feeling. Give him patience to possess his soul and the ability to take charge of it (Luke 21:19). Anoint him with "the oil of joy" (Isaiah 61:3), refresh him with Your Spirit, and set him free from negative emotions this day.

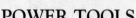

POWER TOOLS

He who trusts in his own heart is a fool, but
whoever walks wisely will be delivered.
PROVERBS 28:26

The eye of the LORD is on those who fear Him,
on those who hope in His mercy, to deliver
their soul from death.
PSALM 33:18,19

I waited patiently for the LORD; and He inclined to
me, and heard my cry. He also brought me up out of
a horrible pit, out of the miry clay, and set my feet
upon a rock, and established my steps. He has put a
new song in my mouth—praise to our God; many
will see it and fear, and will trust in the LORD.
PSALM 40:1-3

He restores my soul; He leads me in the paths of
righteousness for His name's sake.
PSALM 23:3

The LORD redeems the soul of His servants, and none
of those who trust in Him shall be condemned.
PSALM 34:22

CHAPTER TWENTY-THREE

His Walk

*A*man's walk is the way he journeys through life—his direction, his focus, the steps he takes. Every day he chooses a path. One path will take him forward. All others will take him back. The way he walks affects every aspect of his being—how he relates to other people, how he treats his family, how people view him, even how he looks. I've seen men who were unattractive by any standard change radically as they learned to walk with the Spirit of God. As His image became imprinted upon theirs, they developed a richness of soul, a glorious purity, and an inner confidence of knowing what direction they were going. This gave them a strength and a sense of purpose that is not only attractive and appealing, it's magnetic.

The Bible reveals much about the kind of walk we should have. We are to walk with *moral correctness* because "no good thing will He withhold from those who walk uprightly" (Psalm 84:11). We are to walk *without fault* because "whoever walks blamelessly will be saved" (Proverbs 28:18). We are to walk with *godly advisors* because "blessed is the man who walks not in the counsel of the ungodly" (Psalm 1:1). We are to walk in *obedience* because "blessed is every one who fears the LORD, who walks in His ways" (Psalm 128:1). We are to walk with *people of wisdom* because "he who walks with wise men will be wise" (Proverbs 13:20). We are to walk with *integrity* because "he who walks with integrity walks securely" (Proverbs 10:9). Most of all, we are to walk a path of holiness. "A highway shall be there, and a road, and it shall be called the Highway of Holiness. The unclean shall not pass over it, but it shall be for others. Whoever walks the road, although a fool, shall not go astray" (Isaiah 35:8). The best part about walking on the Highway of Holiness is that even if we end up doing something dumb, we still won't get thrown off the path.

Debra's husband, Ben, is a godly man who would not be considered a foolish person. However, he did make an impulsive investment of a rather large sum of money which, in hindsight, proved to be a very foolish move. All that money was lost, and more, because there were added expenses as a result. This matter could have destroyed their finances and possibly even their health and their marriage, but because Ben had a solid walk of obedience and holiness before the Lord, they were spared. The fact that he ran ahead on the path and foolishly didn't wait for God's direction got him into trouble, but not to his destruction.

Jesus said there is only one way to get on the right path, one door through which to enter. "I am the way," He says (John 14:6). The way that leads to destruction is wide and broad and many choose to go that route. But "narrow is the gate and difficult is the way which leads to life, and there are few who find it" (Matthew 7:14). Pray for your husband to find it. Pray that he is guided by God's Holy Spirit. Pray that he stays on the path by having faith in God's Word, a heart for obedience, and deep repentance for any actions he takes that are not God's will for his life. Faith and obedience will get him on the Highway of Holiness; walking in the Spirit, and not in the flesh, will keep him there.

God desires that your husband's every step be led by Him (Galatians 5:25), so He can walk with him and grow him into His image. A man who walks with God is very desirable indeed.

Prayer

"O Lord, I know the way of man is not in himself; it is not in man who walks to direct his own steps" (Jeremiah 10:23). Therefore, Lord, I pray that *You* would direct my husband's steps. Lead him in *Your* light, teach him *Your* way, so he will walk in *Your* truth. I pray that he would have a deeper walk with You and an ever progressing hunger for Your Word. May Your presence be like a delicacy he never ceases to crave. Lead him on Your path and make him quick to confess when he strays from it. Reveal to him any hidden sin that would hinder him from walking rightly before You. May he experience deep repentance when he doesn't live in obedience to Your laws. Create in him a clean heart and renew a steadfast spirit within him. Don't cast him away from Your presence, and do not take Your Holy Spirit from him (Psalm 51:10,11).

Lord, Your Word says that those who are in the flesh cannot please You (Romans 8:8). So I pray that You will enable (husband's name) to walk in the Spirit and not in the flesh and thereby keep himself "from the paths of the destroyer" (Psalm 17:4). As he walks in the Spirit, may he bear the fruit of the Spirit, which is love, joy, peace, patience, kindness, goodness, faithfulness, gentleness, and self-control (Galatians 5:22,23). Keep him on the Highway of Holiness so that the way he walks will be integrated into every part of his life.

POWER TOOLS

Walk worthy of the calling with which you were called, with all lowliness and gentleness, with long-suffering, bearing with one another in love.

EPHESIANS 4:1,2

He who walks righteously and speaks uprightly, he who despises the gain of oppressions, who gestures with his hands, refusing bribes, who stops his ears from hearing of bloodshed, and shuts his eyes from seeing evil: he will dwell on high; his place of defense will be the fortress of rocks; bread will be given him, his water will be sure.

ISAIAH 33:15,16

Having these promises, beloved, let us cleanse ourselves from all filthiness of the flesh and spirit, perfecting holiness in the fear of God.

2 CORINTHIANS 7:1

LORD, who may abide in Your tabernacle? Who may dwell in Your holy hill? He who walks uprightly, and works righteousness, and speaks the truth in his heart.

PSALM 15:1,2

My eyes shall be on the faithful of the land,
that they may dwell with me; he who walks in
a perfect way, he shall serve me.

Psalm 101:6

CHAPTER TWENTY-FOUR

His Talk

*H*ave you ever observed a man who is all talk and no action? There are some men who spend more time bragging about what they are going to do than actually doing it. They typically never get anywhere. "A dream comes through much activity, and a fool's voice is known by his many words" (Ecclesiastes 5:3). Dreams don't come true when more time is spent talking about them than praying and working toward achieving them.

Have you been around a man who is angry, crass, or ungodly in his speech? His bad language gives his listeners a sick, uncomfortable feeling and they don't want to be around him. "Let all bitterness, wrath, anger, clamor, and evil speaking be put away from you, with all malice" (Ephesians 4:31). The good things of life seem to overlook those who have nothing good coming out of their mouths.

Have you known a man who complains all the time? No matter what's happening, he finds something negative to grumble about. "Do all things without murmuring and disputing, that you may become blameless and harmless, children of God without fault in the midst of a crooked and perverse generation, among whom you shine as lights in the world" (Philippians 2:14,15). Negative words bring negative results and things seldom turn out right for a person who continually uses them.

Are you acquainted with a man who is quick to speak yet does not seriously consider what he is saying? He blurts out words without weighing the effect of them. "The heart of the righteous studies how to answer, but the mouth of the wicked pours forth evil" (Proverbs 15:28). "Do you see a man hasty in his words? There is more hope for a fool than for him" (Proverbs 29:20). Much grief is in the future of anyone who doesn't consider the consequences of his spoken words.

Have you seen a man speak discouragement and pain into someone—a spouse, a child, a friend, a coworker? "Death and life are in the power of the tongue, and those who love it will eat its fruit" (Proverbs 18:21). That man will bring *destruction* into his own life because of it.

Our words can justify us or condemn us (Matthew 12:37). They can bring us joy (Proverbs 15:23), or corrupt and dishonor us (Matthew 15:11). What we say can either build up or break down the soul of whomever we are speaking to (Proverbs 15:4). The consequences of what we speak are so great that our words can lead us to ruin or save our lives (Proverbs 13:3).

Everyone has a choice about what he or she says, and there are rewards for making the right one. "Whoever guards his mouth and tongue keeps his soul from troubles" (Proverbs 21:23). Listen to the way your husband talks. What comes out of his mouth has to do with the condition of his heart. "For out of the abundance of the heart the mouth speaks" (Matthew 12:34). If you hear him complaining, speaking negatively, talking like a fool, or speaking words that bring destruction and death into his or anyone else's life, he is suffering from negative heart overflow. Pray for the Holy Spirit to convict his heart, fill it with His love, peace, and joy, and teach him a new way to talk.

Prayer

Lord, I pray Your Holy Spirit would guard my husband's mouth so that he will speak only words that edify and bring life. Help him to not be a grumbler, complainer, a user of foul language, or one who destroys with his words, but be disciplined enough to keep his conversation godly. Your Word says a man who desires a long life must keep his tongue from evil and his lips from speaking deceit (Psalm 34:12-13). Show him how to do that. Fill him with Your love so that out of the overflow of his heart will come words that build up and not tear down. Work that in my heart as well.

May Your Spirit of love reign in the words we speak so that we don't miscommunicate or wound one another. Help us to show each other respect, speak words that encourage, share our feelings openly, and come to mutual agreements without strife. Lord, You've said in Your Word that when two agree, You are in their midst. I pray that the reverse be true as well—that You will be in our midst so that we two can agree. Let the words of our mouths and the meditations of our hearts be acceptable in Your sight, O Lord, our strength and our Redeemer (Psalm 19:14).

POWER TOOLS

Let no corrupt word proceed out of your mouth, but
what is good for necessary edification, that it may impart grace to the hearers.
EPHESIANS 4:29

For every idle word men may speak, they will give
account of it in the day of judgment.
MATTHEW 12:36

Who is the man who desires life, and loves many
days, that he may see good? Keep your tongue from
evil, and your lips from speaking deceit.
PSALM 34:12,13

The words of a wise man's mouth are gracious, but
the lips of a fool shall swallow him up.
ECCLESIASTES 10:12

Those things which proceed out of the mouth come
from the heart, and they defile a man.
MATTHEW 15:18

CHAPTER TWENTY-FIVE

His Repentance

S uzanne prayed every day for years that her husband, Jerry, would stop using drugs. Over and over she caught him doing the same thing. Each time he would confess it, say he was sorry, and swear he wasn't going to do it again. But time and again he fell. She never gave up praying for true repentance to happen in his heart—the kind that turns a man around to walk in a different direction. Unfortunately, Jerry had to learn some hard and painful lessons before God got his attention, but eventually there was a life-changing transformation. Today he is a new man, and together with Suzanne he has a public ministry helping people with similar problems. Suzanne was a praying wife who never stopped believing that God would bring her husband to repentance.

Everyone makes mistakes. That's not the issue. But there is an epidemic in the world today of people who can't admit they did something wrong. God says, "If we confess our sins, He is faithful and just to forgive us our sins and to cleanse us from all unrighteousness" (1 John 1:9). But first we have to be sorry about what we've done.

According to God's way of doing things, there are three steps to changing our behavior. First there is *confession*, which is *admitting* what we did. Next there is *repentance*, which is *being sorry* about what we did. Then there is *asking forgiveness*, which is *being cleansed and released* from what we did. The inability or resistance to do any of these three steps is rooted in pride. A man who can't humble himself to admit he's wrong before God and before man will have problems in his life that never go away. "Do you see a man wise in his own eyes? There is more hope for a fool than for him" (Proverbs 26:12).

Does your husband have trouble confessing his faults? Or is he the kind of person who can say "I'm sorry" twenty times a day, yet the behavior he apologizes for never changes? In either case, he needs a repentant heart. True repentance means having so much remorse over what you've done that you don't do it again. Only God can cause us to see our sin for what it is, and feel about it the same way He does. "The goodness of God leads you to repentance" (Romans 2:4). Repentance is a working of God's grace, and we can pray for it to be worked in our husbands.

Too many men have fallen because of pride and the inability to confess and repent. We see it all the time. We read about it in the newspapers. Unconfessed sin doesn't just go away. It becomes a cancer that grows and suffocates life. Pray for your husband to be convicted of his sin, to humbly confess it before God, then turn from his error and cease to do it. God is "not willing that any should perish but that all should come to repentance" (2 Peter 3:9). This kind of prayer can be very annoying to the one being prayed for, but it's far easier to have God shine His light upon our sin than it is to experience the consequences of it. Your husband will be thankful in the end, even if he won't admit it.

Prayer

Lord, I pray that You would convict my husband of any error in his life. Let there be "nothing covered that will not be revealed, and hidden that will not be known" (Matthew 10:26). Cleanse him from any secret sins and teach him to be a person who is quick to confess when he is wrong (Psalm 19:12). Help him to recognize his mistakes. Give him eyes to see Your truth and ears to hear Your voice. Bring him to full repentance before You. If there is suffering to be done, let it be the suffering of a remorseful heart and not because the crushing hand of the enemy has found an opening into his life through unconfessed sin. Lord, I know that humility must come before honor (Proverbs 15:33). Take away all pride that would cause him to deny his faults and work into his soul a humility of heart so that he will receive the honor You have for him.

POWER TOOLS

If our heart does not condemn us, we have confidence toward God. And whatever we ask we receive from Him, because we keep His commandments and do those things that are pleasing in His sight.

1 JOHN 3:21,22

He who covers his sins will not prosper, but whoever confesses and forsakes them will have mercy.

PROVERBS 28:13

Search me, O God, and know my heart; try me, and know my anxieties; and see if there is any wicked way in me, and lead me in the way everlasting.

PSALM 139:23,24

When I kept silent, my bones grew old through my
groaning all the day long. For day and night Your
hand was heavy upon me; my vitality was turned into
the drought of summer. I acknowledged my sin to
You, and my iniquity I have not hidden. I said, "I will
confess my transgressions to the LORD," and You forgave the iniquity of my sin.

PSALM 32:3-5

A servant of the Lord must not quarrel but be gentle
to all, able to teach, patient, in humility correcting
those who are in opposition, if God perhaps will
grant them repentance, so that they may know the
truth, and that they may come to their senses and
escape the snare of the devil, having been taken
captive by him to do his will.

2 TIMOTHY 2:24-26

CHAPTER TWENTY-SIX

His Deliverance

*M*elissa was concerned about her husband's attraction to alcohol. Mark wasn't exactly an alcoholic, but he was exhibiting symptoms reminiscent of his father, who *was* an alcoholic. She prayed for a breaking of any similar tendency that may have been passed on to her husband, and she also prayed that their children would not inherit the weakness either. She asked God to protect them all from even the *symptoms* of alcoholism. To this day her husband has not become an alcoholic and her teenagers show no signs of it. She feels the power of God in answer to her prayers has played a major part in keeping them from inheriting this condition.

Stephanie had been married to Jason only a short time before she realized he struggled with a spirit of lust. It wasn't that he didn't love her. He was dealing with the sins of his past—a promiscuous lifestyle from which he had never thoroughly distanced himself or renounced. Once she recognized it as something he was captive to, she prayed for his deliverance. Because he wanted that, too, it wasn't long before he was set free from it.

Everyone needs deliverance at certain times, because
there are all kinds of things that can pull us into bondage.
God knows this. Why would Jesus have come as the Deliverer if we didn't need one? Why would He have instructed us to pray, "Deliver us from the evil one"
(Matthew 6:13) if we didn't need to be? Why does He
promise to deliver us from temptation (2 Peter 2:9), the
clutches of dangerous people (Psalm 140:1), our self-
destructive tendencies (Proverbs 24:11), *all* of our troubles
(Psalm 34:17), and death (2 Corinthians 1:10), if He
doesn't intend to do it? He is ready and willing. We just
have to ask. "Call upon Me in the day of trouble; I will deliver you, and you shall glorify Me" (Psalm 50:15).

Isn't it comforting to know that when we feel imprisoned by the death grip of our circumstances, God hears our
cries for freedom? He sees our need. "He looked down from
the height of His sanctuary; from heaven the LORD viewed
the earth, to hear the groaning of the prisoner, to release
those appointed to death" (Psalm 102:19,20). How glorious
to embrace the certainty that when there seems to be no
way out, God can miraculously lift us up and away from
whatever is seeking to devour us (Psalm 25:15). Who
doesn't need that?

Even if your husband finds it difficult to admit he needs
help—some men feel like failures if they can't do it all
themselves—your prayers can still be instrumental in his
finding deliverance. You can pray to the Deliverer to set
him free from anything that binds him. You can stand
strong, through your prayers, against the enemy who seeks
to put him into bondage. "Stand fast therefore in the liberty
by which Christ has made us free, and do not be entangled
again with a yoke of bondage" (Galatians 5:1). The best
way I know to stand strong is to put on the whole armor of

God. That's the way I pray for myself and my husband and I have found it to be most effective. Rather than explain it, let me show you how to pray it.

Prayer

Lord, You have said to call upon You in the day of trouble and You will deliver us (Psalm 50:15). I call upon You now and ask that You would work deliverance in my husband's life. Deliver him from anything that binds him. Set him free from <u>(name a specific thing)</u>. Deliver him quickly and be a rock of refuge and a fortress of defense to save him (Psalm 31:2). Lift him away from the hands of the enemy (Psalm 31:15).

Bring him to a place of understanding where he can recognize the work of evil and cry out to You for help. If the deliverance he prays for isn't immediate, keep him from discouragement and help him to be confident that You have begun a good work in him and will complete it (Philippians 1:6). Give him the certainty that even in his most hopeless state, when he finds it impossible to change anything, You, Lord, can change everything.

Help him understand that "we do not wrestle against flesh and blood, but against principalities, against powers, against the rulers of the darkness of this age, against spiritual hosts of wickedness in the heavenly places" (Ephesians 6:12). I pray that he will be strong in the Lord and put on the whole armor of God, so he can stand against the wiles of the devil in the evil day. Help him to gird his waist with truth and put on the breastplate of righteousness, having shod his feet with the preparation of the gospel of peace. Enable him to take up the shield of faith, with which to quench all the fiery darts of the wicked one. I pray that he will take the helmet of salvation, and the sword of the Spirit, which is the Word of God, praying always with all prayer and supplication in the Spirit, being watchful and standing strong to the end (Ephesians 6:13-18).

POWER TOOLS

The LORD is my rock and my fortress and my deliverer; my God, my strength, in whom I will trust; my shield and the horn of my salvation, my stronghold. I will call upon the LORD, who is worthy to be praised; so shall I be saved from my enemies.

PSALM 18:2,3

Because he has set his love upon Me, therefore I will deliver him; I will set him on high, because he has known My name.

PSALM 91:14

He sent from above, He took me; He drew me out of many waters. He delivered me from my strong enemy, from those who hated me, for they were too strong for me. They confronted me in the day of my calamity, but the LORD was my support. He also brought me out into a broad place; He delivered me because He delighted in me.

PSALM 18:16-19

You have delivered my soul from death. Have You
not delivered my feet from falling, that I may walk
before God in the light of the living?
PSALM 56:13

The Spirit of the LORD is upon Me, because He has
anointed Me to preach the gospel to the poor; He
has sent Me to heal the brokenhearted, to proclaim
liberty to the captives and recovery of sight to the
blind, to set at liberty those who are oppressed.
LUKE 4:18

CHAPTER TWENTY-SEVEN

His Obedience

*L*isa was concerned that her husband, Jonathan, was not growing spiritually the way she was. Her relationship with the Lord was deepening every day while his appeared to be shrinking just as rapidly. She was frustrated with his lack of spiritual commitment, because she longed for them to grow together and have a shared experience in this vital area of their lives. She didn't want to be the spiritual heavyweight in the family. Whenever she said anything about it, Jonathan protested, saying his career kept him too busy to spend time with the Lord and read His Word. Even his business trips often took him out of town on weekends so he missed attending church with Lisa and their children.

The thing that bothered *her* most was that none of this seemed to bother *him*—that is until his work became more challenging than he could comfortably handle. As he grew increasingly stressed, Lisa could see how depleting it was for him. She knew that if he could make the connection between spending time with the Lord every day and finding spiritual strength, his life would be far better. She also was certain he wasn't ready to hear about it from her.

Even though Lisa knew that God was calling Jonathan to this step of obedience, she determined not to say anything. Instead she prayed every day for him to have the desire for more of God in his life. Although she prayed for months without any visible change, one morning he quietly announced, "I'm going to the office earlier today because I need time alone with the Lord before I do anything else."

She silently thanked God.

Since then, with only a few exceptions, he has left home early every week-day morning to read his Bible and pray in his office. That was two years ago and now this spiritual discipline has carried over into areas of physical discipline as well. He is exercising, eating right, losing the weight he wanted to lose, and gaining new stamina. Only God can do that.

If you clearly observe your husband walking down a wrong path, should you say something? If so, how much should you say and when is the right time to say it? The best way I've found to proceed is to take it to God *first* and weigh it on *His* scales. He may instruct you to just be quiet and pray, like He did with Lisa. But if He does direct you to speak to your husband about the matter, there will be a far greater chance of him hearing God's voice somewhere in your words if you've prayed *before* you speak. Anything perceived as nagging will be counterproductive and better left unsaid. Praying that his eyes be opened to the truth and his heart convicted will be far more effective than you telling him what to do. You can *encourage* him to do what's right and *pray* for him to do what's right, but ultimately it's God's voice that will have the greatest impact.

No man can receive all God has for him if he is not living in obedience. Jesus, who was never one to beat around the bush, said, "If you want to enter into life, keep the commandments" (Matthew 19:17). He knew that nothing would give a man more peace and confidence than knowing he is doing what God wants him to do. God's Word promises that by being obedient to His ways your husband will find mercy (Psalm 25:10), peace (Psalm 37:37), happiness (Proverbs 29:18), plenty (Proverbs 21:5), blessings (Luke 11:28), and life (Proverbs 21:21). *Not* living in obedience brings harsh consequences (Proverbs 15:10), unanswered prayers (Proverbs 28:9), and the inability to enter into the great things God has for him (1 Corinthians 6:9).

Walking in obedience has to do not only with keeping God's commandments, but also with heeding God's *specific* instructions. For example, if God has instructed your husband to rest and he doesn't do it, that's disobedience. If He has told him to stop doing a certain type of work and he keeps doing it, that's disobedience. If He has told him to move to another place and he doesn't move, that's disobedience, too.

A man who does what God asks, builds his house on a rock. When the rain, floods, and wind come and beat on the house, it won't fall (Matthew 7:24-27). You don't want to witness the downfall of your house because of your husband's disobedience in any area. While it's not your place to be either his mother or the gestapo, it is your job to pray, and speak *after* you've gotten your orders from God.

If your husband's disobedience to God's ways has already brought down your house in some manner, know that God will honor *your* obedience and He will see that you will not be destroyed. He will pour His blessings on you and restore what has been lost. Just keep praying that your husband not have a hearing problem when it comes to the voice of God, and that he has the strength, courage, and motivation to act on what he hears.

Prayer

Lord, You have said in Your Word that if we regard iniquity in our hearts, You will not hear (Psalm 66:18). I want You to hear my prayers, so I ask You to reveal where there is any disobedience in my life, especially with regard to my husband. Show me if I'm selfish, unloving, critical, angry, resentful, unforgiving, or bitter toward him. Show me where I have not obeyed You or lived Your way. I confess it as sin and ask for Your forgiveness.

I pray that You would give (husband's name) a desire to live in obedience to Your laws and Your ways. Reveal and uproot anything he willingly gives place to that is not of You. Help him to bring every thought and action under Your control. Remind him to do good, speak evil of no one, and be peaceable, gentle, and humble (Titus 3:1,2). Teach him to embrace the stretching pain of discipline and discipleship. Reward him according to his righteousness and according to the cleanness of his hands (Psalm 18:20). Show him Your ways, O Lord; teach him Your paths. Lead him in Your truth, for You are the God of his salvation (Psalm 25:4,5).

Make him a praising person, for I know that when we worship You we gain clear understanding, our lives are transformed, and we receive power to live Your way. Help him to hear Your specific instructions to him and enable him to obey them. Give him a heart that longs to do Your will and may he enjoy the peace that can only come from living in total obedience to Your commands.

POWER TOOLS

My son, do not forget my law, but let your heart
keep my commands; for length of days and long life
and peace they will add to you. Let not mercy and
truth forsake you; bind them around your neck, write
them on the tablet of your heart.
PROVERBS 3:1-3

Not everyone who says to Me, "Lord, Lord," shall
enter the kingdom of heaven, but he who does the
will of My Father in heaven.
MATTHEW 7:21

One who turns away his ear from hearing the law,
even his prayer shall be an abomination.
PROVERBS 28:9

Obey My voice, and I will be your God, and you
shall be My people. And walk in all the ways that I
have commanded you, that it may be well with you.
JEREMIAH 7:23

His Self-Image

W hy do some very capable and talented men consistently find doors of opportunity and acceptance closed to them, while others with equal or less ability have seemingly unlimited opportunities and success in every area of their lives? It doesn't seem fair. Timing, of course, has something to do with it. God has a time for everything and He works in us what needs to be done to prepare us for what is ahead. Having a sense of God's timing brings the peace to wait on the Lord for it.

There can be another important reason for the struggle, however, and that is a man's perception of himself. If he has a poor self-image, he will have doubts about his value that creep into everything he does—even into his relationships. People who are uncomfortable with his insecurity may avoid him, and this will in turn affect how he relates to his family, friends, coworkers, and even strangers. Expecting to be rejected, he will be.

Dan experienced great frustration trying to find his way in life. He didn't know who he was or where he fit in, or if in fact he fit in anywhere. His preoccupation with trying to figure it all out caused great friction between him and his wife, Cindy. She tried to help him, but he resented her advice. He perceived her thoughts and suggestions as mocking his ability to figure things out for himself. His reaction was to dismiss her words, which caused her to strive even more to assert herself. The harder Cindy fought to not feel devalued, the more Dan retaliated, until in the frustration of his own insecurity he rejected her input altogether.

This kind of ever-deepening strife could have led to divorce, but Cindy learned how to pray rather than fight. She asked the Lord to help her understand what was happening with Dan. She wanted to know why he was rejecting her when she was only trying to help. God revealed that Dan's diminished self-image had been learned from his father. He, too, had experienced that same kind of insecurity all of his life. Whatever the source of Dan's behavior, Cindy knew God had the power to change it.

She set herself to pray as long as it would take for God to break the bonds of self-loathing and mold her husband into *His* image. She asked God to help Dan find his identity in the Lord. She also prayed for God to enable her to speak to Dan in the Spirit and not in her flesh, so that her words would be received as encouragement to his soul rather than criticism.

It took a number of months before she saw any changes, but eventually there were major ones. First, Dan learned to trust that his wife was on the same team with him and not his opponent. They agreed to stop fighting and committed to work together. He started going to church more, and she could see he was praying and reading the Bible with new faith. He gradually began to see himself as one of God's much-loved sons and not an evolutionary mistake. The more he sensed his own worth and grew accepting of who he was, the more he was appreciated by everyone else. Not coincidentally, doors of opportunity began to open for him and Dan soon found the kind of acceptance and success he had always dreamed of having.

If your husband's self-image needs a makeover, be patient. The answers don't come overnight when a long-held pattern of thinking has to be broken. But you can appropriate the power of God to fight the enemy that feeds him familiar lies, so he can be free to hear God's truth. You'll find that as you intercede, God will reveal glimpses of the key to unlocking that particular thing in your husband. In other words, as you pray He'll show you *how* to pray.

I firmly believe that the tendency toward a midlife crisis can be hindered by praying along this same line. Any toxicity still in a man's soul after he reaches his fifties will eventually pour out of him like a poison. It's as if the invisible dam holding it back weakens with age. When it breaks, the flood can be strong enough to carry him away. Having his identity soundly established in the Lord will make a major difference in how he gets through that time.

God says our first steps are to be toward Him: seeking His face, following His laws, putting Him first and self-centered pursuits last. When we line up with Him, He leads the way and all we have to do is follow. As we look to Him, the glory of His image gets imprinted upon us. When our self-image gets so wrapped up in God that we lose ourselves in the process, we're free. We want that liberty for our husbands, as well as ourselves.

Your husband will never see who *he* really is until he sees who *God* really is. Pray that he finds his true identity.

Prayer

Lord, I pray that (husband's name) will find his identity in You. Help him to understand his worth through Your eyes and by Your standards. May he recognize the unique qualities You've placed in him and be able to appreciate them. Enable him to see himself the way You see him, understanding that "You have made him a little lower than the angels, and You crowned him with glory and honor. You have made him to have dominion over the works of Your hands; You have put all things under his feet" (Psalm 8:4-6). Quiet the voices that tell him otherwise and give him ears to hear Your voice telling him that it will not be his perfection that gets him through life successfully, it will be Yours.

Reveal to him that "he is the image and glory of God" (1 Corinthians 11:7), and he is "complete in Him, who is the head of all principality and power" (Colossians 2:10). Give him the peace and security of knowing that he is accepted, not rejected, by You. Free him from the self-focus and self-consciousness that can imprison his soul. Help him to see who *You* really are so he'll know who *he* really is. May his true self-image be the image of Christ stamped upon his soul.

POWER TOOLS

Whom He foreknew, He also predestined to be conformed to the image of His Son, that He might be the firstborn among many brethren.

ROMANS 8:29

We all, with unveiled face, beholding as in a mirror
the glory of the Lord, are being transformed into the
same image from glory to glory, just as by the Spirit
of the Lord.
2 CORINTHIANS 3:18

You have put off the old man with his deeds,
and have put on the new man who is
renewed in knowledge according
to the image of Him who
created him.
COLOSSIANS 3:9,10

If anyone is a hearer of the word and not a doer, he is
like a man observing his natural face in a mirror; for
he observes himself, goes away, and immediately forgets what kind of man he was. But he who looks into
the perfect law of liberty and continues in it, and is
not a forgetful hearer, but a doer of the work, this
one will be blessed in what he does.
JAMES 1:23-25

Arise, shine; for your light has come! And the
glory of the LORD is risen upon you.
ISAIAH 60:1

His Faith

I always smile when someone tells me he or she has no faith, because I know it's probably not true. Everyone lives by faith to a certain extent. When you go to a doctor, you need faith to trust his diagnosis. When the pharmacy fills your prescription, you have faith that you'll receive the appropriate medicine. When you eat at a restaurant, you trust that the people serving you have not contaminated or poisoned the food. (Some restaurants require more faith than others.) Every day is a walk of faith on some level. Everyone believes in something. "God has dealt to each one a measure of faith" (Romans 12:3).

We choose what we will believe in. Some people choose to believe in themselves, some in government, some in evil, some in science, some in the newspaper, some in hard work, some in other people, and some in God. The only person I have ever known who didn't believe in anything ended up in a mental hospital because it drove her crazy. Faith is something we can't live without.

Faith is something we can't *die* without either. Our faith determines what happens to us after we leave this world. If you have faith in Jesus, you know that your eternal future is secure. That's because "the Spirit of Him who raised Jesus from the dead . . . will also give life to your mortal bodies through His Spirit who dwells in you" (Romans 8:11). In other words, if the same Spirit who raised Jesus from the dead dwells in you, He will raise you up as well. Having certainty about what happens to us when we die will greatly affect how we live today. Confidence in our eternal future gives us a perspective on living in the present that is laced with confidence as well.

Here's a scary thought! When healing some blind men, Jesus said, "According to your faith let it be to you" (Matthew 9:29). Doesn't that make you want to reevaluate your level of trust in God? The good news is that this means we have a certain amount of control over our lives and can, to some extent, determine how things are going to turn out for us. Our lives don't have to be left up to chance, or allowed to go flapping in the breeze according to whatever wind is blowing at the moment. Our faith will help determine our outcome.

We all have times of doubt. Even Jesus wondered why God had forsaken Him. It wasn't that He doubted God's existence or ability to come to His rescue, He just didn't expect to feel forsaken. Sometimes we don't doubt God's existence, or whether He is *able* to help us, we just doubt His desire to have any immediate impact on our lives. *Surely He is too busy for my problems*, we think. But the truth is, He's not.

Does your husband have times of doubt? If so, your prayers for him to have ever-increasing faith will make a big difference in his life. Even if he doesn't know the Lord, you can still pray for faith to rise in his heart and look for an improvement in his level of peace. There is nothing in your husband's life that can't be conquered or positively affected with an added measure of faith in God. Jesus said of any man who has faith to believe in Him, "out of his heart will flow rivers of living water" (John 7:38). That alone can be enough to wash away a lifetime of pain, trouble, fear, sorrow, apathy, hopelessness, failure, and doubt. Shall we pray?

Prayer

Lord, I pray that You will give (husband's name) an added measure of faith today. Enlarge his ability to believe in You, Your Word, Your promises, Your ways, and Your power. Put a longing in His heart to talk with You and hear Your voice. Give him an understanding of what it means to bask in Your presence and not just ask for things. May he seek You, rely totally upon You, be led by You, put You first, and acknowledge You in everything he does.

Lord, You've said that "faith comes by hearing, and hearing by the word of God" (Romans 10:17). Feed his soul with Your Word so his faith grows big enough to believe that with You all things are possible (Matthew 19:26). Give him unfailing certainty that what You've promised to do, You will do (Romans 4:21). Make his faith a shield of protection. Put it into action to move the mountains in his life. Your Word says, "the just shall live by faith" (Romans 1:17); I pray that he will live the kind of faith-filled life You've called us all to experience. May he know with complete certainty "how great is Your goodness, which You have laid up for those who fear You, which You have prepared for those who trust in You" (Psalm 31:19).

POWER TOOLS

Let him ask in faith, with no doubting, for he who
doubts is like a wave of the sea driven and tossed by
the wind. For let not that man suppose that he will
receive anything from the Lord; he is a double-
minded man, unstable in all his ways.

JAMES 1:6-8

Whatever is not from faith is sin.

ROMANS 14:23

If you have faith as a mustard seed, you will say to
this mountain, "Move from here to there," and it will
move; and nothing will be impossible for you.

MATTHEW 17:20

I have been crucified with Christ; it is no longer I
who live, but Christ lives in me; and the life which I
now live in the flesh I live by faith in the Son of
God, who loved me and gave Himself for me.

GALATIANS 2:20

Therefore, having been justified by faith, we have
peace with God through our Lord Jesus Christ.

ROMANS 5:1

CHAPTER THIRTY

His Future

None of us can live without a vision for our future. If we don't have one, we flounder aimlessly. Without it, life seems pointless and we die a little every day. "Where there is no vision, the people perish" (Proverbs 29:18 KJV).

Having a vision doesn't necessarily mean knowing the specifics about what is going to happen next. It has to do with sensing the general direction you're moving in and having hope that something good is on the horizon. It's knowing that you *do* have a future and a purpose, and that it is bright.

Not every man has that certainty. When he doesn't, you can almost see life draining from him. Even the ones who do, don't necessarily have it all the time. Even the most spiritual man can get overtired, burned out, beaten down, distanced from God, confused about who he is and why he is here, and lose his vision for the future. He can misplace his sense of purpose and become overwhelmed and hopeless because of it. If he loses sight of his dreams and forgets the truth about himself and his situation, he can end up believing destructive lies about his future. "My people are destroyed for lack of knowledge" (Hosea 4:6).

God says not to listen to voices that speak lies, for "they speak a vision of their own heart, not from the mouth of the LORD" (Jeremiah 23:16). Any vision for the future that is full of failure and empty of hope is not from God (Jeremiah 29:11). But God can restore vision where it has been lost. He can give hope to dream again. He can bring His truth to bear upon the lies of discouragement. He can give assurance of a promising future. Prayer is the avenue through which He can accomplish it.

My husband said that one of the times my prayers meant the most to him was when we moved from Los Angeles to Nashville. It was very hard for all of us to leave the people we loved and start over again. There was so much at stake and it was a difficult transition, not to mention a big step of faith. We didn't know how it would all work out, but we moved in certainty that we were following God's leading. We trusted that our lives were safe in His hands. My prayer for Michael during that season was that he not lose the vision God had given him for the future. When circumstances caused him to temporarily lose his spiritual sight, he said my prayers were instrumental in restoring it.

We have to remember that Father God has drawn up His will. His estate is divided equally among His children. All that *He* has, *we* will have. We are "heirs of God and joint heirs with Christ" (Romans 8:17). I've read my copy of the will and it says we don't have any idea of all God has for us, because He has more for us than we ever imagined. "Eye has not seen, nor ear heard, nor have entered into the heart of man the things which God has prepared for those who love Him" (1 Corinthians 2:9). It promises that "the blameless will inherit good" (Proverbs 28:10). It says that not only will we have everything we need in *this* life, but the most significant portion of it will be ours after we die. Then we will be with Him and we will want nothing more.

If your husband's eyes get so focused on the day-to-day details of living that he loses his vision for the future, your prayers can lift his sights. They can help him see that God is his future and he needs to run his life in a way that invests in that. "Do you not know that those who run in a race all run, but one receives the prize? Run in such a way that you may obtain it" (1 Corinthians 9:24). You don't want your husband to be a man who speaks a vision of his own heart and loses the prize. You want him to be able to see from God's perspective.

God doesn't want us to know the future, He wants us to know *Him*. He wants us to trust Him to guide us into the future one step at a time. In order to understand God's leading, we must seek Him for every step. "Those who seek the LORD understand all" (Proverbs 28:5). We must also stay close enough to hear His answer. The Lord is the giver of vision; pray that your husband looks to Him for it. With God, his future is secure.

Prayer

Lord, I pray that You would give (husband's name) a vision for his future. Help him to understand that Your plans for him are for good and not evil—to give him a future and a hope (Jeremiah 29:11). Fill him with the knowledge of Your will in all wisdom and spiritual understanding; that he may have a walk worthy of You, fully pleasing You, being fruitful in every good work and increasing in the knowledge of

You (Colossians 1:9,10). May he live with leading from the Holy Spirit and not walk in doubt and fear of what may happen. Help him to mature and grow in You daily, submitting to You all his dreams and desires, knowing that "the things which are impossible with men are possible with God" (Luke 18:27). Give him God-ordained goals and show him how to conduct himself in a way that always invests in his future.

I pray that he will be active in service for You all the days of his life. Keep him from losing his sense of purpose and fill him with hope for his future as an "anchor of the soul, both sure and steadfast" (Hebrews 6:19). Give him "his heart's desire" (Psalm 21:2) and "the heritage of those who fear Your name" (Psalm 61:5). Plant him firmly in Your house and keep him fresh and flourishing and bearing fruit into old age (Psalm 92:13,14). And when it comes time for him to leave this earth and go to be with You, may he have such a strong vision for his eternal future that it makes his transition smooth, painless, and accompanied by peace and joy. Until that day, I pray he will find the vision for his future in You.

POWER TOOLS

I know the thoughts that I think toward you,
says the LORD, thoughts of peace and not of evil,
to give you a future and a hope.
JEREMIAH 29:11

Mark the blameless man, and observe the upright; for
the future of that man is peace. But the
transgressors shall be destroyed together;
the future of the wicked shall be cut off.

PSALM 37:37,38

Those who are planted in the house of the LORD
shall flourish in the courts of our God. They shall
still bear fruit in old age; they shall be fresh and
flourishing, to declare that the LORD is upright; He is
my rock, and there is no unrighteousness in Him.

PSALM 92:13-15

One thing I have desired of the LORD, that will I
seek: that I may dwell in the house of the LORD all
the days of my life, to behold the beauty of the LORD,
and to inquire in His temple.

PSALM 27:4

There is hope in your future.

JEREMIAH 31:17

The Power of a
PRAYING®
HUSBAND

STORMIE
OMARTIAN

HARVEST HOUSE PUBLISHERS

EUGENE, OREGON

THE POWER OF A PRAYING is a registered trademark of The Hawkins Children's LLC. Harvest House Publishers, Inc., is the exclusive licensee of the federally registered trademark THE POWER OF A PRAYING.

THE POWER OF A PRAYING® HUSBAND
Copyright © 2001 Stormie Omartian
Published by Harvest House Publishers
Eugene, Oregon 97402
www.harvesthousepublishers.com

The Library of Congress has cataloged the edition as follows:

Omartian, Stormie.
   The power of a praying husband / Stormie Omartian.
      p. cm.
   ISBN 978-0-7369-1976-0
      1. Husbands—Religious life. 2. Prayer. I. Title.

BV4528.2 .O48 2001
248.8'425—dc21   2001024262

Printed in the United States of America

*This book is dedicated to my husband,
Michael, whose every prayer for me I have
appreciated and benefited from far more
than words can describe.*

Contents

Acknowledgments

With special thanks:

✢ To the many faithful praying husbands who told me about the joys of seeing their prayers answered for their wives. Especially to Pastor Jack Hayford, Bishop Kenneth C. Ulmer, Bishop Eddie L. Long, Neil Anderson, James Robison, Michael Harriton, Mike Goldstone, Rodney Johnson, and Steven Curtis Chapman for your stories of answered prayer that you contributed to this book. I hold each of you in highest esteem for the kind of husbands, fathers, and men of God that you are.

✢ To the hundreds of praying wives who shared with me the ways they longed to have their husbands pray for them.

✢ To Susan Martinez, my secretary, life manager, sister, and friend, without whom I would never make a single deadline.

✢ To my husband, Michael, for cooking all those great dinners and praying for me to be able to hear God as I wrote this book.

✢ To my daughter, Amanda, for all the meals cooked, errands run, and rooms cleaned so I could have time to work.

✢ To my prayer partners Susan Martinez, Roz Thompson, Katie Stewart, Donna Summer, Bruce Sudano, Michael and Terry Harriton, and Tom and Patti Brussat, without whose prayers I would not have survived this year, let alone written a book.

✢ To my Harvest House family, especially Bob Hawkins Jr., Carolyn McCready, Julie McKinney, Teresa Evenson, Terry Glaspey, Betty Fletcher, LaRae Weikert, Barb Sherrill, and Peggy Wright, for all your prayers, e-mails, letters, calls, and support.

A Word from Michael

Let's face it, men, by the time we marry we bring many years of experiences, habits, personality traits, memories, preconceived notions, and personal ambitions with us into the marriage. Suddenly we are joined, for a lifetime, with a mate who has also brought many years of experiences, habits, personality traits, memories, preconceived notions, and personal ambitions into the marriage with her. We are faced with the need to communicate, compromise, submit to one another, and be unselfish. A tall order, to be sure. Either God has a tremendous sense of humor, or a desire to keep us continually growing. Probably both.

God intends each of our marriages to be a way for us to be totally fulfilled, but we have to live as an example of Christ's love for us. That's why a man's communication with his wife is dependent upon his communication with the Father. Praying specifically for our wives is a powerful thing. God is always listening. He considers every word. Yes, the God of all creation has His ear inclined toward us, and in Him we have the opportunity to defuse bombs the enemy has planted that are set to destroy what God has joined together.

Are there things about our wives we would like to see changed? Praying for those changes invites God to do great things in our lives. Without prayer, the success of our marriages depends on our own wisdom and effort. But what a resource for success awaits us when we pray! We see not only answers to our prayers for our wives, but things happen in us as well.

Throughout my marriage to Stormie I have witnessed miraculous answers to prayer—everything from seeing bondage from her damaged past broken in her, to the saving of her life in a medical emergency, to the flourishing of her ministry as an author. The more I understand how my wife benefits directly from my prayers for her, the more I understand how God uses those prayers to build my faith and how He changes and blesses me in the process.

It is with this confidence in God's answering the prayers of a husband for a wife that I recommend this book to you. And I know you'll enjoy it, because I have been praying for my wife as she writes it.

Michael Omartian

He who finds a wife finds a good thing,
And obtains favor from the LORD.

Proverbs 18:22

THE POWER

Thank you, sir, for reading this book. I'm sure that no one is holding a gun to your head to make you do it, but if she is, tell her to put it down because you intend to keep going.

I don't want to be presumptuous in any way, but I believe it is quite possible that you fit into one of the following categories. See if any of these are true about you:

1. You found this book mysteriously placed on the seat of your favorite chair, on the floor next to the commode, on the pillow on your side of the bed, inside your briefcase or lunch box or toolbox, on the front seat of the vehicle you drive to work, or on top of your desk, worktable, or TV remote.

2. Your praying wife bought this book for you so that you would never again have to feel guilty about not praying enough for her.

3. You bought this book yourself because you've wanted to pray effectively for your wife, but you didn't know where to begin.

4. You have longed to see meaningful and lasting changes happen in your wife, yourself, and your marriage, and you're hoping this book will help.

5. You are already a kind, thoughtful, loving, praying husband, and you want to always be learning new and effective ways to further bless your wife.

6. A friend recommended this book, and although you're skeptical, you're willing to give it a try to see if anything will come of it.

7. Your life has been threatened, and reading this book seems like a small price to pay in order to preserve it.

Whatever the case may be, I salute you, I commend you. You are a giant among men. I say to you that your efforts in reading this book will be well spent, your time will not be wasted, and you will find great rewards ahead.

WHY HER AND NOT HIM?

You may be asking yourself at this very moment, *Why isn't Stormie's husband writing this book?* The answer is simple. He's just like you. He is a busy man, with places to go, people to see, work to do, a family to support, food to eat, a life to live, golf to play, ball games to watch, channels to flip, and a chronic lack of patience when it comes to writing. It's not that he doesn't pray. He does. It's just that he is a man of few words when it comes to prayer. (Quite opposite of the way he is when the Chicago Cubs are losing.) In fact, he has always had one direct response to people who ask him, "Why don't you write a book called *The Power of a Praying Husband?*"

"If I wrote it," he says matter-of-factly, "it would be a brochure."

Double-spaced.

With lots of pictures.

The brochure part doesn't really bother me. Brevity isn't the issue as long as I know he is praying. The truth is, a husband's prayers for his wife don't have to be long and detailed. Short and to-the-point prayers are also powerful. That's because God has given the husband authority in the spirit realm that is unequaled. Whether or not his prayers are answered, however, depends on how that authority is handled. (More about that in the next chapter.)

With the success of my book *The Power of a Praying Wife*, I was afforded the opportunity to travel the country speaking to thousands of women and talking one-on-one with hundreds of them in each city I visited. I heard about their deep longings to have better relationships with their husbands and to see their marriages work successfully and become a source of fulfillment and joy for all concerned. The encouraging part to me was that these wives had found great answers to prayer when they had learned to pray for their husbands the way God wanted them to.

In letters and in person, I was asked countless times by these women to write *The Power of a Praying Husband*. I didn't seriously consider doing it until men started bringing up the same question.

"When are you going to write *The Power of a Praying Husband?*" many of the husbands would ask me.

"Would you actually read it if I wrote it?" I always asked them in return.

"Yes, definitely!" each one of them responded strongly. "I *want* to pray for my wife, I just don't know how."

I was surprised at the consistency of their responses and deeply touched by the honesty and sincerity with which they were spoken.

When I told my husband, Michael, about this repeated request from so many husbands as well as from the praying wives, without even taking his eyes off the TV he immediately suggested that *I* should write the book.

"Do you think maybe *you* should write it?" I asked him. His eyes glazed over and he gave me that same look I see every time I ask him if he wants to go shopping with me.

"No, you're the writer. I'm a musician," he said with finality, using the characteristically few words he spends on a subject he doesn't want to pursue—especially when he's in the middle of watching a game on television.

"GO, GO, GO, GO, GO," he screamed as he leaped up off the couch.

I was about to leave the room to begin writing immediately when I realized he hadn't been shouting at me, but instead at one of the Chicago Cubs who had just made it to first base.

"What about you writing the foreword then?" I probed further after he sat back down.

"Yes, definitely," he answered while riveted to the screen. "WAIT, NO, NO NO! YOU IDIOT."

I wasn't sure how to respond.

Then turning to me he explained, "This umpire is an idiot! That guy was safe!"

Feeling great relief that his character analysis wasn't a commentary on *me,* I pursued the conversation further.

"In that case," I continued, "can you give me a list of all the times you can remember when you prayed for me and God answered your prayers?"

"Not now," he protested. "I'll do it between the seventh and eighth innings."

"I meant sometime in the next few *months,*" I slowly explained.

"YEAH! YEAH! GOOD! GOOD!" he screamed at the top of his lungs, then looking at me said, "Did you say something?"

"Yes. Would you pray for me as I write this book?"

"Not now. Between the seventh and eighth innings."

"I meant throughout this year."

"Uh-huh."

"Is that a firm uh-huh?" I asked.

"Uh-huh," he replied.

So with my husband's enthusiastic endorsement and the encouragement of many husbands and wives, I have been unanimously elected to bring this book to you. I don't take this vote of confidence lightly. And even though my husband declined to write it, he did say he would be more than happy to orchestrate it if it were ever made into a musical.

ANOTHER GOOD REASON TO READ THIS BOOK

When I asked God whether I was really the one to write this book or not, I received some interesting insight. I believe one of the main reasons the Lord wants *me* to write it is that there are ways I am suggesting you pray for your wife that might be viewed as self-serving or selfish if a man were to write them. But I'm inviting you to pray in these ways because I know it will be to your wife's greatest blessing as well as your own.

Also, as I thought about how many husbands had asked me to write this book, I began to see that, if I were taking a poll like they do during political campaigns, I could assume that the men I talked to were a good representation of *all* men. This means that my poll reflects *your* thoughts on the subject. Therefore, I'm sure you can see as well as I do that *THIS BOOK IS ACTUALLY YOUR IDEA!*

THE WAY WE WERE

During the first half of the 28 years Michael and I have been married, we experienced great strife and misery because we tried to do things in the flesh and not in the spirit. We each wanted the other to be a certain way, and we tried to *make* that happen ourselves instead of relying on the power of God to accomplish it. Our methods of forcing things to happen brought far less than satisfying results. Michael used anger as a weapon to control our lives, and I reacted to it by retreating mentally and emotionally.

Of course I had my favorite three-word prayer that I always prayed about the situation. You know the one. It's the "Change him, Lord!" prayer. But God never answered that prayer. Not even once. Then during a time of great strife between us, when I couldn't bear it anymore, I cried out to the Lord desperately for help. And God impressed upon my heart that, if I would be willing to lay down my life in prayer for Michael, He would use me to help Michael become all God had made him to be. In order to do that, however, I had to let God give me a new heart and begin to see Michael from God's perspective. When I consented to that and learned to pray for Michael in the manner God was showing me, I began to understand the source of his misplaced anger.

Michael was raised by a mother who was overbearing, controlling, and too strict with him. She had expectations of him far beyond his capabilities, inclinations, giftings, or the call of God upon his life. She wanted an A student. He was an undiagnosed dyslexic. She wanted a doctor. He was a musician. She wanted success. He struggled in school. She didn't understand his problem. He didn't understand it either.

Whether it was fair or not, there was a good explanation for his mother's attitude toward him. Her family had lived in Armenia, where most of them had been killed by the brutally oppressive Turkish army. Her own mother, Michael's grandmother, had been forced to watch her children be tortured and murdered right in front of her, a situation so horrendous that I can't even bring myself to write out the details for you here. After the slaughter of her family, Michael's grandmother escaped to America and eventually started a new family, into which Michael's mother was born.

The terrifying memories of what had happened, and the dangers and consequences of being poor, uneducated, and part of a minority in a hostile country, permanently marked the heart of Michael's grandmother and ultimately his mother's as well. They believed it was crucial to study diligently and work hard to ensure that this kind of devastation would never happen again. As a result, any member of the family who didn't do well was an embarrassment. Being a musician was even worse since it was not considered a real job that had any kind of real future.

The struggles of the Depression only added to Michael's mother's fears. As she was raising him in the years after that time, she would speak in terms of "survival," "security," "diligence," "accomplishments," and "excellence." She didn't understand words like "learning disability," "artistic temperament," "musical giftedness," or "unique calling of God." She thought he was being difficult and uncooperative. But he was just being who he was, all the while struggling with the belief that it wasn't enough.

I know all this is true because Michael's mother told me so. I became close to her in the months prior to our marriage, and I adored her. She became the mother I never had for that brief time before the ravages of cancer took her life less than a year later. Her struggle to survive had dramatically changed her perspective. She shared that with me too.

"I was way too hard on him," she said to me one day shortly after Michael and I were married. "I see now the mistakes I've made. Facing death makes you understand what is really important. I believe Michael suffers with anger and depression because of the way I was with him."

"Nobody understood those things back then," I tried to comfort her. "You were only doing what you thought was best."

"No, I pushed him way too far. I was overcritical. I expected too much," she answered, and proceeded to tell the same story Michael had told me before we were married.

Because Michael was raised under pressure to be what his mother expected him to be, he was always painfully aware of his inability to meet those expectations. As a result, when he was 19 he had a nervous breakdown. He had been attending college full-time during the day, which is pressure enough for someone with dyslexia, but in addition to that he was working full-time as a musician in clubs at night. The pressure became too much for him to bear. His mother took him to their family doctor, who made the decision to put Michael in a mental hospital because it was near to both the doctor's office and the family's home. He believed it would be a good place for Michael to rest and be medically treated for nervous exhaustion.

"The mental hospital was a big mistake," his mother said to me with tears in her eyes. "He didn't have anything wrong with him that required that type of facility, and yet he was locked in a place where he observed the horrifying actions of those who did need it. The experience did more to damage Michael than it did to help him."

The night before Michael went into the hospital, his cousin led him to receive the Lord. But even though he was then a believer, he still had little spiritual understanding. As a result, his experience in the mental hospital was extremely frightening to him. He thought there might be more wrong with him than there actually was. So what Michael carried with him *out* of that hospital a few weeks later was fear. One of his greatest fears was that he might end up in a mental hospital again. Even 15 years into our marriage, he would still have moments when, overtired and pressured, he would experience anxiety and depression about that very issue.

"The doctor himself later apologized to me," his mother said sadly. "He told me he believed it had been a mistake to put Michael in the mental hospital. I know he was right, because Michael experienced great depression and anxiety from that time on."

All that his mother shared helped me to understand the source of Michael's anger. It even opened my eyes to why he took his anger and resentment toward his mother out on me. He was angry at her, and I was guilty by association. But I was not able to take it very well because of my own past.

I was raised by an abusive mother who was mentally ill and who locked me in a closet for much of my early childhood. Because of this I was filled with fear, depression, hopelessness, and anxiety even into adulthood. I grew up feeling like a failure because my mother repeatedly told me I would be. Her rejection of me made me supersensitive to anything Michael did that also seemed like rejection. Because of the insecurities I brought into the marriage, his harsh words would devastate me, and I would react by withdrawing from him. I viewed him as someone I couldn't trust with my heart because I never knew when he was going to stab it with the knife of criticism or judgment.

When the pain in my marriage became too much for me to bear, I considered separation and divorce. It was at this point God told me that, if I would surrender my desire to escape and submit to His desire to make me an intercessor for Michael, then God would use me as an instrument of deliverance for him. If I would pray for him the way God instructed me to—which required a major change of heart on my part—God would answer my prayers. What I learned over the following years became the basis for my book *The Power of a Praying Wife*.

Even though I desired to do what God wanted, I still asked Him, "Why am *I* the only one who has to change? Doesn't Michael need change too?"

But God spoke to my heart, saying, "It's not a matter of who *needs* to change, it's a matter of who is *willing* to change. If you're willing to change, I can work through you right now."

I don't know if I was all that willing to change, but I *was* willing to do what God wanted me to do. And so I said "yes" to what He was asking of me. And from the time I began to pray for Michael from a right heart and in the way God was directing me to, I started to see changes in him. He became less and less angry. He began to gain a perspective on his past that he hadn't had previously.

"I believe that if my father had covered us spiritually the way he should have, things would have been very different for our whole family," Michael said to me one day. "My dad was a faithful father and husband, and he supported the family financially, but he didn't have much input into my life. I knew he loved me. He wasn't an ogre or anything, he was just very passive. He never took any active interest in who I was. For years I wasn't able to see the situation from my mother's perspective, but now I have new compassion for her. She had to do everything on her own. She had to carry so much weight in the family. He didn't cover her spiritually. There wasn't a balance in the house. She got cancer at 44 and died when she was barely 50, and I believe that was part of what ended up killing her."

This realization has been instrumental in helping Michael to see the importance of praying for his own family. It has motivated him to pray for me. And I know I owe much of the success of my life to his prayers.

THE POWER AND AUTHORITY

The power of a praying husband is not a means of gaining control over your wife. We all know that never really happens anyway. That's because God doesn't want us controlling other people. He wants us to let *Him* control *us*. When we humble ourselves before God and let *Him* control *us*, then He can work through us. God wants to work through you as an instrument of *His* power as you intercede for your wife.

The power in your prayer is God's. When you pray for your wife, you are inviting God to exercise His power in her life. Your prayer enables her to better hear God's voice and respond to God's leading. In spite of that, however,

God will never override a person's strong will. If anyone is determined to live outside of God's will, He will let that person do it. So, although your prayers have the potential to be powerful in your wife's life, there is a limit to what they can accomplish if *her* will—or *your* will—is opposed to the will of *God.* "Now this is the confidence that we have in Him, that if we ask anything according to His will, He hears us" (1 John 5:14).

God wants us to pray about all things, but He wants us to pray according to His will. That's why it's important to ask God to reveal His will to you and help you pray accordingly. Once you have the mind of God as to how to pray, it's easier to pray fervently and persistently. Just as we can't force our spouses to do what we want them to do, we can't force God to do our bidding either. It's *His* will, not ours that will be done.

Your spiritual authority with regard to your wife and family is unequaled. Because your spiritual authority comes from God, it must be used the way God intended. It must be motivated by his love and have His glory in mind. All God-given spiritual authority has as its foundation a humility that desires to serve God more than to control others. God wants you to serve Him by exerting your authority over the enemy. You have been given authority "over all the power of the enemy" (Luke 10:19), and you can devastate His plans on your wife's behalf. If you see the enemy creeping into your marriage in any way, stand up and boldly say:

"I will not permit any plans of the enemy to prevail in our marriage."

"I will not allow the enemy to drive a wedge between us."

"I will not stand by and see my wife deceived by lies of the enemy."

"I will not allow the enemy to attack my wife in any way."

"I will not allow miscommunication to rule our relationship."

"I will not permit the mistakes of our past, even yesterday's, to control our future."

Then pray, pray, pray. Because when you pray, no weapon formed against her or you will prosper (Isaiah 54:17).

DON'T LEAVE YOUR MARRIAGE
TO CHANCE

Remember the Scripture you read in the very beginning of the book? It says that God has already given you favor simply because you have a wife (Proverbs 18:22). There are certain blessings God has for you just because you are married. That's because God has declared the two of you to be one in His sight (Matthew 19:4-6). This means that what happens to one of you will affect the other. If she is happy, you will be happy. If you are blessed, she will be blessed. And of course the reverse is also true. If she is not happy, you definitely won't be either. Her problems are your problems, just as your problems are hers. That's why *your* prayers for her are so crucial. They will affect you both.

Whatever you don't pray about in your life you leave up to chance. And that's not good enough when it comes to your marriage.

The problem with chance in a marriage is, chances are there will be some difficult times. Chances are there will be disagreements. Chances are there will be misunderstandings and hurts. Chances are there will be selfishness and hardness of heart. That's because we are, after all, human. But if we leave the outcome of these things up to chance, we will wind up in trouble down the line. However, all of these things can be turned around through prayer.

If busyness, workaholism, unforgiveness, strife, child-rearing, careers, separate interests, boredom, or miscommunication has crept in between you and your wife, God can work through your prayers to bring down the wall that separates you, melt the armor that has been put on for self-protection, and mold you together in unity. It will give you a vision of hope for how God can redeem, restore, and make things right. Praying for your wife will not only soften her heart, but it will also soften yours as well.

You don't ever have to slip into marital deadness. Misery or divorce don't ever have to be your only two options. No matter what has happened between you, God can fix it. He is the God of wholeness and restoration. You have Him on your side. He has given you the power and the authority. Use them well.

How to Really Love Your Wife

Jesus said that the greatest act of love is to lay down your life for another (John 15:13). There are many ways to lay down your life for your wife without physically dying. One way is to lay down your life for her in prayer. It's sacrificing a relatively small amount of time for her greatest good, which is ultimately yours also.

There are many things a woman wants to hear from her husband. Three of the top four are probably "I love you," "You look beautiful," and "The bills are paid." But I know that one thing every woman wants to hear, the thing that will make her feel more loved than anything else, is "I'm praying for you today."

Whenever a wife hears that her husband is praying for her, it makes her feel loved and protected. It makes her feel she's important to him. If you want to see God soften your wife's heart, or make things right between you, or enrich your life together, or cause your marriage to run more smoothly, then pray for her. If you want your wife to throw herself at your feet, ask her, "How do you want me to pray for you today?" (Don't let me down here, ladies, I know you're reading this.) Okay, maybe that's overstating it a bit. But she will love you for it. Those words speak of your commitment to her and the marriage. Of course, if you tell her you're praying for her and you don't actually do it, I wouldn't go out in any lightning storms if I were you.

WHAT IF SHE'S NOT A BELIEVER?

Most women have a sense of their spiritual side—even those who have no professed religion or organized affiliation with a belief system. They have a recognition that there is a way of life that works and that it's wrapped up in the spiritual.

Prayer touches the heart of anyone for whom we pray. If your wife doesn't know the Lord, you can still pray all the prayers in this book for her and expect to see answers. The Bible says that "the unbelieving wife is sanctified by the husband" (1 Corinthians 7:14). You provide a covering over her. Of course, this doesn't substitute for her knowing the Lord, but it means that your prayers will have a positive and powerful effect on her. Just remember every time you pray for her, ask God to open her heart to the truth of His Word and give her a life-changing encounter with Him.

What Each Chapter Holds

Each of the 20 chapters in this book focuses on one area of prayer in a way I hope will be enlightening, encouraging, and motivating to you. I will share with you what I have learned from experience and what God has taught me. At the end of each chapter will be the following four sections:

1. She Says

   This is the result of a personal survey I made of hundreds of women all over America. I asked them how they wanted their husbands to pray for them. The amazing thing about this is that the results were the same in every city and state I traveled to!

2. He Says

   This is what a number of individual husbands said about how they pray for their wives and about the answers they have seen to their prayers. I was encouraged, amused, touched, and enlightened by their words, and I know you will be too.

3. Prayer Power

   This is a suggested prayer on the subject of that chapter. You can pray it as it is, or include anything personal you want to add. It's there as a guide for you.

4. Power Tools

   This page contains verses from the Bible that lend support to that area of prayer, which will be of great help to you as you pray in depth about it. You can speak these out loud in a declaration of truth over your situation or pray them over your wife.

ONE PRAYER AT A TIME

Don't be overwhelmed by the many ways to pray for your wife. Simply take it one day and one prayer at a time. You can pray through a different chapter each day, or concentrate on praying one each week. I'm not saying how much you should pray, but the Bible says that "he who sows sparingly will also reap sparingly, and he who sows bountifully will also reap bountifully" (2 Corinthians 9:6). The more you pray, the more benefits you will reap. If you want to make room for God to bring about big changes quickly in your wife, yourself, and your marriage, try praying one of these chapters each day for several weeks. See if something good doesn't start happening in your heart and in hers.

Sometimes I have been asked, "Does it really work to pray prayers that someone else has written? In order to truly pray from the heart, shouldn't you make up your own prayers?" My answer to that is, "Does it really work to sing praise songs that someone else has written?" I believe it does. It's good to make up your own praise song, and God delights in that, but the important thing is that what you're praying or singing resonates in your own heart. Is it a prayer that *you* would pray if *you* had thought of it? Do you believe it's a prayer God can answer? If the answer is yes to either of these questions, then that prayer has power. It doesn't matter who thought of it first.

Often when we pray for our mates, we pray about the most urgent need—which is right to do—but we neglect the "maintenance prayers." If you have a high-maintenance spouse, you definitely don't want to do that. Such prayers head off trouble before it happens. They put out small fires before they become roaring flames. Most of the prayers in this book are maintenance prayers. If you pray all of them for your wife a few times a year, you will keep your marriage healthy and enjoy a wife who is happy and fulfilled. They will remind you to pray in ways you might not have had time to think about.

Whether you pray the prayers I have suggested or pray your own, the bottom line is, keep praying and don't give up. Sometimes prayers are answered quickly, but many are not. Jesus said "Men always ought to pray and not lose heart" (Luke 18:1). Keep praying and you *will* see God answer. And don't worry about how the answers will be manifested. You don't have to make them happen. It's *your* job to pray. It's *God's* job to answer. Trust Him to do His job.

CHAPTER ONE

HER HUSBAND

I once saw a football game where the home team was losing and there were less than 15 seconds left in the game. They needed a touchdown to win, but everything was against them making a score in that amount of time. The game appeared to be over, and the opposing team and fans were already celebrating. Some people were even leaving the stadium. But the losing team and coach didn't give up or let their morale fall. Instead they pulled an unlikely play out of their book, and through the most astonishing sequence of events, the home team made a winning touchdown in the last few seconds of the game. It was so amazing that news reports of it even referred to it as a miracle.

Your marriage is like that football game. You and your wife are a team. And she wants the security of knowing that when things are tough and down to the wire—even when the enemy is already celebrating your demise and all appears to be lost—you have the faith to believe that up to the very last second everything can turn around. She needs the assurance you have a play in your pocket that can take you down the field with the ball for a possible winning score. She wants you to trust that with God nothing is impossible, and because of that you will never give up hoping for the impossible to happen.

When your wife knows you are praying, she is confident of all of these things.

In my survey of wives, 85 percent of them said the most important prayer their husband could pray was that he would become the man, husband, and head of the home God wanted him to be. This is the most important place for a man to begin praying.

"THAT YOUR PRAYERS MAY NOT BE HINDERED"

The good thing about prayer—or the problem with prayer, depending on your perspective—is that we have to go to God to do it. This means we can't get away with anything. It means that any negative thoughts, bad attitudes, hardness of heart, or selfish motives are going to be revealed by the Lord. Fervent and honest prayer causes the depths of our hearts to be exposed. That can be uncomfortable. Even downright miserable.

If there is one thing I have learned about prayer, it's that if we have any unforgiveness, bitterness, selfishness, pride, anger, irritation, or resentment in our hearts, our prayers will not be answered. "If I regard iniquity in my heart, the Lord will not hear" (Psalm 66:18). Our hearts have to be right when we pray. We all—men and women alike—jeopardize our own prayers when we don't pray them from a right heart.

What is in our hearts when we pray has more effect on whether our prayers are answered than the actual prayer itself. That's why, when we come before Him to pray, God asks us to first confess anything in our hearts that shouldn't be there. He does that so nothing will separate us from Him.

The Bible says, "Husbands, likewise, dwell with them *with understanding*, giving *honor* to the wife, as to the weaker vessel, and as being *heirs together* of the grace of life, that your *prayers may not be hindered*" (1 Peter 3:7).

Part of dwelling with your wife *with understanding* means recognizing that your wife is in need of your covering, protection, and love. And because you are *heirs together* of God's grace, you need to *honor* her in your thoughts, words, and actions. When you don't, your *prayers are hindered*. This means *all* of your prayers, not just those for your wife. Many men have not seen answers to their prayers because they have not learned this key step. One of the best ways to honor your wife is to pray for her from a heart that is clean before God.

Ask God to show you whatever you need to see about the condition of your heart. You may have the perfect marriage and be sublimely happy, and still be less than what God wants in your attitude toward your wife. Whatever He reveals, confess it to Him. Once we confess our less-than-perfect attitudes to the Lord, He helps us get beyond them. You'll find that the most difficult part about being a praying husband will not be the amount of time it takes to pray for your wife—rather, it will be praying with a heart that's right before God. That's why praying for your wife must begin with praying for yourself.

Don't worry, God taught this same principle to the praying wives. Many women told me that it was at this point in the chapter they threw the book across the room and said, "Forget it! I'm not doing that!" Of course the Holy Spirit wouldn't let them get away with that for long, and so they eventually picked the book back up and kept reading. So if you would like to throw this book across the room and say, "Forget it! I'm not doing that!" this would be a good time to do it. I know you'll pick it back up again, because you're going to get awfully tired of your prayers not being answered.

IT TAKES TWO TO MAKE ONE

When God created Adam, in spite of all the greatness that was in him God knew he still needed a companion, a helpmate who would fit with him, be a complement to him, and complete him (Genesis 2:18). So He created Eve. In spite of all the greatness that is in you, dear brother, God made your wife to be a complement to you and make you complete. You do the same for her.

God says that when you and your wife were married you became one flesh (Genesis 2:24). Isn't it amazing that we were created to be one with our mates? That feels possible when we start out. There is the *anticipation* of oneness in that first moment when you sense you were destined to be more than friends. There is the *sense* of oneness in the courtship. The *promise* of oneness in the engagement period. The *declaration* of oneness in the wedding vows. The *thrill* of oneness on the honeymoon. The *excitement* of oneness as a home is established. Then somewhere along the way, the oneness gets eroded by a subtle separateness.

How does that happen?

The answer is the world, the flesh, and the devil. The world creeps in, along with raising children, pursuing careers, and dealing with the busyness of life. We begin to find more fascination or distraction in *it* than we do in our mates. Our flesh takes over when we decide to be self-centered instead of self-sacrificing. Then there is Satan.

God created marriage at the beginning. Satan has been trying to destroy it ever since. You and your wife are created in God's image (Genesis 1:27). Satan wants to make you over into *his*. Satan doesn't want your marriage to succeed and has in fact set up a plan for its destruction. He is even now making plans to destroy your marriage. But you, my precious brother, have been given the power and authority to put a stop to this through your prayers. When you pray for your wife, it keeps the world at bay, it transforms selfish hearts, and it derails the devil's plans. If God has asked you to pray for your enemies, how much more does He want you to pray for the person you are supposed to love and with whom you have become one? But first you have to pray for *yourself.*

FIVE WAYS TO BE THE HUSBAND GOD WANTS YOU TO BE

In the Bible, God commands, "All of you be of *one mind,* having *compassion* for one another; *love* as brothers, be *tenderhearted,* be *courteous*" (1 Peter 3:8). Paying heed to these five directives can change your life and your marriage and make you the man and husband God wants you to be. It's definitely something well worth praying about.

1. BE OF ONE MIND

It's horrible to have strife in a marriage. It makes us miserable. It affects every area of our lives. And it's probably the closest thing to hell we'll ever know on earth. If it goes on long enough, it can destroy everything. Jesus said, "Every kingdom divided against itself is brought to desolation, and every city or house divided against itself will not stand" (Matthew 12:25). Those are frightening predictions. But prayer is the key by which unity in the marriage relationship can be maintained.

A man and wife cannot live entirely independently of one another without paying a steep price for it. It makes them incomplete. "Neither is a man independent of woman, nor woman independent of man, in the Lord" (1 Corinthians 11:11). But because men and women are different, it's quite easy for them to get off onto completely separate paths. Even in the closest of marriages, the two partners are still not joined at the hip. You and your wife may have separate work, interests, and activities, but if you are praying with and for one another regularly, it will keep you in tune and on the same path. Without this unity of mind and spirit that prayer provides, it's too easy to get used to the other one not being there. And if resentment about that creeps into the heart of either one of you, you can begin to hold yourself apart from one another mentally, physically, or emotionally, without even realizing it.

It is especially important to be of the same faith and beliefs. In fact, this is a good place to begin praying. Your entire relationship is compromised if you are not on the same page in this area. For example, going to separate churches, or going to a church where one of you is not happy, or one of you going to church while the other one consistently does not, all promote a lack of unity.

If you can think of other issues such as this that have caused division between you and your wife, pray specifically about them. Ask God to change your heart where necessary to bring you into unity with your wife. Where your wife's attitude and perspective need to change, pray for her to be able to change them. Your marriage will be a strong force for good if the two of you are of one mind.

2. Be Compassionate

Have you ever seen your wife suffering, but you don't know what to do about it? Some men become impatient with that. Others feel so at a loss or overwhelmed by it that it causes them to withdraw. If you recognize that happening to you, ask God to give you a heart of compassion. To be compassionate toward your wife is to have a deep sympathy for any area in which she suffers and to have a strong desire to alleviate that suffering.

Part of being compassionate has to do with simply listening. That means being able to listen without having that faraway look in your eyes that says, "I have more important things to do. Let's get this over with quickly." Your wife is not expecting you to fix everything. She just needs to know that you hear her heart and care about how she feels.

In the past my husband would stand still and listen to me for no more than three seconds (I timed this) before he would walk out of the room. If I wanted him to hear a complete sentence, I either had to run after him or finish the sentence the next time I saw him. Even when I did get him to actually sit down and look at me while I was speaking, I still had to ask him to give me some indication that he comprehended what I was saying. Usually I said something like "Blink if you can hear me." When he blinked, it meant so much to know he had heard my voice. Now he has a heart for my struggles, and he listens with care. Those moments of listening and indicating compassion have been healing to our relationship.

Pray that God will give you a heart of compassion toward your wife and the patience to listen to her when she needs you to do so. It's a fine art worth cultivating. It can get you places with her where you've dreamed of being.

3. BE LOVING

Jesus loves us with fidelity, purity, constancy, and passion no matter how imperfect we are. If a man doesn't love his wife in that same way, he will abuse his authority and his headship and as a result will abuse *her*. Because you are one with your wife, you must treat her the way you would your own body. You wouldn't do anything to deliberately hurt or destroy it. You love it and care for it. "Let each one of you in particular so love his own wife as himself" (Ephesians 5:33).

Jack Hayford, our pastor for 23 years, always said he could tell when a woman was truly loved by her husband, because she grew more beautiful as the years went on. He recognized an inner beauty that doesn't fade, but rather increases with time when a woman is loved.

You have no idea how much your love means to your wife. Don't withhold it from her, or one way or another you will lose her. The Bible says, "Do not withhold good from those to whom it is due, when it is in the power of your hand to do so" (Proverbs 3:27). Ask God to increase your love for your wife and enable you to show it in a way that makes her beautiful.

4. BE TENDERHEARTED

Is there anything about your wife that bothers you? Is there something that she does or says, or *doesn't* do or say, that irritates you? Do you find yourself wanting to change something about her? What happens when you try to *make* those changes occur? How does she respond when you show your irritation? Have you ever just given up and said, "It's no use. She's never going to be any different"?

The truth is, we all have a hard time changing. Try as we may, we can't change ourselves in any significant way. Only God can make changes in us that last. Only *His* power can transform us. That's why prayer is a more tender and more certain way to see changes happen in your wife.

For example, does your wife always run late, while you like to be on time? She's probably not doing it on purpose. She may either be a poor judge of time or else she is trying to do too much. Pray that God will help her to organize things better or not take on more than she can handle, or that she will gain a clearer concept of time. Above all, don't let anger, harshness, or demeaning attitudes creep in. Criticism intended to make your wife change doesn't work. It will never give you the results you want. The only thing that works is prayer.

So rather than be impatient with your wife's weaknesses, ask God to give you a tender heart so you can pray for her about them. Ask Him to show you how they are a complement to your strengths. And remember that, though the ways you and your wife are the same can unite you, the ways you are different can keep things interesting.

5. BE COURTEOUS

Do you ever talk to your wife in a way that would be considered rude if you were speaking to a friend or business associate? Are you kind to everyone all day at work, but then you take out your frustration, exhaustion, and anger on your wife when you get home? Do you ever allow criticism of your wife to come out of your mouth in front of other people? If so, as a sister in the Lord who deeply cares about both you and your wife, allow me to give you your first serious assignment in this book:

STOP THAT!

Marriage is hard enough without one of the parties being rude, cruel, or inconsiderate. Nothing makes a marriage feel more like hell on earth. Nothing is more upsetting, defeating, tormenting, suffocating, or emotion-provoking, nothing does more to bring out the worst in us, than a marriage where one of the partners is lacking in common courtesy. I have heard of more marriages dissolving because the wife had been treated rudely for so long that she felt herself becoming resentful, angry, bitter, and hopeless. In other words, she was turning into the kind of person she never wanted to be. We have to care enough about our mates to stop doing things that hurt or upset them.

There is nothing more wonderful than the male voice. It is strong and deep and rich. And the sound of male voices singing together is one of the most beautiful sounds on earth. But the male voice can also be terrifying, especially to women and children. Most men have no idea about the power of their voice. When a man speaks, his words have the power to create and the power to destroy. His words can be like a sharp knife that wounds and kills, or a soothing balm that heals and brings life.

I'm not saying that you shouldn't talk honestly and openly with your wife about the issues in your lives. By all means, put your thoughts and feelings on the table. But don't let your words turn into weapons of criticism that destroy what you want to preserve. Even when we don't mean to, our impatience or exhaustion can make our words seem less than courteous. Remember that "the kingdom of God is not in word but in power" (1 Corinthians 4:20). It's not the words you speak, it's the power of God behind them that will make the difference. Praying first, *before* you talk about a sensitive subject, will give your words power and ensure that you speak them from a right heart.

Your wife was created as a gift from God to complete you. "Nor was man created for the woman, but woman for the man" (1 Corinthians 11:9). But she must be treated as the gift from God that she is, in order for that complete blessing to happen in your life. Your wife will prove to be your greatest asset if you value and honor her. The Bible tells us that "whatever we ask we receive from Him, because we keep His commandments and do those things that are pleasing in His sight" (1 John 3:22). Pray for God to help you speak to your wife in a courteous way that is pleasing in His sight, and to convict your heart when you do not.

Praying about these five simple biblical directives will transform your life and your marriage. And no matter how great your marriage is, God wants it to be better. Since God tells us to "be transformed," that must mean there is always room for improvement (Romans 12:2). Therefore it stands to reason that, as we improve individually, our marriages will also improve. Next to your love for her, the greatest gift you can give your wife is your own wholeness. Her most fervent desire for you is that you become the man God created you to be. It must be your desire also. God has given you strength, brilliance, power, authority, and the wonderful and admirable traits that come with being a man. Ask God to help you use them well and to His glory. Ask God to make you everything He created you to be so you and your wife will always be a winning team.

SHE SAYS...

Please pray for yourself that:

1. You will be the husband God wants you to be.
2. You will know how to really love your wife.
3. You will be led by the Holy Spirit in all decisions.
4. You will be delivered from negative behavior.
5. You will speak words that build and not destroy.
6. You will have the desire to pray for your wife.
7. You will grow spiritually, emotionally, and mentally.

HE SAYS...
BY MICHAEL OMARTIAN

Michael is a record producer and songwriter. He and Stormie have been married for 28 years, and they have three grown children.

I just heard the sad story of yet another woman who lived in a marriage where she had to endure the overbearing actions and declarations of her husband. It has ended in a divorce. It was a marriage in which her opinions were not valued or needed, and she was made to feel disrespected, unloved, powerless, and useless. The worst part is that such things are happening alarmingly often even in Christian marriages. The reality is that many men have been taught strange interpretations of portions of the Bible. These misinterpretations have been spread through ignorance and because of some men's need to feel powerful as the "priest" of the home. No wonder the feminists have had a field day.

Although some women have been hurt and damaged through the extremism of the women's liberation movement, I can certainly see how it got started. We men can do a much better job of loving our wives as Christ loved the church. I know *I* can, and I pray that I will. I believe that through prayer God will give us men the tools we need so we can regard our wives with great respect and affection and become the instruments of support that they need.

Christ died for the church. We need to ask God to help us rise to the standard He has for us so that we will consider our wives before ourselves. That way our marriages can be a very different story.

PRAYER POWER

Lord, create in *me* a clean heart and renew a right spirit within me (Psalm 51:10). Show me where my attitude and thoughts are not what You would have them to be, especially toward my wife. Convict me when I am being unforgiving. Help me to let go of any anger, so that confusion will not have a place in my mind. If there is behavior in me that needs to change, enable me to make changes that last. Whatever You reveal to me, I will confess to You as sin. Make me a man after Your own heart. Enable me to be the head of my home and family that You created me to be.

Lord, show me how to really cover (<u>wife's name</u>) in prayer. Enable me to dwell with her with understanding and give honor to her so that my prayers will not be hindered (1 Peter 3:7). Renew our love for one another. Heal any wounds that have caused a rift between us. Give me patience, understanding, and compassion. Help me to be loving, tenderhearted, and courteous to her just as You ask me in Your Word (1 Peter 3:8). Enable me to love her the way that You do.

Lord, I pray that You would bring (<u>wife's name</u>) and me to a new place of unity with one another. Make us be of the same mind. Show me what I need to do in order to make that come about. Give me words that heal, not wound. Fill my heart with Your love so that what overflows through my speech will be words that build up, not tear down. Convict my heart when I don't live Your way. Help me to be the man and husband that You want me to be.

POWER TOOLS

A MAN SHALL LEAVE HIS FATHER AND MOTHER AND BE JOINED TO HIS WIFE, AND THE TWO SHALL BECOME ONE FLESH...LET EACH ONE OF YOU IN PARTICULAR SO LOVE HIS OWN WIFE AS HIMSELF, AND LET THE WIFE SEE THAT SHE RESPECTS HER HUSBAND.

EPHESIANS 5:31,33

ONE WHO TURNS AWAY HIS EAR FROM HEARING THE LAW, EVEN HIS PRAYER IS AN ABOMINATION.

PROVERBS 28:9

HUSBANDS, LOVE YOUR WIVES, JUST AS CHRIST ALSO LOVED THE CHURCH AND GAVE HIMSELF FOR HER.

EPHESIANS 5:25

CONFESS YOUR TRESPASSES TO ONE ANOTHER, AND PRAY FOR ONE ANOTHER, THAT YOU MAY BE HEALED. THE EFFECTIVE, FERVENT PRAYER OF A RIGHTEOUS MAN AVAILS MUCH.

JAMES 5:16

HUSBANDS OUGHT TO LOVE THEIR OWN WIVES AS THEIR OWN BODIES; HE WHO LOVES HIS WIFE LOVES HIMSELF. FOR NO ONE EVER HATED HIS OWN FLESH, BUT NOURISHES AND CHERISHES IT, JUST AS THE LORD DOES THE CHURCH.

EPHESIANS 5:28,29

Chapter Two

Her Spirit

Your wife is like an automobile. She may be high maintenance like an Italian sports car. She might be as refined and expensive as a German luxury sedan. She may be solid and sturdy like an SUV, or delicate like a Pebble Beach Concours d'Elegance show car. She could be an efficient six-cylinder type, or be a faster but costlier V-8 model. She may be dependable in all kinds of weather like a four-wheel drive, or she may have no downhill traction control at all, even on a good day. Whatever she is, whether she is tiny like a compact car or full-size and beyond, she needs fuel to make her run smoothly.

Your wife's spirit is the gas in her car. She may have the greatest chassis, a fine interior, fabulous sleek lines, an engine that purrs like a kitten, a wonderful back seat, a roomy trunk, a beautiful nose, and all the standard accessories, but if she doesn't have fuel then she's not going to run. Her exterior will still look good, but her power supply will be diminished And not only must her tank be full, but her battery needs to be charged, her oil kept clean, her brake fluid replenished, and yes, she must have a good supply of antifreeze for those cold nights.

Without the daily infilling of the Holy Spirit, we all run on empty. Your wife may be running on empty right now and not even realize it. Some women don't ever take time to check their gauges, so they're completely surprised when they suddenly run out of fuel. If a woman doesn't spend enough time every day with the Lord in prayer, worship, and the Word of God, she will lose ground, and the enemy of her soul will run her down.

Your wife may be too solid in the Word of God to doubt her salvation, or His promise of eternal life, or His grace and goodness. But Satan may be able to get her to doubt that God created her with valuable gifts and a calling of her own. Or there may be times when she questions whether all things really do work together for good. When she experiences these kinds of attacks, and all women do at one time or another, it will deplete her. Many women can get eroded physically, emotionally, and mentally by unrelenting attacks of the enemy and not even be aware that it's happening. And the effects of it will carry over into your marriage. Your wife's relationship with God will affect her relationship with you more than anything else.

Because you are the head of the home and have been given authority over "*all* the power of the enemy" (Luke 10:19), you can inform him that he cannot lie to your wife or twist the truth of God in her mind. You can pray that your wife will be so solid in the truth that she can immediately identify a lie of the enemy, cast it aside, and listen only to the voice of God.

In my survey of women, the number-one area in which women most want their husbands to pray for *them* is their spiritual walk. Your wife wants to be a strong woman of God. She desires a relationship with God that is solid, and faith that is unshakable. And because women feel pulled in so many directions, they need prayer for patience, love, peace, and all the other fruits of the spirit to be manifested in their lives.

Your wife also wants to know God's will and be certain she is in the center of it. Having clarity about what God is calling her to do, and then doing it, gives her peace. For example, if God is calling her at this time in her life to stay home and take care of her children, she needs to hear from God about it so that she will be satisfied to do that. Your prayers will help her hear from God and be content no matter what state she is in.

Another good reason to pray for your wife's spiritual walk is that it is far better if both of you are putting your expectations in God. That keeps you from putting all your expectations on each other and becoming disappointed when they are not met.

When your wife's tank is empty, her sound system will still work, and she may appear to be in good shape, but her wheels won't turn because she can't accelerate, let alone get up to full speed. Her steering will go out, so she can't navigate. Her brakes won't function, so she can't stop when she needs to. She must be filled afresh with the fuel of the Holy Spirit each day. She must be charged with the power of God. When her tank is full, she'll have automatic climate control, she'll be able to go the distance, and the ride will be smooth.

Does your wife have enough of what she needs for the distance she has to go today? Has she filled up with the finest? Ask God about this, and He will show you.

SHE SAYS...

Please pray for your wife that:

1. She will be strong in faith.
2. She will grow spiritually.
3. She will spend time in the Word and in prayer.
4. She will have discernment and revelation.
5. She will become a mighty woman of God.
6. She will be a light to others.
7. She will know God's will and live in it.

HE SAYS...
BY MICHAEL GOLDSTONE

Michael is the owner of a lighting distribution company. He and his wife, Debra, have been married for 28 years, and they have two grown children and one grandchild.

I have prayed for my wife nearly every day for many years now. Before we leave each other in the morning, I take her close to myself and cover her, both with my arms and with my prayers. It has been my high priority to give her all the time she needs to update me on all that is going on in her life—her health, her relationships, her ministry opportunities, and all of her feelings. So as I am holding her, I ask God to work in those specific areas that are most meaningful to her for that day. I pray for physical protection. And I pray that God would draw her close to Himself and that she would have a special sense of His presence that day.

It only takes a minute or two, but I have been consistent, by God's grace, in doing this daily for years. God has been faithful to answer my prayers, and it has given Deb tremendous comfort, support, and assurance of how much she is loved by me. We still feel like newlyweds in many respects—so excited to be with each other. I know prayer has a lot to do with that.

PRAYER POWER

Lord, as much as I love my wife, I know You love her more. I realize that I cannot meet her every need and expectation, but You can. I pray that You will give (<u>wife's name</u>) the fulfillment of knowing You in a deeper and richer way than she ever has before. Help her to be diligent and steadfast in her walk with You, never doubting or wavering. Make her strong in spirit and give her an ever-increasing faith that always believes that You will answer her prayers.

Help her to carve out time every day to spend with You in Your Word and in prayer and praise. May Your words abide in her, so that when she prays You will give her the desires of her heart (John 15:7). Help her to increase her knowledge of You. May she turn to You first for everything as You become her constant companion. Give her discernment and revelation and enable her to hear Your voice instructing her. Help her to stay focused on You, no matter how great the storm is around her, so that she never strays off the path You have for her. Keep me aware of when she needs a fresh filling of Your Spirit so that I will be prompted to pray.

It is the desire of her heart to be a godly example to her friends and family, so give her patience with everyone she encounters. Help her to be so filled with Your Spirit that people sense *Your* presence when they are in *her* presence. I know she wants to serve You, but help her to understand when to say no if she is being asked to do more than she should. May she glorify You in all she does.

Your Word says that whoever finds You finds life and obtains Your favor (Proverbs 8:35), so I pray that (<u>wife's name</u>) will find new life in You today and enjoy Your blessings poured out upon her. Guide her in everything she does, so that she becomes the dynamic, mighty woman of God You want her to be. Give her knowledge of Your will and enable her to stay in the center of it. Help her to trust You with all her heart and not depend on her own understanding. May she acknowledge You in all her ways (Proverbs 3:5,6).

POWER TOOLS

BLESSED ARE THOSE WHO HUNGER AND THIRST FOR RIGHTEOUSNESS, FOR THEY SHALL BE FILLED.

MATTHEW 5:6

IF YOU ABIDE IN ME, AND MY WORDS ABIDE IN YOU, YOU WILL ASK WHAT YOU DESIRE, AND IT SHALL BE DONE FOR YOU.

JOHN 15:7

WHOEVER DRINKS OF THE WATER THAT I SHALL GIVE HIM WILL NEVER THIRST. BUT THE WATER THAT I SHALL GIVE HIM WILL BECOME IN HIM A FOUNTAIN OF WATER SPRINGING UP INTO EVERLASTING LIFE.

JOHN 4:14

IF YOU HAVE FAITH AS A MUSTARD SEED, YOU WILL SAY TO THIS MOUNTAIN, "MOVE FROM HERE TO THERE," AND IT WILL MOVE; AND NOTHING WILL BE IMPOSSIBLE FOR YOU.

MATTHEW 17:20

GLORY IN HIS HOLY NAME; LET THE HEARTS OF THOSE REJOICE WHO SEEK THE LORD!

PSALM 105:3

CHAPTER THREE

HER EMOTIONS

Your wife's emotions can be compared to a finely crafted violin. When the instrument is perfectly tuned the result is beautiful music. But because the violin is so delicate and highly sensitive to its surroundings, it doesn't take much for it to be affected dramatically. Any change in temperature, humidity, or altitude—a change so subtle that it may be imperceptible to you—can send it horrifyingly off pitch. And it doesn't have to be out of tune very much to make everyone within listening range completely miserable.

When a violin is played, the end result can be beautiful, rich, deep, pleasurable music. Or it can be harsh, dissonant, screeching, nerve-jolting, cacophonous noise. Whether it is one or the other depends on the condition of the violin, of course, but mostly upon the proficiency of the one playing it. When your wife's emotions are in the hands of the enemy, everything gets out of tune and the results are unpleasant and upsetting. When God is in charge, her emotions are an asset and the end result is soothing.

I'm sure you are already well aware that your life can be dramatically affected by what your wife experiences in her emotions. If she is depressed, anxious, angry, or hurt, chances are you will feel it in some way too. Some men react to their wife's emotions by tuning out. They don't have a clue as to what is going on, so they withdraw and stop listening. Others may make light of what their wives are experiencing, in hopes of minimizing the effect. Then other men will turn up the volume of their lives, hoping to drown out these mysterious problems. But I don't believe men react this way because they don't care. It's because they don't know what to do about it—and that realization alone is overwhelming to them.

The best way to approach the matter of your wife's emotions is to ask God to give you insight into what your wife is feeling and show you how to pray accordingly. Much of what happens in a woman's emotions begins in her mind. The enemy of her soul will feed her thoughts that make her feel depressed, sad, angry, bitter, anxious, fearful, lonely, or full of self-doubt. He will make her think that such thoughts are reality, or that God is giving her revelation for her life. When the enemy screams lies and confusion at her, God will use your prayers to put an end to it and bring the silence, clarity, and peace she needs. Your prayers will clear her mind, calm her emotions, help her to see the truth, and make her better able to hear from God.

Our marriages would all be better if each of us were totally whole before we were married. But achieving wholeness can take a lifetime, and that's longer than most of us are willing to wait before we marry. However, often the very conditions we need for emotional healing are provided in the marriage itself. Emotional healing happens faster within the context of a committed, unconditional love relationship because the hurting person often feels safe enough to face the pain of the past. She doesn't have to try to hold it together, or keep up an image, or pretend there is no hurt.

If you found that after you were married a variety of hurts and emotions began to surface in your wife—things you had never been aware of before—rejoice that you have been deemed trustworthy enough to be her support through the healing time. Don't run from the task or be afraid of it. You are not required to be the healer, or to fix everything, or to have all the answers. Only God can heal damaged emotions, and He will do it from the inside out. But your prayers are crucial to keeping the devil at bay while that is being accomplished.

Because of my own emotional healing from the effects of child abuse (which I described in my book *Stormie*), I have often been asked certain questions by concerned husbands who are married to wives with deep emotional hurts. One man who was typical of many said, "I don't know what to do for my wife when she is depressed. What can I say? How can I help her? Nothing I do seems to make any difference."

I answered him this way.

"So much of what your wife is experiencing in her emotions is a result of things she has experienced in her past," I told him. "And it is hard for you to understand because you have not come out of that same background. But God wants to heal your wife's pain and give her emotional wholeness. He is allowing your wife to go through all this now *because* she is married to you. It's happening because *you* are providing a spiritual covering and a shelter for her so she can feel safe enough to allow the healing process to happen.

"The best thing you can do is to assure her of your unconditional love by your words and actions," I continued. "She needs your support more than ever. Tell her you are praying for her and will pray *with* her whenever she needs you to do so. Ask *God* to help you understand what she is feeling and how to respond in a positive way. Praying about your response to what she is feeling is as important as praying for God to heal her emotions. And when your wife begins to find wholeness, it's important to cheer her on."

Praying for your wife can help to fine-tune that priceless instrument God has put in your care. And it will ensure that you'll be enjoying some mighty fine music at your house.

SHE SAYS...

Please pray for your wife that:

1. She will enjoy emotional stability.
2. She will have a clear, strong mind.
3. She will not believe lies about herself.
4. She will feel secure in your love.
5. She will have the joy of the Lord.
6. You will be able to understand her feelings.
7. She will live in peace.

HE SAYS...
BY JACK HAYFORD

Pastor Jack is the founding pastor of The Church On The Way and chancellor of The King's College and Seminary in Los Angeles, California. He and his wife, Anna, have been married for 47 years, and they have four grown children and eleven grandchildren.

I've been asked how I, as a praying husband, have prayed for my dear wife, Anna, and upon reflection I realize something of a peculiarity. It's that the starting place for my most significant times of prayer for her has been to pray for myself:

- . . . to pray that I might perceive her task as she sees it, in order to appropriately stand with her as a support—someone who understands the emotions she is feeling and the nature of the challenge as she senses it from her viewpoint.

- . . . to pray that I may be patient and gracious, "feeling with her," the same way Jesus is "touched with the feeling" of my weakness (Hebrews 4:15).

More and more throughout the years of our marriage, the Holy Spirit has helped me to recognize that to love my wife as Christ loves the church (Ephesians 5:25) is to gain a Christlike sensitivity to how she feels. So as I have prayed for her day in and day out for the more than four decades of our marriage, I have found that my greatest effectiveness is in learning to let the Spirit of God sensitize my heart to Anna's present moment—her tasks, her weariness, her joys, her trials, her uncertainties, or her needs.

This kind of praying requires one other thing: a constant clarity of soul in my own heart toward her. Irrespective of any stress-prompted irritations caused by our busy life, notwithstanding any impatience I, in my male-style responses, may have with her female-style actions or responses, I cannot allow my soul to become cluttered with any attitude that will cripple my capacity to pray with an understanding of her heart, patience with her trial, or sensitivity to her perspective.

It's been a slow-grow proposition for me, but according to her loving assessment of my effort, I've grown a whole lot! My conclusion on this is that it is just another case of the effectiveness of *her* prayers for *me!*

PRAYER POWER

Lord, I am so grateful that You have made (<u>wife's name</u>) to be a woman of deep thoughts and feelings. I know that You have intended this for good, but I also know that the enemy of her soul will try to use it for evil. Help me to discern when he is doing that and enable me to pray accordingly.

Thank You that You have given (<u>wife's name</u>) a sound mind (2 Timothy 1:7). Protect her from the author of lies and help her to cast down "every high thing that exalts itself against the knowledge of God, bringing every thought into captivity to the obedience of Christ" (2 Corinthians 10:5). Give her discernment about what she receives into her mind. I pray she will quickly identify lies about herself, her life, or her future. Help her to recognize when there is a battle going on in her mind and to be aware of the enemy's tactics. Remind her to stick to Your battle plan and rely on the sword of the Spirit, which is Your Word (Ephesians 6:17). May she turn to You rather than give place to negative, upsetting, evil, or disturbing thoughts.

Keep me aware of when my wife is struggling so I can talk openly with her about what is on her mind and in her heart. Enable us to communicate clearly so that we don't allow the enemy to enter in with confusion or misinterpretation. Help me not to react inappropriately or withdraw from my wife emotionally when I don't understand her. Give me patience and sensitivity, and may prayer be my *first* reaction to her emotions and not a last resort.

Although I'm aware that I cannot meet my wife's every emotional need, I know that *You* can. I am not trying to absolve myself from meeting any of her needs, but I know that some of them are intended to be met only by You. I pray that when certain negative emotions threaten her happiness, You will be the first one she runs to, because only You can deliver her from them. Help her to hide herself in "the secret place of Your presence" (Psalm 31:20).

Lord, I pray that You would restore her soul (Psalm 23:3), heal her brokenheartedness, and bind up her wounds (Psalm 147:3). Make her to be secure in Your love and mine. Take away all fear, doubt, and discouragement, and give her clarity, joy, and peace.

POWER TOOLS

KEEP YOUR HEART WITH ALL DILIGENCE, FOR OUT OF IT SPRING THE ISSUES OF LIFE.

PROVERBS 4:23

THE LORD REDEEMS THE SOUL OF HIS SERVANTS, AND NONE OF THOSE WHO TRUST IN HIM SHALL BE CONDEMNED.

PSALM 34:22

DO NOT BE CONFORMED TO THIS WORLD, BUT BE TRANSFORMED BY THE RENEWING OF YOUR MIND, THAT YOU MAY PROVE WHAT IS THAT GOOD AND ACCEPTABLE AND PERFECT WILL OF GOD.

ROMANS 12:2

TO BE CARNALLY MINDED IS DEATH, BUT TO BE SPIRITUALLY MINDED IS LIFE AND PEACE.

ROMANS 8:6

BY YOUR PATIENCE POSSESS YOUR SOULS.

LUKE 21:19

CHAPTER FOUR

HER MOTHERHOOD

A man's work is clear-cut. He knows when it begins and he knows when it ends. He understands when he is successful at what he does and when he is not. And he knows from his paycheck what his value in the marketplace is. A woman whose main occupation is being a mother doesn't know any of these things. She labors for long hours day and night because the work is never done. There are no sick days off, and there's no place to go if she wants to resign. She finds herself in a highly skilled profession, yet she is given only on-the-job training. She often can't see the fruits of her labor, and she won't *really* know whether she's a success for about 25 years after the job begins. And the pay is quite nebulous, if not nonexistent, even though the benefits are great.

In my survey of wives, women voted motherhood as one of their top three needs for prayer, just under prayer for their spirits and for their emotions. They said that one of the most worrisome aspects of parenting is finding the successful balance between being a good mother and being a good wife. Every mother struggles with that balance daily, and whether she says it or not, she often feels guilty about neglecting her husband or her children. And it is not even an issue of equal time, because there is no way that a self-sufficient husband is going to get equal time with a child who can't do anything for himself. She realizes that her husband can dress and feed himself, get himself off to work, and make wise choices on his own. But her children need her for everything, and the younger they are the more they need her. And, opposite of most other jobs, she cannot successfully delegate much of it to someone else.

Your wife needs your prayers to help her find that balance. When she does, it will not only be better for her, but it will bless you *and* your children in countless ways. Your prayers will also help lift the heavy burden of raising the children off your wife's shoulders before this monumental job becomes wearisome and overwhelming. Most importantly, God will work through your prayers to give her peace in the process. And she must find His peace within herself while she is raising her children, because if she doesn't, she won't survive when they grow up and leave home. Your prayers for her as a mother can make the difference in whether her responsibilities become a daily grind of dirty work or a life-giving labor of love.

THE PAIN OF EMPTY ARMS

In every woman there is a longing to do what she was created to do. One of the things a woman's body was created to do is give birth. Her arms were made to hold a child, and she can feel empty when she is denied that privilege for too long. Even women who for one reason or another have *chosen* not to have children still experience pangs of desire to hold a child in their arms from time to time. For women who very much *want* their own children and have been denied that experience, there is a pain so deep that only God can touch it and soothe it. The "barren womb" is never satisfied (Proverbs 30:15,16).

If your wife is not a mother and wants to be, pray that she will find comfort for that ache, even if she no longer mentions it. If you have decided together to not have children and you are certain it is God's will, there may not be any problem. But if one of you wants a child and the other doesn't, this can lead to frustration, resentment, and unfulfillment that can strain the marriage to the point of breaking. It will never be God's will for the two of you to be in disagreement about this. If you are, seek the Lord wholeheartedly together and pray that the two of you will agree in accordance with God's will.

Surprisingly, healing for infertility was mentioned as one of the top needs for prayer for mothers in my survey of women. So pray that God will do whatever necessary in either you or your wife so that this issue will be completely resolved. And don't give up. I've known many people who have been childless, praying for years for a baby, and who then have seen God answer those prayers in one miraculous way or another. This could not have happened without the long-term fervent prayers of husbands and wives seeking a miracle from God. *Often the greatest miracles happen to those who are desperate for one.*

THE WORKING MOM

Children are a guilt trip anyway ("Have I done enough?" "Did I do too much?"), but if your wife is a mother who works *outside* the home, she has to deal with guilt on an hour-by-hour basis. From the time her children are born or come into her life, a part of *her* is always with *them*. This becomes especially painful when there are long periods of time when *they* are not with *her*. Not being there to greet the children when they come home from school, not seeing them learn something new, not being able to take time off from work when a child is sick, missing special events, performances, games, or field trips, wondering if the person caring for the child is doing a good job while knowing that no one could better care for the child than herself—all these contribute to a mother's pain and guilt.

No matter how good or devoted a mother she is, or how great her parenting skills are, every woman wants prayer that she will be a better mom. Working moms are desperate for those prayers because they have to do more with less time. If your wife is a working mom, pray for the time she has with the children to be maximized. Ask God to provide a way for her to not have to work so much, or maybe not at all. Pray for her to be free from the paralyzing burden of condemnation.

DADS HAVE GUILT TOO

Every man I know wants to be more involved in his children's lives and suffers with guilt when his work occupies too much of his time. Of course, it's important for a man to work and support his family. In fact, it's admirable. Men are often not applauded enough for all they do to provide a secure and safe place for their families. There is great pressure on men to be and do everything successfully, and there is a deep sense of failure when they don't feel they are living up to their own or others' expectations of them. That's one of the reasons I wrote *The Power of a Praying Wife*. I know men need the support of their wives' prayers.

With all that said, I want to encourage you as a father to know that your presence in the home is vitally important. It's more important than you probably realize. When you are at home, it gives your wife and children a sense of security, strength, and love. And in addition to that, if you spend a few minutes of undivided attention a day with your children, looking each of them in the eye and talking to them about their lives in an encouraging way, it enables them to believe they are valuable. You have no idea how important your approval is to your family.

There is a way you can be more involved in your children's lives each day while still providing for their needs in the manner you would like. You can *pray* for them. This does not replace your *time* with them, of course. Kids need *you* more than anything. And they need you to pray *with* them. But when you have to be away from them, tell each of your children that you're going to be praying for them while you're gone, and ask them how they specifically want you to pray. Then pray for them periodically during the day, and they will feel your presence and the presence of God. It's a powerful dynamic.

It's also good to pray for your children together with your wife. "If two of you agree on earth concerning anything they ask, it will be done for them by my Father in heaven" (Matthew 18:19). If one can put a thousand to flight, but two can put *ten* thousand to flight (Deuteronomy 32:30), then praying for your children with your wife is powerful. Ask your wife for any insight she has into each child. She sees so much that you may not have time to notice. She knows their struggles, weaknesses, and strengths, and she wants you to know them too. It will give your wife the greatest peace, confidence, and joy to know you are praying.

No matter how much you are paid in a lifetime for the work you do, the time you spend praying for your wife and children is worth far more. In fact, it's priceless. Whenever you pray for them, you are investing in your future together and storing up treasures in heaven. As far as the worth of your *wife's* work as a mother to your children, let me just quote you some lyrics from a song my husband once wrote with Donna Summer. "She works hard for the money, so you better treat her right." Pray, pray, pray!

SHE SAYS...

Please pray for your wife that:

1. She will be guided by God in raising her children.
2. She will have patience with each child.
3. She will have wisdom when disciplining her children.
4. She will teach her children well about the Lord.
5. She will know how to pray for each child.
6. Her children will be obedient and respectful to her.
7. Her children will rise up and call her blessed.

HE SAYS...
BY STEVEN CURTIS CHAPMAN

Steven is a singer and songwriter. He and his wife, Mary Beth, have been married for 16 years, and they have four children.

Though there have been many instances of the powerful effects of prayer in my relationship with my wife, probably one of the most profound experiences came within the last couple of years. Our daughter Emily, who was 13 at the time, began to talk to us about adopting a little sister. Of course, we explained that in order for her to adopt a little sister, we as her parents would have to adopt another daughter. While we have had a great love for the adoption process since we had experienced it through playing a supporting role for some of our closest friends who had adopted several children, my wife was fairly convinced that ours was to remain strictly a supportive role. I, on the other hand, had always been quietly drawn to the idea of sharing the love of our family with a little one who desperately needed just that...the love of a family. I had often come across the scripture in James 1 that talks about looking after orphans and widows and had wondered what the implications of that should be in my own life.

In the spring of 1999, I was asked to sing at a fund-raising event for an adoption agency that we had been supporting for a couple of years. Emily attended with me that night because Mary Beth had to run taxi service for our boys. That night Emily came home with every piece of informative literature on the subject of adoption she could get her hands on, along with the announcement that there was a great need in China for adoptive families. Mary Beth had made a prior agreement to read anything Emily brought home to her but made it very clear that this was not something she was feeling at all inclined to pursue. And with that, the prayers began. Actually, they had been going on for some time, but they definitely intensified on the part of Emily and me. I had a very strong sense that, though this was something I could get very excited about and could push for, it was going to require God's work in Mary Beth's heart to bring her to a place of peace and even desire for this.

Mary Beth's greatest concern was about love and compassion. She feared that she wouldn't be able to love an adopted child as well as she loved our three birth children. How would she deal with that potential discrepancy, and would it even be fair to bring a child into that enviroment? She would say, "I can hardly change the diaper of one of my own nephews sometimes. It's so different with your own child. What if I feel that way, and it is my own child?" Even as we began to move into the process of filling out papers and walking in the direction of adoption, she would lie in bed and cry many nights, saying she just didn't know if she could really do this. So I prayed, and we prayed.

My prayer usually went something like this: "Okay, Father, You know we've done some pretty crazy things before and this may just be the craziest of all. This seems like something You keep placing in our path and I don't want to miss what You have in Your perfect plan for us. But if this really is Your will for us, then You will have to reveal that to Mary Beth and give her faith to believe it for herself. I don't think I'm supposed to force the issue or even strongly encourage this. She knows where I stand and I'm leaving the rest up to You. If this is not for us to do, then that's okay too. Please have Your way and do the work that only You can do."

And work He did. Some day we'll write the book and tell the whole story, but for now, let me jump way ahead and say that on March 16, 2001, Emily, Caleb, Will Franklin, and I got to see a real-life miracle take place right before our eyes. A precious little bundle of life named Shaohannah was placed in Mary Beth's arms for the first time—and there was no shadow of doubt in her eyes that this was *her* daughter. In fact, I am sure that at that very moment Mary Beth would have just as quickly laid her life down for Shaohannah as for any of our other children. Now, Mary Beth will be the first to tell you she has had a hard time believing those words of doubt ever came from her lips. Yes, God did the thing that only He could do, and we are so grateful that He did. And you know what else? The diapers are nothin'!

PRAYER POWER

Lord, I pray that You will help (<u>wife's name</u>) to be the best mother to our children (child) that she can be. Give her strength, and help her to understand that she can do all things through Christ who strengthens her (Philippians 4:13). Give her patience, kindness, gentleness, and discernment. Guard her tongue so that the words she speaks will build up and not tear down, will bring life and not destruction. Guide her as she makes decisions regarding each child. By the authority You have given me, as a believer as well as a husband and father, I break any rebellion or area of disobedience that would erect a stronghold in our children (child) (Luke 10:19). Specifically I lift up (<u>child's name</u>). I bring before You my concern about (<u>name any area of concern that you have for that child</u>).

Lord, I know we cannot successfully raise our children without You. So I ask that You would take the burden of raising them from our shoulders and partner with us to bring them up. Give my wife and me patience, strength, and wisdom to train, teach, discipline, and care for each child. Help us to understand each child's needs and know how to meet them. Give us discernment about what we allow into the home through TV, books, movies, video games, magazines, and computer activities. Give us revelation and the ability to see what we need to see. Show us Your perspective on each child's uniqueness and potential for greatness. Give us a balance between being overprotective and allowing our children to experience life too early.

If we, being evil, know how to give good gifts to our children, how much more will You, our heavenly Father, give good things to us when we ask it of You (Matthew 7:11). So I ask You for the gifts of intelligence, strength, talent, wisdom, and godliness to be in our children. Keep them safe from any accident, disease, or evil influence. May no plan of the enemy succeed in their lives. Help us to raise our children (child) to be obedient and respectful to both of us and to have a heart to follow You and Your Word. I pray that my wife will find fulfillment, contentment, and joy as a mother, while never losing sight of who she is in You.

POWER TOOLS

HER CHILDREN RISE UP AND CALL HER BLESSED; HER HUSBAND ALSO, AND HE PRAISES HER.

PROVERBS 31:28

BEHOLD, CHILDREN ARE A HERITAGE FROM THE LORD, THE FRUIT OF THE WOMB IS A REWARD.

PSALM 127:3

THEY SHALL NOT LABOR IN VAIN, NOR BRING FORTH CHILDREN FOR TROUBLE; FOR THEY SHALL BE THE DESCENDANTS OF THE BLESSED OF THE LORD, AND THEIR OFFSPRING WITH THEM.

ISAIAH 65:23

POUR OUT YOUR HEART LIKE WATER BEFORE THE FACE OF THE LORD. LIFT YOUR HANDS TOWARD HIM FOR THE LIFE OF YOUR YOUNG CHILDREN.

LAMENTATIONS 2:19

FOR THIS CHILD I PRAYED, AND THE LORD HAS GRANTED ME MY PETITION WHICH I ASKED OF HIM.

1 SAMUEL 1:27

CHAPTER FIVE

HER MOODS

I know what you're thinking. You're wondering why I didn't include "Her Moods" in the chapter on "Her Emotions." The reason for this is that the chapter on emotions is very concrete. Solid, identifiable emotions have names like depression, sadness, anxiety, or anger. Moods, as I am referring to them here, are far more difficult to pin down. They are often very hard to recognize, identify, or understand. They can, in fact, seem so nebulous, unexpected, unwarranted, or irrational that many a husband has been reluctant to venture into this unfathomable territory to try and comprehend their cause. But I would like to attempt an explanation of a woman's moods that may help you gain understanding and—who knows—might even make *sense* to you.

First of all, you must keep in mind that there is a process always going on in a woman's mind and soul, unbeknownst to her unsuspecting husband—and perhaps all others in the vicinity. What is happening is that all her thoughts, fears, hormones, responsibilities, memories of previous offenses, the amount of sleep she got last night, the devil's plans for her life, her entire past, and how her hair is behaving that day, are simultaneously competing for her attention. When all these things converge at one moment in time, it can be unbearable. It doesn't matter what might have been happening just a few moments ago, or the last time you talked to her. That was *then*. This is happening *now*. You may find yourself completely taken by surprise because you were not privy to the process. But don't feel bad about that, because even your wife herself may not have recognized it.

Try to understand that as a man you have simple, clearly defined needs, such as food, sex, success, appreciation, and recreation. Your wife, on the other hand, is a complex being. Her needs are so intricate that even she is at a loss for words to explain them to you. Only God, her Creator, can fathom it all.

Her cycle of hormones alone is beyond comprehension. A woman can be emotionally sensitive in the days before, during, and after her monthly cycle. That leaves about three days in the middle when she is normal, and on one of those days she is ovulating, so it's up for grabs how she is going to be that day. So I figure a guy has two good days when it's safe. In addition to that, if there is any stress in her life, if her husband is too busy for her, if she is over 30 and feels like life is passing her by before she ever gets to realize her dream, if her kids are small and need her every second, if her kids are grown and don't need her like they used to, if she is creative and has no way to express it at the moment, if she has gained weight, or if the devil is telling her she has no purpose, then the atmosphere in and around her can be charged with overwhelming frustration. It seems impossible to cope with it all.

If you ever find this phenomenon occurring in your wife, it's best not to say, "What in the world is the matter with you *now?*"

It's better to first pray, "Lord, reveal to me what is happening in my wife and show me what I can do about it."

Then say to your wife, "Tell me what's going on in that pretty head of yours."

She may not be able to articulate an answer that is remotely understandable to you, but the important thing is that she sees you are listening. If she tells you how horrible she thinks she is and she doesn't know what you see in her, don't agree with her. If she says she hasn't forgotten how you have let her down, don't deny it. If she shares with you that she feels like running away or murdering someone, put your arm around her and say, "How can I help you find a more suitable option?"

Then do everything in your power to keep your eyes from glazing over. Don't glance at your watch or the TV remote. Don't allow your head to turn back in the direction of the newspaper or whatever project you are working on at the moment. And above all, keep your mind from thinking about the *more important* things you could be doing. Women have a special ability to spot that from 50 yards away.

Here is some advice that can help you navigate these waters successfully, including a few good lines that always work. Say them to your wife in any order, and then pray for her.

1. "I love you."
2. "You are the greatest woman in the world to me."
3. "You're beautiful when you're moody." (Maybe you shouldn't use the word "moody." "Upset" might be a better choice.)
4. "Tell me what's on your mind, and I promise not to get mad."
5. "How have I let you down?"

6. "How can I make it up to you?"
7. "Have you been getting enough sleep?"
8. "What would make you happy right now?"
9. "I don't have all the answers. But God does."
10. "Do you want to pray about this together?"

This whole process, prayer included, could take less than 15 minutes of your undivided attention, and it will dissipate the power of all those converging forces. What a small investment of time in order to have such great rewards!

Whatever you do, don't ask your wife, "Is it that time of the month again?" She doesn't want her suffering to be dismissed or explained away so easily. Even if that has everything to do with it, she is not able to see that now. And it will do no good to try to force the issue.

In the midst of the complex manifestations of your wife's moods, there will come forth a simple message. It may be a cry for intimacy. It could be a desire to be known and appreciated. Perhaps it is a deep longing for reassurance that everything is going to be okay. Ask God to help you hear the message and show you how to pray accordingly.

SHE SAYS...

Please pray for your wife that:

1. She will have the peace of God.
2. She will not be subject to mood swings.
3. Her hormone levels will be balanced.
4. She will express her feelings openly to you.
5. She will believe that you love her.
6. You will listen and hear what she is saying.
7. She will rely on the Lord more.

HE SAYS...
BY MICHAEL HARRITON

Michael is a music composer. He and his wife, Terry, have been married for 23 years, and they have three grown children.

Men, when your wife screams "Don't touch me!" at the top of her lungs and then crawls into bed and turns off the lights at 7 P.M., it really means, "Don't leave me. Come and get me. Save me. Help!" If she withdraws her hand when you reach out to touch it, that means, "Please keep trying. This is working. Follow the trail of depression and bad vibes. Find me and rescue me."

My beautiful and talented wife picks up after me, does her studio singing, teaches voice lessons, runs my errands, cooks healthy gourmet meals, keeps a spotless house, does laundry, entertains my clients, serves at church, and still manages to sparkle as my dream date! But some days it doesn't take much to send her into an emotional tailspin. It's usually my fault. I'll do something like getting upset at her because my favorite sock has suddenly become an orphan in its drawer.

On those days my wife has thoughts of running away from home, joining the circus or the space program, or buying a one-way ticket to some remote island. She tells me so. One day in particular I reached out to her, and she recoiled as though I were contagious. I tried again, with only slightly better results. (Do women go to school somewhere to learn this stuff?) Finally she said, "I am NOT pretty. I am NOT talented. I am NOT good at anything, nobody wants me, and there is NO PLACE for me ANYWHERE! I am such a disappointment. Such a failure. What do you see in me?"

Guys, when you hear those tough questions, struggle hard for a positive comeback. She may just be testing you. Pass the test with flying colors by reciting a long list of her good qualities and then praying for her. When I remember to do that, along with any necessary apology, it always works.

PRAYER POWER

Lord, I pray for (<u>wife's name</u>) and ask that You would calm her spirit, soothe her soul, and give her peace today. Drown out the voice of the enemy, who seeks to entrap her with lies. Help her to take every thought captive so she is not led astray (2 Corinthians 10:5). Where there is error in her thinking, I pray You would reveal it to her and set her back on course. Help her to hear Your voice only. Fill her afresh with Your Holy Spirit and wash away anything in her that is not of You.

Balance her body perfectly so that she is not carried up and down like a roller coaster. Give her inner tranquility that prevails no matter what is going on around her. Enable her to see things from Your perspective so that she can fully appreciate all the good that is in her life. Keep her from being blinded by fears and doubts. Show her the bigger picture, and teach her to distinguish the valuable from the unimportant. Help her to recognize the answers to her own prayers. Show me how to convince her that I love her, and help me to be able to demonstrate it in ways she can perceive.

Lord, I know that You have "called us to peace" (1 Corinthians 7:15). Help us both to hear that call and live in the peace that passes all understanding. I say to my wife, "Let the peace of God rule" in your heart, and "be thankful" (Colossians 3:15).

POWER TOOLS

THUS SAYS THE LORD: "BEHOLD, I WILL EXTEND PEACE TO HER LIKE A RIVER."

ISAIAH 66:12

SURELY I HAVE CALMED AND QUIETED MY SOUL.

PSALM 131:2

PURSUE RIGHTEOUSNESS, FAITH, LOVE, PEACE WITH THOSE WHO CALL ON THE LORD OUT OF A PURE HEART.

2 TIMOTHY 2:22

WEEPING MAY ENDURE FOR A NIGHT, BUT JOY COMES IN THE MORNING.

PSALM 30:5

THE PEACE OF GOD, WHICH SURPASSES ALL UNDER-STANDING, WILL GUARD YOUR HEARTS AND MINDS THROUGH CHRIST JESUS.

PHILIPPIANS 4:7

CHAPTER SIX

HER MARRIAGE

I lived on a farm and cattle ranch until I was eight years old. We raised *all* our own food. The winter before I turned nine, a severe blizzard killed our cattle. The following spring, hail killed all our crops. We were completely wiped out. By the time summer came, my dad had decided that farming and raising cattle was too hard, and so we moved to the city and what promised to be an easier life.

One of the main things I learned from life on the farm was how carefully you must plant and tend a garden when you know that your life depends on what it produces. If you don't reap a successful crop, there won't be food to eat.

I learned that if you want anything to grow in your garden, you have to start with the right soil. Just as you cannot build a house without a foundation, you can't have a productive, life-giving garden without good, rich soil. Next, you must have the right seeds. What grows in your garden depends on the seeds you plant, so you need to plant what you want to see come up in the harvest. Once you get the garden planted, you have to carefully water the seeds, diligently pull out the weeds around the sprouts that appear, and be on the lookout for pests, bad weather, and other conditions that can destroy it.

Your marriage is like a garden. The soil is enriched and prepared through prayer. Then you have to plant the right kind of seeds—the good seeds of love, fidelity, respect, time, and communication.

SEEDS OF LOVE

Seeds of love are some of the easiest seeds to plant, and their growth is so rapid that you can sometimes see results instantaneously. If seeds of love are planted by our marriage partner, then hope, peace, and happiness will grow in us. These things will give us courage to face our fears, failures, and inabilities. They will give us strength to stand up and resist the things that oppose us.

Of course, you do have to pull out anything growing in the garden that shouldn't be there. Weeding is not the fun part of gardening, but it is one of those necessary chores that must be done. If weeds of hurt, strife, misunderstanding, criticism, selfishness, and anger are allowed to flourish in the marriage garden without being uprooted, they will choke out anything good that is planted. If seeds of lovelessness are planted, we wither and slowly die from the inside out. Sometimes a garden can still look like a garden, but the plants are dead on the inside. They just haven't fallen over yet. Marriages can get that way too. They look fine on the outside, but within, they are dead. This does not fulfill God's plan for our lives, and it certainly doesn't glorify Him.

If you and your wife do not produce enough love to allow each of you to grow into all God created you to be, then your relationship needs to be examined for selfishness, fear, pride, control, or whatever other weed of the flesh is stifling it. If you have serious problems in your marriage, know that

God can work miracles when you pray. He can change hearts and perspectives in an instant. He can uproot seeds of sin, resurrect love where it has died, and make it not only grow again, but flourish.

The Bible says, "Let love be without hypocrisy. Abhor what is evil. Cling to what is good" (Romans 12:9). Cling to what is good in your marriage with all sincerity of heart. Despise what the devil is trying to plant there. Pray that God will show you how to plant *new* seeds of unconditional love. (A garden has to be replanted every year.) With proper care, those seeds of love will produce a great harvest.

SEEDS OF FIDELITY

In order for a garden to not become a salad bar for hungry animals, it needs a fence around it to keep them out. In the same way, the boundaries of marriage are set up for its protection. If we don't watch over the boundaries, something is sure to be stolen from us. Too often people carelessly plant seeds outside the boundaries, and what grows up attracts the attention of creatures that come to devour. They wait outside the garden, and if the fence falls into disrepair because it isn't maintained, they find a way in through the weakest part. When we plant seeds of infidelity, we break down the boundaries and invite unwanted creatures of prey to come in.

A dear Christian friend of mine had a husband who sowed seeds of infidelity outside the garden of his marriage. This attracted a creature of prey who was hungry to take over the garden for herself. That man and this creature scattered their seeds in fields that were not their own, seeds of weeds and briars from which nothing good could ever grow. This eventually destroyed not only one but two marriage gardens, and it was never possible to regain what was lost.

Everyone gets tempted to sow outside his own garden. The ones who resist, and instead deliberately plant seeds of fidelity, reap a harvest of plenty. Even if you have the most perfect marriage ever known to man, the enemy will still try to tear down the fence and destroy it by one means or another. The devil will always look for ways to set a snare for one of you. So your marriage soil is never too good to be beyond the need for enriching prayer. If we think our marriage is so strong that we don't ever need to pray about it, we are deceived. "Therefore let him who thinks he stands take heed lest he fall" (1 Corinthians 10:12).

Pray that God will keep you and your wife from planting anything you will live to regret. Ask Him to show you how to plant seeds of fidelity and build a fence so solid it will be the envy of all your neighbors.

SEEDS OF RESPECT

One of the main reasons marriages fail is that the husband or wife does not seek the other's best interest. The Bible says, "Let no one seek his own, but each one the other's well-being" (1 Corinthians 10:24). When we sow seeds of disrespect in a marriage, we are not seeking the other's well-being, and we will reap a crop of bitterness and strife. Putting our mate's well-being before our own is not only very difficult, it's simply impossible to do on a consistent basis without the Holy Spirit enabling us. That's why we must pray about it.

Because you are a dear brother in the Lord, I want to share something with you that women don't always verbalize to their husbands. This is, your wife does not want to be your mother, nor does she want to be your maid. The former will cause *her* to lose respect for *you;* the latter will make her feel that *you've* lost respect for *her.* I know there are countless things your wife will do that a mother or maid would do also. But if that expectation becomes a way-of-life attitude on your part, she will begin to think of you as a child or as a boss, and it will adversely affect your relationship. The more your wife feels like your mother or your maid, the less she will feel like your lover. Ask God to help you see things from your wife's perspective and show you how to plant seeds of respect in your marriage.

Seeds of Time

You can't have a successful garden if you don't spend enough time in it. It takes many hours to plant, water, feed, nurture, and harvest. In successful marriages the husbands and wives spend time together alone. If your schedules never allow time for you and your wife to be alone with each other, then you are too busy. You need that time of togetherness to talk, to work things out, to share interests and dreams, to just be together in silence, and to have intimate times that are not rushed. I know there are seasons in everyone's life that are especially busy. But when busyness becomes a lifestyle, you've got to consider exactly what it is you're planting. Pray that God will help you plant seeds of time together.

Seeds of Communication

Words are like seeds. They start out small and grow into something big. If a person plants words of anger, indifference, criticism, impatience, or insensitivity in his marriage, the fruit of those words will be lack of intimacy and warmth, loss of harmony and unity, and the silencing of laughter and joy. These seeds can grow into something big enough to choke out everything else around them.

One of the biggest problems in many marriages is a lack of communication. Wives say, "My husband doesn't really hear what I'm saying. He doesn't listen." Husbands say, "My wife doesn't understand me. She misinterprets things I say." This comes about because men and women think differently. It's one of the ways we complete one another. If a man and a woman inevitably see things from different perspectives, then it stands to reason that they should ask God to help them both see things from *His* perspective. That way they can see them together, from the same viewpoint.

In the garden of a marriage relationship, there will always be a harvest time. "Whatever a man sows, that he will also reap" (Galatians 6:7). If we don't like the crop we're reaping, then it's probably time to plant seeds of a different nature. Seeds are planted through actions, but mostly through words—and when a husband and wife can't communicate well with their words, bad things start growing.

If bad word-seeds have already been planted in your marriage, and fast-growing weeds are choking the life out of your relationship, know that God has given you the tool of prayer to uproot them. Get to the bottom of whatever you see growing out of control, such as bitterness, anger, or unforgiveness, and pray for those things to be dug up and thrown away.

Marriage can seem like heaven. Or it can seem like hell. For most people, it's somewhere in between. That's because it's not easy becoming one with another person, even if that person is the one God created especially for you. There is a lot of growing required. But it's not about causing our mate to grow into *our* image, it's about both husband and wife growing into *God's* image, together.

God can cause a husband and a wife to grow together in a way that makes them more compatible while allowing the two partners to develop their individual gifts and retain their own uniqueness. Marriage does not need to be stifling, forcing two people to lose all individuality. Rather, it can actually provide the perfect environment for the gifts of each person to be developed to the fullest. When the two people in a marriage partnership relate to one another in the way God wants them to, it brings about a fulfilling of each one's purpose that will not happen otherwise. Through prayer, each one can *release* the other rather than control; *encourage* rather than condemn.

God will not bless our disobedience. He doesn't approve when selfishness, deceit, strife, neglect, and cruelty are permitted to grow unchecked in a marriage garden. When we treat our marriage partner in a way that is less than what God wants us to do, not only are we rebelling against the Lord, but we are working against what God wants to accomplish in us as individuals and as a couple.

Ask God to help you and your wife appreciate your differences. Ask Him to show you where you complement each other. Is one of you strong where the other is weak? The very thing that is designed to be our greatest blessing can often become an irritant because we don't ask God to let us see it from *His* perspective. Is there something your wife does or says that bothers you? Tell God about it. He'll show you how to pray.

Divorce doesn't happen because people don't want their marriages to work out. It's usually because the husband or wife believes that things will never change. Ask *God* to change what needs to be changed in either of you. Even if it appears that irreparable damage has already been done in your marriage, that the garden has been hopelessly blighted, know that God can and wants to work a miracle. We have no idea of the wonderful things God has for us when we humble ourselves and love God enough to live His way (1 Corinthians 2:9). This is never more true than in a marriage.

Through prayer you can invite the light of the Lord to bathe and invigorate the garden of your marriage. Then it will bud, blossom, bloom, and grow into a harvest of joy and fulfillment for both of you.

SHE SAYS...

Pray for your marriage that:

1. Love will grow between you and your wife.
2. You and your wife will resist temptation to stray.
3. You will practice mutual respect for one another.
4. The two of you will not live separate lives.
5. You will be friends as well as lovers.
6. You will work together as a team.
7. There will be no divorce in your future.

HE SAYS...
BY MICHAEL OMARTIAN

"A threefold cord is not quickly broken" (Ecclesiastes 4:12). That verse was "manna" to Stormie and me during tough times in our marriage. It seemed that our difficulties often arose out of superficial circumstances, but the enemy of our souls would use anything to destroy the threefold cord that our marriage represented. Confronting, arguing, and trying to reason with each other always came up short. What didn't come up short was praying together. But what a hurdle we had to face just to get to that.

Prayer requires forgetting your own agenda and letting God set the agenda. Many times prayer would focus my attention away from the need to see Stormie change and become more accommodating to me, to instead how *I* could change and be more accommodating to *her*. Scary stuff for the ego! But through prayer we have been able to make changes and work things out. Now we have been married for 28 years and I can't imagine anyone else as my mate. But our problems only work themselves out when she and I join with God to solve them. That threefold cord will not be easily broken.

PRAYER POWER

Lord, I pray that You would establish in me and (<u>wife's name</u>) bonds of love that cannot be broken. Show me how to love my wife in an ever-deepening way that she can clearly perceive. May we have mutual respect and admiration for each other so that we become and remain one another's greatest friend, champion, and unwavering support. Where love has been diminished, lost, destroyed, or buried under hurt and disappointment, put it back in our hearts. Give us strength to hold on to the good in our marriage, even in those times when one of us doesn't *feel* love.

Enable my wife and me to forgive each other quickly and completely. Specifically I lift up to You (<u>name any area where forgiveness is needed</u>). Help us to "be kind to one another, tenderhearted, forgiving," the way You are to us (Ephesians 4:32). Teach us to overlook the faults and weaknesses of the other. Give us a sense of humor, especially as we deal with the hard issues of life.

Unite us in faith, beliefs, standards of morality, and mutual trust. Help us to be of the same mind, to move together in harmony, and to quickly come to mutual agreements about our finances, our children, how we spend our time, and any other decisions that need to be made. Where we are in disagreement and this has caused strife, I pray You would draw us together on the issues. Adjust our perspectives to align with Yours. Make our communication open and honest so that we avoid misunderstandings.

May we have the grace to be tolerant of each other's faults and, at the same time, have the willingness to change. I pray that we will not live two separate lives, but will instead walk together as a team. Remind us to take time for one another so that our marriage will be a source of happiness, peace, and joy for us both.

Lord, I pray that You would protect our marriage from anything that would destroy it. Take out of our lives anyone who would come between us or tempt us. Help us to immediately recognize and resist temptation when it presents itself. I pray that no other relationship either of us have, or have had in the past, will rob us of anything in our relationship now. Sever all unholy ties in both of our lives. May there never be any adultery or divorce in our future to destroy what You, Lord, have put together. Help us to never cast aside the whole relationship just because it has developed a nonworking part. I pray that we will turn to You—the Designer—to fix it and get it operating the way it was intended.

Teach us to seek each other's well-being first, as You have commanded in Your Word (1 Corinthians 10:24). We want to keep You at the center of our marriage and not expect from each other what only *You* can give. Where either of us have unrealistic expectations of the other, open our eyes to see it. May we never waver in our commitment and devotion to You and to one another, so that this marriage will become all You designed it to be.

POWER TOOLS

TWO ARE BETTER THAN ONE, BECAUSE THEY HAVE A GOOD
REWARD FOR THEIR LABOR. FOR IF THEY FALL, ONE WILL
LIFT UP HIS COMPANION. BUT WOE TO HIM WHO IS ALONE
WHEN HE FALLS, FOR HE HAS NO ONE TO HELP HIM UP.

ECCLESIASTES 4:9,10

IF TWO OF YOU AGREE ON EARTH CONCERNING ANYTHING
THAT THEY ASK, IT WILL BE DONE FOR THEM BY MY FATHER
IN HEAVEN.

MATTHEW 18:19

WHOEVER DIVORCES HIS WIFE AND MARRIES ANOTHER COM-
MITS ADULTERY AGAINST HER.

MARK 10:11

TAKE HEED TO YOUR SPIRIT, AND LET NONE DEAL TREACH-
EROUSLY WITH THE WIFE OF HIS YOUTH.

MALACHI 2:15

BE KINDLY AFFECTIONATE TO ONE ANOTHER WITH BROTH-
ERLY LOVE, IN HONOR GIVING PREFERENCE TO ONE
ANOTHER.

ROMANS 12:10

CHAPTER SEVEN

HER SUBMISSION

Submit is a verb. *Submitting* is a voluntary action. That means it is something *we ourselves* do. It's not something we make *someone else* do. Just as we can't force another person to love us, we can't force someone to submit to us either. Of course we can *make* that person do what we want. But then that's not true submission.

Submission is a *choice* we make. It's something each one of us must decide to do. And this decision happens first in the heart. If we don't *decide in our hearts* that we are going to willingly submit to whomever it is we need to be submitted to, then we are not truly submitting.

This may be shocking news to you, but an overwhelming majority of wives in my survey said they *want* to submit to their husbands. They *want* their husbands to be the head of the home, and they have no desire to usurp that God-given position of leadership. They know what the Bible says on the subject, and discerning wives want to do what God wants because they understand that God's ways work best.

However, problems often arise in this area because a wife is afraid to submit to her husband for two reasons:

- Reason #1. Her husband thinks submission is only a noun, and he uses it as a weapon.

- Reason #2. Her husband has himself not made the choice in his heart to be fully submitted to God.

Okay, okay! I know that God did not say a wife needs to submit to her husband only if he proves to be worthy. Submission is a matter of trusting in *God* more than trusting in man. But a wife will more easily make the choice to submit to her husband if she knows that he has made the choice to submit to the Lord. It will be a sign to her that it is safe to submit to him. And the goal here is to *help* her, not *force* her, into proper alignment.

Many a wife has a hard time trusting that her husband is hearing from God if he doesn't appear to be submitted to God in the way he treats her. Wives know that after the verse "Wives, submit to your own husbands" (Ephesians 5:22), the Bible says "Husbands, love your wives, just as Christ also loved the church and gave Himself for her"(verse 25). Christ doesn't neglect, ignore, demean, or abuse the church. He doesn't treat her rudely or disrespectfully. He never acts arrogantly or insensitively toward her. Nor does He criticize her and make her feel she is not valuable. Rather He loves her, protects her, provides for her, and cares for her. So while God gives the husband a position of leadership in relationship to his wife, He also requires the price of self-sacrifice from him.

The big question in many women's minds is, "If I submit myself to my husband, will I become a doormat for him to walk on?" The answer to that question depends entirely upon whether her husband believes he should love his wife like Christ loves the church and willingly sacrifices himself for her—or thinks that submission is a noun and that it is something owed him. In other words, does he only consider *his* desires and opinions, to the exclusion of *hers*?

A wife has a hard time giving her husband the reins to her life if she doesn't believe she can trust him to have her best interests at heart as he steers the course of their lives together. She has trouble going along with his decisions when he refuses to consider her thoughts, feelings, and insights on the subject. And if she has submitted to a male in the past and her trust was violated in some way, it is even more difficult for her to trust now.

On the other hand, a woman will do anything for a man who loves her like Christ loves the church. Submission is easy under these conditions. I know a number of women who are married to unbelieving husbands and who have no problem submitting to their husbands, because in each case the husband loves his wife like Christ loves the church, even though he doesn't even know Christ.

Too often people confuse "submit" with "obey." But they are not the same thing. The Bible give commands about obeying other people only in regard to children and slaves, and in the context of the local church. "Children, obey your parents in the Lord, for this is right" (Ephesians 6:1). "Bondservants, be obedient to those who are your masters according to the flesh" (Ephesians 6:5). "Obey those who rule over you, and be submissive, for they watch out for your souls, as those who must give account" (Hebrews 13:17). Since a wife is neither her husband's child nor his servant, and the local church isn't part of a marriage, the word "obey" has no application to the relationship between a husband and a wife.

Submission means "to submit yourself." In light of that, when a husband *demands* submission from his wife, it is no longer true submission. And his demands can become intimidating and oppressive, which breeds resentment. When a husband is more interested in his wife's submission to *him* than he is in his own submission to *God*, then submission becomes a tool to hurt and destroy.

I have seen too many marriages between strong Christian people—high-profile Christian leaders, in fact—end in divorce because the husband *demanded* submission and resorted to verbal or physical abuse in order to get it. My husband has even counseled men like that, men who refused to hear that losing their family was a horrible price to pay for being "right." How much better it would have been for the husband to submit himself to God's hand and then pray for his wife to be able to come into proper order. This kind of situation occurs far too often.

When we submit to God, He doesn't suppress who we are. He frees us to become who we're made to be, within the boundaries of His protection. When a wife submits to her husband, she comes under his covering and protection, and this frees her to become all God created her to be. And trust me, you want that for your wife. Her greatest gifts will prove to be your greatest blessing.

If you feel that your wife is not submissive, pray for her to have a submissive heart, first toward God and then toward you. Then ask God to help you love her the way He does. I guarantee that you will see her submission level rise in direct proportion to the unselfish love you exhibit for her. And let her see that you are seeking God for guidance. If she knows that you are asking God to show you the way, she will follow you anywhere.

SHE SAYS...

Please pray for your wife that:

1. She will understand what submission really is.
2. She will be able to submit in the way God wants her to.
3. You will be completely submitted to God.
4. She will trust God as He works in you.
5. You will take your position as spiritual leader.
6. She will trust you to be the head of the family.
7. Submission will not be a point of contention in your marriage.

HE SAYS...
BY MICHAEL OMARTIAN

I vividly remember, from the time I was a young man, watching my father help my mom with the dishes, throw clothes into the washing machine, make beds, and prepare dinner with my mother. He worked a regular job by day, but he never used that as an excuse for sharply dividing the roles in the family. His actions modeled to me a man who respected, revered, and cherished his wife. He wanted me to know that submission was not a one-sided dynamic, but an action shared equally between two people who both sacrificed for the achievement of one another's goals. I believe that too much has been made of the concept of submission. Where males have taken the heavy-handed approach, it has spawned a woman's movement with justifiable complaints.

Where love, unselfishness, and prayer prevail, the concept of submission is allowed to live and breathe naturally. We men have failed in this area by holding onto notions of some special power we think we have simply because we are men. We are then tempted to lord it over our wives with this power. Yes, God gives us authority, but He also created us equal with our wives and makes us to be one flesh with them. I would be warring with myself if I attempted to gain unbalanced authority over my wife. Again, prayer is the equalizer. I pray for both my wife and myself that we would be in right order toward one another and toward God.

PRAYER POWER

Lord, I submit myself to You this day. Lead me as I lead my family. Help me to make all decisions based on Your revelation and guidance. As I submit my leadership to You, enable (<u>wife's name</u>) to fully trust that You are leading me. Help her to understand the kind of submission You want from her. Help me to understand the kind of submission You want from me. Enable me to be the leader You want me to be.

Where there are issues over which we disagree, help us to settle them in proper order. I pray that I will allow You, Lord, to be so in control of my life that my wife will be able to freely trust Your Holy Spirit working in me. Help me to love her the way You love me, so that I will gain her complete respect and love. Give her a submissive heart and the faith she needs to trust me to be the spiritual leader in our home. At the same time, help us to submit "to one another in the fear of God" (Ephesians 5:21). I know that only You, Lord, can make that perfect balance happen in our lives.

POWER TOOLS

WIVES, SUBMIT TO YOUR OWN HUSBANDS, AS TO THE LORD. FOR THE HUSBAND IS HEAD OF THE WIFE, AS ALSO CHRIST IS HEAD OF THE CHURCH; AND HE IS THE SAVIOR OF THE BODY. THEREFORE, JUST AS THE CHURCH IS SUBJECT TO CHRIST, SO LET THE WIVES BE TO THEIR OWN HUSBANDS IN EVERYTHING. HUSBANDS, LOVE YOUR WIVES, JUST AS CHRIST ALSO LOVED THE CHURCH AND GAVE HIMSELF FOR HER, THAT HE MIGHT SANCTIFY AND CLEANSE HER WITH THE WASHING OF WATER BY THE WORD, THAT HE MIGHT PRESENT HER TO HIMSELF A GLORIOUS CHURCH, NOT HAVING SPOT OR WRINKLE OR ANY SUCH THING, BUT THAT SHE SHOULD BE HOLY AND WITHOUT BLEMISH.

EPHESIANS 5:22-27

HE WHO FINDS HIS LIFE WILL LOSE IT, AND HE WHO LOSES HIS LIFE FOR MY SAKE WILL FIND IT.

MATTHEW 10:39

BE OF THE SAME MIND TOWARD ONE ANOTHER.

ROMANS 12:16

CHAPTER EIGHT

HER RELATIONSHIPS

Awoman needs close friendships with other
women. She doesn't need many—it's the
quality that counts more than the quantity. But
the right caliber of friends is very important.

Your wife doesn't need friends who use her, wear her
down, are jealous of her, don't really like her, talk dis-
paragingly about her behind her back, are trying to get
close to you, or are so needy and dependent that they are
draining. She needs friends who build her up and enrich
her life, and allow her to do the same for them. She needs
trustworthy and faithful companions to talk to, to pray
with, to offer help when she needs it, and with whom she
can discuss important topics about which you may not
have the slightest interest. She needs friends who will pull
for her, contribute to her life, and keep her on the right
path, and who always give her a standard to which she can
aspire. These kinds of friends will help your wife to grow,
and ultimately add to your marriage relationship. Your
wife wants you to pray that she will have good, godly
friendships.

Relationships with family members are extremely important and must be covered in prayer as well. People are sensitive, and things can get in the midst of *any* relationship
and cause it to misfire. But family members in particular

have a history of expectations and disappointments, which makes relationships with them very complex.

In-law relationships can be especially delicate. That's why you can't assume that your wife's relationship with your family is going to be fine. In fact, the type of relationship she has with them will depend a lot on you. Your answers to the following questions will reveal how you should be praying.

1. Does your family fully accept your wife, or do they still think that someday you will come to your senses and find the wife of their choice?

2. Do you say good things about your wife to your family members, building her up in their minds?

3. Do you ever complain about your wife in front of your family members or side with them against her?

4. Does your family think of your wife as a blessing, an asset, a valuable person, and a gift from God to you?

5. Is your wife ever viewed by your family as a threat, an endurance test, a mistake, a thorn in their sides, or a cross they have to bear?

6. Does your family welcome your wife with open arms, or do they keep her at arm's length?

7. Has your wife ever indicated to you that her relationship with your family is not what she would like it to be?

Ask God to show you the truth about your wife's relationship with your family. Ask your wife to share her feelings about whether or not she feels accepted by all your family members. Many a wife has suffered in silence for years over not feeling accepted by her in-laws. And many a husband has refused to hear his wife's feelings on the subject because he blamed her for the entire problem.

If your wife reveals something of that nature to you, don't be defensive about it—cover it in prayer. Ask God to show you the truth about the situation. Sometimes it's just that people are different and they don't understand one another. Your wife can't *force* people to love her, yet you might be able to say something to her or your family that would make a difference. But pray about it first. When a husband brings a wife into his family, he owes it to her to pray that she will find favor with each of his family members. Just because *he* fell in love with her doesn't mean *they* will.

Besides good relationships with friends and family members, every married couple needs to have at least two or three other couples with whom they can spend time. It's not always easy to find two people who are married to each other whom you and your wife equally enjoy, so it may require flexibility on someone's part to make it work. But it's worth praying for these couples to come into your lives. If you already have these kinds of friends, pray for the friendships to grow.

The Bible says we should not be "unequally yoked together with unbelievers" (2 Corinthians 6:14). This doesn't mean you can't have any unbelieving friends, but the relationships that influence you the most should be with people who strive to live God's way. We all know unbelievers who make better "Christians" than certain Christians. So pray that God will take out of your lives anyone who will not prove to be a positive influence.

FORGIVENESS IS CRITICAL

Crucial to any relationship is having and maintaining a forgiving heart. It's easy to find something to be unforgiving about, so we have to choose to be a forgiving person. If we don't, our unforgiving heart can overflow at any time into our relationships. For example, have you and your wife ever gone to dinner with other couples and heard a husband or wife make disrespectful, critical, or unflattering remarks about their spouse in front of everyone? It makes everyone at the table feel very uncomfortable. No matter how graciously people might respond, they secretly glance at their watches, design an early escape plan in their minds, and cross that couple off the guest list for their next dinner party. Even if something was said jokingly, everyone there feels the embarrassment or hurt of the person who was ridiculed. The husband or wife may have a legitimate complaint, but will appear like a weakling for dealing with it in such a cowardly way. Everyone knows that the consequences of those words will be evident the next time the offending person wants to be intimate—and the spouse has no interest.

Comments such as these reveal an unforgiving heart on overflow. And an unforgiving person affects everyone around him or her. When husbands and wives are unforgiving toward one another and don't treat each other with respect, not only do *they* suffer, but so do their children, family members, friends, co-workers, and anyone else with whom they come into contact. When a person has unforgiveness in his or her heart toward anyone, people who are around them pick up on it, even if they don't know exactly what it is.

If your wife has any unforgiveness in her heart toward anyone, pray for her to be free of it. If she doesn't get free, it will affect every relationship she has and keep her from becoming all God made her to be.

She Says...

Please pray for your wife that:

1. She will have close friendships with godly women.
2. She will have good relationships with all family members.
3. She will find favor with her in-laws.
4. She will not be an "injustice collector."
5. She will be able to release hurts from the past.
6. She will forgive others completely.
7. She will experience reconciliation where there is now estrangement.

He Says...
by Kenneth C. Ulmer

Bishop Ulmer is the senior pastor of Faithful Central Bible Church in Inglewood, California. He and his wife, Togetta, have been married for 24 years, and they have 3 children.

The area of prayer that has claimed my most consistent fervent attention is the relationship between my wife and my children. I have been married for almost 25 glorious years, and I have seen the power of God move in our relationship, exemplifying the truth that God is able to do exceedingly abundantly above all that we could ever ask or think. God has especially moved mightily and miraculously in the bond between my wife and my daughters.

My girls were five and three when my wife and I were married. I had been married before, and the prospects for a blended, ready-made family were not good. I saw from the outset that we would need the covering of God on the tender, fragile connection between my old life and the second chance God was graciously giving me. From the very beginning I began to pray against bad stepmother-stepdaughter relationships! And I have seen the Lord form a bond of honesty, understanding, patience, and respect that never could have been created in the natural. Now my daughters are 29 and 27. They and my wife have a real relationship of love and respect. They don't hang out together because they have their own lives, but I have seen God create a closeness that only He could produce.

The Lord has also allowed us to adopt the world's greatest son, who is now 14. He is my beloved son, in whom I am well pleased! I thank God that all of my children are saved and love the Lord. All of us have struggled together, cried together, and prayed together for the protective hand of God on our home and family. We are in many ways the typical pastor's family, but in other ways we are a miracle testimony to the power of God to heal, deliver, and bind together relationships for His glory.

I have also prayed that God would send a few godly women into my wife's life whom she could trust and with whom she could be close. I find that pastors' wives are often the loneliest women because they have no real friends with whom they can be open and honest. They do not know whom they can trust. I prayed for women who would love my wife, pray with her, and stand with her. And I thank God for the friends He has given her with whom she can laugh, cry, and rejoice. I have even found myself thanking God for the friends she can shop with (at least until I get the bills!), knowing that these are times of refreshing fellowship. God has been faithful to answer these prayers.

PRAYER POWER

Lord, I pray for (<u>wife's name</u>) to have good, strong, healthy relationships with godly women. May each of these women add strength to her life and be a strong prayer support for her. Take away any relationship that will not bear good fruit. I also pray for good relationships with all family members. May Your spirit of love and acceptance reign in each one. I pray for a resolution of any uncomfortable in-law relationships for either of us. Show me what I can do or say to make a positive difference. Specifically I pray for my wife's relationship with (<u>name of friend or family member</u>). Bring reconciliation and restoration where that relationship has broken down.

Lord, I pray that (<u>wife's name</u>) will always be a forgiving person. Even if she doesn't feel like it at the moment, help her to forgive out of obedience to You. Show her that forgiveness doesn't make the other person right, it makes *her free*. If she has any unforgiveness that she doesn't realize she has, reveal it to her so that she can confess it before You and be released from it. I especially pray that there would be no unforgiveness between us. Enable us to forgive one another quickly and completely. Help us to remember that You, Lord, are the only One who knows the whole story, so we don't have the right to judge. Make my wife a light to her family, friends, co-workers, and community, and may all her relationships be glorifying to You, Lord.

POWER TOOLS

THE RIGHTEOUS SHOULD CHOOSE HIS FRIENDS CAREFULLY, FOR THE WAY OF THE WICKED LEADS THEM ASTRAY.

PROVERBS 12:26

WHENEVER YOU STAND PRAYING, IF YOU HAVE ANYTHING AGAINST ANYONE, FORGIVE HIM, THAT YOUR FATHER IN HEAVEN MAY ALSO FORGIVE YOU YOUR TRESPASSES.

MARK 11:25

A MAN WHO HAS FRIENDS MUST HIMSELF BE FRIENDLY, BUT THERE IS A FRIEND WHO STICKS CLOSER THAN A BROTHER.

PROVERBS 18:24

LET ALL BITTERNESS, WRATH, ANGER, CLAMOR, AND EVIL SPEAKING BE PUT AWAY FROM YOU, WITH ALL MALICE. AND BE KIND TO ONE ANOTHER, TENDERHEARTED, FORGIVING ONE ANOTHER, JUST AS GOD IN CHRIST FORGAVE YOU.

EPHESIANS 4:31,32

JUDGE NOT, AND YOU SHALL NOT BE JUDGED. CONDEMN NOT, AND YOU SHALL NOT BE CONDEMNED. FORGIVE, AND YOU WILL BE FORGIVEN.

LUKE 6:37

CHAPTER NINE

HER PRIORITIES

Your wife is constantly on trial. Or at least she can often feel that way.

It is the unwritten law of the land that she be judged on how well her children behave, perform, succeed in school, and ultimately turn out in life. She will be silently indicted if she is not active in the church, school, neighborhood, and community. Society holds her responsible for and will pass judgment on how the interior of her house looks, even though there is only hearsay evidence that it always looks that way. (The exterior is blamed on you.)

If she is employed, this further complicates things because there is an unspoken ordinance that says she must serve notice to the rest of her life that her job takes precedence. Above all, she will be held accountable to be a great wife, mother, daughter, friend, and neighbor. And if she fails at even one of the above, she will be put on trial and judged on circumstantial evidence by a not-so-impartial jury. During all the time she spends on any one of these priorities, she worries that she is recklessly endangering the others. She can sometimes feel she has to daily prove her innocence, or else she must plead guilty and suffer the consequences.

It doesn't help matters that she has the prosecutor of her soul forever providing expert witnesses of her failure.

It seems that all of his accusations are sustained, that every one of her objections is overruled. The cross-examination going on in her mind is ruthless. The charges are pressed so hard that they hurt. All infringements of which she stands accused seem too minor to warrant such harsh punishment. She is, after all, only trying to do her best. Why does it never seem to be enough?

Society expects a lot of women. Society expects a lot of men too, but in different ways. Men, for example, have more pressure than women to provide for their families. A woman may *help* provide for her family, but the expectations are not ultimately on her to do it. Even when a woman is the sole provider for her family, if she doesn't make much money or get a great promotion or become successful in her field, no one thinks less of her. A man is not allowed that much slack. But no matter how much a wife contributes to the family income, even if she is the only one working to provide for the family and her husband stays home with the children, she will still be held responsible if her children don't do well socially or academically.

Sometimes your wife may feel the pressure of so many expectations at once that it overwhelms her, and this makes her less effective in getting done what she needs to do. She may even get discouraged and short-circuit. Understanding all this will help you pray for her.

Another one of those great pressures on a woman is that of creating and maintaining a pleasant, inviting, clean, attractive, nurturing, safe haven of a home for the family. A man may be actively involved in making a nice place to live, but he doesn't feel put on trial by it like a woman does. And when a woman feels insecure about her ability to create a comfortable and inviting home, or she has limited time and finances to do it, the home then becomes a source of unending pressure.

For instance, if people walk into Bill and Sara's home and it is messy, unkempt, and unattractive, they don't think Bill is a slob, they think Sara is a bad housekeeper. That's why your wife may be far more upset than you are when family members don't clean up after themselves. Or when you invite someone over to dinner at the last minute without notifying her. She may get irritated about that, not because she doesn't want to see the person, but because when the house is not guest-ready or the dinner is not guest quality, she feels that *she* is the one who will be judged for it. And for many a woman, setting a fine table and serving great food is something that gives her a sense of accomplishment and fulfillment. She is robbed of the chance to do it as well as she knows she can by the element of surprise.

The Bible says it's futile to try to establish a home without asking God to build it. Taking care of a home includes countless small tasks that have to be done again and again, and some tasks are so menial that we don't even think of asking God to be in the midst of them. But He will lighten our load if we yoke up with Him in *all* that we do. Most women have a life outside housekeeping, and they would like to live it. It would take so much of the pressure off of your wife if you would pray that the burden of caring for the home would be lifted. Don't hesitate to ask God what *you* can do to help lighten her load as well. (One of the things I most appreciate about my husband is that he helps around the house.)

Keeping a home can be a very thankless job for a woman, especially if no one is, well, *thanking* her. So remember to show her your appreciation for all she does in the home. She needs to know that you approve, and that you will not thoughtlessly increase her workload.

In setting priorities, a women will generally put everything and everyone before herself. This creates a constant drain on her that may not be noticeable until, one day, she cracks like a bone that has been drained of its calcium. If she is constantly doing for everyone else and never taking time for herself, it will deplete her emotionally and physically. Eventually she will not have anything to give. Pray for her to take time for herself. It will not make her self-centered, it will make her *God-centered.*

It's very difficult for a woman to find the right priorities for her life when so many things are pleading for her attention. Your wife desperately needs your prayers. And if you have been one of those who has passed judgment on her and pronounced sentence, I'm sure you did it with no malice aforethought. Retract your charge, exonerate your wife, and refuse to allow any further miscarriage of justice. Serve notice on the enemy that your wife has been pardoned by the ultimate Judge, the highest legal Authority in the universe, and therefore he has no jurisdiction over her. Her testimony of God's grand acquittal in her life will assure other law-abiding women that they, too, can be free of the rule of high expectations. Then pray that God will reveal to your wife what her priorities should be. As to whether she can actually achieve that perfect balance, the jury is still out.

I rest my case.

SHE SAYS...

Please pray for your wife that:

1. She will remember to put God first.
2. She will take time for you.
3. She will balance her time with the children.
4. She will take needed time for herself.
5. She will be able to create a warm and inviting home.
6. She will always use her time wisely.
7. She will understand what her priorities are.

HE SAYS...
BY MICHAEL OMARTIAN

I know how debilitating life can be when it has no order or priority. Our tasks as men may seem complicated, but I believe they are relatively simple compared to what our wives take on. I spend a lot of my prayer time for Stormie asking God to bring an order to her life so that she may experience joy and peace in the midst of all she has to do. The absence of joy and peace in either one of us directly affects our marriage.

Each of us needs to encourage his wife. "Thank you for doing such a great job," "Thank you for taking good care of the kids," "Thank you for being my wife," are words that cannot be spoken enough. In addition, we must each pray for our wife to seek God and hear from Him what He has given her to do. If we don't pray, we can short-circuit the path and the priorities the Lord has for her. Praying and supporting God's purposes in my wife helps clear a pathway for her to be effective.

I always used to believe that stress was chiefly the domain of us guys. Yeah, right! *I* was sitting in the golf cart, waiting at the eleventh tee, telling my golf partner how happy and relieved I was to be able to take a few hours off to play a round of golf. *Stormie* was in the middle of a book deadline, all the while home-schooling our daughter, taking care of the house, juggling speaking engagements, and taking time for her always-complaining husband.

Our wives probably have more to deal with than we do. Men tend to handle fewer decisions—the larger, more obvious ones. A wife has to make decisions about many details, both small and large. I have asked God to help Stormie set clear priorities so that she isn't drained of life and energy. And God has answered that prayer countless times.

PRAYER POWER

Lord, I lift up (<u>wife's name</u>) to You today and ask that You would be in charge of her life. Show her how to seek You first in all things, and to make time with You her first priority every day. Give her the wisdom to know how to effectively divide up her time, and then to make the best use of it. Show her the way to prioritize her responsibilities and inter-ests and still fulfill each role she has to the fullest. Show her how to find a good balance between being a wife, being a mother, running a home, working at a job, serving in the church and com-munity, and finding time for herself so that she can be rested and refreshed. Release her from the guilt that can weigh her down when these things get out of balance. In the midst of all that, I pray that she will take time for me without feeling she is neglecting other things. Give her the energy and the ability to accomplish all she needs to do, and may she have joy in the process.

Lord, I pray that You would help (<u>wife's name</u>) to make our home a peaceful sanctuary. Regardless of our financial state, give her the wisdom, energy, strength, vision, and clarity of mind to transform our dwelling into a beautiful place of refuge that brings joy to each of us. I ask You to lift from her the burden of caring for our home and give her peace about it. Show me how I can encourage and assist her in that.

Holy Spirit, I invite You to fill our home with Your peace, truth, love, and unity. Keep it safe, and let no one enter our home who is not brought here by You. Through wisdom let our house be built, and by understanding may it be established. By knowledge may the rooms be filled with all precious and pleasant riches (Proverbs 24:3,4). Reveal to us anything that is in our house that is not glorifying to You, Lord. I say that "as for me and my house, we will serve the LORD" (Joshua 24:15).

Give (<u>wife's name</u>) the grace to handle the challenges she faces each day, and the wisdom to not try to do more than she can. Teach her to clearly recognize what her priorities should be, and enable her to balance them well.

POWER TOOLS

TO EVERYTHING THERE IS A SEASON, A TIME FOR EVERY PURPOSE UNDER HEAVEN.

ECCLESIASTES 3:1

SEEK FIRST THE KINGDOM OF GOD AND HIS RIGHTEOUSNESS, AND ALL THESE THINGS SHALL BE ADDED TO YOU.

MATTHEW 6:33

UNLESS THE LORD BUILDS THE HOUSE, THEY LABOR IN VAIN WHO BUILD IT.

PSALM 127:1

SHE WATCHES OVER THE WAYS OF HER HOUSEHOLD, AND DOES NOT EAT THE BREAD OF IDLENESS.

PROVERBS 31:27

THE LAW OF HIS GOD IS IN HIS HEART; NONE OF HIS STEPS SHALL SLIDE.

PSALM 37:31

CHAPTER TEN

HER BEAUTY

I don't care how young or old, perfect or imperfect, confident or fearful, or mature or immature she is, every woman would like to be more beautiful than she is now. And most women don't think they are as beautiful as they really are. I have never met a woman who would not enjoy being told that she is beautiful, especially by the man in her life. If you find a woman who doesn't want to be told she is beautiful, it's probably because she has gone too many years without hearing it, or perhaps when she did hear it she was violated in some way because of it. Whatever the case, she is responding out of hurt.

God made women beautiful. The women of the Bible, such as Sarah, Rachel, Rebekah, and Esther, were exceptionally beautiful, and who can doubt the beauty in Mary and Eve. Inherent in a woman is the desire to see beauty, both in herself and in her surroundings. It is a natural instinct God has put there because He wants her to desire *Him*, the most beautiful of all. He wants her to look to Him so she can reflect *His* beauty (Psalm 27:4).

The main thing that makes a woman beautiful is knowing that she is loved. That's why having God's Spirit living in her and spending time in God's presence in praise and worship is the most effective beauty treatment available. His love beautifies her inside and out.

Her husband's love also makes a woman beautiful. A woman who is not loved will wither and die. One of the reasons raising children can be such a great fulfillment to a woman is that love and affection are flowing through her and to her all day long. But as great as that love is, she needs her husband's love more. His love fulfills her as a person. It makes her rich. It causes her to *feel* beautiful. And all that goodness flows back into his life in return. (My husband has always told me that I am beautiful, even when I was at my worst. Sometimes I tell him I hope he'll never get his vision checked. But I always feel beautiful when he says it.)

Your wife is beautiful. Even though she may not be perfect, there is beauty in her. I know this because you would not have married her if you had't seen her beauty. No man marries a woman if he can't find anything beautiful about her. She has to appeal to him in some way. And no matter how long you are married, you will always be able to find that beauty in your wife if you love her enough to look for it and tell her when you see it. The more a man encourages a woman to feel beautiful, the more beautiful she will become.

Now you may be thinking about that song from *My Fair Lady* called "Why Can't a Woman Be More Like a Man?" In fact, you may even be singing it to yourself at this very moment. But let me remind you that women are *different* than men. There is a popular book out with a title suggesting that men and women come from different planets. I believe that is a serious understatement. Men and women are actually from two different *galaxies*. That's why there is no way a woman can be more like a man and still be a woman. So even though you may not be able to fathom the importance of praying for your wife's beauty, you'll just have to trust me on this one. I know what I'm talking about, so please hear me out. How your wife feels about herself is ultimately as important to *your* happiness as it is to hers.

Although you cannot be responsible for the image of herself that your wife brought into your marriage, you *can* contribute either positively or negatively to the image she grows into. Your words have more power to bring out the beauty in your wife than you ever dreamed possible.

My friend Terry was shopping with her husband one day in a department store and she asked him, "Is there anything you want here?"

Her husband, Michael, turned to her and said, "I don't want anything in this place but you."

Who can doubt that those words made her feel beautiful? Those are the kind of words I'm talking about.

If your wife was devalued and made to feel unattractive by her parents, siblings, or peers when she was young, she may not attribute beauty and worth to herself now. Even though many people may tell her differently, there are only two who can actually make her *believe* she is beautiful—God and you. But even *you* will not be able to convince her if *God* doesn't speak to her first. No matter how much a man tells a woman she is beautiful and valuable, if she doesn't believe it inside herself, it will never be enough. That's where your prayers can make all the difference. Your prayers can set her free from lies of the past and enable her to hear God speak the truth to her heart.

Your prayers will also help your wife find that balance between arrogance and self-flagellation. And every woman must find it in order to have a healthy self-image. No one wants to be around a person who constantly berates herself over how unattractive she is. And no one can tolerate a woman who conceitedly believes she is more beautiful than anyone else.

While most women don't fall into either of those extremes, far too many women do not consider themselves as attractive as they are. That's because women are bombarded with the world's image of what a beautiful woman is supposed to look like. Unless she is a certain size, with certain measurements, with a certain type of hair, eyes, lips, skin, and fingertips, she is made to feel she is not attractive. Pray for your wife to be free from the tyranny of the world's spirit and to get her eyes focused on the beauty of the Lord. His reflection will make her more beautiful than anything else.

A female's need for this kind of affirmation starts early in her life. When my daughter was only two, every Sunday I would get her dressed for church in one of her pretty dresses. I would tell her she looked beautiful, and I could see that it pleased her. But then I always sent her out to the other room to show her dad. If *he* noticed her and told her she looked beautiful, she lit up like a light. No matter what age a woman is, receiving that kind of approval from the man in her life makes her glow. So not only should you tell your wife how beautiful she is, but you should tell your daughter also. She needs that from you more than you will ever know. And while you're at it, tell your mother and your grandmother. It doesn't matter whether a woman in your life is 2 or 102—you have the power to turn on the light.

SHE SAYS...

Please pray for your wife that:

1. She will know that she is loved by God.
2. She will sense the beauty of the Lord in herself.
3. She will feel loved by you.
4. She will value herself.
5. She will find time to take care of herself.
6. She will know how to make herself more attractive.
7. You will always think she is beautiful.

HE SAYS...
BY MICHAEL OMARTIAN

We men have a tendency to discount the importance of our wives' feeling beautiful. Sometimes I wonder why Stormie makes such an effort to keep herself attractive. Make no mistake, I appreciate the results—but the point is that she views her beauty as an integral part of her being, as do most women, so therefore it's important for me to pray that she sense the beauty that God has put in her. In addition to that, my wife never had parents or family members tell her she was beautiful, in fact quite the opposite. So she grew up being convinced that she wasn't attractive.

After a recent emergency surgery, Stormie said to me in a rather discouraged tone, "Michael, today you are seeing me at my worst," to which I responded, "Honey, you see me at my worst every day!" We men have a profound effect on our wives' self-esteem when we build them up and tell them how beautiful they are. In the area of beauty, my prayer for Stormie is that God will reflect His beauty through her. Trust me, it's working!

PRAYER POWER

Lord, I pray that You would give (wife's name) the "incorruptible beauty of a gentle and quiet spirit, which is very precious" in Your sight (1 Peter 3:4). Help her to appreciate the beauty You have put in her. Help me to remember to encourage her and speak words that will make her feel beautiful.

Where anyone in her past has convinced her that she is unattractive and less than who You made her to be, I pray that You would replace those lies with Your truth. Keep any hurtful words that have been spoken to her from playing over and over in her mind. I pray that she will not base her worth on appearance, but on Your Word. Help her to see herself from Your perspective. Convince her of how valuable she is to You, so that I will be better able to convince her of how valuable she is to me.

Show my wife how to take good care of herself. Give her wisdom about the way she dresses and adorns herself so that it always enhances her beauty to the fullest and glorifies You. But remind her that time spent in Your presence is the best beauty treatment of all. Make my wife beautiful in every way, and may everyone else see the beauty of Your image reflected in her.

POWER TOOLS

CHARM IS DECEITFUL AND BEAUTY IS PASSING, BUT A WOMAN WHO FEARS THE LORD, SHE SHALL BE PRAISED.

PROVERBS 31:30

DO NOT LET YOUR ADORNMENT BE MERELY OUTWARD—ARRANGING THE HAIR, WEARING GOLD, OR PUTTING ON FINE APPAREL—RATHER LET IT BE THE HIDDEN PERSON OF THE HEART, WITH THE INCORRUPTIBLE BEAUTY OF A GENTLE AND QUIET SPIRIT, WHICH IS VERY PRECIOUS IN THE SIGHT OF GOD.

1 PETER 3:3,4

THE KING WILL GREATLY DESIRE YOUR BEAUTY; BECAUSE HE IS YOUR LORD, WORSHIP HIM.

PSALM 45:11

GIVE UNTO THE LORD THE GLORY DUE TO HIS NAME; WORSHIP THE LORD IN THE BEAUTY OF HOLINESS.

PSALM 29:2

HE HAS MADE EVERYTHING BEAUTIFUL IN ITS TIME.

ECCLESIASTES 3:11

CHAPTER ELEVEN

HER SEXUALITY

Be honest, now. Did you skip right to this chapter without reading the previous ten? If you did, don't feel bad about it. It's quite understandable and totally natural. Sex is not only a man's strongest drive, but also one of his greatest needs. (You may already know that.) In my book *The Power of a Praying Wife*, I put the things dearest to a man's heart at the beginning. "His Sexuality" is the fourth chapter. (I didn't make it the first chapter because it is, after all, a Christian book.) In the book you're reading now, I have put the greatest concerns of a *woman's* heart in the beginning. That's why "Her Sexuality" falls in about the middle. (Remember, I chose these chapters according to the results of my survey of women.)

There's a reason that sexuality doesn't rank as high on a woman's list as it does on a man's, and I believe it's because sexuality is a *very* complex issue for a woman. It is extremely hard for her to separate herself from emotions, memories, thoughts, and experiences and just be strictly physical. She doesn't seek to gratify only a physical need, there's an emotional one as well.

Your wife's sexuality is wrapped up in two things:

1. How she feels about herself

2. How she feels about you

The way a woman feels about *herself* has a lot to do with how she has been treated by men throughout her life. If she has been abused, ignored, demeaned, disrespected, violated, or simply not valued, she will not value herself. Even if it was not her husband who perpetrated this cruelty, the fact that she endured it will still cause her to have a hard time responding to him. As unfair as that may seem, if a woman doesn't *feel* attractive or sexy, it's difficult for her to act like she is. However, a man can reassure his wife of how attractive she is to him and how much he loves her, and feeling attractive and loved makes a woman want to share herself with her husband in the most intimate ways.

The way your wife feels about *you*—if she is angry, unforgiving, disappointed, wounded, or bitter—will immensely affect her desire for intimacy. If you have hurt her in one way or another, even if it was completely unintentional, it may cause her to withdraw physically in self-protection. It doesn't matter that the wound was inflicted 30 days ago and you haven't even thought about it for the past 29. If it has not been resolved satisfactorily in *her* soul, it will affect your sexual relationship. When she's upset with you, intimacy is the furthest thing from her mind.

For a woman, sex comes out of affection. She has no desire to be affectionate with a man who makes her feel hurt and neglected. Though it's possible for a man to perform sexually without feeling emotionally involved, it's not that way with a woman. She can do it, but it makes her feel like she should be getting paid. A woman's true sexuality is wrapped up in how loved and valued she feels, and it's very difficult for her to give herself to someone who has made her feel bad.

Trust is also a huge factor in a successful sexual relationship. Your wife must be able to trust you. She can tolerate mistakes in other areas if she knows you are truthful. If either of you has violated the other's trust, pray for complete repentance, forgiveness, and healing. A woman never fully gives her body, mind, and emotions to a man she doesn't trust.

If there has been sexual infidelity in your relationship, you need the prayers and support of strong, qualified, trustworthy Christian counselors who believe in the power of God to transform, renew, and bring total restoration. The betrayal must be fully confessed and thoroughly repented of, and forgiveness must be sought. Pray for sexual purity to be restored in the heart of each of you and for fidelity to be an uncompromising way of life. If these things are not the case, all unresolved hurts will be brought to the marriage bed. There has to be complete healing in this area before trust returns, and only God can heal you both and restore that trust.

Many couples have sexual problems in their marriages because one or both of them had improper sexual experiences *before* they were married. If that happened to either of you, pray to have those soul ties broken so you can be set free from their effects. You don't need the ghosts of former relationships brought into the bedroom.

According to the Scriptures, a husband and wife cannot rightfully withhold their bodies from one another. But at the same time, they have to be sensitive to each other's needs and conditions. If one of them is ill or in pain, this should be considered and respected. Often a woman will be too exhausted, but it's nothing personal. There is so much vying for your wife's attention—from raising children and taking care of a home, to work and finances, to emotional stress and hormone ups and downs—and she wants you to be considerate of this. But allowing this part of your life to become neglected is not good either. A woman can get sidetracked by many things and end up neglecting the sexual relationship with her husband. That's why it's important to pray about it.

Sex needs to be a priority in a marriage. Men already know that. Women don't always see it that way. Far too often a wife does not understand how great her husband's need for sex actually is. That's why it's good for you to pray that your wife will gain a clear understanding of this and give you the physical intimacy you need. And you don't have to feel like you're being selfish in doing that. You're not. You are watching over and spiritually covering a vital part of your marriage that, if neglected, could lead to your marriage's destruction. You can't leave this highly important aspect of your relationship up to chance.

I know this may sound strange to you—and don't get mad at me for saying it, because it's what the women in my survey said—but women want to be able to share affection with their husband without always having it lead to the sex act. Your wife wants a sense of togetherness—a hug, a kiss, a simple touch, an embrace—that doesn't always lead to physcial intimacy. Sometimes she needs emotional connection, affirmation, and closeness without having to perform.

There is nothing more attractive to a woman than a man who is strong in the Lord. It makes him irresistible. I have seen unattractive men become quite handsome and appealing when they come to know the Lord, grow in His ways, and become more like Him. If you want to be more attractive to your wife, grow deeper in the Lord. Let God mold your heart, and He will also enhance your appearance as you are transformed into His likeness. There must be 50 ways to *keep* your lover, and this is definitely one of them. And I'm sure, with God's help, you can think of 49 more.

SHE SAYS...

Please pray for your wife that:

1. Your sexual relationship will be fulfilling for both of you.
2. You will be unselfish with one another.
3. Romance will stay alive in your marriage.
4. There will be great affection and desire between you.
5. She will be understanding of your needs.
6. She will not be too exhausted to be intimate.
7. You will be able to please one another sexually.

HE SAYS...
BY MICHAEL OMARTIAN

My wife is a "babe"! She was the first day I met her, and she continues to be so to this very moment. (Let's face it, men, most of us married over our heads.) But Stormie's beauty is not her sole responsibility though, because, believe it or not, *I* have something to do with it. It begins when I vow to revere her in marriage and not violate our sexual trust at any time. I purpose to not allow Satan to destroy our bond. I'm not perfect, and at times I fail in my thoughts, but I do recognize the power of our culture, as orchestrated by the enemy, to make us view our mates as somehow less beautiful and interesting physically, especially after many years of marriage. We're being pushed to fantasize and to dabble in sin. But God will keep us sexually pure if we ask Him. He will keep us away from temptation and infidelity if we seek Him for that.

I pray that our sex life will be beautiful and fulfilling, just as it always has been. No fantasy could ever compete with what God has for us. I also pray for my wife to feel good about who she is. That's very important too.

PRAYER POWER

Lord, I pray that You would bless (<u>wife's name</u>) today, and especially bless our marriage and our sexual relationship. Help me to be unselfish and understanding toward her. Help her to be unselfish and understanding toward me. Teach us to show affection to one another in ways that keep romance and desire alive between us. Where one of us is more affectionate than the other, balance that out. Help us to remember to touch each other in an affectionate way every day. I pray that how often we come together sexually will be agreeable to both of us.

Show me if I ever hurt her, and help me to apologize in a way that will cause her to forgive me completely. Any time we have an argument or a breakdown of communication, enable us to get over it quickly and come back together physically so no room is made for the devil to work. If ever the fire between us dies into a suffocating smoke, I pray that You would clear the air and rekindle the flame.

Help me to always treat my wife with respect and honor and never say anything that would demean her, even in jest. Help me to be considerate of her when she is exhausted or not feeling well. But I also pray that she would understand my sexual needs and be considerate of those as well. Only You can help us find that balance.

Make our sexual relationship fulfilling, enjoyable, freeing, and refreshing for both of us. May our intimacy bond the two of us together and connect our hearts and emotions as well as our bodies. Help us to freely communicate our needs and desires to one another.

Keep our hearts always faithful. Take out of our lives anyone or anything that would cause temptation. Where there has been unfaithfulness in thought or deed on the part of either of us, I pray for full repentance, cleansing, and release from it. Keep us free from anything that would cause us to neglect this vital area of our lives. May our desire always be only for each other. Renew and revitalize our sexual relationship, and make it all You created it to be.

POWER TOOLS

THE WIFE DOES NOT HAVE AUTHORITY OVER HER OWN BODY, BUT THE HUSBAND DOES. AND LIKEWISE THE HUSBAND DOES NOT HAVE AUTHORITY OVER HIS OWN BODY, BUT THE WIFE DOES. DO NOT DEPRIVE ONE ANOTHER EXCEPT WITH CONSENT FOR A TIME, THAT YOU MAY GIVE YOURSELVES TO FASTING AND PRAYER; AND COME TOGETHER AGAIN SO THAT SATAN DOES NOT TEMPT YOU BECAUSE OF YOUR LACK OF SELF-CONTROL.

1 CORINTHIANS 7:4,5

BECAUSE OF SEXUAL IMMORALITY, LET EACH MAN HAVE HIS OWN WIFE, AND LET EACH WOMAN HAVE HER OWN HUSBAND. LET THE HUSBAND RENDER TO HIS WIFE THE AFFECTION DUE HER, AND LIKEWISE ALSO THE WIFE TO HER HUSBAND.

1 CORINTHIANS 7:2,3

MARRIAGE IS HONORABLE AMONG ALL, AND THE BED UNDEFILED.

HEBREWS 13:4

THIS IS THE WILL OF GOD, YOUR SANCTIFICATION: THAT YOU SHOULD ABSTAIN FROM SEXUAL IMMORALITY; THAT EACH OF YOU SHOULD KNOW HOW TO POSSESS HIS OWN VESSEL IN SANCTIFICATION AND HONOR, NOT IN PASSION OF LUST, LIKE THE GENTILES WHO DO NOT KNOW GOD.

1 THESSALONIANS 4:3-5

FLEE SEXUAL IMMORALITY. EVERY SIN THAT A MAN DOES IS OUTSIDE THE BODY, BUT HE WHO COMMITS SEXUAL IMMORALITY SINS AGAINST HIS OWN BODY.

1 CORINTHIANS 6:18

CHAPTER TWELVE

HER FEARS

Anyone who has ever watched the news on TV or read the daily newspaper knows there is plenty to be afraid of in this world. Even the strongest, most godly, faith-filled man or woman has something to fear at one time or another. Women feel especially vulnerable and have their own special set of "what ifs" that have to do with threats to their safety and security and that of their families: "What if someone breaks into the house?" "What if we don't have enough money to pay the mortgage?" "What if my husband dies or is injured?" "What if something bad happens to my children?" "What if I get sick and can't care for my family?" These are very real and legitimate concerns. But when fear about them grips and torments and rules a woman's life, it can become a spirit of fear that is paralyzing.

We can give place to a spirit of fear when we experience something traumatic or frightening. Or when we *witness* something that is. Whether we admit it or not, it causes us to doubt that God is really in control and that He will protect us. When the power and presence of fear outweighs our assurance of the power and presence of God, we can become tormented by a spirit of fear.

The opposite of fear is faith—something we all could use more of in our lives. But getting from fear to faith is a lot harder to do when fear has become a controlling factor. That's why a person who has been overtaken by fear needs prayer. And a husband's prayer for his wife to be set free from fear is powerful. Your prayers for your wife can help her recognize that fear does not come from God (2 Timothy 1:7), and that the perfect love of God removes fear from her soul (1 John 4:18). Your prayers can also help her have faith strong enough to believe that God loves her, is in control of her life, and will not leave or forsake her.

Besides being weighed down by her fear of physical danger and lack of provision for herself and the people she loves, a woman may also suffer from fear of man. There are few women who don't care what anyone thinks about them, their children, their homes, their work, their appearance, their husbands, or their abilities. A certain amount of caring is normal, but when a concern over what other people think adversely affects how a woman behaves, it becomes a fear of man. The fear of man can keep your wife driven to be perfect, or so intimidated that she is afraid to do anything for fear of making a mistake. Your prayers can help your wife to be ruled by the fear of God and not the fear of man.

Even if it doesn't appear to be a full-fledged fear, the thing a woman struggles with most—such as food, weight, relationships, self-worth, appearance, finances, guilt, or self-doubt—usually has its root in the fear of something. The Bible says to "watch and pray, lest you enter into temptation. The spirit indeed is willing, but the flesh is weak" (Matthew 26:41). If your wife has something she considers to be a constant struggle, a weakness of her flesh, or temptation in her life, she needs you to pray with her that God will give her the strength to resist it and be set free.

Do you know what your wife's greatest struggle is? Are you aware of her deepest fears? You may already have a good idea, but if you're not absolutely sure, ask her. Say, "Tell me what you struggle with or fear most in your life, because I want to pray for you about it." You may be completely surprised at her response. Many of us have deep fears that we never share. When I asked my husband that same question years ago, he said he was afraid of not being a good father. I was very surprised to hear that because he had never given any indication it was a particular concern. His fear prompted me to pray specifically for his relationship with his children.

Too often, women carry burdens in their lives that are far heavier than their delicate shoulders were created to bear. Remember, no matter how strong your wife appears to be, she is fragile. Even though a woman may appear strong to the point of hardness, it's usually because she felt she had to be for one reason or another. Ask God to show you whether your wife is carrying something she shouldn't. If so, you can bear part or all of the weight of that thing in prayer.

Another ploy of the enemy of your wife's soul is to put deep discontent in her heart. It's one thing to see where your life needs to improve, and then pray for that and be patient to wait on God for His answer. It's another thing to hate your life. That makes us sick and bitter. Sometimes a woman fears that the difficult spot she's in at the moment is as good as it gets, and that things will never change. That hopeless mindset is torturous for any woman, and I believe it is one of the tactics the enemy uses to create unrest and strife and keep a woman in constant fear. Often women struggle with deeply wanting certain things to happen, yet having to wait such a discouragingly long time for prayers about those things to be answered. Pray that your wife can see her struggles and fears as an opportunity to depend on God in a greater way. Pray that she will be content with her life and be able to trust that God has her where she is for a purpose.

Fear that prompts us to pray is beneficial. Fear that paralyzes and torments us is destructive. Don't allow fear in your wife to keep her from moving into all God has for her.

SHE SAYS...

Please pray for your wife that:

1. She will not be ruled by a spirit of fear.
2. She will submit her struggles to God.
3. She will have no fear of man.
4. She will be able to resist any temptation.
5. She will find her security in the Lord.
6. She will depend on God and not fear the attacks of the enemy.
7. She will have the peace of God.

HE SAYS...
BY JAMES ROBISON

James is an evangelist, the president of Life Outreach International in Fort Worth, Texas, and the co-host of the Life Today *television program. He and his wife, Betty, have been married for 38 years, and they have three children and eleven grandchildren.*

I have been blessed by God with the most wonderful wife. Only God could have designed such a perfect mate, friend, mother, grandmother, and now, miraculously, co-host of the *Life Today* television program.

Betty was plagued with a spirit of fear for much of her life. It manifested itself in feelings of low self-esteem, a horror of failure or disappointment, and an overwhelming desire to perform in some way in order to gain acceptance. But the fear of failing in the attempt to perform caused her emotions and her mind to jam. She used to explain that, even before tests in school, she would experience what she considered serious panic attacks. She felt that she had little to offer others, so she simply dedicated herself to being a devoted wife and a committed mother. She accomplished this worthy mission to great effect, but her feelings of inferiority about sharing with others basically kept her closed off, and kept her mostly to herself as far as the public was concerned.

In my heart, I knew that if the world could see the beauty, spiritual depth, and true wisdom that filled this woman's inner being, she would be an indescribable blessing. I prayed for many years that God would grant her the peace of mind and the confidence to willingly open herself to others so that the river of life which ran so deeply within her could spill over and impact others. As I prayed, I could sense her desire to overcome, and God gave me the insight to constantly encourage her. As I poured on the praise and confidence-building encouragement, it was like watering a beautiful flower.

Every time she would share just a little in a small group, I would point out how mightily others had been blessed. I would keep telling her that the beauty God had placed within her would inspire others to trust Him to enable them to overcome whatever difficulties they faced in life. God answered the prayer, and we saw Him release a life-giving flow that brings admiration and expressions of gratitude from millions of people throughout North America and the mission fields of the world. I sincerely believe, based on the comments of others, that Betty is one of the most loved and respected women alive today. She is living proof of the power of prayer. Because of this miraculous transformation of the life of Betty Robison, millions will live in fullness on this earth and then for all eternity in the presence of our great God and Father!

PRAYER POWER

Lord, I pray that You would help (<u>wife's name</u>) to "be anxious for nothing" (Philippians 4:6). Remind her to bring all her concerns to You in prayer so that Your peace that passes all understanding will permanently reside in her heart. Specifically I pray about (<u>anything that causes your wife to have fear</u>). I ask You to set her free from that fear and comfort her this day.

Teach me to recognize the ploy of the enemy every time he tries to steal life from my wife by bringing fear to torment her. I stand against any enemy attacks targeted at my wife, and I say that a spirit of fear will have no place in her life. Strengthen her faith in You, Lord, to be her Defender.

I pray that (<u>wife's name</u>) will not be tormented by the fear of man. Enable her to rise above the criticism of others and be delivered from fear of their opinions. May her only concern be with pleasing You. I say to my wife, "Be strong in the Lord and in the power of His might" (Ephesians 6:10). "In righteousness you shall be established; you shall be far from oppression, for you shall not fear; and from terror, for it shall not come near you" (Isaiah 54:14). Enable my wife to rise up and say, "The LORD is my light and my salvation; whom shall I fear? The LORD is the strength of my life; of whom shall I be afraid?" (Psalm 27:1).

Lord, give (<u>wife's name</u>) strength to stand strong in the midst of the tough times of her life. Sustain her with Your presence so that nothing will shake her. Enable her to rise above the things that challenge her. Specifically I lift up to You (<u>your</u>

wife's greatest need, weakness, struggle, or temptation). Help her separate herself from that which
tempts her. I say to (wife's name) that "no temptation has overtaken you except such as is common
to man; but God is faithful, who will not allow you
to be tempted beyond what you are able, but with
the temptation will also make the way of escape,
that you may be able to bear it" (1 Corinthians
10:13). "Wait on the LORD; be of good courage, and
He shall strengthen your heart" (Psalm 27:14).
Lord, enable my wife to endure temptation and
receive the crown of life which You have promised
to those who love You (James 1:12).

Give my wife patience while she is waiting for her
prayers to be answered and for all things to be
accomplished. Help her to wait upon You instead of
waiting for things to change. Cause her to fear only
You and to be content where she is this moment,
knowing that You will not leave her there forever.
Perfect her in Your "perfect love" that "casts out
fear," so that fear has no room in her soul (1 John
4:18).

POWER TOOLS

GOD HAS NOT GIVEN US A SPIRIT OF FEAR, BUT OF POWER AND OF LOVE AND OF A SOUND MIND.

2 TIMOTHY 1:7

THERE IS NO FEAR IN LOVE; BUT PERFECT LOVE CASTS OUT FEAR, BECAUSE FEAR INVOLVES TORMENT. BUT HE WHO FEARS HAS NOT BEEN MADE PERFECT IN LOVE.

1 JOHN 4:18

THE FEAR OF MAN BRINGS A SNARE, BUT WHOEVER TRUSTS IN THE LORD SHALL BE SAFE.

PROVERBS 29:25

BLESSED IS THE MAN WHO ENDURES TEMPTATION; FOR WHEN HE HAS BEEN APPROVED, HE WILL RECEIVE THE CROWN OF LIFE WHICH THE LORD HAS PROMISED TO THOSE WHO LOVE HIM.

JAMES 1:12

I SOUGHT THE LORD, AND HE HEARD ME, AND DELIVERED ME FROM ALL MY FEARS.

PSALM 34:4

CHAPTER THIRTEEN

HER PURPOSE

Everyone has gifts and talents. Your wife needs to understand what hers are. That's because she will be truly fulfilled only when she is using the gifts God gave her, for the purpose for which God called her. If she doesn't understand what that purpose is, she will always have a certain amount of unrest and frustration. And that will affect your relationship in a subtle but important way.

Of course, a married woman's first call is to be a good wife to her husband. The Bible says that "an excellent wife is the crown of her husband" (Proverbs 12:4). We wives do want to be the crown that our husbands wear proudly. But too often the woman we are *called* to be and *want* to be— and know we *can* and *should* be—and the person we *are,* don't match up.

We try to be self-controlled, peaceful, serene, pleasant, strong, gracious, full of good humor, and attractive—all the things we know we have the potential to be and can clearly picture in our minds. But in weak moments—which happen with alarming regularity in a marriage relationship—our good intentions are overpowered by our flesh, and everything we have tried to build can be torn down by careless words and actions. We come face to face with the person we are at the moment, and we feel saddened and powerless to do anything about it.

Let's face it. None of us can be who we need to be without the power of God transforming us and enabling us to change. Marriage certainly won't transform any of us into a new person. However, wonderful changes *can* occur in us after we are married because now we are one with our mate and our prayers for one another have amazing new power. Miraculous things can happen. But often they don't because *we* try to make things happen in our mates instead of asking *God* to do it.

We can't force someone to be a certain way. That's why it's usually futile to demand that someone be different than he or she is. In fact, that kind of pressure can eventually ruin a relationship. But *praying* for your mate to become all she was created to be invites *God* to make changes that *last*. Putting the process of change entirely in the Lord's hands means you can trust that His timing and methods are perfect—and then you become free to enjoy the process.

Your wife *wants* to be the wife God created her to be and you need her to be. She wants to know how to best honor you and be a true helpmate. Pray for her to be able to do all that. And in the process, tell the Lord about any area of frustration you have. Be honest. Tell Him what you need more of (or less of) from your wife. If there's something you could change about her, what would it be? Tell God. Then ask Him to mold your requirements and her abilities into a mutually acceptable package.

No matter how good a wife she is, no matter how great a mother, no matter how perfectly she runs your home, your wife has other gifts and talents as well. These gifts are also part of who God made her to be. Whether she has used those gifts or not, they are there. Even if it has been years since she used them because she had to lay them aside to do other important things, they are still there. If you recognize her gifts, tell her what you see. What is obvious to you may not be obvious to her. She needs you to remind her that she was created for a high purpose. Don't let her deny who she is in order to try to become who she thinks you want. This will have serious consequences down the line. Pray that God will show her who He created her to be and enable her to become that.

Don't worry. This kind of praying will not threaten your marriage. Quite the contrary—it will enhance it. When you have a wife who is fulfilled because she is able to use her God-given gifts for His glory, it will be to your benefit. God will use her gifts in a way that is compatible with her being your wife and the mother of your children. God always makes our gifts fit into the life He has given us. Your wife's gifts will complement yours.

Another reason your wife needs to recognize her gifts and calling is so that she will not be seeking after something God is not calling her to be or do. That produces constant frustration and ultimate defeat. You would never take your favorite golf club and use it to drive nails into the deck of your home. That would be a grave misuse of the club because it would not be fulfilling the purpose for which the club was created. Your wife, too, can be hitting her head against a hard place if she doesn't discover the truth about who God made her to be. There will be a frustration in her that won't go away, and it may manifest itself as an unspoken resentment.

Women have a tendency to think that because they are mothers and have children at home, they have missed out on what God has called them to do. But this isn't true. It's in the doing of these immediate assignments God has given your wife that His ultimate purposes in her life will be realized. And there are ways for her to fulfill her calling even during the seasons of her life when not much time can be devoted to it. If your wife doesn't see how God's calling can ever be realized in the midst of her life as it now is, it's because she is trying to accomplish His purposes in her own strength. It must be *God* who does it all. Declaring her complete dependence on Him is the first step toward realizing His call on her life. Your prayers can help her to understand that.

In order to become all she was created to be, your wife needs love, support, and encouragement from you more than anyone else on earth. The richest, most famous, beautiful, successful, talented, acclaimed, and seemingly independent woman on earth still wants to know that her husband loves and values her. If she believes that he doesn't, she dies inside, no matter who else is singing her praises. Your prayers, as well as your words spoken to her, can help her to know how valuable she is to you. And when she knows that you love and appreciate her, it will give her life purpose like nothing else can.

SHE SAYS...

Please pray for your wife that:

1. She will understand God's purpose for her life.
2. She will recognize her gifts and talents.
3. She will be the wife God wants her to be.
4. She will be a wife deserving of honor and respect.
5. She will be the wife you need her to be.
6. She will use her gifts to help others.
7. She will fulfill God's call on her life.

HE SAYS...
BY MICHAEL HARRITON

Michael is a music composer. He and his wife, Terry, have been married for 23 years, and they have three grown children.

It's always tempting to eat from the tree of the knowledge of good and evil, the tree of judgment. We men feel so intelligent, so superior in our insight when with smug satisfaction we point out the flaws in our wives. But God has allowed us all to be flawed, and He uses our differences to complement one another. Instead of judging my wife for her emotionalism, for example, I try to remember that God has made my wife to be a *very sensitive barometer,* a very accurate gauge of what is really going on in my world. I wish I could say I heed her warnings all of the time. When I don't, I inevitably wish I had.

Just recently, my wife pointed out a situation in my business that she recognized was out of hand. She could see the dangers, but I couldn't see them at all. I thought she was flat-out wrong. In fact, I prayed for God to show my wife that she was in error. And as an afterthought, I prayed that if there was by any remote chance some deception or shortsightedness in me, God would remove it.

About two days later, the realization came flooding in on me that my wife was absolutely right and had been right all along. If I had not heeded her warning, the consequences could have been disastrous. These kinds of insights are unexpected fringe benefits of praying for our wives to be all God wants them to be. I pray for my wife to achieve 100 percent of her potential in Christ. (I also pray for myself that I would be healed of male pattern blindness.)

Prayer Power

Lord, I know that You have placed within (<u>wife's name</u>) special gifts and talents that are to be used for Your purpose and Your glory. Show her what they are, and show me too, Lord, that I may encourage her. Help her to know that You have something in particular for her to do and have given her a ministry that only she can fulfill. Give her a sense of Your call on her life, and open doors of opportunity for her to develop and use her gifts in that calling.

I pray that You would give my wife understanding that Your plan for her life has a specific and perfect timing. Even though she may not know the details of that plan, help her to rest in the confidence of knowing that You will bring it to pass as she seeks You in the details of her life.

Lord, I pray that (<u>wife's name</u>) will be the wife You have called her to be and the wife I need her to be. What I need most from my wife right now is (<u>name the need most pressing on your heart</u>). Show me what my wife needs from me. Help us to fulfill one another in these areas without requiring of each other more than we can be. Keep us from having unrealistic expectations of each other when our expectations should be in You. Help us to recognize the gifts You have placed in each of us and to encourage one another in their development and nurture.

Thank You, Lord, for the wife You have given me (Proverbs 19:14). Release her into Your perfect plan for her life so that she will fulfill the destiny You've given her. Use her gifts and talents to bless others.

Bring her into alignment with Your ultimate purpose for her life, and may she be fulfilled in it. I say to her, you are "like a fruitful vine in the very heart of your house" (Psalm 128:3). "Many daughters have done well, but you excel them all" (Proverbs 31:29). "Let your light so shine before men, that they may see your good works and glorify your Father in heaven" (Matthew 5:16). Lord, grant my wife according to her heart's desire, and fulfill all her purpose (Psalm 20:4).

POWER TOOLS

I...DO NOT CEASE TO GIVE THANKS FOR YOU, MAKING MENTION OF YOU IN MY PRAYERS: THAT THE GOD OF OUR LORD JESUS CHRIST, THE FATHER OF GLORY, MAY GIVE TO YOU THE SPIRIT OF WISDOM AND REVELATION IN THE KNOWLEDGE OF HIM, THE EYES OF YOUR UNDERSTANDING BEING ENLIGHTENED; THAT YOU MAY KNOW WHAT IS THE HOPE OF HIS CALLING, WHAT ARE THE RICHES OF THE GLORY OF HIS INHERITANCE IN THE SAINTS, AND WHAT IS THE EXCEEDING GREATNESS OF HIS POWER TOWARD US WHO BELIEVE, ACCORDING TO THE WORKING OF HIS MIGHTY POWER.

EPHESIANS 1:15-19

THE GIFTS AND THE CALLING OF GOD ARE IRREVOCABLE.

ROMANS 11:29

...WHO HAS SAVED US AND CALLED US WITH A HOLY CALLING, NOT ACCORDING TO OUR WORKS, BUT ACCORDING TO HIS OWN PURPOSE AND GRACE WHICH WAS GIVEN TO US IN CHRIST JESUS BEFORE TIME BEGAN.

2 TIMOTHY 1:9

IN HIM ALSO WE HAVE OBTAINED AN INHERITANCE, BEING PREDESTINED ACCORDING TO THE PURPOSE OF HIM WHO WORKS ALL THINGS ACCORDING TO THE COUNSEL OF HIS WILL, THAT WE WHO FIRST TRUSTED IN CHRIST SHOULD BE TO THE PRAISE OF HIS GLORY.

EPHESIANS 1:11,12

Chapter Fourteen

Her Trust

Have you ever felt like your wife doesn't trust you? With finances? With taking care of your children? With that attractive woman at work? With important decisions? With your ability to hear from God?

If so, I'm sure it's not because she doesn't *want* to trust you. It's probably because her trust has been violated in the past. And not necessarily by you. Maybe her dad let her down. Or it could be that her first husband or boyfriend was untrustworthy. Or perhaps something you've done or *not* done, something you're not even aware of, has caused her to be hesitant to trust. Or maybe frightening things have happened to her because she trusted someone once. Or possibly her relationship with God is not as intimate as it could be, and she has not yet learned the safety of trusting *Him*. Whatever it is, ask the Lord to reveal it to both of you. You may discover something about yourselves that neither of you has ever realized. Something that could be healed through prayer.

Keep in mind that there are three extremely important areas in which a husband needs to be completely trust-worthy. Failure in any one of these areas will cause his wife's trust to be weak in all the others.

1. *His absolute fidelity to his wife and his marriage.*

There is nothing that violates trust like adultery. If a woman has been cheated on once, it changes her forever. She may forgive, but to forget, she would need a frontal lobotomy. Restoration takes a long time and requires a miraculous touch from God. Even if her husband has never actually done anything wrong, yet his actions around other women make her feel insecure about his ability to stay faithful to her in the future, then his wife cannot trust him.

2. *His responsibility to make a decent living and be wise with the family's finances.*

No matter how much a man loves his wife and how well he treats her, if he is irresponsible with money, it undermines her faith in him. If, for example, he won't keep a steady job, so he is out of work most of the time while his family suffers. Or if his wife is the only one providing for the family, and this was not mutually agreed upon as their way of life. Or if he gambles away their money in any number of ways. In all such cases, his wife will feel that she cannot trust him.

3. *His consistent efforts to treat his wife and children with love and respect.*

I know a number of women who can't trust their husbands to treat them and their children well. Although the husband is faithful and provides a good living, his wife never knows when he is going to explode in anger and be abusive over some insignificant thing. She simply can't trust him.

However, when a husband is consistently trustworthy in these three important areas, his wife finds it far easier to trust him in all the others. But trust must be *mutual* in a marriage. When one person can't or won't trust the other, neither of them can grow into all God has for them. That's why you also need to pray that *you* can trust your *wife.* "The heart of her husband safely trusts her; so he will have no lack of gain" (Proverbs 31:11). Much of the arguing and strife that goes on between marriage partners has to do with a lack of trust on the part of one or the other. The goal is to get to the point where both of you are so committed to the Lord that you can trust *Him* as He works in your mate.

Pray as well that God will give you the wisdom to lead your family and make right decisions. Often your wife's hesitancy about following you is not because she doesn't trust you, but rather because she trusts God more. She believes that only *He* knows certain things, and she wants to know that you have sought *Him* for wisdom and will make decisions based on *His* will. She needs to be certain that you have your future together as a family firmly in mind when you make all decisions. Pray that *your* trust in God will be so evident that *your wife* can in turn trust God to have her best interests at heart as He works through you.

Be patient in praying about this. Trust is broken quickly but takes time to restore. "Let us not grow weary while doing good, for in due season we shall reap if we do not lose heart" (Galatians 6:9). God *will* answer.

SHE SAYS...

Please pray for your wife that:

1. She will trust the Lord with her whole heart.
2. She will be able to completely trust you.
3. She will forgive anyone who has violated her trust.
4. You will be a trustworthy husband.
5. She will trust God working in you.
6. She will be a trustworthy wife.
7. She will be a woman of strong faith.

HE SAYS...
BY RODNEY JOHNSON

Rodney is a real-estate agent. He and his wife, Valerie, have been married for 18 years, and they have three children.

Trust...how hard we strive for it and desire it in our relationships and how easily it is broken. As a real-estate agent in Los Angeles, I have experienced the extremes. One client so trusted me that he and his wife left me a $30,000 check made out to my company and gave me the power of attorney to buy them a particular million-dollar home if it became available while they went out of the country on a three-week vacation. On the other extreme, I had a client from outside the U.S. who was so suspicious of everything I did that ultimately she sabotaged the sale of one of the two homes she was trying to sell.

Guys, wouldn't you like your wife to be like the couple in my first example—willing to trust you to handle the finances, provide a home, and take her on her dream vacation without a care in the world? Sometimes, though, we all find ourselves thinking like the woman in my second example, who became suspicious of everyone and everything. If a woman is suspicious of a man, it is most likely because a male authority figure in her life has done something to break her trust. Now that I have been praying for my wife about this, our mutual trust has never been better.

Men, women need to know that they can trust us. The feminist movement notwithstanding, women want a man to lead, and they want to know that he can be trusted. Therefore, as you pray today for your wife's trust to grow, you must in turn pray to become more trustworthy yourself. If, for example, you have been doing things with the family finances secretively, without consulting your wife, this is a trust-buster. To win back her trust in this area, go to her with a repentant heart and a plan of action as to how you are going to change your untrustworthy behavior. Ultimately, you are a picture of our Father God to your wife and your children. If you can be trusted, it will be easier for your spouse and your kids to trust their heavenly Father.

PRAYER POWER

Lord, I pray that You would give (<u>wife's name</u>) the ability to trust me in all things. Most of all, I want her to trust Your Holy Spirit working in me and through me. Where I have not been worthy of that trust or have violated it, show me, and I will confess that before You as sin. Help me not to conduct myself that way anymore. Make me always be worthy of her trust. Show me how to convince her that I am in partnership with You and will do all I can to be trustworthy.

Where she has lost trust in me unjustly, I pray You would help her to see the truth. If she doesn't trust me because of something someone else has done to her, help her to forgive that person so she can be free. I pray that she will not project those failures onto me and expect that I will do the same thing. Specifically I pray about (<u>name any area where there is a lack of trust</u>).

In any place where we have broken trust with one another, help us to reestablish it as strong. May we both trust You, Lord, working in each of us. Break any unholy bonds or soul ties between me and any other woman in my past. Break any unholy bonds or soul ties between my wife and any other man in her past. Help us to fully repent of all relationships outside of our own that were not glorifying to You.

Lord, I pray that You would deepen my trust of my wife. Show me if there are places where I don't trust her judgment, her abilities, her loyalty, or her decisions. I pray that she will always be a trustworthy person and that I will be able to trust her completely.

Help me to be the kind of spiritual leader of our home and family that You want me to be. Increase our faith, for I know that You are a shield to those who put their trust in You (Proverbs 30:5). I say this day on behalf of my wife and me that You are our refuge and our fortress. You are our God, and in You will we trust (Psalm 91:2).

POWER TOOLS

AS FOR GOD, HIS WAY IS PERFECT; THE WORD OF THE LORD IS PROVEN; HE IS A SHIELD TO ALL WHO TRUST IN HIM.

2 SAMUEL 22:31

TRUST IN THE LORD WITH ALL YOUR HEART, AND LEAN NOT ON YOUR OWN UNDERSTANDING.

PROVERBS 3:5

LET ALL THOSE REJOICE WHO PUT THEIR TRUST IN YOU; LET THEM EVER SHOUT FOR JOY, BECAUSE YOU DEFEND THEM; LET THOSE ALSO WHO LOVE YOUR NAME BE JOYFUL IN YOU. FOR YOU, O LORD, WILL BLESS THE RIGHTEOUS; WITH FAVOR YOU WILL SURROUND HIM AS WITH A SHIELD.

PSALM 5:11,12

IT IS BETTER TO TRUST IN THE LORD THAN TO PUT CONFIDENCE IN MAN.

PSALM 118:8

LET HIM TRUST IN THE NAME OF THE LORD AND RELY UPON HIS GOD.

ISAIAH 50:10

CHAPTER FIFTEEN

HER PROTECTION

In football, the perfect offense protects the quarterback from attack and frees him to do what he needs to do. He can either pass the ball to a receiver, hand off the ball to the running back, or run the ball to the goal line himself. This is exactly how your prayers of protection work for your wife. They create a strong wall around her so that no attack of the enemy can break through the lines to harm her. This allows her to do what she needs to do confidently and in safety. No matter what tricks the enemy has up his shoulder pads, they won't succeed.

So when your wife is out on the playing field of life facing a mean line of 350-pound demons, you as the captain can mobilize your team of angels through your prayers and see to it that she reaches the goal line without a scratch on her.

Now that our children are grown, I travel frequently on book tours and speaking engagements. But I wouldn't even consider leaving home without my husband praying over me for protection. In fact, I wouldn't be traveling at all if he weren't in agreement that I should be and then giving me his prayer support. And whenever *he* has to be out of town, he prays for my safety at home. (I do the same for him, but that's another book.)

There are few places completely safe anymore. Even in our own homes, evil and danger can intrude upon our lives with devastating swiftness. I knew a man who was killed in a car accident a few blocks from his home when he was coming back from the bank in the middle of the day. I knew a woman who was robbed and murdered when she pulled up in front of a neighbor's house to pick up her daughter from a Bible study. I know of a woman who was killed and whose car was then stolen, all in the parking lot of her local supermarket in the middle of the morning when she was getting groceries for her family. We can never take the safety of our loved ones for granted. Accidents happen suddenly and when we least expect them. It will give your wife the greatest comfort to know you are praying for her safety.

It's also important to pray for your wife to have good physical health. Taking care of her body is not easy for a woman. I don't know any woman who doesn't struggle with that in some way. And many women are almost blatantly negligent about it.

If someone were to present you with the car of your dreams, how would you take care of it? Would you neglect to have it serviced? Would you go out to the garage every day thinking, "What a waste of time to take care of this"? I know you wouldn't. Yet that's what your wife does to herself when she doesn't take care of her body. She may have many excuses, such as lack of time, lack of motivation, or lack of understanding about what to do, but your prayers can help her find the time, be motivated to do something, and gain the knowledge she needs.

Health decisions and body care can be complicated and confusing. There's an abundance of sometimes-conflicting information out there, and it makes us all want to go have a candy bar and forget the whole thing. But your prayers will have a positive effect on your wife's ability to hear God about what's right for her.

Permit me to again compare your wife to a car. (It's the only analogy that really speaks to my husband, so I've learned to communicate in these terms.) Your prayers will help your wife to value her chassis and keep it in good working order. They will enable her to exercise her engine enough to keep it in perfect running condition. They will help motivate her to keep up on the regular maintenance the owner's manual calls for, and not wait till she falls apart before she has a checkup. She won't think, "I'm just an old clunker, I'm not worth expensive repairs."

She needs your support in this area, but just talking to her about it won't work. You know how much good it does to go out and yell at your car when it needs to be serviced, and the same is true with your wife. If she is not taking care of herself properly, it's not because she doesn't want to. It's because she either doesn't know the correct things to do, doesn't realize the need for it, doesn't value herself enough, is too busy, or finds discipline in that area extremely difficult. She needs you to ask God to help her.

Tell her you are praying for her to have the strength, knowledge, wisdom, and motivation to take care of herself. And that you're doing it because she is the most valuable gift God has ever given you and you can't bear to see her sick. If she is a vintage model, all the more reason to pray that she will be completely restored.

If your wife is suffering from a specific health problem, ask God for healing. My husband has prayed for me for healing from so many different ailments over the past 30 years. But his finest hour of intercessory prayer came not long ago, when I felt something explode in my body and was doubled over in pain so excruciating that I knew I would die if a doctor didn't figure out the cause and do something about it quickly. It was three o'clock in the morning and Michael was the only one praying for me, except for me as I feebly groaned, "Help me, Jesus." I was completely dependent on my husband's prayers to move the hand of God and save my life. (He will tell you more about it at the end of this chapter.)

Our greatest efforts can't keep us well forever. Even on the best teams, the quarterback still gets sacked. God knew this, and that's why He sent Jesus as our Healer. So ask for healing on behalf of your wife. And don't stop praying until you see an answer. We can't afford to give up too soon when it comes to our health.

SHE SAYS...

Please pray for your wife that:

1. God will protect her body.
2. God will protect her mind and emotions.
3. She will have energy, strength, and endurance.
4. She will be motivated to take care of herself.
5. She will understand how to take care of her body.
6. She will be disciplined.
7. She will be protected wherever she goes.

HE SAYS...
BY MICHAEL OMARTIAN

My wife has the wonderful opportunity to travel and speak to women all over the country. I am painfully aware of the anxiety that creeps up on me at the thought of her getting on airplanes, going to strange towns and cities, staying in hotel rooms, dealing with bad food, being strained by many hours on her feet, and suffering normal anxiety over wanting to do well. There is no option for me but to pray over her before she goes and to continue to pray throughout the days that she is gone. But I have learned the importance of praying for her safety while she is home too.

At no time have my prayers ever been more urgent than when I was awakened at three o'clock one morning by the terrifying screams of my wife. She was doubled over in pain. She said she felt something had exploded within her. She's not one to complain, so I knew something was terribly wrong. The situation was so urgent, in fact, that we couldn't even take the time to wait for an ambulance. I was shaking as I managed to find her shoes and a warm coat to put over her pajamas. Our daughter Amanda and I helped a very doubled-over Stormie into our car, and I rushed down the freeway to the emergency hospital. I could do nothing to comfort her. She was in excruciating pain.

I knew enough to begin singing choruses of healing and praying fervently that she would be attended to immediately. When we arrived, I ran into the emergency admitting room, and thankfully a nurse was right there to rush to the car with a wheelchair. She sped Stormie into an examination room, and after a number of tests, a surgeon came and rushed her into surgery.

I prayed over her continuously, asking God to spare her life. I called others to pray, and they in turn called others as well. When the operation was completed and the surgeon came out to me, he said that her appendix had burst and she was dangerously close to death. He had been forced to take extreme measures to save her life, which meant the recovery would be long and difficult. It didn't matter. She was alive.

I have never experienced such fervency in praying as I learned that night. When we face a life-and-death issue it gives intercessory prayer new meaning. And I have never been so aware of the power and importance of my ongoing prayers for my wife's protection. All of those prayers for her safety over the years were answered. What if she had been out of town on a speaking engagement or on an airplane when that happened? It was God's grace and an answer to prayers for her protection that she wasn't.

PRAYER POWER

Lord, I pray that You would surround (<u>wife's name</u>) with Your hand of protection. Keep her safe from any accidents, diseases, or evil influences. Protect her in cars, planes, or wherever she is. Keep her out of harm's way.

Lord, You have said in Your Word that even though "the wicked watches the righteous, and seeks to slay him…[the] Lord will not leave him in his hand" (Psalm 37:32,33). Protect my wife from the plans of evil people. I pray that when she passes through deep waters, You will be with her, and when she passes through the rivers, they will not overflow her. When she walks through the fire, she shall not be burned nor shall the flame scorch her (Isaiah 43:2). I pray that (<u>wife's name</u>) will make her refuge "in the shadow of Your wings" until "these calamities have passed by" (Psalm 57:1).

Lord, I pray that You would help (<u>wife's name</u>) to truly see that her body is Your dwelling place. Enable her to be disciplined in the care of her body, and teach her to make right choices in what she eats. Give her the motivation to exercise regularly so that she has endurance. Help her to get plenty of rest so that she is completely rejuvenated when she awakens. May she acknowledge You in all her ways—including the care of her body—so that You can direct her paths.

Let no weapon formed against my wife be able to prosper (Isaiah 54:17). Keep her at all times under the umbrella of Your protection, and deliver her from the enemy's hand so no evil comes near her. Give Your angels charge over her to keep her in all her ways (Psalm 91:11). I say to my wife that God will "cover you with His feathers, and under His wings you shall take refuge; His truth shall be your shield and buckler. You shall not be afraid of the terror by night, nor of the arrow that flies by day, nor of the pestilence that walks in darkness, nor of the destruction that lays waste at noonday. A thousand may fall at your side, and ten thousand at your right hand; but it shall not come near you" (Psalm 91:4-7).

Thank You, Lord, that this day You will cover (wife's name) and help her to lie down in peace, and sleep; for You alone, O Lord, make her to dwell in safety (Psalm 4:8).

POWER TOOLS

THE LORD IS MY ROCK AND MY FORTRESS AND MY DELIV-
ERER; MY GOD, MY STRENGTH, IN WHOM I WILL TRUST; MY
SHIELD AND THE HORN OF MY SALVATION, MY STRONGHOLD.
I WILL CALL UPON THE LORD, WHO IS WORTHY TO BE
PRAISED; SO SHALL I BE SAVED FROM MY ENEMIES.

PSALM 18:2,3

BECAUSE YOU HAVE MADE THE LORD, WHO IS MY REFUGE,
EVEN THE MOST HIGH, YOUR DWELLING PLACE, NO EVIL
SHALL BEFALL YOU, NOR SHALL ANY PLAGUE COME NEAR
YOUR DWELLING; FOR HE SHALL GIVE HIS ANGELS CHARGE
OVER YOU, TO KEEP YOU IN ALL YOUR WAYS. IN THEIR
HANDS THEY SHALL BEAR YOU UP, LEST YOU DASH YOUR
FOOT AGAINST A STONE.

PSALM 91:9-12

I WILL RESTORE HEALTH TO YOU AND HEAL YOU OF YOUR
WOUNDS.

JEREMIAH 30:17

DO YOU NOT KNOW THAT YOUR BODY IS THE TEMPLE OF THE
HOLY SPIRIT WHO IS IN YOU, WHOM YOU HAVE FROM GOD,
AND YOU ARE NOT YOUR OWN? FOR YOU WERE BOUGHT AT A
PRICE; THEREFORE GLORIFY GOD IN YOUR BODY AND IN YOUR
SPIRIT, WHICH ARE GOD'S.

1 CORINTHIANS 6:19,20

THE PRAYER OF FAITH WILL SAVE THE SICK, AND THE LORD
WILL RAISE HIM UP.

JAMES 5:15

CHAPTER SIXTEEN

HER DESIRES

The last person I ever desired to marry was a man addicted to football, who had to spend his evenings and weekends on the couch listening to every sports channel. That's why one of the things that I found most attractive about Michael when we were dating was that he claimed to have no interest whatsoever in televised sports. So it was quite shocking to me when, a few years into our marriage, Michael not only became interested in sports, he became obsessed. He dressed in Bears T-shirts and Cubs hats. He screamed in front of the TV until everyone around him was deaf. He took me to a few games, but I thought it was ridiculous to see a bunch of grown men falling all over each other, fighting over a ball that wasn't even round. The hot dogs held more interest for me. I was upset that I had been deceived before the wedding.

Once I learned to pray for my husband the way God wanted me to (as I shared in *The Power of a Praying Wife*), God gave me a new perspective on this situation. But for some unfathomable reason, He did not take away my husband's obsession for sports like I had prayed. Instead Michael and I came to an agreement that I would not look upon his avid interest in football with disdain and disrespect if he would not pressure me to feign interest in it.

This truce was tolerable, and the practicality of it was livable for quite some time. But Michael wasn't content with that, and so he started praying for me behind my back. He prayed that I would go to football games with him once in a while and actually enjoy it. He knew this was a lot to ask of God, but He *had* parted the Red Sea and all.

For some amazing reason, one day my eyes were suddenly opened and I got a picture of what the game was about and how fascinating it was. The thrill of a completed pass. The utter disappointment when the quarterback is sacked. The art form of precision teamwork. The joy of an unexpected play that the other team isn't prepared to stop. Now I never miss a game, and I don't even care about the hot dogs.

Is there an interest you wish your wife would share with you? Pray for her to develop that interest. Obviously, nothing is impossible with God. He can even open your wife's eyes to the thrills and wonders of your favorite pastime. All she needs is a little prayer. But there is more to pray about than just interests and activities. There are dreams and desires that should be prayed about too.

Everyone has dreams. Some of them come from our flesh, but many are put in our hearts by God. It's vitally important to know which is which, because it is miserable when we mistake our own dreams for *His*. When we pursue our own dreams and make idols out of them, we become unfulfilled. When we *don't* pursue the ones *He* gives us, we become bitter.

It's not that God doesn't want us to dream. He does. God says we can't live without a dream or vision. But He doesn't want us to leave *Him* out of it. And if the dream we are dreaming is not from the Lord, we will be forever frustrated by the fact that it is never realized. He wants us to surrender our dreams to Him. When we do that, it will seem as if they are completely dead. But God will resurrect the ones that are from Him and release us from the ones that are not.

It's amazing how we can live in the same house with a person for years and never know the deepest desire of his or her heart. And all because we don't ask. Often our dreams and desires are so deep that we don't even verbalize them. Or we believe that the possibility of them ever happening is so remote that we lose hope.

I know a woman who had the deepest desire to travel and see other interesting places. She was married to a husband with a very strong and controlling personality. He was the CEO of his company, and business was his life. He devoted himself to it without a moment's thought about what her dream or desire was. He wasn't a bad man. He was actually a good man who had never inquired about his wife's dream. He only thought about *his,* and he was living it.

His wife was lonely and unfulfilled, and her children were grown-up and didn't need her much anymore. So she often sat alone with travel magazines and books and soap operas, and dreamed of another life. One day, another married man looked into her eyes and saw *her.* He wanted to know what she thought and what her dreams were. It turned into an affair that nearly destroyed both marriages. When it all came to light, it was a major wake-up call for her husband. Determined to save the marriage, they both went to Christian marriage counseling. To the husband's credit, he confessed that he had been neglectful of his wife, and he started to really listen to the cries of her heart. They began to travel together to wonderful places, fulfilling her lifelong dream. Their marriage was eventually healed, but it took years of gut-wrenching struggle to repair it.

I know another woman who has artistic talent, and had a dream of painting pictures that were worthy of the finest walls. She was sinking daily from the frustration of unfulfillment of it. When her wise husband asked her about the dream or desire of her heart, she shared all that with him. He prayed with her about it, and she released her desire to the Lord. Soon after that, he suggested that she take an art class while he watched their two small children. It changed her life. She bought art supplies for herself and her children, and the three of them painted together every day. To be able to express the gift within her and fulfill a desire she'd had released her so much that it gave new purpose and energy to her personality.

Sometimes the answers to life's frustrations are so simple. As simple as asking a loved one about her dream and then praying it into existence or completely out of her life. Husbands, if you want a happy and fulfilled wife who is a joy to be around, ask her if there is a dream deep within her heart that she longs to see fulfilled. Listen openly as she describes it, with no judgment, no condemnation, and no lecture on why it's not possible. Then pray for her to be able to surrender it to the Lord. When she is able to surrender her dream to God, He will either take the desire for it away or else bring it to full fruition in His way and in His time. Either way, she will find peace.

If the dream your wife shares with you is of the Lord and He opens a door, encourage her to walk through it. If her dream is not of God, He will use your prayers to release her into something far better and more rewarding. And the rewards of a released wife are ones you will thank me for later on.

SHE SAYS...

Please pray for your wife that:

1. She will know if the dreams in her heart are from God.
2. She will be able to share her dreams with you.
3. Her dreams will be compatible with yours.
4. She will take an interest in what interests you.
5. The two of you will have interests you share together.
6. She will be able to surrender her dreams to the Lord.
7. She will have the desires of her heart.

HE SAYS...
BY MICHAEL OMARTIAN

Oh no, she's going to give me that look again, I thought. *That look that says, "Do you ever get enough of sitting in front of that stupid TV watching football?"* Of course my answer was, "Why no, dear, you know I'm just a Neanderthal kind of guy whose interests never drift beyond caveman pursuits." I would endure the look, feeling that the possibility of her ever approving of this "waste of time," let alone sharing it, was beyond the scope of possibility. I now know better!

A simple prayer—and I mean *simple*—was all that it took, and 27 years of football disapproval was replaced by an enthusiasm I never thought possible and I'm not sure I want at this point! Stormie is now a Tennessee Titan fan to the max. She has the sweatshirts, the T-shirts, the hats, and she screams when the action gets close. She even raves about her favorite players on the team. There might have been a time when I would have felt threatened by such declarations, but now I'm just too tired to put up a fight. And besides, it's fun to go to games with my enthusiastic wife. Another amazing answer to prayer. Who would have thought it possible?

I have also prayed for her about her dream of seeing the books she has written go all over the world. They have now been translated into 11 languages. As she says, this has gone beyond her wildest dreams. Only God can do that. And I know I had a part in it because I prayed.

PRAYER POWER

Lord, I pray that You would touch (<u>wife's name</u>) this day and fulfill her deepest desires. Help her to surrender her dreams to You so that You can bring to life the ones You have placed in her heart. I pray that she will never try to follow a dream of her own making, one that You will not bless. Help her to surrender *her* plans so that You can reveal *Your* plan. I know that in Your plan, timing is everything. May she reach for her highest dreams in Your perfect timing.

Lord, I pray that in the midst of all my wife has to do, there would be time for what she enjoys most. Help me understand the things that interest her. I also pray that You would make a way for us to share (<u>name a specific activity or interest you would like to do together</u>). Help her to understand my enjoyment of it, and may she develop an appreciation for it too. Show me how to encourage her in this area. Give me words without any negative undertones that will inspire her. If this is not an appropriate activity for us, show us one that would be. I pray we will have common interests we can enjoy together.

Lord, I know that You would not give us dreams that aren't compatible. I pray that the desires of our hearts will be perfectly knitted together. May we not only be caught up in our own dreams but in each other's as well. Help us to always share with one another the deepest desires of our hearts.

POWER TOOLS

DELIGHT YOURSELF ALSO IN THE LORD, AND HE SHALL GIVE
YOU THE DESIRES OF YOUR HEART.

PSALM 37:4

HE WILL FULFILL THE DESIRE OF THOSE WHO FEAR HIM; HE
ALSO WILL HEAR THEIR CRY AND SAVE THEM.

PSALM 145:19

WHERE THERE IS NO VISION, THE PEOPLE PERISH.

PROVERBS 29:18 KJV

YOU OPEN YOUR HAND AND SATISFY THE DESIRE OF EVERY
LIVING THING.

PSALM 145:16

THEY CRY OUT TO THE LORD IN THEIR TROUBLE, AND HE
BRINGS THEM OUT OF THEIR DISTRESSES. HE CALMS THE
STORM, SO THAT ITS WAVES ARE STILL. THEN THEY ARE
GLAD BECAUSE THEY ARE QUIET; SO HE GUIDES THEM TO
THEIR DESIRED HAVEN.

PSALM 107:28-30

Chapter Seventeen

Her Work

The perfect woman, according to the Bible, is a hard worker. This woman creates, manages, and provides. She buys and sells property (a real-estate agent?). She plants a vineyard (a gardener?). She makes clothing (a seamstress?). And she sells it (a retailer?). She is a woman of strength, energy, and vision, who works into the night and knows that what she has to offer is good. In the midst of it all, she takes care of her family, gives to the poor, and makes her husband proud. He is blessed by the excellence of all she does (Proverbs 31). If this is what your wife aspires to, she needs your help. Frankly, I'm exhausted just reading about it.

Every woman works. But some are more appreciated for what they do than others. Many wives work because they want to contribute financially to the family. Many work simply because they enjoy what they do. Others have abilities that are valuable to people who are willing to pay for them. For many women, maintaining a home and raising children *is* their work. And they take it seriously and want to do it well. For other women, ministry opportunities or volunteer activities are their work. No matter what the particulars of your wife's work, it gives her fulfillment and the satisfaction of accomplishment if it makes life better for her, her family, or someone else. But she needs your prayers and support.

Don't be hesitant to encourage your wife to be all she can be in her work. It won't mean that she will no longer need you when she is successful. In fact, quite the opposite. It will cause her to need you even more. If you support your woman in prayer, she will not get arrogant and cocky when the blessings roll in. She will not think, "Look how great I am. I don't need him. Why, I can do better without him." That's what women think who are married to men who *don't* encourage and support them in prayer. Your wife will never become so complete that she doesn't need you. Her success will never undermine your position in her life. It will elevate it. Your prayers will mean so much to her that she will become "addicted" to them. Remember, the two of you are one and what happens to her happens to you. You need never feel intimidated by her success.

Because my husband is a producer in the music business, we have come to know many women who have had phenomenal success. The couples who have been able to see this success as a blessing from God for them both have dealt with it the best. The husbands who have resented their wife's success have destroyed the marriage. Limiting a woman's potential will destroy her. That's why her achievements must be covered in prayer.

A woman needs to have a sense of accomplishment, just like a man does. However, if a man doesn't have it, he feels like a failure. If a woman doesn't have it, she experiences frustration and unfulfillment. This will in turn affect all the other areas of her life—especially her relationship with her husband. A woman whose work is raising children and running a successful home still needs that sense of accomplishment and the recognition for a job well done. Unlike her sisters in the workplace, the only one she can really hear that affirmation from is her husband. That's why his prayers for her are so important. They breed affirmation.

No matter what kind of work your wife does, she needs your prayers and encouragement, and God's guidance and blessings. Pray for her to find that perfect balance of confidence in her abilities but total reliance upon the Lord to enable her to do what she needs to do.

SHE SAYS...

Please pray for your wife that:

1. She will glorify the Lord in her work.
2. She will do her work well.
3. She will be respected for the work she does.
4. She will be compensated well for her work.
5. She will have strength to get her work done.
6. You will approve of her work.
7. Her work will bring fulfillment to her.

HE SAYS...
BY MICHAEL OMARTIAN

I remember that early in our marriage, during our child-raising years, Stormie expressed the desire to write books. She had written the lyrics to many songs, and we collaborated frequently. She was comfortable with writing songs since it required only a relatively small time commitment, but she felt strongly that to sacrifice time to write a book, time that would be spent away from raising the children, was out of the question. That impressed me to no end. I began praying that God would bless her more than she could imagine for her faithfulness to our children in their early years.

Psalm 37:4 says, "Delight yourself also in the LORD, and He shall give you the desires of your heart." My wife delighted herself in the fulfilling of the responsibilities God had given to her. My prayer was for her to have strength and patience. When the children were older and she had more time available, God gave her the desire of her heart to write books. Of course, I prayed her through each one. Now she is the author of many successful books, and God has blessed her work because she relied on Him every step of the way.

PRAYER POWER

Lord, I pray that You would help (<u>wife's name</u>) to be successful in her work. No matter what her work is at any given time, establish it, and help her to find favor. Thank You for the abilities, gifts, and creativity You have placed in her. Continue to reveal, develop, and refine those gifts and talents, and use them for Your purposes. May her skills increase in value, and may she excel in each of them. Open doors for her that no man can shut, and bless her with success.

Keep us from ever being in competition with one another, and help us to always rejoice in each other's accomplishments. Help us to build one another up and not forget that we are on the same team. If what she is doing is not in Your perfect will, show her what Your will is. Keep pride far from her so that the enemy will never be able to make her fall. Show me how I can encourage her.

Lord, Your Word says when we commit our work to You, the financial blessing we receive will not bring misery along with it (Proverbs 10:22). You have also said "the laborer is worthy of his wages" (1 Timothy 5:18). I pray that (<u>wife's name</u>) will be rewarded well for her labor and that it will bless us, our family, and others. Give her the gift of work that she loves and establish the work of her hands (Psalm 90:17). Enable her to accomplish great things so that You are glorified.

POWER TOOLS

LET THE BEAUTY OF THE LORD OUR GOD BE UPON US, AND ESTABLISH THE WORK OF OUR HANDS FOR US; YES, ESTABLISH THE WORK OF OUR HANDS.

PSALM 90:17

THE LABOR OF THE RIGHTEOUS LEADS TO LIFE.

PROVERBS 10:16

THIS BOOK OF THE LAW SHALL NOT DEPART FROM YOUR MOUTH, BUT YOU SHALL MEDITATE IN IT DAY AND NIGHT, THAT YOU MAY OBSERVE TO DO ACCORDING TO ALL THAT IS WRITTEN IN IT. FOR THEN YOU WILL MAKE YOUR WAY PROSPEROUS, AND THEN YOU WILL HAVE GOOD SUCCESS.

JOSHUA 1:8

HE WHO HAS A SLACK HAND BECOMES POOR, BUT THE HAND OF THE DILIGENT MAKES RICH.

PROVERBS 10:4

IN ALL LABOR THERE IS PROFIT, BUT IDLE CHATTER LEADS ONLY TO POVERTY.

PROVERBS 14:23

CHAPTER EIGHTEEN

HER DELIVERANCE

Picture yourself out sailing on a beautiful, clear, sunny day. A gentle wind is blowing in your face and rustling the sails. The water is calm as you glide along peacefully. You sense the open sea giving you life. You can feel it seeping through your pores and into your innermost being. You have a renewed sense that life is good. You can relax and enjoy the moment as you sail to your destination.

Carefree sailing like that only happens when it's done right. The sails have to be positioned perfectly to catch the wind so the boat can move forward. If they don't catch the wind properly, the boat can be tossed unpredictably. You can end up going around in circles revisiting the same old territory, and never actually getting anywhere. Or worse yet, you can lose control and capsize.

The same is true for us. If we are not positioned right in our relationship to the Lord, we never catch that wind of His Spirit that enables us to sail against the tide of our limitations and circumstances and arrive at our destination. We keep coming back to the same old places, and we never get free. And the ride can get rough and unpleasant. We sometimes lose control and get the feeling that we're sinking. But when we move with the Spirit of God, He never leaves us to wander around where we are. He moves us on to where we are supposed to be.

The problem is, we can't move on to where we are supposed to be if we have dropped anchor in the past. Whether it's something that happened 30 years ago or only as recently as yesterday, the past can keep us where we are if we don't pull in our anchor. God wants us to sail freely. He wants us to leave those old broken places behind so we can become whole people. This is especially important in a marriage, because that's where the mirror of our lives is held up to us daily. We see what we're made of, good or bad, moment by moment. The more whole we are individually, the better our marriages will be. But if we don't seek that fresh wind of God's Spirit to carry us, we never arrive at that place of wholeness and peace.

MOVING AWAY FROM HURTS OF THE PAST

No matter what your wife's past is, unless she has been able to step out of it, she won't be able to live successfully in the present or move into the future God has for her. Whatever hurt from the past that your wife has brought into your marriage will affect the present and the future of your life together. It could be something that someone said or did to her, or the trauma of things that happened to her, or something she did herself. Whatever it is, if it keeps her from having peace about the past, present, or future of her life, then she needs to get free of it. And she needs your prayers to help her do that.

After I wrote the book *Stormie* about my life of devastation and the road I took to find total restoration in the Lord, I received countless letters from men married to women who had come from abusive or emotionally damaging childhoods. In each case, the woman seemed fine when the man married her, but after they were married she fell apart. The husband felt helpless in the face of the depression and turmoil his wife was going through and was at a loss as to how to help her. Her emotional swings were too confusing for him. He didn't feel up to the task at hand, even if he could figure out what it was. He found it impossible to relate to what his wife was experiencing. This is what I advised each one of those men:

"Because of the love you have for your wife, and the fact that you have committed yourself to her in marriage, you have provided a safe haven for her," I wrote. "Your love tangibly represents God's love. She now feels loved enough and safe enough to face the frightening issues of the past and let them be exposed to the healing light of God's presence and power so she can be released from them. She feels secure enough to fall apart so that the Lord can put her back together again. What she wants from you is to know you will continue to stand by her with love and support—even if you don't fully understand what she's feeling or going through. She needs your prayer covering because it will 'break the back' of the enemy and provide a place of protection while she heals."

THE NEED FOR FORGIVENESS

We can never sail smoothly out of our past and into the future God has for us without forgiveness. That's because our greatest hurts usually come from people. If there are negative relationships in your wife's past (especially old boyfriends, or an ex-husband), pray for her to be delivered from the effects of them so she won't bring ghosts from the past into your life together now. Those ghosts can appear at your most intimate times together without your even knowing what's happening. You don't want to be constantly trying to prove that you are not like the person with whom she had a bad experience before she knew you.

Another important area of healing to pray about is your wife's relationship to her earthly father. The way he treated her will affect how she relates both to God and to you. Was he strong and there for her? Did he abandon or abuse her? If she had a father who molested or mistreated her, or who made her feel bad about herself in some way, she may have a hard time trusting you. It's not that she doesn't want to, it's just that the man who was *supposed* to protect and love her didn't. If she doubted her earthly father's love, she may doubt her heavenly Father's love, which may cause her to doubt your love as well. This is where your prayers can make a major difference.

There are also traumatic events that can affect a woman so profoundly that she needs prayer to get free from the memory of them. For example, I once witnessed a man bleed to death after a terrible car accident. I didn't see the accident happen, but I drove by immediately afterward and stopped to help and report it on my cell phone. The man was alone and trapped in his car, and as I prayed I saw the life drain out of him before the ambulance even arrived. It was so traumatic for me that I had nightmares for days afterward. My husband finally had to pray for me to be delivered from the grip of that memory, and then the nightmares stopped.

FINDING FREEDOM

We all need to get free of anything that binds us. It could be anger, resentment, bitterness, or depression. The number of women who struggle with depression is staggering. But God doesn't want women struggling with any of these things. He wants them to be set free. If your wife is tormented by depression, for example, she needs you to stand with her in prayer until she receives freedom from it, no matter how long it takes.

The struggle many women have with food is a deep and troubling problem for them, one that requires deliverance. They desperately need their husbands to pray for them until they find victory in this tormenting issue.

The great thing about praying for your wife to get free is that *you* don't have to have all the answers. She's not expecting that anyway. And you don't have to understand everything. She may not even understand it herself. But God understands everything and has all the answers, so put *Him* in charge. Your wife just wants to know that you will continue to love and support her when you see what she's been holding inside.

If you have a wife who needs a lot of freedom and healing, you may be thinking, "I don't have it in me to deal with all of my wife's problems. I just want to sail along peacefully, and she's stirring up the waters." But that's why opposites attract—so they can complete each other. Do you have any idea how boring it would be to live with someone who was exactly like you? Where would the spark be? The challenge? You would be able to predict your wife's every word, her every move, because it would be the same as what *you* would say or do.

I'll never forget the time I was involved in a seminar where the host and hostess divided us into personality groups. The outgoing people who needed to be the center of attention were all together. The sensitive, deeply thoughtful people were all put together, and so on. It was completely miserable. The outgoing people were constantly trying to outdo one another. The sensitive, deeply thoughtful people were depressing each other. I couldn't wait to get back into a mixed group. Being exactly alike is boring.

You may be thinking that you would gladly trade all the excitement you've been having for a little more boredom. And I understand that. But when we are challenged by our mate's problems, it makes us stretch. So even though your wife may be going through a difficult time that seems like more than you have the patience to bear, just remember how privileged you are to be an instrument of God's healing, and thank Him for allowing you to grow along with her.

THE DELIVERANCE PROCESS

The most startling thing I discovered about being pregnant was that from the moment I conceived, a process was set in motion. And there was no way I could stop it, outside of doing something that would terminate it. It was entirely out of my control. The process was going to go on, with or without my cooperation. That sense of being completely out of control of your body is a strange feeling. Sometimes that's exactly the way the deliverance process feels. It's going on whether you want it to or not. But that's because you have submitted your life to the Lord, and He wants you to be free. When God decides you are ready to go through it, He plants the seed, and it becomes a force that grows until you give birth to freedom. And just as with delivering a baby, there's a certain amount of pain that is a part of the deliverance process. But when it's over, you're glad you went through it.

Emotional hurts and bondage usually come off in layers, just the way they got there in the first place. That's why, even though your wife may have achieved a breakthrough in a certain area, the whole thing may come back with even greater force. It will appear to be the same old thing all over again, only worse this time. If that happens, don't be intimidated or disappointed by it. Don't think that things are getting worse instead of better. It just means that there are new layers of hurt or bondage that are coming to the surface for healing, and that God is leading your wife into a deeper level of deliverance. Often the deepest layers are the most painful. Just cling to God in the midst of the storm, and He will bring you through it safely.

Just as with giving birth to a baby, the worst pain comes right before the greatest deliverance of our lives. Things are the most difficult right before the biggest blessing is about to come forth. But God's timing is perfect. If women were able to deliver babies whenever *we* wanted to, we would deliver them sometime in the second month when the morning sickness kicked in. But the baby would not survive because it would be premature. The same is true with deliverance. We have to provide the best conditions we can, give it time, and try not to do anything to terminate it once the process has been set in motion.

Only God has the kind of love that can calm the storms of our lives. Only He can set our sails and move us in the right direction. Pray that your wife can pull up the anchor from her past and allow the fresh, calm wind of the Holy Spirit to get her sailing smoothly where she needs to go.

SHE SAYS...

Please pray for your wife that:

1. She will find deliverance and freedom in the Lord.
2. Nothing will separate her from all God has for her.
3. She will have emotional and mental wholeness.
4. She will be able to release the past completely.
5. She will forgive anyone she needs to forgive.
6. You will always love and support her in prayer.
7. Her life will become a testimony of God's healing power.

HE SAYS...
BY NEIL T. ANDERSON

Neil is the president of Freedom in Christ Ministries and author of Victory Over the Darkness *and* The Bondage Breaker. *He and his wife, Joanne, have been married for 33 years, and they have two children and two grandchildren.*

In the spring of 1986 my wife had eye surgery to replace a defective lens. It should have been a fairly routine surgery, but Joanne did not respond well to the anesthetic. She suffered a phobic condition, which led to a major depression lasting 15 months. Nothing her doctors did reduced her symptoms. In the midst of it, I got caught in a major role conflict. Was I her pastor, discipler, or counselor (which I had been for many people)? Or was I her husband? I realized I could only be the latter. I was in a situation I could not fix or control.

During this trial we lost everything we had. We were stripped down to nothing, and I realized for the first time that if God is all I have, then God is all I need. My ministry was to hold onto Joanne every day and say, "This too will pass." And it did pass, through prayer and humble dependence on God. The Lord brought me to the end of *my* resources so I could discover *His*. It's only God who can bind up the brokenhearted and set the captive free. Out of this period of brokenness, Freedom in Christ Ministries was born. And our marriage has been greatly strengthened.

PRAYER POWER

Lord, I pray that You would set (<u>wife's name</u>) free from anything that holds her other than You. Deliver her from any memory of the past that has the power to control her or keep her trapped in its grip. Help her to forgive any person who has hurt her so that unforgiveness will not be able to hold her captive.

Set (<u>wife's name</u>) free from everything that keeps her from being all You created her to be. Keep her protected from the plans of the enemy so that he cannot thwart the deliverance and healing You want to bring about in her life. Restore all that has been stolen from her until she is lacking no good thing. I know that in Your presence is healing and wholeness. Help her to live in Your presence so that she can be made totally whole.

Lord, I know that "though we walk in the flesh, we do not war according to the flesh. For the weapons of our warfare are not carnal but mighty in God for pulling down strongholds" (2 Corinthians 10:3,4). In the name of Jesus I pull down any strongholds the enemy has erected around (<u>wife's name</u>). Specifically I pray that my wife will be set free from (<u>name a specific area of struggle from which your wife needs to find freedom</u>). Set her free from this in the name of Jesus. I pray that for her sake You "will not rest, until her righteousness goes forth as brightness, and her salvation as a lamp that burns" (Isaiah 62:1). Make darkness light before her "and crooked places straight" (Isaiah 42:16). You have said in Your Word that "whoever walks wisely will be delivered" (Proverbs 28:26). I pray she will walk with wisdom and find full deliverance. Show me how to love and support her well in the process.

POWER TOOLS

DO NOT REMEMBER THE FORMER THINGS, NOR CONSIDER THE THINGS OF OLD. BEHOLD, I WILL DO A NEW THING, NOW IT SHALL SPRING FORTH; SHALL YOU NOT KNOW IT? I WILL EVEN MAKE A ROAD IN THE WILDERNESS AND RIVERS IN THE DESERT.

ISAIAH 43:18,19

THE LORD WILL DELIVER ME FROM EVERY EVIL WORK AND PRESERVE ME FOR HIS HEAVENLY KINGDOM. TO HIM BE GLORY FOREVER AND EVER.

2 TIMOTHY 4:18

...YOU HAVE HEARD HIM AND HAVE BEEN TAUGHT BY HIM, AS THE TRUTH IS IN JESUS: THAT YOU PUT OFF, CONCERNING YOUR FORMER CONDUCT, THE OLD MAN WHICH GROWS CORRUPT ACCORDING TO THE DECEITFUL LUSTS, AND BE RENEWED IN THE SPIRIT OF YOUR MIND, AND THAT YOU PUT ON THE NEW MAN WHICH WAS CREATED ACCORDING TO GOD, IN TRUE RIGHTEOUSNESS AND HOLINESS.

EPHESIANS 4:21-24

IF ANYONE IS IN CHRIST, HE IS A NEW CREATION; OLD THINGS HAVE PASSED AWAY; BEHOLD, ALL THINGS HAVE BECOME NEW.

2 CORINTHIANS 5:17

FORGETTING THOSE THINGS WHICH ARE BEHIND AND REACHING FORWARD TO THOSE THINGS WHICH ARE AHEAD, I PRESS TOWARD THE GOAL FOR THE PRIZE OF THE UPWARD CALL OF GOD IN CHRIST JESUS.

PHILIPPIANS 3:13,14

CHAPTER NINETEEN

HER OBEDIENCE

One year my husband bought me a set of golf clubs and a series of golf lessons as a Christmas gift. I took the lessons and learned how frustrating it was to try to hit a ball that was so small it was impossible to even find it in a patch of weeds. And I wondered why on earth grown men would spend hours doing this every week. That is, until one day I went out to the golf course, placed my ball on the tee at the first hole, gripped my driver, eyed the fairway, looked down at that tiny ball, and did everything in my swing that I had learned how to do. When the head of my club connected squarely with the ball, there was the most glorious sound. It was like nothing else I'd ever heard, except for maybe the sound of Sammy Sosa's bat hitting a home run at Wrigley Field. My swing was completely right, and the ball sailed straight down the fairway for 170 yards. In that instant I understood why men spend so much time on the golf course. They want to hear that sound. They want to experience how it feels to do it right.

That's the same way it is with obedience. You get the most wonderful feeling when you know that you have just obeyed God and it pleases Him. It's seeing that, when you do things God's way, the right way, life works. That feeling keeps you coming back and trying harder, because you want to do whatever it takes to experience it.

The greatest thing we feel when we obey God is a deeper sense of His presence. That's because there is a link between obedience and our experience of the presence of God. Jesus said, "If anyone loves me, he will keep my word; and my Father will love him, and we will come to him and make our home with him" (John 14:23). He manifests Himself to those who love and obey Him. So often we sacrifice the *fullness* of His presence operating in our lives because of disobedience. Your wife longs to feel that fullness of God's presence on a regular basis. She wants to experience the thrilling sense of God's pleasure when she has obeyed Him. She needs you to pray that she will consistently be able to live God's way.

No matter what game you are playing, there are consequences and penalties for not playing by the rules. One of the consequences for disobedience is not getting our prayers answered (Proverbs 28:9, Psalm 66:18). You don't want your wife to neglect some of the rules and not get her prayers answered. Pray for the eyes of her understanding to be enlightened so that she is clear about the rules of the game.

One of the most common ways women can be disobedient is with our speech. The Bible is very clear on this subject.

- *We are not to be too quick to speak.* "Do you see a man hasty in his words? There is more hope for a fool than for him" (Proverbs 29:20).
- *We are not to say everything we feel, when we feel like it.* "A fool vents all his feelings, but a wise man holds them back" (Proverbs 29:11).

- *Our words can destroy people.* "Death and life are in the power of the tongue, and those who love it will eat its fruit" (Proverbs 18:21).
- *Timing is everything.* "The heart of the righteous studies how to answer, but the mouth of the wicked pours forth evil" (Proverbs 15:28).

Most women love to talk. That's because nearly any woman is overflowing with thoughts, feelings, emotions, revelations, insights, hurts, and joys, and it feels as if she will burst if she does not share them with someone. Out of the overflow of her heart her mouth speaks, and some women overflow more than others.

Communication is a woman's greatest joy. It also can be one of her greatest assets. By her speech alliances are formed, emotions are healed, knowledge is imparted, relationships are restored, mysteries are unraveled, and world problems are solved. She loves to talk things out. Show me a woman who will not talk, and I'll show you a woman who has had people in her life who never listened to what she had to say.

Every woman is well aware of the power of her words and what a long-lasting effect they can have (after all, a wife remembers things her husband said years ago, which he forgot 30 seconds afterward). She agonizes over words she has spoken if she thinks they may have hurt someone. If she says something that is interpreted differently than what she intended, or if she speaks too harshly to her children or to a friend, she has deep regrets. That's why women have specifically asked to be prayed for in this area. Your wife needs your prayers that God will create in her a clean heart and give her words that edify and bring life. She needs discernment from God about what to say and when to say it. And she needs to recognize when it is time to keep silent.

No woman wants to be a complainer, but in her attempt to make life good for her husband, her children, herself, and others, she often sees things that are wrong and tries to change them with her words. If you ever find your wife saying the same thing over and over to you out of the frustration of her heart, pray with her about it. It will give her peace to know that you understand her concern well enough to put it in a prayer. And she'll feel relieved knowing that you have committed it to God. She may even stop talking about it.

Speaking words that bring life is only one of *many* areas of obedience. Your wife wants you to pray that she will be able to do well in *all* of them. She wants to get to the point in her walk with God that she can hit those perfect long drives down the fairway of her life without a slice or a hook. She may not always hit a hole in one, but at least she won't end up in any of those embarrassing sand traps either. Pray for her to hear that wonderful sound of God's voice saying, "Well done, good and faithful servant."

SHE SAYS...

Please pray for your wife that:

1. She will have a heart to obey God.
2. She will understand what God requires of her.
3. She will choose to live God's way.
4. The Holy Spirit will control her actions.
5. Her words will always edify and bring life.
6. God will help her to obey Him.
7. She will please God by her obedience.

HE SAYS...
BY MICHAEL OMARTIAN

My wife has a heart to obey God. But it's not always easy. Sometimes there are choices to be made and it's not clear what God wants her to do. She asks me to pray that she will hear God's voice and have His leading about which way to walk. I also pray for her to have the strength to stand strong and not slack off in her obedience to the things she already knows to do. I pray that the Holy Spirit will lead her in all things so that obedience comes naturally.

One time in particular I felt that God was leading us to move to a different state. My wife did not feel that leading and said so. I realized that if this was what God wanted us to do, He needed to speak to her as clearly as He had spoken to me. I knew it would be better for me to pray that she would hear from God than it would be to force the issue. So that's the way I prayed. And one afternoon a few weeks later, she sensed a clear leading from God that we were to make that move.

God makes it clear that our obedience to Him is vitally important to our spiritual health. He says that it's better than sacrifice. One of the most comforting things in my marriage is to know that my wife is walking in obedience to God. With that obedience comes a settled peace not only for my wife, but which gives a sense of well-being to our entire family. I know it inspires our children as well to walk in obedience to God. God can speak profoundly into each of our lives and give us a great sense of purpose when we seek Him and walk in obedience to what He wants. I pray for my wife to forsake anything that stands in the way of her obeying God. Not only do I want to pray that for her, but I want to personally model that to her as well.

PRAYER POWER

Lord, I pray that You would enable (<u>wife's name</u>) to live in total obedience to Your laws and Your ways. Help her to see where her thoughts and actions are not lined up with Your directions as to how she is to live. Help her to hear Your instructions, and give her the desire to do what You ask. Remind her to confess any error quickly, and enable her to take the steps of obedience she needs to take.

I know that one of the consequences for not living in obedience to Your ways is a sense of distance from You. Keep my wife from doing anything that separates her from the fullness of Your presence and Your love. Show her where she is not living in obedience, and help her to do what she needs to do. Your Word says, "He who obeys instruction guards his life" (Proverbs 19:16 NIV). Bless her mind, emotions, and will as she takes steps of obedience. Give her the confidence that comes from knowing she has just obeyed You.

Lord, You have said that "out of the overflow of the heart the mouth speaks" (Matthew 12:34 NIV). Fill my wife's heart with Your love, peace, and joy this day so that it overflows in her words. May Your Spirit control her tongue so that everything she speaks brings life. Help her to say as David did, "I have resolved that my mouth will not sin" (Psalm 17:3 NIV).

Lord, Your Word says, "No good thing will He withhold from those who walk uprightly" (Psalm 84:11). I pray that my wife will walk uprightly and that You will pour out Your blessings upon her. Especially bless her with the peace and long life You speak of in Your Word (Proverbs 3:1,2). I pray this day that my wife will walk in obedience to You and that You will reward her with an abundance of good things. Let the words of her mouth and the meditation of her heart be always acceptable in Your sight, O Lord, our strength and our Redeemer (Psalm 19:14).

POWER TOOLS

DO NOT FORGET MY LAW, BUT LET YOUR HEART KEEP MY COMMANDS; FOR LENGTH OF DAYS AND LONG LIFE AND PEACE THEY WILL ADD TO YOU. LET NOT MERCY AND TRUTH FORSAKE YOU; BIND THEM AROUND YOUR NECK, WRITE THEM ON THE TABLET OF YOUR HEART.

PROVERBS 3:1-3

SHE OPENS HER MOUTH WITH WISDOM, AND ON HER TONGUE IS THE LAW OF KINDNESS.

PROVERBS 31:26

HE WHO GUARDS HIS MOUTH PRESERVES HIS LIFE, BUT HE WHO OPENS WIDE HIS LIPS SHALL HAVE DESTRUCTION.

PROVERBS 13:3

THE PATH OF THE JUST IS LIKE THE SHINING SUN, THAT SHINES EVER BRIGHTER UNTO THE PERFECT DAY.

PROVERBS 4:18

WHO CAN FIND A VIRTUOUS WIFE? FOR HER WORTH IS FAR ABOVE RUBIES.

PROVERBS 31:10

CHAPTER TWENTY

HER FUTURE

I used to follow the stock market to see which companies were doing well and which ones were not. "Look at that," I'd say to myself. "If I had bought stock in this company I would have made so much money by now." I was great at picking stocks, but because I didn't invest anything I never made any money. It wasn't until I learned to invest something that I saw good returns.

The same is true for our future. When we invest in it wisely, we see greater dividends. However, unlike the stock market, when we *don't* invest anything, we can still lose. And those losses can be devastating.

The most profitable way to invest in the future is to pray. That way you can never lose. God promises to give us a future and a good reason to have hope, but we have to pray about it (Jeremiah 29:11). Your prayers for your wife's future are an investment that is guaranteed to reap benefits for the rest of your lives together.

Women can get very fearful about the future. It's probably because we feel quite vulnerable at times. A woman's most common fears about the future are over losing a child, becoming seriously ill or disabled, losing her husband, being alone, not being able to defend herself against an assailant, having no purpose or relevance, not being attractive, not being able to support herself, or not being needed. If her fears get to the point where she's afraid she doesn't have a future worth living, she can become confused, overwhelmed, and hopeless. Only the truth of what God says about who she is and why she's here can set her free from all that.

God says that your wife is His child (John 1:12) and she will never be alone (Matthew 28:20) or forsaken (Hebrews 13:5). She will always be loved (John 15:9), and she will live a victorious life (Romans 8:37). And everything that happens in her life will work together for good (Romans 8:28). Pray for your wife to believe that the things God says about her future are true.

WHEN YOUR WIFE IS IN MINISTRY

Having a wife in ministry requires much prayer from you. That means if your wife is serving the Lord by teaching, touching, or speaking into the lives and hearts of people in some way, it is crucial that she have your prayer covering. Whether she is singing to thousands of people, or teaching five children in a Sunday school class, or telling her elderly neighbor on the corner about the Lord, she needs your prayers. Whether she is so high-profile that people all over the country know her, or her ministry is one-on-one and the only person who knows the true extent of what she does for the kingdom of God is you, she needs your prayers. Without them she is the target of an enemy who is out to destroy her. The more powerfully the Lord is using her, the greater Satan's plans for her destruction. Don't ever underestimate the significance of your prayers for her. God will hear them. They will save her life and secure her future.

If *you* are in ministry, your wife may be the enemy's target just because she is at your side helping you with what

God is calling *you* to do. The devil will try to destroy *you* by destroying *her*. Show me a married man who is powerfully doing the Lord's work, and I'll show you a wife who has probably been attacked in some way by the enemy. If you and your wife are working *together* in ministry, that is more of a threat than the realm of darkness can bear. The enemy will pull out all the stops to see you both brought down. Be prepared by praying for one another daily, and have other strong believers covering you as well.

THE WISDOM TO GET THERE

One of the most important things your wife needs for the future is the wisdom to get there. Life can quickly get out of control and we can get off the path when we don't have wisdom and revelation from God. Your wife needs wisdom with finances, wisdom to distinguish between truth and lies, wisdom to know whether someone is trustworthy, wisdom to do the right thing, and wisdom to be at the right place at the right time. The perfect woman in the Bible was filled with wisdom, but that doesn't happen without prayer (Proverbs 31:26).

Most of a woman's decisions have to be made quickly, throughout the day. She needs to have the wisdom of the Lord in order to be able to make those decisions well. "If any of you lacks wisdom, let him ask of God, who gives to all liberally and without reproach, and it will be given to him" (James 1:5). If you ask God for wisdom, discernment, and understanding on behalf of your wife, she will be given the knowledge of God. Knowledge will help her to see who she is in the Lord. Wisdom will get her where she needs to go. What more does she need for her future?

When you have wisdom, discernment, understanding, and the knowledge of God, you don't have to worry about the future. I used to be despairing about mine because all I could ever see was my circumstances at the moment. But one day Pastor Jack Hayford said to me, "Don't let where you are become a prophecy of where you're going to stay."

Don't you love that? If your life isn't the way you want it to be right now, that doesn't mean it's always going to be that way. We women have a tendency to fear that things will never change.

Pastor Jack also said, "Don't judge your future by the people who are betting you don't have one."

We don't have to be concerned about whatever terrible thing someone might have predicted for our future. We don't have to worry about what the newspaper, the stock market, the neighbor next door, the guy at work, or Aunt Bessie, has said about our future. We just need to know what *God* says about it.

God says we need to have a vision. So we must ask Him for it. But getting a vision from God for our future doesn't mean He is going to reveal all the details of what's ahead. He only promises to reveal *Himself* to us, when we seek Him. That's because He doesn't want us to know the future—He wants us to know *Him. He* is our future. When we know *Him,* He guides us into the future He has for us.

So praying for your wife to have a vision for her life doesn't mean she's going to know all that's ahead for her. It just means that she'll see that she *does* have a future and that it is *good.* And that is enough.

The future is so uncertain that, even when things are going well, we can never get too cocky about it. Everything can change in one moment, and then our lives are forever different. That's because the enemy never stops making plans for our future. We have to be continually watchful in prayer to make certain that our future is securely in *God's* hands so *His* plans will prevail.

As you pray for your wife's future, remember that it's *your* future too. That's because your future is not independent of hers, nor is hers separate from yours. They are intertwined. This is the reason that the prayers you pray for your wife are guaranteed to yield a return that will make you secure for the rest of your lives. If you keep investing in your wife's future with prayer, I guarantee that your lives are going to be rich with blessings from God.

SHE SAYS...

Please pray for your wife that:

1. She will not fear the future.
2. She will have wisdom in all things.
3. She will have a vision and hope for her future.
4. She will be able to make quick decisions wisely.
5. She will not listen to lies of the enemy about her future.
6. She will bear fruit into old age.
7. Her future will be secure.

HE SAYS...
BY EDDIE L. LONG

Bishop Long is the senior pastor of New Birth Missionary Baptist Church in Lithonia, Georgia. He and his wife, Vanessa, have been married for 11 years, and they have four children.

My wife is regarded as a mother to many people—more than 22,000 parishioners in our church at last count. She is an articulate, educated, kind, demure, God-fearing lady who does not seek the limelight. But Vanessa's destiny is tied to mine, and because she is my wife, many times she winds up at center stage where all eyes are upon her. She has an innate ability to handle any situation with grace, and I continually pray that she will hear clearly from God and follow His destiny for her life.

I have witnessed several changes in my wife over the years. She has stretched out her hand and addressed issues that touch the women of our congregation and others connected to our ministry. She has decided to get to the heart of women's issues by dealing with grassroots problems. I believe the answers to my prayers for my wife are seen each day as she helps heal the broken hearts and homes of those she touches. Without prayer, I don't believe the Heart to Heart Women's Ministry under her leadership would touch the hearts of women and change the lives of families worldwide as it does today.

I will not take any credit for God's plan or the prayers that have been prayed by our family and friends, but I know I pray for my wife. As her husband, I believe that my prayers help sanctify her for God's use. Prayer changes things. Prayer brings an increased measure of God's power. Much prayer, much power; little prayer, little power; no prayer, no power.

I continue to pray for my wife while reaping the benefits, because she is a blessing to all who have the good fortune to know her. I know that as God is ongoingly magnified in her life, she will continue to grow in glory. My wife is my glory, a gift from God. Praying for her in turn affects my life as we grow together in Christ.

"I love the LORD, because He has heard my voice and my supplications. Because He has inclined His ear to me, therefore I will call upon Him as long as I live" (Psalm 116:2).

PRAYER POWER

Lord, I pray for (<u>wife's name</u>) to have total peace about the past, present, and future of her life. Give her a vision for her future that makes her certain she is safe in Your hands. Keep her, and the people she loves, protected from the plans of the evil one. Free her completely from the past so that nothing interferes with the future You have for her. Help her to see her future from Your perspective and not believe any lies of the enemy about it. May she trust Your promise that the plans You have for her are for good and not evil, to give her a future and a hope (Jeremiah 29:11 NIV). Give her confidence that the future is something she never has to fear.

Lord, I pray that You would give (<u>wife's name</u>) wisdom in all things. When she has to make any decision, I pray that You, Holy Spirit, will guide her. Give her wisdom in her work, travels, relationships, and finances. Bless her with the discernment to distinguish the truth from a lie. May she have the contentment, longevity, enjoyment, vitality, riches, and happiness that Your Word says are there for those who find wisdom (Proverbs 3:16-18). May she also find protection, grace, rest, freedom from fear, and confidence in You (Proverbs 3:21-26). Take my wife from glory to glory and strength to strength as she learns to depend on Your wisdom and not lean on her own understanding.

For the decisions we must make together, give us wisdom to make them in unity. Specifically I pray for (<u>name a decision you must make together</u>). Help us to know Your will in this matter. I pray that we will make godly choices and decisions that are pleasing to You.

I pray that (<u>wife's name</u>) will be planted in Your house and flourish in Your courts. May the fruit of her life be seen every year, and even into old age may she be fresh and flourishing (Psalm 92:13,14). Bless her with long life, and when she comes to the end of her life, may it not be one moment before Your chosen time. Let that transition also be attended with peace and joy, and the absence of suffering. Let it be said of her that she was Your light to the world around her.

I say to (<u>wife's name</u>) this day, "You are complete in Him" (Colossians 2:10). I am confident that "He who has begun a good work in you will complete it until the day of Jesus Christ" (Philippians 1:6). "Arise, shine; for your light has come! And the glory of the LORD is risen upon you" (Isaiah 60:1).

POWER TOOLS

EYE HAS NOT SEEN, NOR EAR HEARD, NOR HAVE ENTERED
INTO THE HEART OF MAN THE THINGS WHICH GOD HAS PRE-
PARED FOR THOSE WHO LOVE HIM.

1 CORINTHIANS 2:9

THERE IS SURELY A FUTURE HOPE FOR YOU, AND YOUR HOPE
WILL NOT BE CUT OFF.

PROVERBS 23:18 NIV

KEEP SOUND WISDOM AND DISCRETION; SO THEY WILL BE
LIFE TO YOUR SOUL AND GRACE TO YOUR NECK. THEN YOU
WILL WALK SAFELY IN YOUR WAY, AND YOUR FOOT WILL NOT
STUMBLE. WHEN YOU LIE DOWN, YOU WILL NOT BE AFRAID;
YES, YOU WILL LIE DOWN AND YOUR SLEEP WILL BE SWEET.
DO NOT BE AFRAID OF SUDDEN TERROR, NOR OF TROUBLE
FROM THE WICKED WHEN IT COMES; FOR THE LORD WILL BE
YOUR CONFIDENCE, AND WILL KEEP YOUR FOOT FROM BEING
CAUGHT.

PROVERBS 3:21-26

HOUSES AND RICHES ARE AN INHERITANCE FROM FATHERS,
BUT A PRUDENT WIFE IS FROM THE LORD.

PROVERBS 19:14

I KNOW THE THOUGHTS THAT I THINK TOWARD YOU, SAYS
THE LORD, THOUGHTS OF PEACE AND NOT OF EVIL, TO GIVE
YOU A FUTURE AND A HOPE. THEN YOU WILL CALL UPON ME
AND GO AND PRAY TO ME, AND I WILL LISTEN TO YOU. AND
YOU WILL SEEK ME AND FIND ME, WHEN YOU SEARCH FOR
ME WITH ALL YOUR HEART.

JEREMIAH 29:11-13